THE ELEMENTS
OF BANKING

F. E. PERRY

THE ELEMENTS
OF BANKING

SIXTH EDITION

Revised by
GERALD KLEIN
FCIB, Cert. Ed.

R

Routledge
in association with
The Chartered Institute of Bankers
LONDON

First published in 1975 by Methuen & Co. Ltd
Reprinted with revisions and supplementary notes 1976
Second edition 1977
Reprinted with revisions and supplementary notes 1978 and 1979
Third edition 1981
Fourth edition 1984
Reprinted 1984 and 1985
Fifth edition 1986
Reprinted 1989 by Routledge
Sixth edition 1989
11 New Fetter Lane, London EC4P 4EE

Typeset by Scarborough Typesetting Services
and printed in Great Britain by
Richard Clay (The Chaucer Press) Ltd
Bungay, Suffolk

British Library Cataloguing in Publication Data

Perry, F. E. (Frank Ernest), 1912–1983
The elements of banking. – 6th ed. revised
by Gerald Klein
1. Great Britain. Banking
I. Title   II. Klein, Gerald   III. Chartered Institute
of Bankers
332.1'0941

ISBN 0–415–04466–9

Contents

Preface

It seems only a short time ago that I wrote the fifth edition of this book, but since 1986 so much has happened in the field of banking that it has become necessary to revise the book yet again.

In essence, the core topics, customers, negotiable instruments, etc. have on the whole remained the same, but it has been necessary to completely rewrite such topics as the Stock Exchange, the role of the building societies, and incorporate the Financial Services Act 1986, the Banking Act 1987, and generally update where necessary.

As in previous editions, I have continually borne in mind that this book will be used by graduates who although are exempt from Stage I of the Chartered Institute of Bankers examinations will use the book as background reading. It is also relevant to students of the Business and Technical Education Council (BTEC) Diploma or Certificate, as well as those studying for the Banking Certificate or the Bankers Foundation Course.

My thanks to the Office of the Banking Ombudsman for the updated material, to Don Strutt, Barclays Bank plc, Clearing Department for his assistance on the chapter on the Clearing system and the APACS for the provision of the clearing statistics and permission to use them in the book. Once again I am obliged to the Bank of England for permission to reproduce the list of recognized banks, to National Westminster for their permission to use their opening account form and balance sheet. I would like to thank the editor of the *Banking World* for allowing me to reproduce as an appendix the elements of the Jack Committee Report.

I am also indebted to Lesley Kay, Finance Houses Association; Agnes Hockey, Publications Branch, Girobank; Alwyn Jones, Group Corporate Communications, Royal Bank of Scotland; Trevor Fossey, TSB; and Laurence Klein, Stock Exchange and savings media, for their guidance and assistance. Finally, my grateful thanks to my wife Anne for her support and to the many friends who have encouraged me in this undertaking.

G.K.

1

What is money?

Many parents have children at school who do not seem very bright at their schoolwork. Annual reports contain phrases such as 'tries hard, but finds it difficult to take in' and 'finds this subject hard to understand'.

Yet the parents observe that, however dull their offspring may appear to their school teacher, there is one subject over which they have complete mastery, that is money. They have had no difficulty in learning the subdivisions of the pound, they recognize the coins instantly, they can check their pocket money in a twinkling of an eye, and they know exactly how much their money will buy. Moreover, they learn all this at a very early stage. But what exactly is money? To answer that question, we have to go back in time.

Barter

Today we buy, say, bread or clothes with money in the appropriate shop. These are goods; we exchange our money for goods which others sell to us. Today we travel on a train or bus, or maintain a banking account, or consult our solicitor about some legal matter, and we pay the charge or fee demanded. These are services; we exchange our money for the services which others provide for us.

But in a primitive community where there was no money, goods and services were obtained by barter – we called it 'swapping' at school. In very early times the Phoenician traders of the Mediterranean reached Cornwall and the Scilly Isles to barter their spices and dyes for the tin mined in the West.

But as primitive communities develop into more advanced societies people specialize in what they can do best, and barter becomes a clumsy method of exchange. The cobbler who wanted to advertise his shoes had to find not only a printer to print the hand-bills, but also a printer who happened to want a pair of new shoes. This was called the 'double coincidence of wants'. Even then, what is to be the 'rate of exchange'? How many handbills should be printed for a pair of shoes?

There had to be some commodity which could be used as a medium of exchange. Anything would do as long as everyone accepted it in payment. This acceptance was crucial. The 'money' did not have to be attractive for its own sake, although it often was. In this connection everyone instantly thinks of cowrie shells, which were rather handsome rose-tinted shells found in the Indian and Pacific oceans. But other parts of the world found other things to use as a medium of exchange. In early Rome men used sheep, and in Greece, cattle. In ancient Egypt if a man was well disposed towards another, or wished to impress him, he would make him a present of one or more slaves, for there a man's status was measured by the number of slaves he had.

These were rather large units, difficult to match up with some small article the herdsman or farmer might want. Neither were con-venient for carrying about. Also of course, there were healthy, fat cows; and poor, thin cows. There might be trouble from a seller expecting to be paid ten fat cows when he was offered ten thin ones.

Nowadays we know that the units of money must be homogen-eous – that is, they must all be of the same kind, look the same, weigh the same, all be of the same type, shape, size and quality. They must also be durable. Cows die sooner or later. Many things have been used as the medium of exchange – corn, furs, rice, tobacco, salt, tea, rum – there is no end to them. Man is an animal with a gift for trading, and when conditions are primitive – i.e. when there is no money – barter will reappear. Thus cigarettes were used in prisoner-of-war camps and in the black markets in post-war Germany. They are still used by inmates of HM prisons.

On an international scale barter is accepted because each country is keen to export its own goods and services and, in exchange, import such goods and services as are needed by the population to maintain or improve its standard of living. Barter is expanding. In fact it is estimated that about 40 per cent of all international trade is done either by compensation trading or counter purchase – which is basi-cally barter by grander names. Such deals take place when countries are short of hard convertible currency, e.g. US dollars, Swiss francs, sterling, etc. In the main, it is the Eastern bloc and Third World countries that resort to this type of trade and are willing to take plant, machinery or grain in exchange for products grown or manufactured in their own country.

Early money

In time it was generally realized that metals were superior to the commodities previously mentioned, because coins made from metal are homogeneous, portable, and easily divisible by weight. However, coins were not introduced immediately, and sellers had to be in a position to check the weight of a bar of the metal offered in payment. So every market-place sported its weights and scales, and we can find many instances of their use in the Bible and in other records of early times. Metals also had the advantage that if they were not required as money they could be melted down and used to make something else, such as spear blades, ploughshares or goblets.

Among the Ancient Britons, and in Greece, iron was used, and copper in Rome, but gradually silver and gold emerged as better than the other metals because they keep indefinitely – iron rusts – and they provided a greater value in smaller bulk. That meant that merchants had to carry less weight about with them. Another advantage was, and is, that all gold and silver of a certain weight and fineness is the same.

Coinage

The early British coinage was based on silver, probably because gold was scarce and expensive. There were, however, gold coins from time to time, but it was not until the reign of Edward III that a regular gold currency was instituted in England. One in particular, struck by Henry VIII, bore his figure and was called a sovereign. The name persisted, to describe our chief gold coin in later years.

Towards the end of the seventeenth century gold became more plentiful and golden guineas and florins were struck. The guinea was first coined from gold brought back from the coast of Guinea, whence its name. The florin (now 10p) is named from the city of Florence, where florins were first coined.

Copper and bronze coins, the farthings, halfpennies and pennies, originated because of the shortage of coins of small values. Tradesmen got into the habit of issuing copper tokens for small transactions, much as drapers' shops used to give out a packet of pins as change in place of a farthing. Of course people could not be allowed to issue their own coinage and the tradesmen's tokens were stopped. But a need had been recognized, and in 1672 the mint began to issue copper coins. In 1860 bronze coins were substituted, containing ninety-five parts copper, four parts of tin, and one part of zinc. These bronze coins were very much better, and were in use up to the changeover to decimal coinage, except the farthing which was discontinued in 1961. Some years after this the sixpenny piece ($2\frac{1}{2}$p) was gradually phased out, while in 1984 we find the introduction of a new £1 coin, which has replaced the £1 note. Additionally, with effect from 14 February 1989, a new coin – a £2 piece – has been introduced as legal tender. Two versions of this coin have been struck, the first to honour the Tercentenary of the Bill of Rights and the other the Tercentenary of the Claim of Right in Scotland.

Debasement of the coinage

Coins are free from most of the disadvantages of earlier forms of money, but if the coinage is to retain its value and the confidence of those who use it, certain dangers must be guarded against. But before we see what these are, we must be clear what sort of coins we are talking about. The original or early coinage was more or less worth its stated face value in its content of metal. Thus if you melted down a number of silver coins, you could sell the silver for about the same amount as the face value of the coins. While this was so the merchants who used them no longer had to check their weight on scales, but could rely on the guarantee of the government implicit in the imprint, and check them only by the much quicker process of counting them.

The later coinage tended to be token coinage, that is to say, it might be made from cupro-nickel instead of silver. The value of the metal in the coin would be nowhere near the face value of the coin. Nevertheless the governmental imprint still appeared on it, certifying that it was a true coin of the realm, issued under governmental authority. In this case the value of the coin depended upon the confidence of the public in the government and its conduct of the monetary system. Token coinage is used in mature and developed communities. Let us call these the earlier coins and the later coins.

The earlier coins had intrinsic – genuine – value, and if they could be copied cheaply, and the cheap copies substituted for the genuine article, there would be a profit for those who made the substitution.

So forgeries appeared. Bad forgeries gave themselves away, good forgeries could be detected only by weighing or bending them. The danger was that such tampering with the coinage would result in the public losing confidence in the coins, thereby hampering trade. The State therefore imposed severe penalties for the crime of forgery.

Another profitable operation used to consist of clipping or shaving a little metal from the edge of the coin, and then passing it on to the next person a little smaller than it was before. To defeat this, the device of the milled edge was introduced and from the second half of the seventeenth century all coins coming from the London Mint were so protected. Then there is, of course, normal wear and tear. Coins get steadily thinner and lighter as they are continually handled. When wearing away had got to a point where the coin was no longer acceptable, the government had to recall it and replace it with a new coin. The maintenance of the coinage is an expensive business which no government wishes to carry out more often than is absolutely necessary, and the practice grew up of minting coins with an alloy of harder wearing metal to give longer life without, however, significantly reducing the amount of valuable metal in the coin.

Finally, there was the risk that the government itself would deliberately mint the coins with a value less than their face value. In a way, it is a disadvantage that the government of a country is responsible both for issuing the coinage and for maintaining its value.

Kings, emperors and governments in need of money have never been reluctant to debase coinage. That is, they have withdrawn good coins containing the proper amount of metal, and have replaced them with lighter coins containing less metal, pocketing the difference. Any such manoeuvre has always resulted in a depreciation in the value of the coins, forcing merchants to resort again to the practice of weighing the metal. The depreciation in the value of the coinage is shown by a general rise in prices. It was not really that prices were going up so much as the fact that the value of the coinage was going down.

While this process of debasing the currency is under way, coins of the proper weight and value will circulate side by side with the 'light' coins ('good' money and 'bad' money). When this happens people will tend to hoard the good coins and pass on the bad ones. This tendency for debased coins to drive good coins out of circulation is called Gresham's Law, after Sir Thomas Gresham, financial adviser to Queen Elizabeth I. He seems to have been the first official to note the working of this tendency.

It is not necessary for the metal content of all coins to be worth their full face value. This would be possible only if the metals used maintained their prices unchanged, i.e. if the country were on a gold or silver standard. So we come to the 'later' or token coinage.

These coins are free from the risk of forgery, for that is not worth anyone's while. Nor is anyone going to bother to clip the edges. In spite of this the token coinage may well still incorporate the milled edge, partly through convention and habit and partly to make the coins look as much as possible like the old ones which had intrinsic value. Nor is the government likely to embark on the sterile project of trying to debase them. Wear and tear will still continue, but this cannot be avoided. These are all advantages. The disadvantage is that there is no automatic check on the value of the coinage, which is therefore free to depreciate according to the inflationary conditions which in recent decades have come to be regarded as quite normal throughout the world.

Development of paper money

After coins came notes. These were developed almost by accident. Accustomed as we are in these days to the security of our banking system, we find it hard to imagine a time before there were any banks, and to understand that the hardest problem then for anyone with money was to find somewhere safe to keep it. In the seventeenth century many people in this country held their wealth in gold, for a great deal of that metal had been brought back from America during the Elizabethan Age. During the Civil War people were very frightened of being robbed.

If they lived in or near a large town it therefore seemed sensible to look around for someone who had to have vaults and safes for their own business, and then to ask them to look after the money. Gold- and silversmiths had such safes, for their trade was traffic in coin and bullion, and they needed somewhere secure to keep their stocks. (Bullion is uncoined, refined gold or silver, generally in bars called ingots; or gold or silver, including coined metal, when exported or imported.)

So it came about in the seventeenth century that goldsmiths took these deposits for safe keeping, issuing a receipt which acknowledged the deposit of the money and incorporated a promise to return it on demand. More and more people came to hold these receipts and they began to circulate for value among merchants. Originally merchant A, wishing to buy something from B, would take his receipt back to the goldsmith, surrender it, and get his money back. Then he would buy the article from B. As like as not, B would then take his money and deposit it with a goldsmith, either the same one or another.

It was quicker and more convenient for A to pass the goldsmith's receipt on to B, who could either keep it or 'cash' it at the goldsmiths. Where the goldsmith's name was well known and his reputation good, such circulation was commonplace. To pass the right to the ownership or title on to B, and to guarantee that the transaction was bona fide and in order, the merchant 'endorsed' the receipt before passing it on to B, that is, he signed his name on the back of it.

From goldsmiths' notes to banknotes

The movement from goldsmiths' notes to bank notes could probably be traced back to the establishment of the Bank of England in 1694. Although the Bank will have a chapter devoted to itself, it is worth while mentioning here that it was established in order to assist – financially of course – the government to conduct the war of the Grand Alliance. The Bank was to have the power to issue its own notes.

The Bank was a success from the word go. There was no difficulty at all in finding the necessary capital. It had limited liability, by Royal Charter. It was larger than any other bank existing at that time and, lastly, it had the confidence of government.

The early banknotes were convertible on demand, that is, they could be exchanged at the Bank for gold coins. Because everyone knew that this could be done, they did not often bother to do it. Instead, they used the notes in their trading, confident that a £5 note was indeed worth £5 in gold. Such convertible paper is not strictly money, only a claim to money.

In 1708 the Bank was given a near monopoly of the issue of notes in England. No other corporate body, or banking partnership of more than six persons, within a radius of 65 miles of London could issue notes payable on demand, or payable at any time less than six months ahead. Thus parliament protected the Bank from possible competition from other banks.

The Bank of England monopoly did not extend to Scotland. There, a similar monopoly given to the Bank of Scotland was not renewed in

1716 when the Bank's charter was renewed. The result was that in 1727 the Royal Bank of Scotland, a joint stock banking company, was founded. Other joint stock banks were subsequently formed and made rapid progress, all issuing their own notes. These however, were not legal tender in England. Legal tender is any means of payment that a creditor is obliged by law to accept in settlement of a debt. Thus while a debt may be settled by cheque, or by postal order, this is at the option of the creditor. He cannot be compelled to accept a cheque, or a postal order, for neither are legal tender. He can be compelled to accept Bank of England notes, for they are legal tender.

After the Act of 1709 the goldsmiths and the private bankers in or near London deposited their cash with the Bank and used its notes instead of their own. In the country areas banking had been slower to develop, and the banking partnerships there were on a smaller scale. Limited to partnerships of not more than six persons, hundreds of small banking businesses had come into existence, all issuing their own notes, many of them with quite inadequate financial resources and doomed to fail at the first economic or monetary crisis.

The Gold Standard

Around the beginning of the eighteenth century, there were the banknotes of the Bank of England, the banknotes of the country bankers, and gold coins circulating together. The coins were gold florins and guineas until 1816, when the gold sovereign was substituted for them as the legal standard unit. All the notes were convertible into gold. They all incorporated a promise to pay the bearer. Those of the Bank of England were signed by the Chief Cashier, as they still are today.

This system of notes backed by gold was called the Gold Standard. The system was in use in most developed countries abroad, and this facilitated the settlement of international trading debts because all the countries concerned had confidence in gold as a unit of value, and were willing to accept payment for their exported goods in gold or claims to gold.

The three essential conditions for a gold standard to work properly are:

(1) that there must be free mintage of gold into the standard legal coins (i.e. any person may take a bar of gold to the mint and

require it to turn the bar into legal gold coins of the realm, without charge, and to hand the coins back to him);

(2) that gold must be allowed to come into the country, or go out of it, without restriction;

(3) that the legal paper money of the country must be convertible into gold at the central bank on request.

Apart from the period 1797–1821, when the Bank was forced to suspend payments of gold because of the Napoleonic wars, this system lasted until the outbreak of the Great War in 1914, when gold payments were again suspended. A modified form of the Gold Standard, called the Gold Bullion Standard, was reintroduced in 1925. Single notes could no longer be exchanged at the Bank, for there was by now no gold coinage, but a gold bar of 400 oz could be obtained in exchange for notes to the value of about £1,555.

In this way important economies were made in the use of gold, while at the same time the currency was still kept convertible. The value of gold was fixed at £3 17s 10½d, or in decimal currency £3.89, per standard ounce, eleven-twelfths fine. The Gold Bullion Standard was an excellent scheme but it had a short life, for in 1931, in the worst economic crisis the world has ever known, the Bank was again forced to suspend gold payments. The reason for this was the same as on the previous occasions – the gold reserves of the country were not sufficient to meet the demands from foreign financial centres.

Since 1931 the banknotes of this country have been inconvertible. In themselves they have no value, they are just bits of paper. The promise to pay still appears on the front, but since 1931 the only way in which the Bank of England could pay a £5 note would be by two £5 notes, or £10 worth of coins. As with the milled edges of our cupro-nickel coinage, the promise to pay is a relic of former days.

People still accept the paper notes as good. Banknotes are now money in their own right, no longer merely claims to money. The nation which uses banknotes daily has a massive belief that they will be accepted in payment for goods supplied, or services rendered, in the full assurance that they may in turn be passed on to others in exchange for their goods or services.

Although the link with gold of a specified weight and fineness has been broken, and although the number of notes in circulation is no longer limited by the amount of gold which the central bank formerly had to keep by way of cover for the note issue, the public confidence in the banknote issue shows that it does not matter whether the medium of exchange is gold, paper, rice, tea or cigarettes, as long as it is generally acceptable in exchange for goods and services.

The form which money takes is irrelevant, so long only as it commands the confidence of those who use it. If people lose confidence in banknotes, it is either because they have lost faith in the bank which issued them, or because they have lost faith in the currency of the country as a whole. In the great expansion of banking in the eighteenth and nineteenth centuries many of the smaller private banks, particularly in the provinces, got into difficulties through lending so much out, usually in the form of their own notes, that they left themselves insufficient reserves to meet the demands for repayment of their notes, or deposits, or to pay bills falling due. On these occasions word quickly got around and the unthinkable happened – all their depositors demanded the repayment of their balances at the same time. There was a run on the bank, and confidence in the bank's note issue rapidly diminished. Eventually the bank was forced to close its doors and announce that payment was suspended. This was a local loss of confidence, often unhappily only too well founded.

On a national scale the result is infinitely worse. What happens then was demonstrated in Germany after the First World War, when prices rose with such speed that the tickets in shop windows had to be altered several times daily, and stamp collectors saw with amazement that over a period of weeks, then days, the cost of posting a parcel in Germany escalated from 50 marks to a fantastic 50,000 million marks. At that point the currency collapsed completely. Nobody would accept the notes any longer for anything at all. They had become completely worthless.

This has never happened in this country. The notes issued by the Bank of England have sometimes lost part of their value through devaluation against gold or foreign currencies, or because of inflation, but the public have never lost confidence in them to the point of refusing to accept notes in payment of debts.

The functions of money in a modern economy

From previous reading, you will have realized that, in the main, money consists of notes and coins. For the time being at least, accept that this is the major method of payment for goods and services. Whether we use certain notes or certain coins, the commodity that we give to settle the debts must be acceptable to the recipient. ACCEPTABILITY is the first and perhaps the most important function of money. Should people not be willing to accept the money that is in use, then it ceases to operate as money and some other commodity will take its place.

Secondly, money must function as a UNIT OF ACCOUNT. This enables a person to compare one commodity with another in terms of money. Further it enables us to maintain financial records of who owes us money and to whom we owe money.

The third function of money is to act as a STORE OF VALUE. These days this function does not always operate successfully, as money kept in a bank current account for a year will not have the same purchasing power as it did originally. However confident we are that money held from one salary day to another will maintain its purchasing power, inflation will over a period of time reduce the value of money if money does not earn interest to maintain its value.

Lastly, money must act as a STANDARD FOR DEFERRED PAYMENTS. In order for society to function, contracts between one person and another will be made showing the amount to be paid or received. These deferred payments will be stated in monetary terms.

The qualities of money in a modern society

In order to perform all the above functions, the commodity which is considered money must have the following qualities.

(1) Stability

The value of money must be fairly stable, that is, it will only change its value slowly. Should it fluctuate wildly, people will not be keen to hold it or use it. They will not know how much to pay for goods.

(2) Transferability

To perform the function of money, it must be easily exchanged for goods and services. Money must be transferred without any legal processes and have the confidence of the public and have legal acceptability.

(3) Durability

No person will want to hold money if it perishes or loses its value quickly. The Bank of England's notes have a life expectancy of about six months, so although the notes perish quickly, they are quickly replaced by the authorities.

(4) Divisibility

As goods are quoted in different prices, money, in order to perform its functions, must have different values and the sum of its parts must add up to the whole unit, e.g. 20 fivepence pieces must equal £1.

(5) Portability

Money should be easily carried by people. With inflation the number of notes in circulation can at times be a nuisance (as with the Italian lira), so that the authorities will sooner or later issue a note of higher denomination to make money more portable.

(6) Recognizability

To have acceptability of money, the various units must be immediately recognizable by the public, so that all units must have the same shape, weight, size and content.

Legal tender

By law the only units of money that have unlimited legal tender are Bank of England notes. That is, when a debt has to be settled, the debtor offers the creditor Bank of England notes in settlement. He is bound to accept, no matter what the amount is.

Limited legal tender means that only a certain number of coins need be accepted by the creditor. Under the Coinage Act 1971, up to 20p in bronze need be accepted, £5 worth of 5p or 10p, and £10 of 20p or 50p.

Bank deposits

So far we have identified as money, banknotes and coins – cash. The balances held by banks and building societies in their customers' names are also money, providing those funds are repayable on demand, and these balances are much greater in total than all the banknotes and coins put together.

Since the major building societies now have cheque accounts available to their customers, the possibilities for persons to have debts settled by having funds deducted from these accounts are parallel to the services offered by banks on current account. From this point, building society deposits are synonymous with bank current accounts. For the remainder of this chapter, bank deposits should be read as including building society accounts.

The argument that bank deposits are money is quite a simple one. Suppose that A has £100 in £5 notes. With these he opens a banking account. When A has paid his money to the cashier and all the formalities are complete, A has no money in his pocket, but he has, or can have on request, a bank statement to the effect that he has £100 deposited with the bank. He will also have a cheque book. He can get all or any of his money out when he wants to, by drawing a cheque for some or all of the balance.

The bank which now has his money has nowhere put into writing its promise to repay (as did the Chief Cashier of the Bank of England on A's twenty £5 notes), but this promise is nevertheless a well-understood term of the banking contract between A and his bank.

Not only are bank deposits money, created when bank customers pay sums into the bank, but banks themselves can be said to create money when they agree to lend.

Suppose A negotiates an overdraft of £500 from his bank. What happens? The bank marks A's account to the effect that his cheques may be honoured up to a total of £500 more than he has actually got. A goes away from his bank knowing that he can now draw cheques, up to £500, which will be honoured by the bank although they would not have been so honoured before the agreement on the overdraft facility.

No new money has been created yet, but as soon as A draws the first cheque – say £200, payable to B – the process begins. B gets the cheque and pays it in to his bank. A's account now shows the balance to be overdrawn, but B has £200 worth of disposable money which was *not* there before and would not be there had it not been for the decision of A's bank to lend money to A.

Where did this money come from? Not from A, for he did not have any. It has come from the bank who marked A's account. By this marking the bank has created money. So far it has created the equivalent of £200 which is now to be found in B's bank.

But the story does not end there. We know that bankers rely on the fact that not all their depositors will come in at the same time to demand the return of their money, but only a proportion of them. Therefore the bankers do not have to keep all the deposits ready to repay, but only a proportion of them. The rest they can lend out profitably just like the goldsmiths did. By long experience the bankers discovered that only about 5 per cent of their deposits need be actually in their tills in cash, ready to honour their depositors' cheques over the counter as and when they are presented.

So coming back now to B's bank, which has just received £200 from B, we know that B's bank will keep £10 in cash in its till in case B wants to draw some of his money out across the counter; but if it wishes, it can then lend the other £190 to someone else. This deposit would in its turn create a further lending liability of £180.50, and so on.

So is A's money any less money because it is now in a banking account? Let's try again.

A and B both have banking accounts in credit. A owes B £100. Some of the ways in which A can pay B are as follows.

(1) A can draw £100 out of his account in cash and take it to B at B's office. B can then take the £100 to his bank, and pay it in to his account.

(2) A can send B a cheque for £100. When B gets this he will pay it in to his banking account and his bank will collect the proceeds of the cheque on his behalf from A's bank. When this has been done, A's account will be less by £100, and B's account more by the same amount, just as in (1) above.

(3) A can write a letter to his bank asking it to transfer £100 from his account to the credit of B's account at B's bank, and A's bank will comply. Again the result is exactly the same – money has been deducted from A's account and added to B's. In the first case actual notes were used, in the other two cases the matter was settled by book transfer between the two banks.

We can conclude from the examples given above that bank deposits serve the same ends as banknotes, or can be made to when it comes to transactions between parties where one pays another. The bank deposit has acted as a medium of exchange, and, as the saying is, 'money is as money does'. It is money if it does the work of money.

We can learn one or two more lessons from these examples. First, the cheque itself in example (2) is not money. It is a claim to money. In this it resembles the early convertible banknotes. Like them it is only a piece of paper. So was the letter from A to his bank in example (3).

Perhaps we can identify one common factor which is responsible for the remarkable effects these pieces of paper have.

The banknote is worth its face value because the public rely on the government to maintain the value of the note issue – more or less – in terms of other commodities. In other words, the government's credit is good in the eyes of the public.

The cheque is taken by B because he has confidence that when it is presented on his behalf to A's bank, it will be duly paid. If he did not think this, he would not accept payment by cheque. He does not have to for cheques since they are not legal tender. But with him, A's credit is good.

The letter would not be acted upon by the bank unless it had confidence in its customer A. This does not necessarily mean that A has to have at least £100 on his account with the bank. He might have less than that, but the bank knows that A is both willing and able to see that the bank does not lose over the transaction. A's credit is good at the bank. The common factor, then, is credit.

Those of a mathematical turn of mind may care to work out what is the maximum amount of new money that can be created from the decision of A's bank to lend A £500. As it is quite a considerable sum it is clear that this decision by the bank cannot have been taken lightly, and on reflection we can come to the conclusion that the factor of overwhelming importance for the bank was that A's credit was good. Without that belief in A's credit no money would have been created. In one way then, A and his bank acted together to create the new money, and both credit and willingness to lend were factors.

An even simpler way of summarizing it would be to say that credit was turned into money. In this way banks, by lending money to creditworthy customers, create money, or spending power. However, a bank cannot create spending power indiscriminately. As we shall see later on there are many checks and controls. One of the most important of these limiting factors is the bank's liquidity ratio. This is the relationship between those assets of the bank which are in money or in securities which can very quickly be turned into money (the liquid assets), and the total balances which the customers of the bank have on their banking accounts (described in the bank's balance sheet as 'Current, deposit and other accounts'). The bank must always keep a certain minimum percentage of its assets in a liquid form to be sure of being able to meet any possible demands on it, and it must bear this in mind when lending money, so creating debts (or claims or assets) which may not be particularly liquid. Furthermore, a general expansion of credit, which will show up in the system as a whole, is subject to the overall control of the central bank. It cannot rest on the decisions of any individual bank.

Money substitutes

So far you have read that banknotes, coins and bank and building society deposits are regarded as money. That is, in popular terms all are likely to be accepted in settlement of a debt. However, you will notice in advertisements on TV, in newspapers, etc., that many companies and retail outlets will offer/accept other items in place of money. Perhaps one of the most popular forms of 'near money' would be luncheon vouchers; others would include gift tokens, and vouchers either cut out from a newspaper or pushed through the letter box showing some monetary value and used specifically for the purchase of a named product. All these items are in given circumstances classified as 'near money', as they perform some functions of money. Other items could include travellers' cheques, bills of exchange, credit cards, and a fairly recent innovation, EFTPOS (Electronic Funds Transfer Point of Sale). This is a system whereby the insertion of a card into a machine, followed by the pressing of certain keys, will enable you, or the card holder, to purchase goods, and will instantaneously debit the bank account of the card holder and credit the retailer.

This may be all very easy to understand, but is this sufficient to describe money in the modern Western economy?

At the other end of the scale, such instruments as Treasury bills and certificates of deposit, which are short-term investments, are highly liquid and can easily and readily be converted into money.

All this can be very confusing to the reader. In fact the Bank of England, in order to define the various stocks of money held by individuals, companies, financial institutions, whether short term or long term, or in any other currencies, has devised certain monetary measures which not only define the type of money but indicate the movement of money from one sector to another and assist the Bank to control the money markets.

The base measure of money is known as M0. This consists of notes and coin in circulation and cash in tills of banks.

From this base measure stem all other monetary measures and components. They are:

M1   This consists of the non-interest-bearing components plus private-sector interest-bearing sterling sight deposits. They are the cheque accounts that attract interest but withdrawals do not require any notice to be given (e.g. 7 days).

M3   This consists of the components of M1 plus the private-sector sterling time bank deposits. These are the normal deposit accounts held by banks, plus the private-sector holdings of sterling bank certificates of deposit (see Chapter 5).

M4 consists of M3 plus the private-sector holdings of building society shares, deposits and sterling certificates of deposits, *less* building society holdings of bank deposits, bank certificates of deposit and notes and coin. The reason for this deduction is that such funds that are held by building societies in their accounts with banks have already been included as part of M3.

M5 equals M4 plus holdings by the private sector of money market instruments (bank bills, Treasury bills, local authority deposits), certificate of tax deposits and saving certificates). This measure will not include the holdings of building societies of money market instruments.

The alert reader will be aware that we have discussed M0, M1, M3, M4 and M5. We must now show the meaning of the aggregate of M2.

M2 is the non-interest-bearing component of M1 plus private-sector interest-bearing retail sterling bank deposits plus private-sector holdings of retail building society shares and deposits and National Savings Bank ordinary accounts. In this context the word 'retail' refers to deposits of less than £100,000.

The last measure is called M3c. The 'c' refers to currency.

M3c is M3 plus the private-sector holdings of foreign-currency bank deposits.

When financial editors, economists or bank officials wish to comment on the movement of any area of the money supply they will refer to the various monetary aggregates mentioned above.

The Elements of Banking

Revision test 1

Place a tick against the letter you consider is the correct answer.

1 Token coins in order to have acceptability must have recognizability. Does this mean they are
   (a) easy to mint?
   (b) all of the same type?
   (c) easily portable?

2 Which of these is money:
   (a) a luncheon voucher?
   (b) a cheque?
   (c) a banknote?

3 Is a banknote
   (a) a receipt?
   (b) written proof of a link with gold?
   (c) a promissory note?

4 Token coins
   (a) have milled edges to prevent 'clipping'
   (b) are free from the risk of forgery
   (c) have metallic content equal to face value.

5 Inflation is shown by
   (a) bad coins driving out the good
   (b) a run on the bank
   (c) a rise in general prices.

6 A coin which has intrinsic value
   (a) is worth near its face value
   (b) can only be paid into a bank
   (c) is worth nothing.

7 Between 1821 and 1914 the country was on
   (a) the Gold Bullion Standard
   (b) the Gold Standard
   (c) no standard.

8 The note issuing authority in England and Wales is
   (a) the government
   (b) the Bank of England
   (c) any clearing bank.

9 Which of the following normally constitute legal tender in the UK:
   (a) English bank notes?

(b) Scottish and Irish bank notes?
(c) postal and money orders?
10 For anything to be used as money it must be
(a) intrinsically valuable
(b) readily acceptable
(c) fixed in supply.

Questions for discussion

1 State in which monetary aggregate the following are classified, giving reasons:
(a) Building society deposits
(b) Current accounts with banks
(c) Certificates of deposits issued by banks
(d) Investments in a unit trust.
2 On the assumption that a large number of wealthy persons and cash-rich companies transfer funds from their accounts in building societies and banks and sell their certificates of deposits and with these funds open currency accounts in US dollars, Deutschmarks and yen, what effect could this have on the monetary aggregates?
3 Describe some of the methods used in modern society to settle debts between people, other than by the use of notes and coins.

2

What is a bank?

It may seem strange that in a book on 'the elements of banking' the question 'What is a bank?' should be asked, but if you look around the high streets of any large town or city, you will notice not only the branches of the four largest clearing banks, but probably the Royal Bank of Scotland and the TSB will have a presence as well. Additionally, there may be branches of banks that have foreign-sounding names and other institutions that try to attract depositors.

In the City of London, where the head offices of nearly all the banks are situated, you will find banks that employ only about 20 people, others that have a staff of about 200, the larger banks may have about 2,000 employees and the major clearing banks have a total City-based staff exceeding 20,000. What have all these banks in common? How is a bank defined?

Legally speaking there is no act of parliament that gives a definition of a bank. The following are a few examples of legislation that refer to banks.

The Bills of Exchange Act, 1882. This is a most important Act for bankers, yet it merely describes a banker as: 'Any body of persons whether incorporated or not, carrying on the business of banking'.

The Exchange Control Act, 1947, now repealed, but important to bankers for over thirty years, did not define a bank.

The Protection of Depositors Act, 1963, whose purpose at that time was to protect the public from the attention of dubious financial organizations, did not define a bank.

The Companies Act, 1948, now consolidated into the 1985 Act, perhaps one of the most important Acts since the Second World War, gave certain exemptions to organizations provided they satisfied the Board of Trade that they ought to be treated as a bank or a discount house. But the Act did not define a bank.

The Consumer Credit Act, 1974, mentioned the granting of licences to institutions which could satisfy the authorities that they carry on the business of banking.

It is possible to continue in this manner, but the above evidence is sufficient to show how difficult it is to define a bank.

However, all is not lost. Dr Hart in his *Law of Banking* (1931) said: 'A banker or bank is a person or company carrying on the business of receiving money and collecting drafts for customers subject to the obligation of honouring cheques drawn upon them from time to time by customers. . .'. This definition, though wide in its description, was given recognition and accepted as an opinion from a learned person. Some thirty years later, in United Dominions Trust Ltd v. Kirkwood (1966), Lord Denning, Master of the Rolls, said that the duties of a banker must be to:

(1) ensure the safe custody of funds;
(2) maintain some form of current account in which to record transactions;
(3) act as an agent for collection; and
(4) honour cheques drawn on the bank.

Ensure the safe custody of funds

This service is fundamental to any organization that wishes to be known as a bank. Even before the days of the goldsmiths when banking was a basic crude service this was the first act of a banker. In fact, in early civilizations, it was found that bankers were the priests. They accepted this role because they were trusted by the population they served. Often they were the only people who were literate and numerate, and consequently were the only ones who could keep records of the transactions between themselves and the other parties – customers. Lastly, the churches and temples were safe places to store valuables such as gold and silver without fear of loss by theft, as these holy places were well guarded and not desecrated by vandals. These days, customers who deposit funds with banks must have the same confidence in the banks – not that they expect to suffer personal loss if the bank is burgled, but they trust that the bank will not get involved in speculative activities that will incur major losses.

Maintain some form of current account

This type of account is perhaps the most basic and the most popular. With it, a cheque book and a paying in book are issued to the customer free of charge. Funds may be paid into the account either at the branch where the account is held or at another branch of the same bank, and many other banks are willing to accept credits for another bank. Funds may also be withdrawn with ease and little formality, either by the use of a cheque payable to oneself or payable to a third party. These days, funds may be withdrawn by using a cash dispenser card.

Other services are available to customers who maintain a current account. However, a charge for using the account may be imposed, but this will depend on the bank's policy at the time, which will take into consideration such matters as the minimum/average balance and the number of debit and credit transactions during the particular period.

Statements are sent out at regular intervals, the usual minimum period being every six months, but customers may request their despatch more frequently – say monthly. These statements are also sent by post free of charge. Customers whose premises are very close to the bank may have their statements delivered or they can collect them from the branch counter.

Act as an agent for collection

This function refers to the collection of cheques and other financial documents which the bank will credit to the customer's account immediately on receipt and present to the drawee banker for payment. The normal method for presentation of cheques is through the clearing system which is discussed more fully in chapter 10.

Banks will also act as agents for collection when the customer is an exporter and wishes to send documents abroad with the intention of collecting the proceeds from the importer. In this case the bank can either credit the customer's account immediately or await the advice of final payment from his correspondent bank/branch abroad.

Whenever the bank credits the customer's account it usually does so on the understanding that should the item not be paid then the bank has the right of recourse, that is, to debit the account and return the cheque or bill to the customer.

Honour cheques drawn on the bank

As the bank holds customers' funds, so it must on receipt of written instructions pay these funds away. The normal method of demanding payment is by drawing a cheque which instructs the bank to whom it is addressed to pay a specified person or bearer a stated sum of money. This the bank must do, provided the cheque is in order and there are funds on the account to meet this payment, or arrangements have been made to pay the cheque in question. Usually, cheques drawn in favour of a third party are presented by that person to his own bank, which, acting as an agent for collection, will present the cheque to the drawee banker and will receive payment on behalf of its customer. Other mandates such as standing orders and direct debits will also be honoured, but arrangements must be in writing so that the bank can comply with the mandate of the customer.

Banks defined

The courts having given a broad indication of what is meant by a bank and the services it should offer, one would have thought that the authorities would be quite happy to allow banks, under the supervision of the Bank of England, to continue a successful and happy relationship that has in the past made London the largest financial centre in the world. After all, banking in this country has been successful and expanding for about three hundred years, both in the number of banks and the range of services offered.

True, during the past three centuries banking, like any other commercial enterprise, has had its failures, but in the main the banking system in this country was far more efficient than most. More recently, the banks have been subject to the provisions of various Acts of Parliament. In particular, the Bank of England Act, 1946, nationalized the Bank of England and gave it legal powers to enforce its directives. However, since the end of the Second World War, many companies have set themselves up in London and elsewhere and called themselves banks. At that time the Bank of England gave little thought to control of their activities. All the banks that came to London had freedom to develop, few restrictions were imposed, and the financial markets, particularly in Eurocurrency and foreign exchange, were developing rapidly. London was an attractive place for international banks.

Matters did not rest. Between 1972–4, there was a banking crisis when some of the small banks went into liquidation and the viability of many others was brought into question. This crisis took place at a time of high inflation and rising interest rates, conditions which undermined commitments by banks in the foreign currency and property markets, some of a rather speculative nature. Under the authority of the Bank of England, potentially viable banks were rescued by the launching of 'lifeboats' by the major banks which gave financial support to allow them to overcome their problems. The crisis was surmounted but it left demands for a banking act. To quote Lord O'Brien (Ernest Sykes Memorial Lecture, 1979):

> I believe that the central bank ought to have ample opportunity to assess the integrity, performance and financial soundness of those who aspire to this status [of being a bank], and have the assurance that the market as a whole is satisfied that they are worthy of it. In the past too many of the aspiring deposit-taking institutions grew up too fast, with over-exalted ideas of their place in the world, and considerable impatience with the caution and conservatism of the long-standing banker. We need brilliant bankers and we need cautious bankers, but above all we need sound bankers.

Other factors influenced the creation of the Banking Act.

Public confusion about what banks were

In the 1960s and early 1970s, all sorts of institutions were coming into being, calling themselves banks and using titles which seemed to indicate that they were large and well-established financial institutions. Bureaux des changes at that time often had the word 'bank' in neon lights outside their premises. The ordinary man in the street could not readily identify one type of institution from another.

Lack of supervision of the fringe institutions

The crisis in the banking sector drew attention to the fact that the fringe banks were not subject to the same rigorous supervision that the front-line banks received, so that they were able to operate speculatively and indeed often recklessly with the funds belonging to customers. This convinced the authorities that some form of statutory control was necessary to ensure that the debacle should never happen again.

The internationalization of banks

Large banks have found it necessary to open branches or representative offices in the major financial centres of the world. Thus UK banks have sought new and expanded business abroad, while banks from overseas have greatly expanded their representation in the UK. This has added new dimensions to the problem of exercising control over banking activities. Additionally, it must be realized that banks have extremely efficient systems of communication. They have the ability to move large sums of money around the world and can if necessary have these same funds back in London on the following morning ready for dealing in the international money markets.

Directive from the EEC

As a member of the European Economic Community, the UK must sooner or later conform to standard Community practice. A directive was issued from the EEC Commission in 1977 which set out banking objectives, the most important one being that banks and financial institutions must be licensed.

Looking back, I believe that the banks of this country were by the late 1970s ready to accept supervision providing that it was fair and evenly distributed.

The purpose of the Banking Act, 1987

Although the Banking Act, 1979, on the whole worked well it was found that it was necessary for a number of reasons, in particular the distinction between 'banks' and 'licenced deposit takers' which caused some confusion and difficulties, to abolish this act and bring in the Banking Act, 1987. Therefore, for all practical purposes, the 1987 Act has replaced the 1979 Act and this latter act is now only history.

All institutions that wish to become banks must receive the authority of the Bank of England who will, under the Act, be responsible for supervising the operations of that bank. From the day authority is given to an institution to become a bank, it is allowed to take deposits.

The first question to ask is 'What exactly is a deposit?' Would a regular payment to a gentlemen's outfitter be considered as a deposit? After all, he may receive hundreds of deposits each working day. By definition, his receipts from the various sources are not, for the purposes of the Banking Act, considered deposits, since his day-to-day business is not the receipt of funds from depositors but the selling of clothing to members of the public. In the same way, a hotelier or a travel agent who receives a vast number of deposits from persons who wish to stay at the hotel or go on holiday need not apply to the Bank of England for a licence to accept deposits, as his everyday business is to provide food and accommodation. The acceptance of a deposit in this instance is to show good faith by the person making the reservation and is ancillary to the main job of the hotelier or travel agent.

For the purposes of the Act a deposit is a sum of money paid on terms that it will be repaid:

(a) with or without interest and

(b) on demand, at an agreed time or on the occurrence of an agreed event.

While those organizations that are banks are controlled by the Banking Act, there are other institutions, e.g. building societies, which also take deposits; the National Savings Bank, the building societies, local authorities, and others that are permitted to take deposits are subject to acts of parliament relevant to their operations and therefore exempt from the supervision of the Bank of England. In order to receive authorization the Act lays down four criteria, namely

(i) Every director, controller, and manager must be a fit and proper person to hold his position;

(ii) The business must be conducted in a prudent manner. This covers, amongst other things, adequate capital, liquidity provisions for bad debts, accounting, and other records and internal controls;

(iii) The business must be carried on with integrity and the appropriate professional skills;

(iv) Paid-up capital and reserves of £1 million (£5 million if called a 'bank').

The Bank of England may at its discretion refuse authorization, and anyone taking deposits illegally may be fined or imprisoned. Under the Act the Bank must be notified of any changes in directors, controllers, and managers. Any person who can be classified as a 'significant' shareholder, i.e. holding between 5 and 15 per cent of the voting rights, must notify the Bank. Any person proposing to hold more than 15 per cent of the voting rights must give the Bank *advanced* notice. Failure to do so is a criminal offence.

All banks are supervised by the Board of Banking Supervision which meets monthly and consists of the Governor and Deputy Governor of the Bank of England, the Executive Director responsible for banking supervision, and six external members. It is a criminal offence to provide the Board of Banking Supervision with false or misleading information. Nor is an institution allowed to withhold any information that is required by the Board. The information provided is strictly confidential; provision has been made for the exchange of information with other regulatory bodies and with government departments.

While it is usual for banks to have auditors, since the Act any changes in auditors or their resignation must be notified to the Bank of England. Auditors must also give notice to the Bank if they intend to qualify their opinion on the institution's accounts. It is also possible that the Bank may require the auditor to disclose information obtained in the course of the audit, provided such disclosure is made in good faith and is relevant to the Bank's supervision.

All institutions authorized as banks under the Act are covered by a Depositors Protection Scheme and cover is 75 per cent of the first £20,000 of sterling deposits.

A list of recognized institutions can be found in Appendix IV.

Revision test 2

Put a tick against the letter you consider is the right answer.
1 Before 1979 the definition of a bank was to be found in
   (a) the Bills of Exchange Act, 1882
   (b) the Companies Act, 1948
   (c) no definition available on the statute books.
2 In the case of United Dominions Trust Ltd v. Kirkwood, the basic service of a bank was

(a) the safe custody of funds
(b) the issue of a cheque book
(c) investment advice.

3 The function of a bank as 'agent for collection' refers to the collection of
   (a) information for customers
   (b) financial documents
   (c) government statistics.

4 The 'lifeboats' launched by the Bank of England during the 1972–4 crisis refer to
   (a) the Royal National Lifeboat Institution
   (b) financial assistance from major banks
   (c) financial assistance from nationalized industries.

5 The purpose of the Banking Act, 1987, was to
   (a) publish a list of banks
   (b) standardize the size of banks
   (c) give the Bank of England authority to supervise all commercial banks.

6 A deposit can be defined as
   (a) funds deposited with a bank
   (b) funds deposited with the Department of National Savings
   (c) any funds deposited with any commercial organization.

7 Paid-up capital and reserves for a bank means a minimum capital of
   (a) £5 million
   (b) £25 million
   (c) £50 million.

8 A basic criterion necessary for recognition under the Banking Act, 1987, is that the manager/controller/director
   (a) must be a holder of the Banking Diploma
   (b) must be in possession of a university degree recognized in the U.K.
   (c) must be a fit and proper person to hold his position.

9 The Depositors Protection Scheme will protect depositors up to
   (a) 75% of £20,000 of sterling deposit
   (b) 75% of any deposit
   (c) 100% of £20,000.

10 The following banks are exempt from the Banking Act, 1987:
   (a) all clearing banks
   (b) National Savings Bank
   (c) foreign banks in London.

Questions for discussion

1 You have been approached by a major employment agency which offers you a job with a salary which you find impossible to resist. The job is to be part of a three-person team to set up a new bank in London. Ms A will be responsible for recruiting staff, Mr B will be responsible for obtaining premises, fixtures, and fittings, while you will be responsible for establishing the bank as a limited company in London.

   Describe the procedure you would adopt to ensure that you are able to operate as a bank in six months time.

2 It has been said that a 'bank' must be an agent for collection. Describe operations other than cheque collection that involve the bank as an agent for collection.

3 Describe the criteria necessary for a financial institution to be recognized as a bank.

3

The central bank

Having discussed in the previous chapter what a bank is, it is now necessary to describe the different types of banks that operate in the UK. The first, demanding a chapter to itself, is The Bank of England – the central bank. Chapter 4 will deal with the other types of banks.

Establishment of the central bank

The first and most important function of a central bank is to accept responsibility for advising the government on the making of the country's financial policy, and then to see that it is carried out. The government must decide how much money there shall be in the country at a given time, and the central bank must take steps to increase or decrease the supply accordingly.

This was by no means clear when the Bank of England was founded in 1694. The specific reason then for its formation was to provide money for the government during the war of the Grand Alliance against France (1689–97). War had become too expensive to be financed out of current taxation.

The Royal Charter of Incorporation was granted in the first instance for eleven years, but only three years later an Act provided for an increase in the Bank's capital and extended the charter until 1711, after which date it was periodically renewed. In 1709 the Bank was constituted the only joint stock bank in England and Wales. Its business at first was the receiving of money on deposit, the discounting of approved bills of exchange, and the lending of money against satisfactory security.

At first this lending was nearly all to the government, and gradually the Bank came to perform other services on behalf of the government; it thus became regarded as 'banker to the government'. In this role it undertook on the government's behalf the circulation of Exchequer bills, which were simply promissory notes of the government, first issued in 1696, and constituting the floating debt of the country for the next century and a half. They were the forerunners of the present Treasury bills. In 1718 subscriptions for government loans were for the first time received at the Bank and thereafter it undertook the management of the issue of government securities. In 1751 it took over the administration of government accounts and the National Debt.

There had been many crises in these early years, but the Bank survived them all by one means or another, although sometimes it had to suspend payment of its notes in gold. In 1821 there were more than 500 banks in England. Because of the prohibition of any joint stock bank other than the Bank of England, and because of the monopoly held by the Bank on the issue of notes in London, most of these banks were country banks limited to not more than six partners. The result was that most of these banks had inadequate resources. Sometimes they issued notes too freely. This was the main cause of a crisis in 1825 when the Bank again passed through a very severe time. In the country as a whole there were 73 banking failures; this fact was ammunition for the advocates of joint stock banking, who still had to fight hard against the vested interests of the Bank and the hostility of the surviving private bankers. We are told that the credit of the Bank was saved by the providential 'finding of a box containing some £1 notes'.

Whatever really happened, the credit of the Bank remained good and its notes respected. In the country areas there was general suspicion of the notes of many country banks. Accordingly the Bank of England was empowered to open country branches for the purpose of restoring confidence by issuing notes in the country. Branches were duly opened at Gloucester, Swansea and Manchester. The present-day branches of the Bank are to be found at Birmingham, Bristol, Leeds, Liverpool, Manchester, Newcastle and Southampton.

In 1826 an Act permitted joint stock banks with note issuing powers to be set up outside a radius of 65 miles from London. Another Act in 1833 permitted joint stock banks without note issuing powers to be set up within the 65-mile radius. The Bank of England's monopoly of joint stock banking was over. Its monopoly of note issuing was about to begin.

The Bank Charter Act, 1844

It is difficult for us today to realize the instability of the banking structure at this time. In the first quarter of the nineteenth century nearly 300 country banks went bankrupt. This instability was attributed to the over-issue of notes, and a demand for reform led to the passing of the Bank Charter Act, the object of which was to control the issue of notes and so to control inflation and thus restore confidence. It was the damage to confidence in the notes of these many small banks which led to periodical 'runs' on the banks. These crises forced the banks in question to draw on their balances with London banks, who in turn were obliged to draw on the Bank of England, which was the ultimate source of cash in the monetary system.

The Bank Charter Act gave the Bank of England a monopoly of note issue and provided that no new bank thereafter was to be allowed to issue notes. The note issue of existing banks was to be limited and the right to issue notes was to be given up by any bank deciding to amalgamate with another. The last amalgamation of a note issuing bank took place in 1921 when Lloyds Bank took over Fox Fowler. The Treasury issued £1 and 10s notes until 1928, but thereafter the Bank of England was the sole issuing authority in England and Wales.

The Act of 1844 also provided that the Bank might continue its existing issue of £14 million in notes not backed by gold – called the fiduciary issue – but that all notes issued in excess of this figure were to be fully covered by gold and silver. The fiduciary issue of notes was to be covered by securities.

So that the issue of notes could be more closely checked the Bank was to publish a weekly balance sheet (the Bank Return), and was to be divided into two departments – the Issue Department and the Banking Department. One of the earliest returns made after the Act is shown on p. 33 in simplified form.

The fiduciary issue can be seen at a glance from the Issue Department's figures. The total of the fiduciary issue was allowed to increase by two-thirds of the amount of any note issuing powers given up by other banks. In the Banking Department the 'Capital' is that of the Bank's stockholders. The item 'Rest' is the Bank's reserve, accumulated out of undisclosed profits and never allowed to fall below £3 million. 'Public deposits' is the balance in the government's account; when taxes are collected, for example, they

ISSUE DEPARTMENT

	£ millions		£ millions
Notes issued	28	Government debt	11
		Other securities	3
		Gold coin and bullion	13
		Silver bullion	1
	—		—
	28		28
	=		=

BANKING DEPARTMENT

	£ millions		£ millions
Capital	14	Government securities	14
Rest	3	Other securities	8
Public deposits	4	Notes	8
Other deposits	9	Gold and silver coin	1
Bills	1		
	—		—
	31		31
	=		=

are paid into this account. 'Other deposits' included the money left at the Bank by other bankers and by the Bank's private customers.

The Bank was originally intended to carry on the two roles of central note-issuing banker and fully competitive commercial banker, but experience has shown that the central bank functions are all-important and that the Bank ought to concentrate on them. Its activities as a commercial bank have been curtailed and it now undertakes only a very small amount of private business and will not normally accept new private accounts.

In passing the Bank Charter Act, parliament thought it was establishing control over inflation by strictly limiting the supply of money at its source. The quantity theory of money was understood – the more money which is issued, the less it is worth. Prices will go up (really the value of money going down) and, in today's terminology, there will be inflation.

Two new variables to the theory were introduced in 1920, namely the volume of production and the velocity of circulation. In its refined form the theory is expressed as $MV = PT$. In this formula, M stands for the quantity of money (here the total of bank deposits, notes and coin); V represents the velocity of circulation of money; T represents the total of all transactions causing transfers of money (and is related to the level of economic activity); and P represents the general level of prices.

What was not understood by parliament was that bank deposits were also money. The Bank Charter Act gave no control over them, and during the years that followed the total quantity of money available increased substantially, as did Britain's trade. For bank deposits – a third type of money besides bank notes and coin – were being used to carry on the bulk of the expanding Victorian commerce.

In 1928 the fiduciary issue, which between 1844 and 1921 had increased only from £14 million to £20 million, had reached the figure of £260 million, a measurement of the post-war inflation. This tendency was to increase and gather momentum. In 1952, after another war, the figure was £1,450 million and in 1983 £10,900 million.

Control of the fiduciary issue is placed, by the Currency and Bank Notes Act, 1954, in the hands of the Treasury, with the proviso that any upward change lasting for more than two years has to be confirmed by parliament. The banknotes of the Scottish and Northern Irish banks are issued under licence of the Treasury.

Present-day functions

In the twentieth century the work and responsibilities of the Bank have been considerably increased by the growth in government expenditure, by the management of the currency following the suspension of the Gold Standard in 1931, and by the introduction of exchange control in 1939. (Exchange control was abandoned in 1979.)

The Bank was nationalized by the Bank of England Act, 1946, the existing stockholders being compensated by the receipt of government stock. That Act included the clearest possible indication that the government was to make itself henceforth solely responsible for the implementation of the country's monetary policy.

Section IV of the Act provides that the Treasury may from time to time give such directions to the Bank as, after consultation with the Governor of the Bank, they think necessary in the public interest. The Bank, in turn, is empowered to make requests of, and issue directives to, the clearing banks and other financial institutions.

However, the regulations laid down to control the monetary policies have changed quite drastically in the last fifteen years or so.

Pre-1971

Prior to 1971 the Bank of England was primarily concerned with the control of bank lending by maintaining a Bank Rate, which was the rate whereby the Bank imposed a penal interest rate as lender of last resort. The clearing banks also had to keep a cash ratio – that is, cash in hand and balances at the Bank of England – at a minimum level of 8 per cent and a liquidity ratio – covering a wider range of relatively liquid assets – of 28 per cent. There were frequent impositions of Special Deposits to be placed by the banks with the central bank, and from time to time quantitative and qualitative 'requests' were issued to the banks. These indicated that the government either wished to have ceilings on overall lending and/or wished to influence the pattern of lending, e.g. to curb personal lending while encouraging lending for exports or capital investment in industry.

1971–81

In May 1971 the Bank of England produced a consultative document called 'Competition and Credit Control' which set out a new system designed to encourage freer competition between the banks, and allow credit to be allocated more by price and less by control of the central authority. All banks were included in the scheme. Competition was also introduced into the discount market with changes to the system of bidding for Treasury bills. The basic points of this paper were as follows.

(a) Quantitative directives to the banks would end.

(b) Banks and discount houses would abandon their mutual agreements on various interest rates so as to allow for freer competition.

(c) Bank overdraft and loan rates were no longer linked to the official Bank Rate, but each bank would calculate them by reference to its own 'base rate', which it would vary as it wished.

(d) Instead of keeping a liquidity ratio of 28 per cent, the clearing banks would maintain day by day a minimum 'reserve asset ratio' of $12\frac{1}{2}$ per cent of 'eligible liabilities'. The new ratio would apply uniformly to a wide spectrum of banks and finance houses, not just the clearing banks.

Eligible liabilities was a new name for deposits. They were defined as the short-term sterling deposits of a bank or finance house.

Reserve assets were defined as balances at the Bank of England, Treasury bills, and money at call with the London Money Market. Cash in tills was not included even though it had counted towards the former liquidity ratio.

(e) All financial institutions with eligible liabilities of £10 million or more must keep $\frac{1}{2}$ per cent of their eligible liabilities with the Bank of England on a non-interest-earning account. The amount of these balances would be adjusted twice a year in line with the average eligible liabilities in the previous six months. Additionally the clearing banks would maintain other accounts as appropriate for inter-bank clearing purposes.

(f) The Minimum Lending Rate which replaced Bank Rate would be based on the average rate of discount for Treasury bills plus $\frac{1}{2}$ per cent rounded off to the nearest $\frac{1}{4}$ per cent above.

As can be realized, these measures gave all banks greater freedom to lend, and within a short space of time it was necessary to impose Supplementary Special Deposits (nicknamed 'The Corset'). This system did not work effectively for either the commercial banks or the Bank of England.

1981 – control of the money supply

With the suspension of the Minimum Lending Rate (MLR) in August 1981, new arrangements were instituted by the Bank of England to ensure the adequacy of liquidity in the banking sector, and influence interest rates through open market operations – involving buying and selling eligible bills of exchange – rather than by lending directly to the discount houses.

To make the market in Treasury bills and commercial bills of exchange large enough to allow interest rates to be influenced there rather than by direct lending to the discount houses, the Bank widened the field of 'first-class names' by accepting many more banks into the group, which formerly consisted of the London and Scottish clearing banks, the members of the Accepting Houses Committee and a handful of overseas and Commonwealth banks.

Those banks included for the first time in the privileged list of 'eligible names' had to have already a substantial high quality bill business in London. They included American, Japanese, Swiss, German and French banks. They can now issue bills which are eligible for re-discount at the Bank of England through the intermediary of the discount market. This privilege makes the bills particularly attractive as investments to the discount houses, which are consequently prepared to pay a premium.

The banks that applied for 'eligible' status had to meet the following criteria:

(1) the applicant has and maintains a broadly based and substantial acceptance business in the UK;

(2) its acceptances command the finest rates in the market for ineligible bills;

(3) in the case of foreign banks, British banks enjoy reciprocal opportunities in the foreign owners' domestic market.

Banks granted eligible status undertook:

(1) to maintain 5 per cent of eligible liabilities on a secured basis with members of the London Discount Market Association and/or with money brokers and gilt-edged jobbers;

(2) that the proportion held with members of the LDMA would not fall below $2\frac{1}{2}$ per cent of eligible liabilities on any one day.

The Bank's intention is to keep very short-term interest rates within an unpublished band which it believes to be consistent with the monetary targets. From time to time the band may be revised, but the Bank has said that it will follow rather than lead money market interest rates, although it reserves the right to announce changes which it thinks desirable in the interests of the country, just as though MLR were still in operation. In fact MLR was reintroduced for one day only on 14 January 1985 at a rate of 12 per cent when the authorities wished to move short-term interest rates up sharply.

The former function of the reserve asset ratio is replaced by requirements for the banks to hold prescribed averages of liquid assets. There are special provisions for discount houses and certain banks with money trading departments.

These changes have been gradually introduced over the last two years, and only after prolonged discussions with the banks. They are tentative only, and the Bank meanwhile will aim at collecting improved statistics of bank retail deposits, the relatively stable bank branch liabilities, which might point the way to much more fundamental changes.

So far the system is working well. The Bank purchases bills as its main way of relieving money market shortages, and these purchases have kept bill rates down to money market levels, and have had some success in the double aim of keeping short-term interest rates down and reducing the growth of sterling M3 (see Chapter 1). The Bank estimates every morning the amount of money which the banks will require during the day and buys, through the discount houses, a sufficient number of bills to satisfy the needs of the market at a rate of interest which it thinks ought to be the right rate for the conditions appertaining at that moment. Sometimes it makes further purchases in the afternoon as the experience of the morning points to a revised target figure. Sometimes it lets the banks know, unofficially, whether or not it thinks they ought to raise or lower their base rates – a system used over many years and given the description 'nods and winks'. But the banks, while closely considering these requests, do not have to follow them.

Now, much more than previously, the banks themselves have to take a view as to the future movements of short-term interest rates. The banks are considering the matter principally from the aspect that they are in business to make a profit. They look at this from two points of view, domestic and foreign. They always have been concerned about the exchange rate of sterling, but now that the major banks have developed into very big international institutions they are very much involved in this field; they also have to bear in mind that if the going rate of interest gets above overdraft rates, they will suffer from the activities of arbitrage operators. The Bank of England, too, is always having to keep an eye on sterling exchange rates, for it is concerned with the implementation of the policy of the government.

Although the Bank of England may try on its own to check major fluctuations in sterling (e.g. a drop from \$1.80 to \$1.40 against the £) by market intervention through the use of the Exchange Equalization Account, it has limited influence. It is perhaps by requesting the co-operation of other central banks in market operations, or by changing the level of interest rates that the Bank of England can have the most steadying influence on sterling exchange rates.

Conclusions and assessment

The changes made to the way in which the Bank deals with the discount houses and the banking system are worth summarizing.

They include the abolition of the Reserve Asset Ratio (see Appendix III) and the suspension of the Minimum Lending Rate, the widening of the range of eligible banks, and the requirement that these banks maintain 5 per cent of their eligible liabilities in the form of secured money with the discount market and/or with money brokers and gilt-edged jobbers. The proportion held with the discount market must not fall below $2\frac{1}{2}$ per cent on any one day. The Bank's principal means of relieving shortages or absorbing surpluses is now by way of dealing with the discount market in eligible bills.

Other present-day functions of the Bank of England

Acts as banker to the government

All the main accounts of the central government are kept at the Bank of England. Funds are received from individuals and companies through direct and indirect taxation. Government expenditure comes from the distribution of these funds through the accounts of the various ministries. Finally, the short-term and long-term government borrowings are arranged by the Bank of England, which also keeps the registers of the various government stocks, pays the interest at the appropriate times to the stockholders, amends the registers when purchases or sales are made, and at maturity refunds the sums due to the current stockholders.

Manages the Exchange Equalization Account

At the beginning of the Second World War the government imposed strict exchange control regulations which later became the Exchange Control Act, 1947, in which the government did not allow any person or corporate body to hold gold or foreign currency. Any funds held or received had to be surrendered to an Authorized Depository – usually a bank – for transfer to the Bank of England. Such foreign currency and gold were placed to a special account called the Exchange Equalization Account. Originally this account was used to pay the country's external debts, but since returning to a peacetime economy the account is now used for the official reserves of currency and gold. It is through this account that the Bank enters the foreign exchange market in order to prevent any undue fluctuations of the pound sterling against the other major currencies of the world.

Note issuing authority

As a result of the Bank Charter Act, the Bank of England has become the only authority to issue notes in England and Wales. The Bank of England maintains its own printing presses, so that notes may be printed and circulated as needed. The circulation of such notes to members of the public is in the main carried out by the clearing banks who draw their requirements from the various branches of the Bank. Additionally, the clearing banks will collect old and unusable notes from the public and return them, via their head offices, to the Bank of England for destruction.

Handles the issue of Treasury bills

Treasury bills are placed on offer every Friday by the Bank of England for issue in the following week. In return for the Bank acting as 'lender of last resort', the London Discount Market Association will take up the whole issue of Treasury bills offered. Treasury bills are negotiable instruments issued generally with a maturity of 91 days, and at a discount. The purpose of these bills is to cover the short-term borrowing needs of the government.

Acts as banker to other banks and financial institutions

All the clearing banks maintain accounts to be used for interbank indebtedness resulting from the daily settlement of debit and credit clearings. Under present regulations all banks must maintain $\frac{1}{2}$ per cent of their deposits with the Bank.

Maintains the sterling accounts of other central banks and international organizations such as The World Bank, IMF, etc.

These accounts are used by central banks and international institutions for the purpose of receiving and paying funds in sterling.

Supervises the banking institutions in the UK

Under the powers given to the Bank of England under the Banking Act, 1987, the Bank of England is the only institution that can authorize a company to accept deposits, i.e. become a bank, providing certain criteria have been attained (See Appendix III). The Bank also has the right to request information and documents from any bank and any withholding of information or misleading statements can be regarded as a criminal offence. The Bank also has the right to request auditors to disclose any information that is relevant to the Bank's supervision.

In this way the Bank can monitor the liquidity, capital adequacy, internal controls, etc., to ensure that each bank has available funds to meet the demands of its customers.

Lender of last resort to the discount houses

As part of its relationship with the discount market, the Bank of England is always prepared to lend funds to the discount houses so that at the end of each day they may balance their books. While the authorities are prepared to lend funds, they will only do so at a penal rate of interest. This interest rate is not advised until the discount house goes to the Bank to request funds.

Supervision under the Financial Services Act, 1986

This Act has taken some time to be implemented in full and, although its main purpose is the protection of the private investor, it was laid down in the Act that a Securities Investment Board (SIB) was to be set up jointly by the Bank of England and the Secretary of State.

The SIB in its turn would be responsible for establishing Self-Regulating Organizations (SROs). Although the conduct of the members of the SROs is not the direct responsibility of the Bank of England, the Bank is aware that it is responsible for orderly money markets and can wield such influence to ensure compliance with the regulations.

The secondary banking crisis

During the 1960s the strict lending controls over the main banking system had encouraged the growth of a number of fringe institutions varying widely in size and in the banking type of business which they undertook. Unhampered by the controls, they were able to flourish in the developing wholesale money markets, charging the higher interest rates needed for profitable growth, particularly to finance property development. They benefited from the increased resources available in the inter-bank market after the introduction of competition and credit control, and continued to expand. However, the sharp rise in interest rates in the second half of 1973, the collapse of the property market, beset by a rent freeze and the prospects of a heavy development gains tax, and a generally poorer economic climate, left some weak positions exposed.

The failure of one secondary bank brought into question the liquidity of others, leading to a withdrawal of funds from many secondary banking companies. To protect depositors and to prevent a further spread of mistrust, the Bank of England and the clearing bank joined together in a rescue operation – the 'lifeboat' – to provide support which eventually reached a peak of some £1,200 million. Although it was originally hoped that such support would be required for only a few months, it soon became clear that the problems would take much longer to solve. Most of these arose from the fall in property values and the difficulties of the property companies to which the secondary banks had lent long-term funds on the basis of short-term deposits. Other banks suffered too from the fall in property prices, not only those who had lent direct to property companies, but also those relying heavily upon property as security for advances in the normal course of business. The situation was further aggravated by the collapse of the stock market as the prospects for industrial and commercial companies became increasingly bleak, and fears arose of world recession in the wake of the oil crisis. Adding to these problems were the repercussions of banking failures overseas, through losses in the more volatile foreign exchange markets of floating exchange rates.

Although conditions subsequently improved and the worst fears proved unfounded, the shocks were considerable and have had long-term effects on the banking system. Closer attention has been given to the adequacy of bank capital and liquidity. Risk assessment is now given high priority by the banks themselves and by the Bank of England which, in 1975, formally affirmed its responsibility for the regulation and supervision of UK banks and took steps to make such regulation and supervision effective.

Revision test 3

Place a tick against the letter you consider is the right answer.

1 The Bank of England was established in 1694 to
   (a) keep up with the banking systems in other countries
   (b) finance the King for the wars of the Grand Alliance
   (c) improve banking services.

2 The object of the Bank Charter Act was to

(a) force the Bank to present its accounts more clearly
(b) nationalize the Bank of England
(c) control the issue of banknotes.

3 At the present time the fiduciary issue is
(a) fully covered by securities
(b) fully covered by gold
(c) partly covered by gold and securities.

4 The Bank of England is
(a) the sole note issuing authority in England and Wales
(b) a publicly owned commercial bank
(c) a privately owned merchant bank.

5 The item 'public deposits' in the Bank Return refers to
(a) money which has been temporarily taken away
(b) money deposited by the government
(c) money maintained by the banks to make daily adjustments between themselves.

6 When the Bank of England wants to borrow money over a short term, it issues Treasury bills. They are tendered for by
(a) the clearing banks
(b) the foreign banks
(c) the discount houses.

7 The ratio between a bank's deposits and its liquid assets is called
(a) the cash ratio
(b) the reserve asset ratio
(c) the lending ratio.

8 If the authorities want to support sterling on the foreign exchange markets, they will
(a) issue more banknotes
(b) make a call for special deposits
(c) raise interest rates.

9 A bank with 'eligible' status must have
(a) substantial acceptance business
(b) a wide spread of banking services
(c) a large number of banking branches.

10 A Treasury bill is
(a) an IOU issued by the Bank of England
(b) a bill of exchange issued by the Bank of England at a discount
(c) a certificate issued by the Bank of England on which a dividend is paid.

Questions for discussion

1 Describe the effect the introduction of competition and credit control had on all banks in the UK.
2 Discuss the present method by which the Bank of England controls the activities of the banking system.
3 What effect did the Bank Charter Act, 1844, have on the banking system?

4

Other banks

As there is some confusion between the various descriptions of banks, and many are used without a great deal of thought, it is perhaps helpful to begin with a few descriptions that are in common use.

Bank

A deposit-taking institution which is recognized as a bank by the Bank of England under the provisions of the Banking Act, 1985.

Deposit taking institutions other than banks, that is those that have a capital and reserves of less than 5 million, must receive a licence from the Bank of England in order to accept deposits. The division between authorised banks and licensed deposit takers was effectively abolished by the Banking Act, 1987.

Deposit bank

This description applies to all banks since, having been given a licence to accept deposits, all banks are deposit banks.

Clearing bank

This often refers to the 'Big Four', which is erroneous as there are now a considerable number of banks involved in the clearing system. There are seven banks who form the Committee of London and Scottish Bankers (CLSB). This body has replaced the Committee of London Clearing Banks as the trade association for the major 'high street' banks.

The members of the new committee are the Chairmen of the Bank of Scotland, Barclays, Lloyds, Midland, National Westminster, The

Royal Bank of Scotland, Standard Chartered, and eventually the Trustee Savings Bank. The Committee of Scottish Clearing Banks (Clydesdale, Bank of Scotland and the Royal Bank of Scotland) continue to handle those affairs of particular relevance to Scottish banking.

Commercial bank

This refers to banks engaged in all aspects of commercial activities. They deal with trade within the country, remit funds and receive funds from abroad, and arrange finance for domestic as well as international trade purposes, bearing in mind that their main purpose is to make a profit.

High street bank

This is another name for the major clearing banks. Yet, looking around in the high street of any of the major towns and cities of the country, you will no doubt notice a variety of other banks or other financial institutions such as building societies, that offer banking services.

Joint stock banks

This refers to banks whose shares are available on the Stock Exchange. These are public companies and the members of these banks can be individuals and others who have invested capital in the bank.

Retail bank

Yet another name for a high street bank, but it particularly emphasizes that they take funds from the ordinary man in the street, as well as from major corporations and from the wholesale money markets.

The clearing banks – the 'Big Four'

The first bankers in this country were, as we know, the goldsmiths, who by issuing transferable receipts on the security of gold deposited with them, paved the way for the development of rudimentary current accounts, bill discounting and cheque and loan facilities.

The Bank of England, as the only bank that enjoyed limited liability due to the grant of a Royal Charter, had the monopoly it enjoyed for centuries gradually whittled away, first by an Act in 1826 which allowed joint stock banks to operate outside a radius of 65 miles from London. Seven years later, another Act allowed joint stock banks to be established inside the 65-mile circle, although they were not allowed to issue notes.

With the growth in the use of cheques, the Bank Charter Act, 1844, which was intended to control the supply of money by restricting the note issue, was a factor of ever lessening importance.

The forerunners of the big banks were already established. The London and Westminster Bank opened for business in 1834 with two branches, one in the City and one at Westminster. Barclays had been in existence as a private company with an office in Lombard Street since 1694. Lloyds Bank started in a Birmingham partnership in 1765. Birmingham was also the birthplace of the Midland Bank, where the Birmingham and Midland Bank was founded in 1836. The National Provincial Bank was founded by a timber merchant in Gloucester in 1834. Such were the modest beginnings of the giant banking groups of today. The principle of limited liability was established by an Act of 1855 and extended by the Companies Act of 1862 to banks. From then on the formation of large joint stock banks was unhindered, and a process of amalgamation and expansion progressively swallowed up the smaller banking firms as the big groups sought to achieve nationwide coverage. It was a question of looking at the map, seeing the blank spaces where there were no branches, then trying to buy up, or amalgamate with, a bank well represented in that area.

The scale of amalgamations is suggested by a genealogical tree devised to show the history of the former Westminster Bank (see pp. 48–9).

It was not until the time between the two world wars that banks really started to open their new branches on any scale. By this time there were the 'Big Five' (Barclays Banks Ltd, Lloyds Bank Ltd, Midland Bank Ltd, National Provincial Bank Ltd and Westminster Bank Ltd) and the 'Little Six' (Coutts & Co., District Bank Ltd, Glyn, Mills & Co., Martins Bank Ltd, National Bank Ltd and Williams Deacon's Bank Ltd).

In 1968 a further round of amalgamations took place. Westminster Bank Ltd and National Provincial Bank Ltd (which already owned

WESTMINSTER BANK LIMITED

GENEALOGICAL TREE

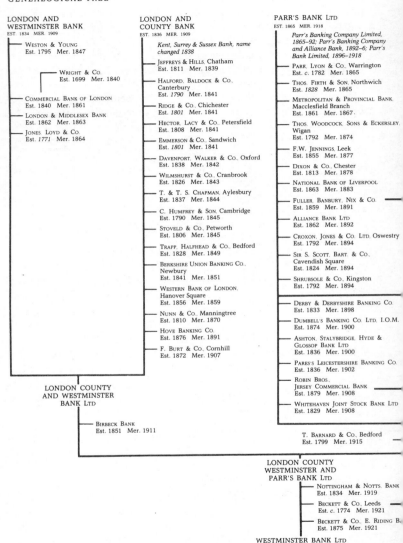

LONDON AND WESTMINSTER BANK
EST. 1834   MER. 1909

WESTON & YOUNG
Est. 1795   Mer. 1847

WRIGHT & CO.
Est. 1699   Mer. 1840

COMMERCIAL BANK OF LONDON
Est. 1840   Mer. 1861

LONDON & MIDDLESEX BANK
Est. 1862   Mer. 1863

JONES LOYD & CO.
Est. 1771   Mer. 1864

LONDON AND COUNTY BANK
EST. 1836   MER. 1909

Kent, Surrey & Sussex Bank, name changed 1838

JEFFREYS & HILLS, Chatham
Est. 1811   Mer. 1839

HALFORD, BALDOCK & CO., Canterbury
Est. 1790   Mer. 1841

RIDGE & CO., Chichester
Est. 1801   Mer. 1841

HECTOR, LACY & CO., Petersfield
Est. 1808   Mer. 1841

EMMERSON & CO., Sandwich
Est. 1801   Mer. 1841

DAVENPORT, WALKER & CO., Oxford
Est. 1838   Mer. 1842

WILMSHURST & CO., Cranbrook
Est. 1826   Mer. 1843

T. & T. S. CHAPMAN, Aylesbury
Est. 1837   Mer. 1844

C. HUMFREY & SON, Cambridge
Est. 1790   Mer. 1845

STOVELD & CO., Petworth
Est. 1806   Mer. 1845

TRAPP, HALFHEAD & CO., Bedford
Est. 1828   Mer. 1849

BERKSHIRE UNION BANKING CO., Newbury
Est. 1841   Mer. 1851

WESTERN BANK OF LONDON, Hanover Square
Est. 1856   Mer. 1859

NUNN & CO., Manningtree
Est. 1810   Mer. 1870

HOVE BANKING CO.
Est. 1876   Mer. 1891

F. BURT & CO., Cornhill
Est. 1872   Mer. 1907

PARR'S BANK LTD
EST. 1865   MER. 1918

Parr's Banking Company Limited, 1865–92; Parr's Banking Company and Alliance Bank, 1892–6; Parr's Bank Limited, 1896–1918

PARR, LYON & CO., Warrington
Est. c. 1782   Mer. 1865

THOS. FIRTH & SON, Northwich
Est. 1828   Mer. 1865

METROPOLITAN & PROVINCIAL BANK, Macclesfield Branch
Est. 1861   Mer. 1867

THOS. WOODCOCK, SONS & ECKERSLEY, Wigan
Est. 1792   Mer. 1874

F.W. JENNINGS, Leek
Est. 1855   Mer. 1877

DIXON & CO., Chester
Est. 1813   Mer. 1878

NATIONAL BANK OF LIVERPOOL
Est. 1863   Mer. 1883

FULLER, BANBURY, NIX & CO.
Est. 1859   Mer. 1891

ALLIANCE BANK LTD
Est. 1862   Mer. 1892

CROXON, JONES & CO. LTD, Oswestry
Est. 1792   Mer. 1894

SIR S. SCOTT, BART. & CO., Cavendish Square
Est. 1824   Mer. 1894

SHRUBSOLE & CO., Kingston
Est. 1792   Mer. 1894

DERBY & DERBYSHIRE BANKING CO.
Est. 1833   Mer. 1898

DUMBELL'S BANKING CO. LTD, I.O.M.
Est. 1874   Mer. 1900

ASHTON, STALYBRIDGE, HYDE & GLOSSOP BANK LTD
Est. 1836   Mer. 1900

PARES'S LEICESTERSHIRE BANKING CO.
Est. 1836   Mer. 1902

ROBIN BROS., JERSEY COMMERCIAL BANK
Est. 1879   Mer. 1908

WHITEHAVEN JOINT STOCK BANK LTD
Est. 1829   Mer. 1908

LONDON COUNTY AND WESTMINSTER BANK LTD

BIRBECK BANK
Est. 1851   Mer. 1911

T. BARNARD & CO., Bedford
Est. 1799   Mer. 1915

LONDON COUNTY WESTMINSTER AND PARR'S BANK LTD

NOTTINGHAM & NOTTS. BANK
Est. 1834   Mer. 1919

BECKETT & CO., Leeds
Est. c. 1774   Mer. 1921

BECKETT & CO., E. RIDING B.
Est. 1875   Mer. 1921

WESTMINSTER BANK LTD
(SO RENAMED 1923)

STILWELL & SONS, Pall Mall
Est. 1774   Mer. 1923

GUERNSEY COMMERCIAL BANK
Est. 1835   Mer. 1924

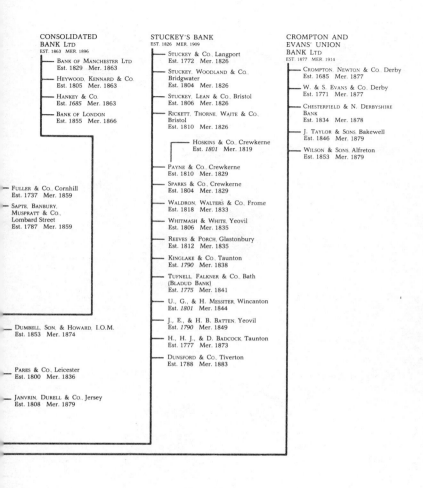

CONSOLIDATED
BANK LTD
EST. 1863 MER. 1896

- BANK OF MANCHESTER LTD
  Est. 1829 Mer. 1863
- HEYWOOD, KENNARD & CO.
  Est. 1805 Mer. 1863
- HANKEY & CO.
  Est. *1685* Mer. 1863
- BANK OF LONDON
  Est. 1855 Mer. 1866

- FULLER & CO., Cornhill
  Est. 1737 Mer. 1859
- SAPTE, BANBURY,
  MUSPRATT & CO.,
  Lombard Street
  Est. 1787 Mer. 1859

- DUMBELL, SON, & HOWARD, I.O.M.
  Est. 1853 Mer. 1874

- PARES & CO., Leicester
  Est. 1800 Mer. 1836

- JANVRIN, DURELL & CO., Jersey
  Est. 1808 Mer. 1879

STUCKEY'S BANK
EST. 1826 MER. 1909

- STUCKEY & CO., Langport
  Est. 1772 Mer. 1826
- STUCKEY, WOODLAND & CO.,
  Bridgwater
  Est. 1804 Mer. 1826
- STUCKEY, LEAN & CO., Bristol
  Est. 1806 Mer. 1826
- RICKETT, THORNE, WAITE & CO.,
  Bristol
  Est. 1810 Mer. 1826

  - HOSKINS & CO., Crewkerne
    Est. *1801* Mer. 1819
- PAYNE & CO., Crewkerne
  Est. 1810 Mer. 1829
- SPARKS & CO., Crewkerne
  Est. 1804 Mer. 1829
- WALDRON, WALTERS & CO., Frome
  Est. 1818 Mer. 1833
- WHITMASH & WHITE, Yeovil
  Est. 1806 Mer. 1835
- REEVES & PORCH, Glastonbury
  Est. 1812 Mer. 1835
- KINGLAKE & CO., Taunton
  Est. *1790* Mer. 1838
- TUFNELL, FALKNER & CO., Bath
  (BLADUD BANK)
  Est. *1775* Mer. 1841
- U., G., & H. MESSITER, Wincanton
  Est. *1801* Mer. 1844
- J., E., & H. B. BATTEN, Yeovil
  Est. *1790* Mer. 1849
- H., H. J., & D. BADCOCK, Taunton
  Est. 1777 Mer. 1873
- DUNSFORD & CO., Tiverton
  Est. 1788 Mer. 1883

CROMPTON AND
EVANS' UNION
BANK LTD
EST. 1877 MER. 1914

- CROMPTON, NEWTON & CO., Derby
  Est. 1685 Mer. 1877
- W. & S. EVANS & CO., Derby
  Est. 1771 Mer. 1877
- CHESTERFIELD & N. DERBYSHIRE
  BANK
  Est. 1834 Mer. 1878
- J. TAYLOR & SONS, Bakewell
  Est. 1846 Mer. 1879
- WILSON & SONS, Alfreton
  Est. 1853 Mer. 1879

- LEATHAM, TEW & CO.,
  Doncaster Branch
  Est. 1800 Mer. 1848
- COOKE & CO., Doncaster
  Est. 1750 Mer. 1868

- BOWER, HALL & CO., Beverley
  Est. 1806 Mer. 1875
- SWANN, CLOUGH & CO., York
  Est. 1771 Mer. 1879

N.B. Dates of establishment in italics indicate only that
the bank was in existence at that time.

Principal subsidiaries of the Midland Bank Group

UNITED KINGDOM

Midland Bank Trust Company Limited

Midland Bank Industrial
Equity Holdings Limited

Midland Bank Group
International
Trade Services Limited

Forward Trust Group
Limited

Clydesdale Bank PLC

Midland Group Insurance
Brokers Limited

Northern Bank Limited

Samuel Montagu
& Co. Limited

The Thomas Cook
Group Limited

OVERSEAS

Associated Midland
Corporation Limited
Australia

Handelsfinanz
Midland Bank
Switzerland

Midland Bank Canada
Canada

Trinkaus & Burkhardt KG
West Germany

Midland Bank
(Singapore)
Limited
Singapore

Midland Finance
(HK) Limited
Hong Kong

Midland Bank SA
France

District Bank Ltd and Coutts & Co.) formed the National Westminster Bank Ltd. A merger proposed about the same time would
have brought together Barclays Bank Ltd, Lloyds Bank Ltd and
Martins Bank Ltd, but permission for this was refused by the
Monopolies Commission on the grounds that such an enterprise
would or might tend to operate against the public interest. It would
have been too big: it would have stifled a lot of the competition and,
while good for the producer or supplier, would have been to the
detriment of the consumer. However, Barclays Bank Ltd was permitted to absorb Martins Bank Ltd.

The 'Big Four' are:

Barclays Bank plc
Lloyds Bank plc
Midland Bank plc
National Westminster Bank plc

The post-Second World War period was the beginning of a time of
rapid expansion for the 'Big Four'. Very gradually but with a gathering momentum, these banks either established subsidiaries or took
over small banks and deposit-taking institutions in order to enter the
fields of hire purchase, merchant banking, unit trusts, factoring,
leasing, export finance, insurance, investment management, and
indeed almost any other activity of a financial nature. For the principal subsidiaries of the Midland Bank, see the chart on p. 50.

About the same time the banks were encouraging the ordinary
man in the street to open accounts with them, and in order to meet
this increased activity computer equipment was being introduced to
improve and extend domestic services. Additionally, banks were
becoming more international, opening branches abroad and from
time to time either entering into consortium banking groups or
buying into banks in foreign countries.

Since 'Big Bang', that is 27 October 1986, when the Stock Exchange changed its method of operation and outsiders were allowed
to have an interest in broking companies, the major banks obtained
ownership of at least one of these in order to expand its services, so
that a comprehensive service involving the purchase and sale of
stocks and shares, portfolio administration, and trust work gave the
ordinary customer the opportunity to invest his money in new outlets, particularly at the time when the government was privatizing
major industries.

With this new climate the role of the banks, which had by tradition
been to borrow short and lend short, was changing as business
customers looked increasingly to the banks not only for working
capital but capital for expansion and the provision of capital for
medium to long-term periods. Either directly from the parent bank,
or through subsidiaries or associated companies, these funds are
available either in sterling or foreign currencies. In recent years, the
banks have entered the private mortgage market, by lending for up
to twenty-five years against the mortgage of owner-occupied residential property. They have also purchased estate agencies in order
to provide customers who are buyers and/or sellers of residential
property with a complete service.

Finally, in order to compete not only with each other, but with
other deposit-taking organizations, the banks are spending huge
sums of money to improve their technology and expand their range
of services.

Other clearing banks

As already mentioned, there are seven banks represented on the
Committee of the London and Scottish Bankers (CLSB). This body is
a constituent of the British Bankers' Association and its concern is to
deal with a wide range of issues on behalf of its members, including
regulatory, legislative and fiscal matters.

Coinciding with the establishment of the CLSB, on 1 December
1985 the Association of Payment Clearing Services (APACS) became
operational. APACS has responsibility for the structuring and
development of the clearing systems and is an independent body. It
is the umbrella organization for three clearing companies. These are:

Cheque and Credit Clearing Co. Ltd – high volume paper clearing
CHAPS and Town Clearing Co. Ltd – high-value same-day
clearing
Bankers Automated Clearing Services Ltd – electronic clearing of
direct debits, standing orders, etc.

In due course a fourth clearing company to cover electronic funds
transfer at point of sale (EFTPOS) will be set up.

The members of the various clearing companies are as follows.

Cheque and Credit Clearing Co. Ltd

Abbey National, Bank of England, Bank of Scotland, Barclays Bank,

Co-operative Bank, Girobank, Lloyds Bank, Midland Bank, National Westminster Bank, Royal Bank of Scotland and the TSB.

CHAPS and Town Clearing Co. Ltd

Bank of England, Bank of Scotland, Barclays Bank, Citibank, Clydesdale Bank, Co-operative Bank, Coutts & Co., Girobank, Lloyds Bank, Midland Bank, National Westminster Bank, Royal Bank of Scotland, Standard Chartered Bank and the TSB.

Bankers Automated Clearing Services Ltd

Abbey National, Bank of England, Bank of Scotland, Barclays Bank, Clydesdale Bank, Co-operative Bank, Girobank, Halifax Building Society, Lloyds Bank, Midland Bank, National Westminster Bank, Royal Bank of Scotland, TSB and the Yorkshire Bank.

It can therefore be seen that APACS has fourteen settlement members, all of whom are members of one or more clearing companies. Other banks and financial institutions providing many transmission services will be eligible for membership of the clearing companies and of APACS in the future, if they meet the relevant criteria.

The Trustee Savings Bank (TSB)

The origins of the TSB date back to 1810 and the foundation of the parish savings bank in Ruthwell, Dumfriesshire, by the Rev. Dr Henry Duncan. The idea of thrift and savings was paramount, and profit was not originally an objective. The TSBs grew and by 1818 there were 465 in the UK. By that time parliament had directed deposits to be placed at the Bank of England in a special account.

By the 1970s the Trustee Savings Bank operated as an association of separate savings banks, closely controlled by government agencies. In June 1971, the British government initiated a report, under the chairmanship of Sir Harry Page, into the National Savings movement and the Trustee Savings Banks which, apart from some minor mergers, had scarcely changed in principle since their formation.

Trustee Savings Bank depositors now required a more sophisticated banking service and in 1973 the Page Report was published, recommending radical changes in the status, operation, and services of the Trustee Savings Banks. As a result, the number of Trustee Savings Banks was slimmed down to twenty by a series of mergers and the range of services was greatly extended to include: mortgages, personal loans, overdrafts, credit cards, life and general insurance, unit trusts, money market services.

Whilst the services were still largely aimed at personal, rather than commercial/corporate customers, nevertheless the new, more market-orientated approach resulted in the rapid expansion of the Bank's business.

By 1982 the number of Trustee Savings Banks had been further rationalized to sixteen – ten in England and Wales, four in Scotland, and one each in Northern Ireland and the Channel Islands. After consultation with the Treasury, it was decided to reorganize the banks further into a company structure with the ultimate aim of a public flotation. In 1983, the Trustee Savings Banks were rationalized into four banks:

TSB England & Wales
TSB Scotland
TSB Northern Ireland
TSB Channel Islands

The four banks were to be wholly owned by TSB Group plc, with the exception of TSB Channel Islands, of which 49 per cent would be offered for sale separately. TSB Group plc would also own the shares of the other principal operating companies:

TSB Investment Management: unit trusts/pensions
TSB Trust Company: life and general insurance
TSB Trustcard: credit card
UDT Holdings: leasing finance company
Swan National: car rental

The flotation took place in September 1986 and was oversubscribed seven times, resulting in 3.1 million share allocations, leaving TSB as one of the most widely owned companies in the UK.

Since flotation, TSB Group plc has sought to expand the range of financial services it can provide and has acquired Target Life (life assurance and pensions), Boston Financial Services (invoice discounting), Hill Samuel (merchant bank), and a series of estate agencies. As a result, TSB Group plc is now able to provide a range of financial services as great as any major UK clearing bank.

TSB Group Structure

TSB Group

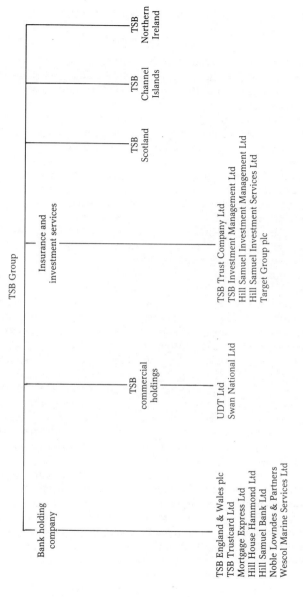

Bank holding company
- TSB England & Wales plc
- TSB Trustcard Ltd
- Mortgage Express Ltd
- Hill House Hammond Ltd
- Hill Samuel Bank Ltd
- Noble Lowndes & Partners
- Wescol Marine Services Ltd

TSB commercial holdings
- UDT Ltd
- Swan National Ltd

Insurance and investment services
- TSB Trust Company Ltd
- TSB Investment Management Ltd
- Hill Samuel Investment Management Ltd
- Hill Samuel Investment Services Ltd
- Target Group plc

TSB Scotland

TSB Channel Islands

TSB Northern Ireland

Girobank

The National Giro, as it was then called, was established by the Post Office in 1968. Factors reinforcing its establishment were the need to modernize the remittance services of the post offices (postal and money orders) and the substantial increase in recent years of the sort of transactions for which a giro system is particularly appropriate: the payments of rates and bills by instalments, hire purchase and mail order remittances, and payments for the renting of consumer durables.

In 1975 the government agreed to a series of measures, which included the provision of more complete banking services, access to government business in fair competition with other banks, and a reconstructed capital structure – measures which were incorporated in the Post Office (Banking Services) Act, 1976. In 1978 National Giro changed its name to National Girobank to reflect more accurately the wide range of services available.

Girobank acquired listed bank status in 1979 and entered the clearing system in 1981. In 1983 it became a full member of the clearing house and now participates in many of the committees which direct much of British banking. It is a sponsoring bank in the Bankers' Automated Clearing Services (BACS), a settlement bank in the Clearing House Automated Payments System (CHAPS), a member of the Society for Worldwide Interbank Financial Telecommunications (SWIFT), a principal member of the VISA International Service Association, and a founder member of the Association for Payment Clearing Services (APACS), the organization responsible for the operation and development of inter-bank payment systems. In 1985 the bank became the first public limited company within the Post Office Corporation and in 1987 adopted the company title of 'Girobank' with a new logo.

All account records are held on computer at Girobank's operational centre based at Bootle, near Liverpool, and the bank uses the national network of almost 20,000 post offices to provide counter services. Personal customers are offered a wide range of financial services including full current account cheque-book banking and a particularly convenient money transfer service for payments between Girobank accounts. The payer sends a completed transfer form, which has a message space on the reverse, to the bank (in a pre-addressed, postage-paid envelope provided). On receipt the payer's account is debited and the transfer form is forwarded, with a credit slip, to the payee. The credit is subject to clearance within two days. For business customers who receive statements on a daily basis, the transfer forms are associated with the relevant credit statement.

Many household bills – gas, electricity, telephone, etc., incorporate a Girobank transfer form as part of the bill, with relevant information such as customer reference and amount pre-encoded. Girobank customers simply complete the form and send it to Girobank. Non-account holders can pay these bills over the counter at post offices.

Regular payments can be made by standing order or direct debit either to another Girobank account or from Girobank to an account with any other bank.

Cheques are used for third-party payments and to withdraw cash at post offices. Cheque card holders have their cheques or transfers for up to £50 guaranteed and can cash a cheque for up to £100 every working day (including Saturdays) at the office named on the card or for up to £50 at any post office. Customers who do not qualify for a cheque card are issued with a withdrawal card which enables them to cash cheques for up to £50 every other working day at either of the two post offices named on the card. Other services for personal customers include: deposit and high interest savings accounts, mortgages, personal and bridging loans, revolving credit and overdrafts, a VISA credit card, automated banking twenty-four hours a day through the network of LINK cash dispensers, a higher interest savings account with access to cash via the LINK network and a range of insurance services.

For travelling abroad customers can obtain travellers' cheques and foreign currency from Girobank, Postcheques to draw in local currency at post offices throughout Europe, and a number of other countries. The Girobank VISA card may also be used for buying goods and services at around five million outlets worldwide and for drawing cash in local currency from VISA banks and VISA ATMs abroad.

Regular detailed statements of account help customers to keep up to date with their accounts.

Applications for accounts and other services are dealt with by post and telephone and decisions are normally made within a few days – there are no interviews.

Girobank has a strong base of business customers and full payment and collection services include cheques, credit transfers, standing orders, and direct debits. Pay, allowances, and expenses to employees and occupational pensions can be made by direct credit. Payment instructions can be sent to the bank in paper list form, on computer tape, or via BACS.

Credit facilities include overdrafts, short- and medium-term loans, acceptance credits and leasing finance, advanced payment and deferred purchase schemes and financing for the purchase of local-authority mortgages.

Other services include money market deposits for short-, medium-, and long-term investments; specialist investment services, including wholesale deposits and certificates of deposit; cash transfer through CHAPS and town clearing, foreign exchange payments, and a full international money-transmission service for payments and receipts, foreign trade, foreign currency, and travel facilities.

In addition the bank provides a nationwide service for deposit of branch or agent takings at post offices during normal business hours, including Saturday mornings. A similar service is provided for local authorities and housing associations enabling their tenants to pay rents, rates, and mortgages at local post offices. The rapid marshalling of these funds into central accounts facilitates efficient cash management and Girobank now handles over one-third of the total retail-sector deposit market.

Statements of account, identifying individual payments, are sent for each day there is a movement – debit or credit on a business account. Statement information can be supplied on magnetic tape for direct input to a customers' own computer systems.

Although relatively new to the banking scene, Girobank is now the sixth largest bank in the UK in terms of numbers of personal current accounts.

Royal Bank of Scotland

One of the oldest names in High Street banking, the Royal Bank of Scotland now operates through a unique nation-wide branch network from Shetland to Devon, from the Isle of Barra to East Anglia.

Today's Bank incorporates some of the most distinguished names in British banking – the Royal Bank, the National Bank, and the Commercial Bank of Scotland, Williams Deacon's Bank and Glyn Mills in England, and the National Bank, originally an Irish bank founded in 1835.

In addition the individual London banks of Child's, Drummond's, and Holt's have been integrated into the Royal Bank of Scotland's network. The Royal Bank of Scotland has a number of overseas operations – in North America, Japan, Hong Kong, Singapore, and Australia. It is a member of the Inter-Alpha group of banks within the EEC. It offers offshore banking in the Isle of Man and the Channel Islands and has a subsidiary company in Switzerland.

The Royal Bank of Scotland is the largest operating division of the Royal Bank of Scotland Group which also includes Charterhouse, the distinguished London merchant bank, Capital House Investment Management, responsible for unit trusts and investment management, Royscot Finance Group, offering a variety of specialist services including leasing, factoring, and hire purchase, and the unique insurance company offering Directline insurance to cover car, home, and creditor insurance.

The merchant banks

Merchant bankers carry on a great variety of business, and each tends to specialize in certain activities or transactions with particular countries. Some activities, however, are basic to all of them. These are acceptance of deposits, underwriting, and management of clients' funds.

The term 'merchant banking' comes from the early years when merchants in London were willing to finance international trade by allowing overseas merchants to draw bills of exchange on them. They acquired a comprehensive knowledge of world markets in the commodities relevant to their trading, and a specialized knowledge of the traders in the appropriate market. This confidence in the London merchants made the bills of exchange readily saleable or discountable in the money markets. The trade in bills became very profitable, which assisted the development of London as the major financial centre of the world. In turn this attracted representatives of foreign merchanting and financial houses to London, where the opportunities for advancement were greater. These men, in their turn, brought with them detailed knowledge of the trading resources and customs of their native countries, and the expertise which has always been the supreme virtue of the merchant banks. Such men were remarkable for their initiative and shrewd ability to develop new financial methods to meet growing demands; they contributed much to the industrial and financial pre-eminence of the United Kingdom at the peak of its power and influence in the nineteenth century.

Merchant banks prefer to be called 'acceptance houses'; indeed, this was made clear by Sir Edward Reid, a past chairman of the Accepting Houses Committee:

> An Acceptance House is a firm or company, an important part of whose business is accepting Bills of Exchange to provide short-term finance for the trade of others. We have in the past been described as Merchant Banks and this description is historically correct as we, or most of us, started as merchants trading on our own account and the business gradually developed into a mercantile bank. The term Acceptance House is a more accurate description.

The work of the acceptance houses made the bill on London so well trusted that it passed readily from hand to hand and became the nearest thing there was to an international currency. The acceptance business continued to flourish until the world recession in the 1930s, but long before then the merchant bankers, with their ability to raise large sums of money, had found another remunerative outlet for their skills. Between 1870 and 1914 London was the chief centre for the raising of long-term loans for imperial and foreign governments, and for companies engaged in the major enterprises of building ports and railways, installing street lighting, water mains, irrigation and sewerage, and constructing tramways, in foreign countries.

Further discussion on the use of term bills as a means of finance, and the market available for the purchase and sale of these instruments, is to be found in chapter 5.

The major activities of the merchant banks are as follows.

New issues

The merchant banks sponsor a substantial amount of capital issues on behalf of their customers, but before so doing they satisfy themselves that the amount required can be raised on conditions which are acceptable to investors, and at a price at which the issue may be expected to be fully subscribed. In all cases they ensure that the total capital to be issued on the market is properly underwritten by other financial institutions. Obviously, the greater the risk, the greater is the underwriting charge made; but in recent times, with such issues as British Telecom, the risk of public subscriptions falling short has been minimal. However, the ultimate responsibility for finding money for the issue rests with the underwriters. The issue of fresh capital is not only undertaken for companies quoted on the Stock Exchange, but will include companies who wish to come on to the Unlisted Securities Market (USM), and provision is made by very many merchant banks for investment by the public in companies approved under the Business Expansion Scheme.

New issues not only take the form of issue of shares to the public by means of a prospectus, but the merchant banks will also be in a position to 'offer for sale' an issue by a company. In this case the issuing house buys the whole of the issue for cash from the company, and itself offers them to the public. In the case of an issue by the company, the issuing house undertakes to find subscribers in full for the whole issue.

New issues may also be 'placed', that is, sold privately to a limited number of investors, usually the big institutions, but in these cases a proportion of securities is allocated to the market to be available to the general public. A further method is for the new issues to be made available by the company to existing shareholders only, by a rights issue or by open offer, usually at a price slightly lower than the recent market price. A rights issue gives the shareholder a right to take up a certain number of shares at a stated price, e.g. one share for every three held at a price of £1.50 per share. A bonus issue is merely the capitalization of reserves and gives the shareholder the right to have, at no cost, the additional shares based on his current holding, e.g. one free share for every two held.

Takeover and merger advice

This area of work came into prominence in the 1950–60s. The entrepreneurial instincts of these institutions came to the fore, so that one acceptance house/merchant bank became an advisor to one company and another became an advisor to the other.

A takeover is a form of amalgamation by a share purchase. This may be done in three ways.

(1) The purchase of all shares in the company. This may be made by an offer of shares in the takeover company or cash or a combination of both.

(2) The control of the composition of the board of directors. To do

this a take-over company need only have 51 per cent of the shares of the company it wishes to control.

(3) Should there be a desire to control the company by special or extraordinary resolution – as in the case of Westland Helicopters plc – it is necessary to obtain 75 per cent of the votes.

A merger can be best illustrated by that of Westminster Bank and National Provincial Bank in 1968. Both these companies were approximately of equal size, so that it made sense to have this merger. The new company was named National Westminster Bank and the shareholders in the old banks were given shares in the 'new' company.

In the 1960s and 1970s there were many takeovers and mergers, not with the intention of greater strength or efficiency, but for 'asset stripping'. Due to this, a report, 'City Code on Take Overs and Mergers', was published. This has been amended from time to time, and is still in existence. To administer this a Panel on Take Overs and Mergers was set up, without legal powers, but able to recommend, for example, a suspension of a Stock Exchange quotation or some disciplinary action by the Department of Trade.

Fund management

This service came about when the decline of the commercial bill as a means of finance led the merchant banks to take a greater interest in domestic matters. It was from the First World War that merchant banks were asked to look after the securities of private individuals. These securities were mainly government and foreign bonds, and the volume of business was small. Nowadays an increasing number of persons seek the expertise of the merchant banks to advise and manage their portfolios in order to variously increase their capital, reduce tax liabilities, or improve income. This service is expanding, and many merchant banks will advertise this service and are happy to advise expatriates or residents on investment either in the UK or abroad in foreign currency or in sterling.

Foreign business

This has been the mainstay of the merchant banks ever since they came into being. Not only are they able to offer the same services as the clearing banks, such as remittance of funds, documentary credits, collections, acceptances, etc., but they are able to offer a specialism and expertise which gives them a competitive edge over their rivals.

Finance

While it has been the tradition for the larger banks to offer short-term finance, it has always been the role of the merchant banks to offer medium-term loans (two to five years) and long-term loans (five years and upwards) to companies who need funds for capital purposes and venture capital. Often this finance could be available by injection of capital, long-term secured loan, syndicated loan, or by any other means suitable to the borrower and in accordance with the guidelines of the Bank of England.

General

With the expansion of their services, the merchant banks offer similar services to those of other banks. It should be realized of course that, in recognition of the value of merchant banking in the financial sector, the large banks do in fact own one or two merchant banks, while in 1985 it was announced that Lloyds Bank was setting up its own merchant bank.

British overseas banks

London is the headquarters of a number of British overseas banks which were originally set up in the days of the British Empire to provide banking facilities for settlers and traders in the colonies. At first, therefore, they opened branches in the main centres throughout the country, offering deposit services and lending for the trade on the pattern of the banks at home. In doing this they naturally built up a specialized knowledge of the financial and trading conditions of the area.

The rapidly changing conditions after the Second World War posed special problems for these banks. Many of them amalgamated, others were taken over in order to strengthen their organizations. One of the biggest overseas banks is Standard Chartered. This is the result of an amalgamation of the Standard Bank, which had earlier absorbed the Bank of British West Africa, and the Chartered Bank, which had previously taken over the Eastern Bank. Barclays Bank International, which has become part of Barclays Bank plc, was at one time known as Barclays Bank (Dominion, Colonial and Overseas). Other problems stemmed from the fact that many countries, particularly in Africa, developed a new national consciousness which resented the financial dominance of foreign banks and sought to rid themselves of it as soon as possible. Great numbers of their staffs came to Britain over the years to learn the business and gain qualifications. As the new countries gathered strength and experience, closer local control was to be expected. In some cases (Libya, Sudan and Tanzania) this amounted to outright nationalization. In any case, local fiscal, monetary and exchange control measures tended to ensure that funds were not as readily switched to London as in the past.

The development of new opportunities for business from 1950 onwards, and the emergence of big international companies requiring advice and long-term finance for exports and for economic development, found the British overseas banks ill-equipped to meet the competition which developed. It became apparent to them that their existing banking business, developed on conventional lines, was no longer enough. They had to be able to provide a broad range of international banking services.

This was done by strengthening the base in London, either by taking over a merchant bank or by amalgamation with other concerns who could open the door to the new money markets in London, and by setting up subsidiaries to offer long-term finance to the developing countries.

These banks have successfully adapted to the new conditions, building up their foreign currency deposits and increasing their participation in the market. Services available include Eurocurrency lending, project finance, bullion dealing and foreign exchange transactions. As UK-based banks their capital is denominated in sterling and their accounts are drawn up in sterling, yet the bulk of their earnings is in foreign currencies.

Many of these banks have built up branches in this country, whilst the reduction of influence in Africa and the Far East has tended to be more than offset by the development of business in Europe and the USA. Additionally, Barclays, Lloyds, Midland and National Westminster have all moved into retail banking in the USA.

The UK overseas banks and some thirty Commonwealth and other foreign banks with London offices are members of the British and Overseas and Commonwealth Banks Association.

Foreign banks

Foreign banks of course have their headquarters in their own countries, but those we are concerned with here have one or more branches in London and perhaps in other towns in the UK. The two world wars checked their growth here for some time, and many shut down on the outbreak, to reopen when peace was restored. Now there are about 450 of these banks in London, if we include subsidiaries, branches and representative offices. They come from 73 different countries and employ about 35,000 staff. The presence of so many foreign banks has ensured the development in London of money markets of unrivalled effectiveness. Foreign banks bring competition for the home banks, but they also bring new business to London and provide a quick intelligence service as to conditions in their own countries. The first foreign banks came to London because the City was the world's premier financial centre and they needed access to London's facilities – particularly sterling resources, insurance and shipping – for the benefit of their own customers. In those early days the foreign banks were engaged in financing international trade, mainly through the acceptance business, and in raising loans for overseas borrowers. They found it convenient to keep large working balances in London.

With the coming of convertibility the foreign banks, like everyone else, acquired freedom to participate in the exchanges and to move capital about the world. They began also to build up some domestic lending. The great bulk of their deposits were in foreign currencies as a result of their participation in the Eurocurrency markets. Thus they are now a central part of London's foreign exchange market.

The largest group is formed by the American banks, who opened branches in London in considerable numbers when the Eurodollar market developed. It is said that there are more American banks in London than there are in New York. Other large groups of banks are Japanese, French and German.

Foreign banks have been successful in obtaining the greater part of the Eurodollar business and can be said to dominate London's foreign currency banking business. But their principal business is to offer a full international range of banking services to customers requiring finance and advice on international operations, preceded perhaps by market research and reports on possible buyers or sellers. They offer many of the services provided by merchant and other banks – credit cards, factoring, travel service, etc.

The easing of exchange control and its eventual suspension gave the foreign banks the opportunity of entering into markets that were previously restricted to the British banks. One area in which the foreign banks marketed their services aggressively was in the UK corporate market. They were particularly aggressive in offering lower domestic interest rates, assisted by the fact they were able to obtain their funds from the wholesale money markets and could afford to quote at a very fine margin over the inter-bank rate. The clearing banks, on the other hand, have to cope with the high cost of gathering together most of their deposits through their branch networks and traditionally quote their lending rates at a margin over their base rates.

The advantages London has as a major financial centre are as follows.

(1) relative freedom from controls
(2) a good orderly market
(3) economic and political stability in the UK
(4) expertise and hard working staff
(5) central time zone
(6) extremely good communication systems between the UK and the rest of the world
(7) common international business language – English
(8) major international markets – insurance, shipping, Stock Exchange, Eurocurrency, foreign exchange, commodities, etc.
(9) innovative approach to financial transactions – LIFFE, development of certificates of deposit, etc.

Foreign banks in London

1967	114
1969	138
1971	201
1973	267
1975	335
1977	355
1980	403
1983	460
1986	447
1988	428

Source: *The Banker*

Consortium banks

With the growth of the Eurocurrency markets and large-scale borrowing by governments, local authorities, multinational companies, etc., it was not the policy of major banks to lend large sums of money to individual concerns. Instead they spread the risk by syndicating loans. That is, they were prepared to offer funds to a large number of organizations rather than one large sum to one large organization. To meet the needs of substantial international borrowers, major international banks, including the British, would inject capital into a new bank formed for the specific purpose of specializing in Eurocurrency syndicated loans. The parent banks often became participants in the various loans arranged by the consortium bank which was the lead manager.

In general, consortium banks have waned in recent years with some being wound up or losing some of the participating banks. Increasing familiarity with the international credit market has brought with it a greater tendency for banks to participate directly rather than indirectly through a jointly owned organization.

Scottish and Irish banks

The four main Irish banks operate a clearing system through the whole of Ireland. Allied Irish Banks and the Bank of Ireland have their head offices in the Republic of Ireland, while the Northern Bank (a subsidiary of Midland Bank) and Ulster Bank (a subsidiary of National Westminster Bank) have their head offices in Northern Ireland. All four banks have branches through the whole country, and of course those branches which are in the Republic of Ireland are subject to Irish law, while those in Northern Ireland are under the supervision of the Bank of England.

The four main banks in Scotland are

The Bank of Scotland
Clydesdale Bank – wholly owned by Midland Bank
The Royal Bank of Scotland
TSB Scotland – linked to TSB England and Wales

With the discovery of oil and gas offshore, many other banks have opened offices in Scotland, particularly the American banks, but the domestic banking scene is still dominated by these major banks.

Other banks

There are a wide variety of banks and licensed deposit takers that have offices in the high streets in major towns and cities. Many of these organizations are from overseas and have entered the retail banking field to provide a service to ethnic minorities. Also in competition with the major clearing banks are quite a few long established small banks, e.g. Yorkshire Bank, Hoare & Co, etc.

Money shops

Money shops are financial retail outlets, financed by major banks. They are not a cohesive group, but fall into two sections according to their objectives and background. Some do not have a large number of retail outlets and prefer to conduct their business by post, while another group will have retail outlets and deal directly with its customers.

In the main, the money shops do not have commercial customers, but prefer to attract individuals.

Their popularity stems from the fact that they are open five days a week and tend to link their opening hours not to the banking system but to retail trade. They offer a less formal attitude to their customers, the offices are bright, comfortable places and are designed to attract the individual.

In the main they accept deposits and offer lending services and saving accounts, offering various rates of interest. One of the chief troubles is the transient nature of their borrowers, many of whom have no other banking account. They are vulnerable to bad debts since many borrowers are poor risks. This is why the loan rates are very much more expensive than those quoted by the clearing banks. Other disadvantages are that there is not such a wide range of advice, and generally staff are not so highly trained.

Revision test 4

Place a tick against the letter you consider has the correct answer.
  1 The basic function of a bank is to
     (a) issue cheque books
     (b) accept deposits
     (c) respond to status enquiries.
  2 The 'Big Four' banks are
     (a) the major banks in the UK

(b) the only clearing banks in the UK
(c) the only recognized banks in the UK.

3 The words 'joint stock'
(a) only refer to banks
(b) refer to private limited companies
(c) refer to public limited companies.

4 The traditional role of a bank was to
(a) borrow long and lend long
(b) borrow short and lend short
(c) borrow any length of time and lend for any length of time.

5 The letters TSB mean
(a) Trustee Savings Bank
(b) Trust Services Branch
(c) Tax Savings Benefits.

6 Merchant banks were originally reputed to have a specialized knowledge in
(a) retail banking
(b) trustee work
(c) bill finance.

7 A British overseas bank can be defined as
(a) a bank which has UK staff but operates entirely abroad
(b) a bank whose head office is in the UK but which has offices abroad
(c) a bank which operates in the UK but only deals with overseas trade.

8 The attraction of London to foreign banks as a financial centre is that
(a) banking supervision is non-existent
(b) property is cheap
(c) there is the opportunity to participate in major financial markets.

9 A 'consortium' is
(a) a decision on monetary policy by the Treasury
(b) a group of financial institutions
(c) a savings scheme for small savers.

10 A new issue is 'placed' when
(a) it is advertised in the press
(b) it is given a quotation on the Stock Exchange
(c) it is sold privately to a limited number of investors.

The Elements of Banking

Questions for discussion

1 Describe the factors that have made London attractive to foreign banks.
2 Looking at the genealogical tree of your own bank, discuss the growth of the bank from the beginning of the twentieth century until the present day.
3 How can the merchant banks compete with the major UK banks?

5

The London Money Markets and financial institutions

The importance of the City of London as a world centre for international financial circles has been built up by a long tradition of innovation, flexibility and, above all, integrity. The financial institutions which have grown up over the centuries are collectively known as the London Money Market. In general terms, this is composed of dealers in money and credit who either have money to lend or want to borrow money.

The Bank of England, which borrows large sums in the money market by its weekly issues of Treasury bills for tender, is closely connected with and indeed an integral part of the market, as also are various London bankers, who, as we have already seen, engage in many varied functions, of which participation in the money market is but one.

Besides the Bank of England and the banks, the market consists of discount houses and the accepting – sometimes called acceptance – houses.

The accepting houses

Bills drawn for a term usually specify three months, but may also of course be for other periods, according to the time estimated to be necessary for goods to reach their destination, be resold, and for the proceeds to become available to meet the due dates of the bills. These periods of time became customary for certain places, thus a usance bill was one drawn at a term governed by the custom in the trade, for example three months' date for bills on Paris, ninety days' date for bills on Lisbon, thirty days' sight for bills on Bombay.

We shall see how banks accepted the bills of the merchants to provide a more widely known name in support of the bills. The merchant banks who are prominent in acceptance credit assist in financing a considerable part of world trade, dealing with the bills of both exporters and importers.

Thus an importer who has to pay for the goods he has bought may accept the bill drawn on him by the exporter abroad, but the acceptance will be more readily dealt with when it reaches the exporter if it has been accepted, not by a merchant in a relatively small way of business, but by a firm of international repute.

The accepting house pays the bill when it becomes due in London, remitting the appropriate currency to the exporter abroad. The importer pays the accepting house the sterling equivalent of the amount of the bill, plus a commission for the service.

An exporter who receives money for his goods sent abroad may stipulate that the bill which he will draw shall be accepted, not by the importer, but by a merchant bank in London. If this is agreeable to the importer, the exporter will draw his bill on the bank, have it accepted, and then either have it discounted, negotiate it or keep it until the due date. The importer will remit the currency equivalent of the sterling bill, plus the commission, to the bank.

Alternatively, the exporter who manufactures the goods and sells them abroad may finance the whole transaction from start to finish by drawing a bill on the acceptance house as soon as the contract with the foreign buyer has been signed, having it accepted, discounting it, and with the proceeds buying the raw materials which he needs to satisfy the contract. Because the name of the acceptance house is on the bill, it will be readily discountable, whereas it would not have been on the name of the drawer alone. As before, the foreign buyer must remit the funds in payment to the accepting house by the due date.

The merchant banks mostly had their origins in the activities of immigrants from Europe, and now they have extensive international contacts. Some have affiliated companies overseas; most have banking correspondents in various parts of the world. Their links are particularly close with the European countries and with the USA.

Bills of Exchange are accepted by any bank recognized under the Banking Act, 1987, but the description 'accepting house' more properly applies to the sixteen members of the Accepting Houses

Committee. The chief qualifications for membership of the committee are that:

(1) a substantial part of the business of each house shall consist of accepting bills to finance the trade of others

(2) the bills, when accepted, can command the finest rates on the discount market, and

(3) the acceptances are freely taken by way of rediscount at the Bank of England.

The last qualification is one which implies long experience and an unquestionable financial standing. To retain this standing an acceptance house has continually to satisfy the Bank of England that it has adequate capital and liquidity.

A bill of exchange drawn on and accepted by an accepting house or an 'eligible bank' has unquestioned financial standing and is known as a 'prime bill'. Prime bills are readily saleable in the London Money Market at a keen price. The banks will buy them as first-class liquid assets, and will accept them as security against their loans to the discount houses. The discount houses themselves are willing to hold them, again not only because they are first-class liquid assets, but also because if need be they can be readily rediscounted with, or used as security for a loan from, the Bank of England.

Thus an accepting house, when accepting a bill, confers on the drawer of the bill (and on anyone who discounts it for him) the certainty of being able to get sterling in exchange for it from any bank or discount house in London.

The discount houses

When a banker discounts an acceptance, he buys it outright for a sum less than its face value. The difference is the discount, which is in effect the interest charged for the loan until the due date of the bill. A bill is usually, though not always, discounted after it has been accepted.

If a merchant has drawn a bill at three months on a buyer abroad, and has had the accepted bill returned, he may find that there are, say, two months and twenty-two days left before the bill is due for payment. If the merchant wants the money immediately, as is often the case, he will wish to discount the bill.

For this there must be two good names, usually those of the drawer and acceptor. Each, by putting his name on the bill, has guaranteed that the bill will be paid on the due date. This very much reduces the risk of loss to a bank which buys the bill, for in the event of dishonour they have two reputable names to fall back on, either one of which should be sufficient. We have seen how any of the accepting houses will always be taken as one of the necessary two good names. As an example, suppose an acceptance at three months for £8,000 is due for payment on 30 June. The drawer takes it in to a discounting bank on 8 April, so that, as suggested above, the acceptance has two months and twenty-two days to run. This is calculated in days. There are twenty-two days left in April (9–30 inclusive), thirty-one days in May, and thirty days in June; a total of eighty-three days. The discount rate will normally be the same as the bank's overdraft rate, for the discounting transaction represents money lent against the security of the bill.

If the discount rate is 10 per cent the discount will be:

$$£\frac{8,000 \times 10 \times 83}{100 \times 365} = £181.92$$

The merchant will be paid £7,818.08 by the discounting bank. The latter may keep the bill until maturity, to present then to the acceptor and receive payment in full. In this case the discounting banker will make a profit of the amount of the discount, for this is the difference between the sum he received for the acceptance when he discounted it and what he gets for it when he presents it for payment at maturity. Or the acceptance may be resold, that is, re-discounted to another banker or financial institution.

When such a bill, bought on the London Money Market, is sold by a discount house, the latter endorses it and so adds its name to the two good names already there, thereby assuming responsibility for the payment of the bill at maturity in the event of default. The rate of rediscount will include a small commission, say ⅛ per cent, to pay for the services rendered and to recognize the liability of the discount evidenced by its endorsement. This has been added to the value of the bill as security. The Bank of England when buying such bills always requires the good names to be 'eligible banks'.

Dealing in commercial bills is a highly specialized business. It requires up-to-date information concerning the credit-worthiness of thousands of customers in many trades, some in countries overseas.

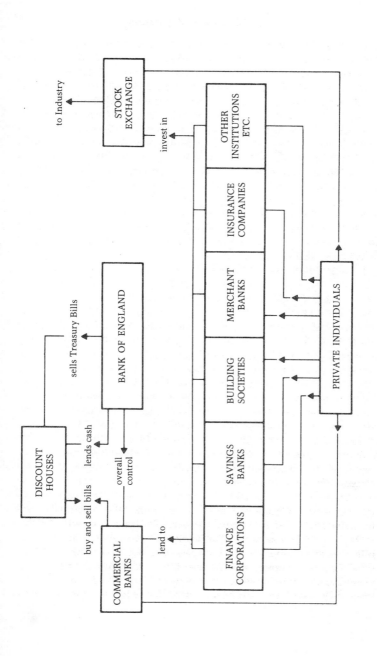

A good commercial bill is one that is self-liquidating on a short-term basis. It is called a first-class bill or first-class paper. Those who discount such bills are often called 'bill brokers'.

When the Bill on London became something approaching an international currency, the discount houses were an essential part of the system for dealing in such bills: in the process they built up an unrivalled knowledge of the names on the bills. When it declined in importance as a result of the First World War, the discount houses became associated with the handling of Treasury bills, which were assuming ever-increasing importance as a method of borrowing by the government. Since then, they have acted as dealers in sterling and dollar certificates of deposits and in the not-too-distant future they will probably act as dealers for Yen certificates of deposit. Additionally they act as brokers and principals in the various money and foreign exchange markets, and as jobbers in the gilt-edged market.

Perhaps their most important functions from the banks' point of view is their willingness to borrow money from the banks at call or at short notice, thus enabling the banks to adjust their liquidity positions whenever required. Such borrowing is always secured and certain of repayment as soon as demanded. These borrowings are secured on the collateral comprising short-term instruments (e.g. Treasury bills, local authority bills, bank bills, sterling certificates of deposit and short-dated British government securities) which they acquire with the money they have borrowed. This activity enables them to play a predominant part in the secondary market, which since the monetary control provision of August 1981 has meant that all 'eligible banks' must keep 5 per cent of their eligible liabilities on a secured basis with members of the London Discount Market Association and/or money brokers and gilt-edged jobbers. Further, the proportion held with the LDMA must not fall below 4 per cent of eligible liabilities on any one day.

There are ten discount houses, each one a public company, owned and operated quite independently, forming the London Discount Market Association (LDMA). This has been described as an organization to provide the best possible secured return on short-term funds. The discount houses make their money by absorbing surplus funds from the banking system and investing them in the wide range of self-liquidating securities mentioned above. They are also engaged in currency transactions, buying and selling London-issued certificates of deposit, bank and trade acceptances expressed in US dollars, bills and notes drawn in foreign currencies, and Euro-currency commercial paper of various kinds.

All the houses are obliged to take part in the weekly tender for Treasury bills, with the firm commitment to cover the whole tender in the case of need. These bills are notes, generally with a term of ninety-one days, issued by the Treasury with the backing of the government. They are similar to commercial bills in that they are issued at a discount and fall due for repayment at specified dates. They represent money borrowed by the government and form part of the country's floating debt.

Each week, except when the government does not wish to borrow in this way, a notice is put in the London Gazette inviting offers – known as tenders – to be received at the Bank of England each Friday, the bills being issued the following week. These bills carry no interest and that, of course, is why they are issued at a discount. Thus if a tenderer (lender) offered £49,000 for a £50,000 Treasury bill, and his tender was accepted, he would pay £49,000 now and receive a bill on which £50,000 would be payable in ninety-one days' time.

If he kept it for the full term and then surrendered it he would have made a profit of £1,000 and the Treasury bill rate would be 8 per cent. If he sold it during its currency he would calculate the selling price according to the number of days the bill still had to run, at the then current Treasury bill rate.

The discount houses used to tender for the bills as a syndicate, each house bidding for a proportion of the total tender, at a price previously agreed amongst themselves, in relation to its capital resources. Since Competition and Credit Control, however, each house is free to tender at a price decided by itself alone. In making the tenders the houses are in competition with other tenderers such as foreign banks and nationalized industries. British clearing banks do not tender directly but buy any bills they may want from the brokers. In this way the London banks can choose bills of the maturity which they want, planning ahead so that the money will become available just at the time they will need it. Treasury bills are part of the banks' liquid assets and so influence their power to create credit.

Treasury bills are issued in amounts from £5,000 to £250,000. No tender may be for an amount less than £50,000, but a proportion only of the tender may be accepted. The total amount of Treasury bills issued each week varies according to the amount of money the government wishes to borrow, and the Treasury bill rate varies with the general level of interest rates on money.

Another way in which the government borrows is by the issue of bonds, more generally referred to as gilt-edged securities or simply 'gilts'. Government bonds are documents whereby the government binds itself to pay a certain sum at a certain time. When an issue is announced the government will indicate the rate of interest payable on the stock, say $10\frac{1}{2}$ per cent. The issue price will either be fixed, for example £98 per £100 nominal, or investors may be asked to tender at a price which they consider appropriate. After the tenders have been submitted, a price is declared consistent with issuing the total amount of stock on offer. Those investors who have tendered at a higher price will nevertheless receive their stock at the declared price, while those who offered less will not receive an allocation. Tender issues have been increasingly popular in recent years, and have the advantage of determining a price which is fair and acceptable to both the issuer and the investor.

Whether a fixed price or a tender issue, the details will state when the government will repay the capital. Sometimes the repayment year will be expressed as a spread, say 1990–92. This gives a choice, so that repayment can be made at the time most favourable to the government. For instance, if the rate of interest on the particular issue is $7\frac{1}{2}$ per cent, but by 1990 the general rate of interest has fallen to 5 per cent, the government may be expected to repay as soon as possible, to get rid of the duty of paying what is by then a high rate of interest. If interest rates rise, the opposite result will ensue.

Bonds are bought and sold during their currency like other stocks and shares, and their prices can be found in any paper with a financial page, under the heading British Funds. They may be there divided into 'shorts' (those repayable within five years), medium-dated (five to fifteen years), and long-dated (over fifteen years).

The discount houses deal in short-dated government stocks, providing a market in them which is very welcome to the government. The Bank of England encouraged the discount houses to develop this market by telling them that such short-dated bonds would be acceptable as security by the Bank when the discount houses wanted to borrow there. The facility was particularly useful to the government during the Second World War, when the discount houses took up large amounts of short-dated national war bonds, issued periodically by the government to raise money to continue the financing of the war.

The discount houses later became involved in the secondary markets for dollar certificates of deposits and then sterling certificates of deposits. These are described on page 86.

To maintain all these activities the discount houses need a great deal of capital. They buy and sell, or keep 'in stock' good commercial bills of exchange, Treasury bills, and short-dated government stocks. They also hold bills and bonds issued by local authorities and public corporations.

The discount houses borrow 'at call' and at short notice from banks and other large financial institutions. 'At call' means that the money is repayable to a lending bank immediately it calls for it. The institutions are pleased to have this outlet for their surplus funds, which otherwise might not earn any interest. The borrowers are undoubted and the money will be promptly returned when wanted.

The discount houses have to consider their position daily, for each day will see acceptances which they hold maturing (money in) while other acceptances have been bought by them (money out). Similarly, they will have bought and sold securities to various people during the day, and finally they will come up with either a surplus for the day, or a deficit.

If it is a deficit they must borrow, at least overnight, to put their books straight. They can try all the head offices of the banks and will usually be able to borrow from at least one of them. The object of this is to take advantage of the difference between the rate of interest payable on funds from the banks and that which the houses earn by trading in the securities mentioned.

When money is in short supply, however, not only may they not be able to borrow, but one or more of the banks may call back an existing loan, thus making matters worse. In such a case the houses are always sure of being able to borrow, against acceptable security, from the Bank of England. They leave the Bank until last, however, because it is more expensive than the other banks.

The Bank of England is the 'lender of last resort'. When discount houses have to borrow from the Bank the 'market has been forced into the Bank'. Discount houses are the only institutions to which the Bank of England lends money at last resort, but to them the Bank will lend up to any necessary amount. This is because of the special importance of the discount houses to the Bank of England. The houses specialize in taking funds from the banks, which they must be ready to repay on demand or at very short notice. The Bank of England has become the lender of last resort to make sure that the discount houses are always able to repay the banks when asked to do so. Thus on some days there is a net outflow from the commercial banking system to the Bank of England, whether as the result of the Bank's intervention in the money markets, or the balance of government tax receipts and disbursements, or official transactions in government stock, or fluctuations in the note circulation. The banks have to meet their shortages and they call in their loans to the discount houses. The houses have to borrow from the Bank to square their books.

On other days the banks have a surplus and they lend to the discount houses, who buy Treasury bills and other assets with the money. In this way the entire banking system receives some protection. The Bank will provide support whenever it is needed, but since 1981 this support has consisted almost exclusively of purchases of Treasury bills and, more especially, eligible bills of exchange at a rate which it considers the right one for very short-term interest rates on that day.

To sum up, then, the principal functions of the discount houses may be described as follows.

(1) They provide a source of short-term funds for commerce and industry by discounting bills of exchange which have been accepted.

(2) They accept funds from the banking system repayable at call or short notice, thus making it possible for the banks to maintain adequate but not excessive levels of liquid assets.

(3) They cover the total tender at the weekly Treasury bill issue.

(4) They provide a secondary market in dollar and sterling certificates of deposits.

(5) They help the Bank of England by dealing in short-term bonds and gilts which are nearing maturity; this assists in funding the public sector debt.

(6) They assist in the control of the money supply by buying or selling Treasury bills and first-class commercial bills from or to the Bank.

Thus, if the Bank wishes to force up interest rates, it can create a shortage of cash in the market. Then the discount houses are 'forced into the Bank'. The Bank will impose the rate it considers necessary to relieve the shortage, which in turn will make the banks increase their base rates.

The Eurocurrency markets

Banking accounts are described as resident or non-resident. Thus non-resident sterling, for example, is a deposit in a UK bank which belongs to someone living abroad. From the early 1950s, markets developed in the foreign currency deposits of non-residents. Residents of the UK were required by law to surrender to banks or other authorized depositaries all foreign currency. Any purchase of foreign currency by UK residents required the sanction of the Bank of England. Gradually the exchange control regulations were eased and they were finally suspended in 1979.

However, there grew up a market in the lending and borrowing of international currencies, particularly the US dollar which accounted for over 80 per cent of the Eurocurrency market. Because of the predominance of US dollars, it is often called the Eurodollar market. The term 'Euro' is a misnomer. This name was given to the market because it started in Europe, particularly in London, but nowadays all major world financial centres trade in Eurodollars.

This market came into being for four main reasons.

(1) The limitation on the amount of interest that American banks might allow upon deposits with them (the Federal Reserve's Regulation 'Q').

(2) The political relationships between the US and the Eastern bloc countries had deteriorated to a low level, so that the communist countries felt that there was a possibility of their assets being frozen in the US. They prudently transferred these funds to friendly banks outside the US, in particular, Moscow Narodny Bank Ltd. From this point Moscow Narodny Bank became a lender of US dollars.

(3) The Eurocurrency market was a supra-national market unaffected by the policies of national governments, although it must be said that exchange controls internationally were being relaxed.

(4) The US had large balance of payments deficits, so that large dollar balances were in the hands of non-residents of the US. The world, being hungry for capital to build up cities, industries, ports

and other major installations, sought these funds for rebuilding and expansion.

As the market grew and prospered, so there was expansion into other currencies. For example, there is Eurosterling, Euroyen, Euro-deutschmark, etc.

Nowadays, nearly all banks in the UK are involved in the Euro-currency market, particularly the Eurodollar market. Many loans are so large that they have to be syndicated. Because of the amounts involved and the policy of risk spreading, each bank will only take a small percentage of any major loan. Loans can be given to one company or institution by a bank. The canons of lending are very much the same as in a domestic situation, but the borrower would be allowed either to borrow at a fixed amount for a fixed term or could be lent funds on a roll-over basis, that is:

(1) on the basis of a revision of the interest rate at each roll-over, e.g. every three months
(2) on the basis of changing from one currency to another at the date of the roll-over
(3) renewing the basis of the loan often for a smaller amount.

Banks will often be involved in bringing to the market Eurobonds. Using dollars as an example, it is possible for a large Swedish company to come to the London market and ask a London bank to arrange a dollar bond issue. The bank or consortium of banks underwrite the issue, and the prospectus is advertised so that insti-tutions may take advantage of the offer and purchase these bonds, which may have a life of anything up to fifteen years or longer. There is a market for the purchase and sale of existing Eurobonds, with prices subject to market fluctuations.

Between banks, the borrowing and lending is of a much shorter period. Often funds will be lent overnight or for a short period. As the transaction is between banks, security is neither requested or given, but each bank will carefully monitor its exposure to any other bank. If it considers that lending to any particular bank is about to exceed a reasonable limit, further loans can be refused.

It is customary for Eurocurrency loans and bond issues to be advertised in the *Financial Times*, so that each working day it is possible to see an advertisement showing the details of some Euro-currency loan or issue. Such advertisements comprise little more than a list of the participating bankers and other financial institutions, and as a result are often referred to as 'tombstones'.

The foreign exchange markets

The Eurocurrency market is a market where foreign currency can be lent and borrowed. The foreign exchange market is a market where foreign currency can be purchased and sold. Neither of these markets has a central marketplace; they rely instead on the telephone, telex and information technology to transmit instructions across London and around the world.

The foreign exchange market consists of banks that buy and sell foreign currency, not only to and from their customers – the retail end of the market – but to and from other banks and financial institutions in London and elsewhere. This end of the market can be considered as the wholesale one.

In order for banks to operate successfully in these markets, all international banks must maintain currency accounts in all major financial centres of the world. For example, all the major UK banks – and that not only includes the Big Four, but merchant, foreign and other banks – will maintain US dollar accounts with all the major banks in New York, Los Angeles, San Francisco, Chicago, etc. This then could amount to hundreds of accounts held in the US by any major bank. Not only that, accounts will be held in Germany, France, Switzerland, Japan, etc. These currency accounts are known by international bankers as '*nostro*' accounts – 'our account with you'. In the same way all major foreign banks, worldwide, will hold accounts with very many banks in London. These accounts are known as '*vostro*' accounts – 'your account with us'. To recap, when a British bank holds a 'nostro' account, the unit of account will be in the currency of that country. When a bank abroad holds a 'vostro' account, then the unit of account will be sterling.

Let us take the retail side of the market first. The bank will, at the customer's request, buy currency from him and credit his account or, alternatively, sell him a given amount of currency and then debit his account. The rates of exchange quoted will fluctuate daily and will depend basically on supply and demand as affected by major trading, political and economic factors. For example, the dollar/sterling rate of exchange can in any single day rise or fall as much as 3 cents. During times of uncertainty, it has moved even a greater amount. The purchase and sale of a currency for settlement on the day of the contract is known as a spot purchase. For example, should you wish to remit 500 Deutschmarks to a person in Hamburg, the bank will quote a rate of exchange; providing the customer's authority is given in writing, the entries will be passed the day the transfer is made. As Deutschmarks are held in Germany, the UK bank will authorize a German bank to debit its 'nostro' account and pay the sum to the beneficiary. In the meantime, the UK bank will debit its own customer in sterling and credit the mirror account in its own books, so that when the statement of account is sent from the German bank to the UK bank the entries can be reconciled.

However, many trading customers cannot inform the bank precisely when they will need currency or, if they wish to sell currency, when precisely they will have these funds available. In this case, in order to avoid the customer carrying the foreign exchange risk, a forward contract can be arranged. This means that a rate of exchange can be assured for a contract that will be settled sometime in the future, and the UK businessman knows the amount in terms of sterling that he will either pay away or receive. Forward contracts can be either at a fixed date in time, i.e. a fixed forward contract, or arranged to be performed between two stated dates, i.e. a forward option contract.

The wholesale side of the foreign exchange market is the dealing between banks. The volume of dealings will depend on the need to sell surplus foreign exchange or the need to buy some in to satisfy the needs of customers, or to make a profit, that is, buy currency at a high figure and sell immediately at a lower figure to someone else. For example, if we purchase US$ at a rate of 1.30 to the £ and sell at 1.25 to the £, the profit on the purchase/sale is 5 cents. Should the amount involved be 1 million dollars, then the profit on the one transaction is considerable. The market deals in spot, which in this case means settlement in two working days' time.

Traditionally, when one bank deals with another bank in London the services of a broker are used, but should a bank in London deal with a bank in another country then generally brokers are not used.

Many factors influence the market.

(1) Speculation – the anticipation of a rise/fall on an exchange rate which will make speculators buy/sell that currency.

(2) Trading figures – the regular publication of the surplus or deficit on a country's external trade.

(3) Interest rates – should the interest rates of a country change in relation to those in other countries, this may cause investors to either buy or sell the currency, either to take advantage of comparatively high interest rates, or to move out because the rates of interest have become unattractive.

(4) Bank intervention – should the central bank of the country enter the market or, as is usual these days, two or more central banks agree to act in concert, buying or selling a particular currency, it can affect the exchange rate.

(5) Economic and political factors – these factors, whether inflation, unemployment, government legislation or even a change of government, will have some effect on the exchange rate.

Looking at the first letter of each factor, you will have the mnemonic word 'STIBE'. This should help you to remember them.

The inter-bank sterling market

In addition to the Eurocurrency and foreign exchange markets, a separate market in sterling caters for the placing and taking of sterling deposits between London banks. Its development was accelerated in 1964 when sterling was weak in terms of other currencies, and therefore foreign banks were reluctant to hold sterling in London in case it depreciated still further.

At the same time British banks were anxious to lend, local authority loans in particular at that time offering good opportunities in terms of a high interest rate coupled with a high degree of safety.

Domestic lending, limited by the amount of money deposited by customers of the banks, began to be less limited when further supplies of sterling could be obtained from the inter-bank market.

The inter-bank market now exercises very considerable influence. Since Competition and Credit Control, the London clearing banks have been very active in it, the proportion of the wholesale deposits at one time reaching over 45 per cent of the clearing bank groups' total sterling deposits. The three-month inter-bank offered rate (LIBOR) has usually been a main factor in the determination of the clearing banks' base rates. Banks still compete within the UK for retail deposits, but they are no longer completely dependent on them.

All transactions on the market are unsecured. They are predominantly short term, the largest amount of dealing being for overnight funds, although it is possible to obtain rates for periods of up to one year. Loans are for £100,000 or more. The market is run by brokers who arrange the transactions between banks, discount houses, local authorities and building societies, who also participate in this market, and earn commission on completed deals; but there is some negotiation between principals. The big banks use the brokers because they act as middlemen and with their experience of the market are able to find, without too much difficulty, a borrower or lender for funds. The brokers act quickly since it is advisable to get large sums of money placed or borrowed before word gets around the market and the rate moves against the individual operator.

The main sources of the funds coming into this market are the overseas and foreign banks, through their London branches, the merchant banks, the savings banks and, of course, the clearing banks and their subsidiaries. Many non-bank organizations also find it convenient to lend to this market, including the finance companies, the big pension funds, the insurance companies and large commercial and industrial companies.

Sterling certificates of deposit

Negotiable sterling certificates of deposit were a logical follow-up to their dollar counterpart. The sterling certificate of deposit market was founded in 1968 and received a boost in the early 1970s following the entry of the clearing banks. As with the dollar certificates of deposit, the sterling certificates are fully negotiable bearer documents, evidencing a sterling deposit with the issuing bank, which is transferable by delivery. They are issued for a minimum period of three months up to a maximum period of five years, though in practice the vast majority of certificates are issued for one year or less.

The minimum denomination of a certificate is £50,000 and the maximum is £500,000. They are issued by practically all UK banks. Their attraction, as with the dollar certificates, is that they assure the lender of instant liquidity by giving him a readily negotiable certificate. Bankers find them attractive as well, because when they have a surplus of funds they will purchase certificates in the market which will for balance sheet purposes represent a reserve asset.

The existence of an efficient secondary market, on which depositors can recover their money before the maturity date if they need it, is of course an essential factor in the issuing of certificates of deposit by bankers. The bankers who hold the certificates issued by other banks are also aware that, should they at any time need liquid funds, they can sell certificates through the market. The main dealers in the secondary markets for both sterling and dollar certificates of deposit are the discount houses.

Certificates based upon the International Monetary Fund's Special Drawing Rights were introduced in 1980. SDRs are a currency unit created by the IMF, which has sought a more stable unit of value than any national currency by using a 'basket' of five leading currencies as a base. SDR certificates of deposit are issued in multiples of SDR 1 million for periods of one to twelve months. These operations have been characterized by stability and a relatively high return. They have been stable because the foreign exchange rate against any reference currency has fluctuated less than the foreign exchange rate of any single currency, and because the interest rates, based on the market rates of interest on the currencies in the basket, have been less volatile than the individual interest rates on the component currencies.

The local authority market

This is the older parallel sterling market, dating back to 1955 when local authorities seeking to borrow funds were denied access to the Public Works Loan Board (a government body) and encouraged to borrow elsewhere; the Public Works Loan Board thereafter acted merely as a lender of last resort. Local authorities as a rule are able to meet only a small proportion of their capital expenditure out of revenue: the rest has to be financed by borrowing.

The local authorities have six main sources of borrowed funds:

(1) direct from the public
(2) from the Public Works Loan Board
(3) through the money market, with the aid of brokers
(4) through the stock market (where variable rate bonds appeared in 1977)
(5) from overseas
(6) from other local authorities with surplus funds.

These sources may be subdivided into short-term borrowing, and long-term borrowing. On a short-term basis the local authorities issue bills which count as eligible security at the Bank of England and are therefore attractive to the discount houses, who are active dealers in these bills. On a longer-term basis the authorities raise money through stock bond and mortgage issues.

Loans are generally in unit amounts of £100,000, are authenticated by means of a deposit receipt, and are repayable at two to seven days' notice on either side. Smaller authorities will advertise for sums as low as £1,000 at one or two years; larger ones will deal in sums of £250,000 or more. The Bank of England maintains close control of local authority bond and bill issues.

The finance houses and the inter-company market

Both of these markets were at their peak just before the secondary bank crisis and since then have declined considerably in importance. The inter-company market had its origin in the credit squeeze of 1969 when some companies, pressed for money and unable to borrow it from other sources, sought out other companies with surplus cash to lend, often provided from unused overdraft facilities at the clearing banks. When the business became significant money brokers appeared who would bring lenders and borrowers together. At the height of the market, before restrictions on bank lending were lifted in 1971, some company treasurers, seeking to maximize the return on their money were able to borrow from banks and re-lend on the market. Such a process is called 'arbitrage' or, more recently, 'round tripping'. In effect, the banks sometimes found themselves borrowing money from the market which they had themselves lent at a lower rate of interest. This profit taking was largely defeated in the end by the banks' decision to lend to these large companies (and other big borrowers such as local authorities, finance houses and other banks) only at rates linked with money market rates, instead of at rates linked to base rate.

Finance houses represent a sector of the London Money Market which until recent years was liable to government measures such as control orders, which specified minimum amounts of initial deposits for hire purchase transactions and maximum repayment periods. The finance houses rely on borrowed money for the bulk of their operations, and their methods of business and the sources of their funds are described in chapter 6.

The London Financial Futures Market (LIFFE)

The first financial futures market was formed in Chicago in 1972, dealing in amalgamations of large selections of individual mortgages guaranteed by the Government National Mortgage Association. The growth of this market was so vigorous that other countries soon began to consider similar operations, tailored to their own particular financial markets.

LIFFE opened in the City's old Royal Exchange in September 1982; contracts were then traded in short-term sterling time deposits, Eurodollar short-term interest rates, and sterling twenty-year rates, linked to a notional gilt-edged stock. Also contracts were traded in five currencies (sterling, the US dollar, the Deutschmark, the yen and the Swiss franc).

The purpose of the market is to enable participants on behalf of their clients to 'hedge' against changes in the cost of finance. Therefore the market deals in financial futures. A financial future contract is an agreement to buy or sell a certain form of money at a stated price on a given date in the future. For example, a company which has funds to invest and knows that interest rates are at their highest may lock into either sterling short-term futures of sterling short-term options. If interest rates were, say, 10 per cent, then he would get a guaranteed investment of 10 per cent. Should interest rates move lower, then he could sell his contract at a profit but, if interest rates move higher, say 11 per cent, then he could sell at a loss, but lock into a higher rate.

In the case of a company treasurer having a borrowing requirement, he can buy a short sterling put option and lock into a borrowing cost. Should interest rates move downwards, then he could let the option expire worthless and then borrow at a lower rate in the market. If rates were to rise, the profits from the appreciation of the put would reduce higher borrowing costs.

In order to trade, an account must be opened with a member of the exchange, who must satisfy himself that that client has the criteria to meet the necessary requirements. Trading on LIFFE is conducted in a central area 'the pit' by 'open outcry' of bids, offers, and quantity. This method of dealing is very competitive and creates competition between the members.

When a broker has executed a deal with another member, the settlement of all deals is made through the International Commodities Clearing House (ICCH). So far as the customer is concerned, he must, on arranging a contract with a LIFFE member, deposit funds with the broker, who in turn will deposit these funds with a clearing member. This deposit is maintained while the contract is outstanding.

The Stock Exchange

A stock exchange has two main functions: its primary function is to enable companies to raise new capital and its secondary function is to provide a market for the trading of existing stocks and shares.

The Stock Exchange, or to give it its full title, The International Stock Exchange, is an integral part of the financial machinery of the City of London.

There are no precise records of its beginnings, but we know that nearly 300 years ago dealers called 'stockjobbers' conducted business in their main market place in the City, the Royal Exchange. By 1698, four years after the founding of the Bank of England, the stock-jobbers had become so numerous, and so noisy, that the other merchants of the Royal Exchange encouraged them to find another home.

The best they could do was the open street in nearby Change Alley. On cold and wet days they used to repair to coffee houses and do business with each other in them. One house in particular, Jonathan's, became their main centre for some years to come.

With the need for increased capital to finance the expansion of trade and to take advantage of the opportunities for overseas trade, joint stock companies began to replace the one-man concerns and partnerships.

In the joint stock company, each investor became entitled to a share in the trading profits, in accordance with the number of shares he held. Such investors could sell their shares to other investors wishing to buy, thus recovering their money without the necessity of withdrawing capital from the company. These transactions were arranged in the various coffee houses or in Change Alley.

In bank stock and in government loans a considerable volume of business built up following the founding of the Bank of England and the establishment of the National Debt. The first foreign government loan, for Austria, was floated in 1706. Thereafter followed a boom period, with optimistic speculation leading to reckless risk taking. The South Sea Company was incorporated by Act of Parliament in 1710 and was given a monopoly of trade in the Pacific Ocean. Unfortunately, Spain placed restrictions on the trade with Spanish colonies in South America, so that the enterprise never really prospered.

The company was also engaged in various financial dealings at home. In particular the directors had worked out a scheme for taking over most of the National Debt from the government. Parliament was persuaded to agree to this, although there was strong opposition. The price of South Sea stock rose dramatically and people rushed to buy shares, recklessly investing their life savings. When the share values reached ten times the nominal value, people began to realize that the shares were not worth nearly as much as their quoted value, and confidence suddenly evaporated. Thousands of people were ruined. The affair was known as the South Sea Bubble. It caused rioting in the streets and the suicide of a minister. It took some time for public credit to be restored. The nation had experienced its first lesson in the economics of share trading.

Over the last 200 years the Stock Exchange has had a number of addresses, but perhaps the most permanent move was that to Capel Court in 1801. This move coincided with a period of great stability in the first part of the nineteenth century, while in 1862 the Companies Act gave a tremendous fillip to trade. There was a growth in loans to foreign governments and in overseas railways financed from London, and an increase in the number of joint stock companies. By 1908, the market had developed to such an extent that the Council of the Stock Exchange decided, in order to protect investors, to segregate the members into two classes, jobbers and brokers.

The brokers were only permitted to act as agents on behalf of their clients and could only carry out their instructions through jobbers, who traded on their own account. Jobbers were essentially market makers, specializing in certain kinds of stocks, and making their money on deals with brokers. This single capacity system, as it is called, survived until 1986 – 'The Big Bang'.

The Big Bang

A new Restrictive Practices Act in 1973 no longer excluded service industries. All broking firms were in the position of having to charge commission on their clients' bargains at rates not less than those laid down by the Council of the Stock Exchange, so preventing price competition for their services. Although the Stock Exchange argued that it was a special case, it was given until the end of 1986 to abolish minimum commissions. This found favour with institutional investors – the pension funds and insurance companies – which felt they were being grossly overcharged for simple, but large, transactions.

Overseas investors were finding ways to buy UK shares without having to go through the Stock Exchange, and so avoid the high charges.

Jobbing firms had to be unlimited liability companies, as had brokers, with a maximum of only 29.9 per cent of their shares allowed to be held by 'outside' companies. They found themselves lacking the capital needed to fund the large-scale market making demanded of them. The number of jobbing firms had shrunk and the market was dominated by just a few companies.

London was in danger of falling behind the rest of the world and losing its position as one of the major financial centres. Happily placed geographically between New York and Tokyo, London has the advantage over other European centres of a long-established reputation and the English language – an international language.

With these pressures, the Stock Exchange began to change. In March 1986 outside companies were permitted to own 100 per cent of Stock Exchange member firms, so providing the capital base that was needed. On 27 October 1986 – the Big Bang – three major changes came into effect:

(1) the abolition of minimum commission.

(2) The abolition of single capacity. There was no longer a division between jobbing and broking firms; all were dual capacity, technically able to deal both as principal and agent.

(3) A new computerized dealing system, called the Stock Exchange Automated Quotations (SEAQ). This meant that a physical trading area, the Stock Exchange floor, was no longer needed as all prices and other information were displayed on computer monitors and dealing was carried out over the telephone.

Dealing

Each market maker displays on SEAQ its buying and selling prices and the number of shares in which it is willing to deal at that quotation for each stock it deals in. So for any stock there will be a list of market makers, prices and sizes, enabling broker-dealers to deal quickly and easily for their clients at the best price available.

The hundred or so most frequently dealt stocks, the alpha stocks, also show the number of shares dealt that day and the prices of the last few bargains. The next most frequently dealt stocks – beta – show prices at which you can deal, as do the alpha stocks, but the prices displayed for the gamma stocks are only an indication, and market makers cannot be held to them.

In the first instance, market makers set their prices according to supply and demand. If there are more sellers than buyers, they will reduce the price in order to discourage sellers and attract buyers. They will also adjust their prices in anticipation of or reaction to an event before any resulting dealing takes place, in expectation of its effect on buyers and sellers. A market maker who has rather too many shares in a particular company might make his selling price lower than that of his competitors, so that any buyers would come to him. In very quiet markets, market makers might move their prices for no other reason than to try to generate some activity.

Most bargains in stocks and shares are subject to the Stock Exchange Account, the most notable exception being gilt-edged (government) stock. An account period starts on a Monday and finishes on the Friday eleven days later. Ten days after it ends – a Monday – all bargains carried out during that account are settled. That Monday is called settlement day or account day. When that would otherwise fall on a bank holiday, the account period is extended for three weeks.

This means that someone can buy shares and sell them in the same account without paying for them, only the difference between the cost of buying and the amount raised on selling would change hands. A person who buys in the hope of the shares going up and selling them in the same account is called a 'bull'. If things do not go according to plan he becomes a 'stale bull'. A 'bear' sells shares hoping to buy them back cheaper before the end of the account. An 'uncovered bear' sells shares he has not got before buying them, a very dangerous operation as there is theoretically no limit to the size of the loss he might incur.

Before the Big Bang, those buying and selling the shares within an account did not have to pay stamp duty and paid commission on only one side of the operation. Although some broker-dealers still allow the commission concession, Stamp Duty Reserve Tax is now payable on the purchase.

'Stags' are speculators who apply for shares in any new company or any new issue, with the sole object of selling any allocations they may get as soon as a premium is obtainable and never intending to hold, or even fully subscribe for the shares.

The securities dealt in on the Stock Exchange are mostly 'registered' stocks and shares. A transfer from one person to another is made by the completion of a stock transfer form, signed by the transferor. This is sent, together with the registered certificate which shows the holding in the transferor's name, by the seller to his broker, then through the intermediary of the Stock Exchange to the registrar of the company whose stock or shares have been traded. The company keeps the register, or list, of shares which it has issued, with the names of the persons to whom the shares were issued.

The purpose of the stock transfer form is to bring about the change on the register. The transferor's name has to be deleted, and that of the new owner – the transferee – inserted. The old registered certificate is discharged or cancelled and filed away, and a new certificate is issued to the new owner of the stock or shares.

With bearer securities ownership can be transferred by mere delivery. There is here a much greater risk of loss through accident or fraud, and greater care has to be taken over the safe keeping of these securities.

The Stock Exchange publishes official daily and monthly lists containing quotations for all the securities in which it deals. The large daily newspapers also quote in their financial columns the day-to-day movements of the major stocks and shares, plus comment on the reasons for some of the movements, and frequently a little crystal-ball gazing.

There are plans to improve the dealing and settlement systems further. The SEAQ Automated Execution Facility (SAEF) will allow dealing in small bargains to be carried out over a computer terminal at the best price without need of a telephone. Ultimately this might be linked to the settlement system to smooth the process further. There are proposals for the Stock Exchange fortnightly account to be replaced by a five-day rolling account period, in line with other major world markets, so that bargains will be settled five business days after they take place. Share certificates will be unnecessary if TAURUS (Transfer and Automated Registration of Uncertified Stock) is introduced.

Government stock

The market in government stock (gilt-edged) is organized in a slightly different way from the equity market. Settlement is for 'cash', that is, settlement takes place on the business day following the transaction. Gilt-edged market makers (GEMMs) have to maintain continuous two-way prices as equity market makers do. They deal with broker-dealers who are dealing on behalf of the public, and also directly with the large institutions.

Stock Exchange money brokers lend stock to the GEMMs so that they can meet settlement needs. The stock is provided by the institutions in return for payment. Inter-dealer brokers allow the GEMMs to deal indirectly and anonymously between themselves, improving market liquidity and enabling large deals to be completed more easily.

Unlisted securities

A company wishing to obtain a full listing on the Stock Exchange must meet rigorous and expensive conditions for entry. In order for smaller, newer companies to have the benefit of a Stock Exchange quotation which they could not otherwise obtain, the Unlisted Securities Market (USM) was set up in November 1980. A company applying for a USM quotation need only have been trading for three years compared with five for a full listing, a minimum of 10 per cent of the equity can be sold (25 per cent full listing) and flotation costs and initial fees are much smaller.

For some years an 'over-the-counter' (OTC) market has operated outside the aegis of the Stock Exchange, providing primary and secondary markets for the shares of companies that could not or would not seek a listing on the Stock Exchange. The market was made by licensed dealers who also provided advice and often had interests in the companies they quoted. Although the Financial Services Act will make provisions for off-market trading the requirements will be much stricter and may well reduce OTC business.

The Stock Exchange also took away some OTC business when it opened the Third Market in January 1987. The requirements for entry are less demanding than those for the USM: companies with little or even no track record can gain admission, and the Stock Exchange Quotations Committee does not vet new companies. This is left to the sponsoring firm, which must be a member of the Stock Exchange, whose reputation may be at stake if it chooses badly.

Unlisted companies are generally small companies whose shares are more volatile and risky than those of a company with a full listing. Growth can be spectacular compared with large conglomerates but the chance of failure can be higher too. Many companies are involved in narrow specialized fields, new technology, and unproven products. The lack of available shares can mean that a small amount of buying or selling pressure can force the share price up and down by large amounts, and this can be exacerbated by poor market knowledge of these companies.

The London commodity markets

Many of the London soft commodity futures markets are still found close by the Tower of London, where they have always been, though how long they have been there is hard to say. The first purpose-built building was opened by Queen Elizabeth in 1571 and named The Royal Exchange. It provided the merchants with a focal point for the many commodities that were bought and sold.

The present Royal Exchange building was opened in 1844 by Queen Victoria and served the country well during the great days of the City's leadership in world trade. However, in 1928 Lloyd's insurance market moved out to its own premises and for many years the building was vacant, until in 1982 the London International Financial Futures Market moved into it.

The members of the London Commodity Exchange (LCE) are as follows:

The Coffee Terminal Market Association of London Ltd
The London Cocoa Terminal Market Association Ltd
The International Petroleum Exchange of London Ltd
The Gafta Soyabean Meal Futures Association Ltd

The London and New Zealand Futures Association Ltd
The London Vegetable Oil Terminal Market Association Ltd
The London Rubber Terminal Market Association Ltd
The United Terminal Sugar Market Association Ltd.

Each of the shareholding members who are allowed on the floor are permitted to deal with each other.

The market is organized and controlled by committees of management who establish the various market rules and ensure that there is close conformity between the futures market and the physical trade. The markets are self-regulating bodies and will take responsibility for contracts, arbitration procedures and trading procedures.

The details of membership in any terminal market association (TMA) will vary from market to market, but generally speaking there are two categories.

Full members are allowed to conduct business on the floor of the market, and in order to so do they must fulfil certain conditions laid down by their committee. As full members they are permitted to vote at meetings.

Associate members are not allowed to trade directly on the floor of the market, nor are they allowed a vote. Applications for associate membership must be approved by the secretary of the TMA concerned.

All contracts traded on the floor of the LCE markets are registered and guaranteed by the International Commodities Clearing House Ltd (ICCH). Thus all members of the TMAs must be members of the ICCH, which is an independent institution owned by various clearing banks but acting independently of its shareholders.

Lloyd's

The name 'Lloyd's' is used, first, to describe a market in insurance where practically any insurable risk can be covered, and, secondly, to refer to a society, incorporated under Act of Parliament in 1871 and known as the Corporation of Lloyd's, which provides the premises, shipping information services, administrative staff and other facilities by which the market is able to carry on its business.

As with the Stock Exchange, the seeds of the insurance market are to be found in the coffee houses of the seventeenth century. There were no insurance companies then, as we understand the term today, but there were people called underwriters, so called because they wrote their names under the wording on insurance policies. In this way cover was provided on a limited and personal basis for merchants' undertakings, particularly ship voyages and cargoes.

One particular coffee house became associated with the insurance business. This was Lloyd's Coffee House, situated near the river Thames and thus usually filled with merchants connected with the sea, ships' captains and mates, and the merchants who specialized in underwriting marine risks. As time went by it became generally recognized that Lloyd's Coffee House was the place to go if you wanted insurance cover.

The exact year that saw the start of this association is not known, but certainly the coffee house was in existence in 1688. Edward Lloyd was not himself an insurer, nor ever became one, but he was a man who knew how to encourage business profitable to himself, and he helpfully provided his customers with writing materials and then with shipping information brought from the waterfront by runners. In 1696 he took the next logical step of publishing a news sheet called *Lloyd's News*, but he got into trouble with this and it had a short life. Still, the idea was good, and it was to be resurrected later by others. Lloyd died in 1713 with no inkling of the international fame and prestige which was one day to be associated with his name.

In 1769 there was a move to another coffee house in Pope's Head Alley. This is believed to have been due to a gambling element among the customers of Lloyd's Coffee House, which was of course quite bad for the reputation of men seeking to provide responsible insurance cover. The new Lloyd's Coffee House was much the same as the old, but without the gamblers. The early London coffee houses were centres of political debate and literature as well as of commerce, and there must have been an advantage in having a house exclusively devoted to the insurance business. As business increased the new coffee house quickly became too small, and in 1774 there was another move, this time to rooms in the Royal Exchange.

In subsequent years there were other moves in search of adequate space; but in 1957 the present site of the market was opened in Lime Street, with a bridge at first-floor level communicating with earlier premises in Leadenhall Street.

The Act of Parliament which incorporated Lloyd's was passed in 1871. Lloyd's had then been in existence in one form or another for nearly two centuries, but the growing scope and complexity of the business it undertook made it desirable for the organization to be placed on a legal footing.

Underwriters and brokers

Lloyd's is now an international market for almost any type of insurance. Ships, aircraft, cargoes, oil rigs, space capsules, personal accident and third-party liability, civil engineering projects, houses and buildings are a few examples of the risks covered. Some of the sums involved are truly impressive. Every step forward in technology demands the formulation of new policies to meet new circumstances.

The enormously increased values have naturally brought about a change in the old system whereby each underwriter personally transacted his own insurance business. Today there are more than 7,000 underwriting members of Lloyd's who are formed into syndicates, which are represented at Lloyd's by underwriting agents. When a syndicate underwriter accepts (or 'writes') a risk he can do so for a very much larger amount than if he were acting on his own behalf alone.

There are four main sectors of the market – marine, non-marine, aviation and motor. The non-marine sector of the market currently transacts more business than the marine. The underwriters for syndicates sit with their staffs in the Underwriting Room at 'boxes', pew-like desks which, together with liveried staff called 'waiters', recall the origins of the business. They cannot be approached directly by members of the public, but only by brokers approved by the Committee of Lloyd's and known as Lloyd's brokers. This measure is based on practical considerations, for it requires specialized knowledge to find the appropriate underwriter and to place the business at the most advantageous terms and rates. Lloyd's brokers are thus an essential link in the chain between the assured and Lloyd's underwriters. The broker represents his client, and if he cannot deal satisfactorily with the underwriters he can place the business with other insurance companies.

Lloyd's intelligence system

Lloyd's has always been closely connected with the sea. Its early business was almost wholly concerned with marine insurance, and it was not until the 1880s that other forms of insurance were pioneered – burglary cover, block cover for jewellers, and insurance for loss of profits due to fire were examples. The first aviation insurance was written in 1911, two years after Bleriot flew across the English Channel.

As a result of this early link with the sea, Lloyd's has developed a world-wide shipping intelligence system of agents and sub-agents who are constantly sending news of shipping movements and other information relating to their own ports, towns and areas. Edited, printed and published at Lloyd's, *Lloyd's List* is London's oldest daily newspaper, a descendant of the original *Lloyd's News* of the coffee house. It contains shipping, insurance, air and general commercial news, together with reports of the latest shipping movements received, and casualty reports – ships and cargoes damaged or sunk. *Lloyd's Shipping Index* contains an alphabetical list of 16,000 merchant vessels, giving details of each vessel, its current journey and latest position as known at Lloyd's. It is the only publication of its kind in the world, requiring some 5,000 alterations daily in order to keep the information up to date. Copies are flown to New York on the same day as publication.

Other publications include *Lloyd's Weekly Casualty Lists, Lloyd's Law Reports, Cargo by Air* – a monthly publication giving details of scheduled flights from the United Kingdom and Europe – and *Lloyd's Loading List*, an alphabetical list of ports throughout the world, showing vessels loading for these ports from United Kingdom and continental ports. This is all a far cry indeed from the system of news brought back to the coffee houses by runners from the waterfront!

Details of marine and aviation casualties and reports of non-marine losses such as fires, floods and robberies are posted on the Casualty Boards in the Underwriting Room at intervals throughout the day. The Casualty Book in the centre of the Underwriting Room contains names of vessels which have become or are likely to become total losses. This information enables Lloyd's' underwriters to be kept informed of vessels which have sustained serious damage and in which they may have an insured interest.

Above the rostrum hangs the Lutine Bell, which is for many of the public a symbol of Lloyd's. It was salvaged from HMS *Lutine*, a frigate which sank off the coast of Holland in 1799 while carrying a cargo of gold and silver insured at Lloyd's and valued at over a million pounds. It is not known when the bell was first rung in the Underwriting Room, but it is thought to have been in the late 1890s when Lloyd's was in the Royal Exchange. There is a widespread belief that the bell is rung for a major disaster, or each time a ship sinks. This is not true. The sounding of the bell signifies that an important announcement is about to be made to the market. It is struck once to indicate bad news and twice for good news, as for example when two 'out of control' space capsules were brought back from outer space, thereby saving Lloyd's millions of dollars.

Lloyd's, it can be seen, is an organization of many different kinds. It is a corporation; a society of underwriters covering risks from a film star's legs to a space capsule; an international market; printers and publishers of shipping information; and the world centre for marine intelligence. It has a world-wide name for always paying up. However, this reputation has suffered in the recent past from the emergence of a series of disputes which in time reached a peak; this prompted a well known national newspaper to comment that the scandals unearthed at Lloyd's meant that the whole method and efficiency of market surveillance and enforcement techniques used by market authorities was in doubt.

The Fisher Committee, reporting in June 1980, recommended the formation of a new council to take over the rule making and strategic work until then handled by a general meeting of members. An Act of Parliament was necessary for this, and after considerable opposition, which wished to exclude from the bill the thorny issue of divestment (the forced sale by brokers of their underwriting interests in Lloyd's), the bill was eventually passed. The questionable practices which some underwriters had adopted when placing their own reinsurance business were at the root of the matter, but parliament had made it clear that the distinction between principal and agent, that is between underwriter and broker, must be made absolute as soon as possible.

The Act came into force on 1 January 1983 and a series of radical reforms have been carried out. They include the strengthening of the ruling body by the admission of respected and impartial outsiders to act in a supervisory role, the insistence on disclosure of possible conflicts of interest, and increased powers for Lloyd's' auditors.

Considerable damage has been done to Lloyd's' reputation, but nothing which has happened has in any way undermined or injured Lloyd's' ability to meet claims anywhere in the world. Whatever may be going on behind the scenes, Lloyd's always pay up promptly when called upon.

The London gold market

The gold market consists of five firms dealing in gold bullion. One of the members also melts, refines, processes and assays gold. The five firms meet twice on each working day for the fixing of the London gold price. The market tries to absorb all new production or any other gold which may be offered at the fixing. Operations on the market are not confined to gold changing hands at the official fixing. A fair amount of business is done outside the fixings at varying prices.

Since April 1969 the London gold market has been functioning without official support or intervention. Gold coming on to the international markets is newly mined gold which has not been taken into official reserves, together with gold from private sources.

It is illogical that gold should be so highly regarded; it pays no interest and, after all, is only a metal like any other. Yet through history it has aroused man's deepest admiration and greatest stupidity. As a base for a currency system it did well in the days when everyone was on the Gold Standard, but in these modern times things are different. So there arose, particularly in America, an anti-gold lobby. Efforts were made in 1977 to get gold phased out of the international monetary system, but these met with considerable resistance from European countries for economic, financial and political reasons. There was still a belief that the most effective way of achieving the global restoration of monetary law and order lay in organizing a new world monetary system in which gold would be given a central part to play. The gold price is widely seen as an index of international opinion – the higher it goes, the less the faith in national currencies, and vice versa. But of course those mundane factors supply and demand have got something to do with it all as well.

Residents in the United Kingdom have a number of choices. They can invest in Krugerrands and other gold coins, the value of which climbs as the price of gold climbs, or in speculative gold shares in mining, or in specialized unit trusts. Since the lifting of exchange control restrictions in October 1979, there are no limits on the holding of gold bullion or gold coins, though in 1985 the import of further Krugerrands was banned as a form of embargo against South Africa.

Europe's first exchange for forward trading of gold was opened in the City of London in 1982; it is attractive not only for London-based operators but also for traders in Switzerland and the Middle East. Unfortunately, gold contracts were initially offered in sterling, although the international bullion price is traditionally quoted in US dollars. The pricing basis was altered, after experience of a flagging market, from sterling to the dollar in October 1982, thus relieving speculators of worry over the sterling/dollar exchange rate.

Finance houses

It was in the 1860s that the first hire purchase contracts were written, when railway companies provided only the railway lines and the customers had to provide the rolling stock. The biggest users were the coal mine operators, who needed trucks to take their coal from the mines to the main industrial centres. 'Wagon companies' were formed to buy the railway wagons, which were then leased to the mine owners with an option to purchase at the end of a certain term.

'Payment by instalments' is a phrase familiar to most people. Usually three parties are concerned. A sells something to B, who elects to pay by instalments, and signs the necessary paper. A is paid at once by C, a finance company. B repays C over a period, paying interest.

It was after the First World War that cars were first available on instalment or hire purchase terms. This came about as the original wagon companies moved away from the financing of railway wagons and turned their attention to motor vehicles. Hire purchase was subsequently extended to gramophones, radios and other consumer equipment such as gas and electric cookers, refrigerators, washing machines, etc. Now almost anything can be obtained in this way.

At the time of the world slump in 1930 hire purchase was given as one of the causes. The view then current was that it is wrong to anticipate one's income. If an article is desired, the thing to do is to save up until one can afford it. The only exception was if the article was to be used in a way which would reduce the owner's outgoings. It was all right to buy a motor cycle to go to work on, because this would save train fares. When the motor cycle instalments were all paid, the owner still had the motor cycle as a capital asset, and the savings (not outgoings) would continue.

Nevertheless, hire purchase survived and expanded. Since the end of the last war there has been a steady annual increase in the figure representing hire purchase debt. Legislation was passed to protect the consumer, and credit sale agreements were invented.

In a hire purchase agreement the contract is one of hire. The property in the article sold does not pass to the hirer until the last payment is made. Thus it was possible for the finance company, until restricted by legislation, to repossess the article at any time up to the final payment.

With a credit sale agreement (sometimes known as an instalment trading agreement) there is no right of recovery by the finance company, because the contract is one of sale. The ownership of the article passes immediately to the purchaser, although he does not pay the full price immediately, but by instalments.

In the case of 'sale and lease back' a company may raise immediate finance by selling a capital asset, whether property or capital equipment, to a finance company, then leasing it back and continuing to use it as before. The ownership of the asset passes to the lessor, the finance company. The leasing rental will contain an element of the cost of the asset purchased from the lessee company, plus an interest charge to cover administrative and service charges. Sale and lease back arrangements are usually found only where the asset to be purchased is worth £50,000 or more.

Leasing is now the largest single type of external finance employed for the acquisition of plant and equipment in the UK economy. As a result of changes in the tax laws it is to the interest of both lessor and lessee that equipment should be financed by leasing rather than by medium-term borrowing. It has played a major part in the development of the North Sea oil project, including the leasing of a complete oil refinery.

In the boom years of 1976–9 the tax benefits for lessors – and indirectly for the lessees – were of paramount importance. All lessors were able to write off the cost of assets for leasing immediately, through the ability to charge 100 per cent first-year capital allowances against tax. Where leasing was done to bodies which could not have claimed the capital allowances if they had bought the assets themselves, the leasing company was able to pass on some of the benefit. In any case the allowances created valuable tax losses which provided tax shelter for profits from other sources and were used up by companies through group relief claims.

These tax reliefs were substantially cut down in the Finance Act, 1980, which provided that the first-year capital allowance was limited to 25 per cent in cases in which the lessee company could not have claimed capital allowance had it bought the asset itself.

However, it was expected that these changes which the Act provided for a gradual change from 1983 onwards would have a harmful effect on leasing in this country, as it was thought that leasing was based purely on the tax advantages of lessors making use of the first-year allowances. These predictions were confounded. While the pre-1984 tax system played a critical role in bringing the leasing industry to its present size, it is now proceeding under its own steam, on the merits of its natural advantages to lessees in industry and commerce. In cash terms, leasing business had doubled in the period 1983–7.

In Great Britain there are hundreds of companies engaged in instalment credit business. The banks, whether directly, indirectly, in partnership with another, or through subsidiaries, can be said to have the lion's share. The major finance houses are owned by the large banks, which find them a useful source of profit at times when their own profits are on a downward trend. Thus, when interest rates are high, the current account balances of banks generate good profits. The cost of funds to the finance houses, however, is pushed up, and the potential customers tend to be reluctant to take on fixed-interest commitments. On the other hand, when interest rates fall bank profits from their domestic current account business tend to fall, whereas finance houses find it cheaper to borrow money and their customers tend to be more willing to borrow at fixed rates. This cyclical effect is now less marked as more and more finance houses link their lending to Finance House Base Rate.

Forty-seven of the larger and better known of these finance companies are members of the Finance Houses Association, which represents over 90 per cent of all finance house business. The Finance Houses Base Rate (FHBR) of interest is calculated on an agreed formula based on the inter-bank three month rate. As new services developed and the base rates of the banks tended to changes with greater frequency, the finance houses were aware that their own base rates had a built-in time lag, so that there is now a tendency for a number of finance houses to use clearing bank parents' base rates instead of FHBR for some or all categories of variable rate lending.

The growth of the business of equipment leasing led to the formation in 1971 of the Equipment Leasing Association, whose aims are to represent to the authorities the views of its members on any proposed or actual legislation which may affect the leasing industry; to increase awareness of leasing and its role in helping the economic development of the country; and, because leasing in the United Kingdom is closely linked to the system of taxation, to keep taxation and monetary policy under special and continuous review. Currently there are about seventy members of this association.

Between 1957 and 1960 there was a growing demand for funds by medium-sized businesses, property developers and others. The finance houses, as a result, expanded the banking side of their business. The banks realized that their traditional lending would suffer from this competition, and accordingly the clearing banks acquired interests in leading finance houses, which in many cases they built up until the finance house became a subsidiary. They would perhaps have done this earlier had it not been for the veto imposed by the Capital Issues Committee on finance houses seeking to raise fresh capital (removed in July 1958) and, perhaps, for their feeling that hire purchase was not in the ordinary course of their business. However, the profit element was all-important, and when one bank chairman proclaimed that nearly everyone had to buy their houses by instalments, i.e. on mortgage, so what could be wrong with buying by instalments the things that went in them, hire purchase had become respectable. The sums involved became so considerable that the government had to exercise control from time to time by stipulating minimum initial payments and maximum periods for repayments. These regulations were issued by means of control orders which sought to limit the volume of trade in non-essential items of equipment or luxuries.

Over the last twenty years important changes have been taking place in consumer credit. The habit of buying goods on credit has been acquired by many people in all walks of life, not just the lower income groups as in earlier years. The services of the finance houses have been used by an increasing number of companies, retailers and suppliers of consumer durables, motor cars, office equipment and other standard manufactured goods. Industry has also been turning to the finance houses for assistance with machinery and plant. New schemes have been devised such as the leasing of plant and equipment. Some items cannot be bought at all, only leased. A maintenance obligation may be assumed by the manufacturer by agreement with the finance company and the lessor. The finance company may be a subsidiary of the manufacturing company.

Leasing is effected by a contract under which the lessee has possession and use of a specific asset on payment of specified rentals over a period, while the lessor retains ownership. The asset is chosen by the lessee. It is this selection by the lessee before purchase which distinguishes leasing from hiring.

The idea, of course, is not a new one: companies and individuals have rented premises for their business operations, houses and flats are rented to live in, television sets are rented from dealers. Since 1960 leasing operations by finance houses have expanded rapidly; the system is suitable for large and costly assets such as computers, aircraft, containers and container ships, and specialized plant and equipment.

Leasing is an alternative to purchase of an asset by instalment credit or through the aid of a mortgage or term loan. It has the following advantages:

(1) The lessor retains ownership of the asset which is being financed. This gives him better security than the lender has, who generally take only a floating charge on the assets of the borrower, in most types of loan facility.

(2) The lessee can benefit from the rather more competitive financing rates which a lessor can offer, as a result of this enhanced security.

(3) Due to the fixed nature of a lease contract – which applies to the lessor as well as the lessee – there is a certainty of cash flow which is not associated with such facilities as overdrafts, which are repayable on demand and are subject to credit squeezes or changes in economic conditions, so that there can be no acceleration in payment of the agreed rentals.

(4) Unlike other credit facilities, the implied interest rate built into leases is in most cases fixed throughout the lease term. Though on longer-term leases, lessors may offer rentals variable with changes in money costs, leases on fixed terms are common for periods of up to three years, while in other cases the lessor may offer an option of fixed or variable rates.

(5) Many leases are negotiated on tailor-made terms between lessor and lessee, with the lessee able to negotiate terms to match

his particular needs. He is responsible for selecting the equipment from the supplier of his choice, and the terms may be adjusted to take account of any part-exchange allowances. The benefit of discounts offered by suppliers is still available where leasing is used, and is passed to the lessee through the terms of lease rentals.

(6) Leasing normally provides finance for the entire cost of the equipment, with no initial cash outlay except perhaps for a quarterly or monthly rental in advance. Hundred-per-cent finance on similar terms may not always be available by using alternative credit lines.

(7) Leasing extends the range of facilities available; leasing is one among several facilities that can be employed simultaneously to finance capital requirements. As leasing does not involve any capital outlay, it therefore does not count as borrowing for the purpose of the company's Memorandum and Articles of Association (off-balance-sheet finance). However there is need to be aware of the implications of Statement of Standard Accounting Practice 21 (SSAP 21) 'Accounting for leases and hire-purchase transactions' where lessee companies making use of finance leases are required to capitalize the leased assets on their balance sheets. Operating leases can remain off balance sheet to the lessee.

(8) Leasing removes the need to tie up resources in fixed assets. By means of a lease, the use of an asset can be obtained without capital outlay. If we assume that the need for the asset has been established, the income generated by the use of the asset should be more than sufficient to meet the series of rentals. Thus, the commitment can be self-financing.

Within the broad definition of leasing there is a distinction between a lease where the lessee has no option to purchase the asset (a 'finance lease', sometimes called a 'full pay out financial lease') and certain other types of lease that are termed 'operating leases' and include those schemes dealing with assets for which there is an established second-hand market.

Leasing under either a finance lease or an operating lease is not usually subject to early termination; if one is requested, then it could be subject to substantial penalties. In such cases the lessee is relieved of the risk of obsolescence, and will often cover his own residual value risk through a buy-back arrangement with the dealer. This structure will of course remain an operating lease from the lessee's standpoint, though not necessarily for the lessor.

A finance lease usually stipulates two periods of payment. The first (the 'primary' or 'basic' period) calls for rentals to be paid monthly or quarterly until the cost of the asset and the charge made by the finance company has been paid; this might involve a period of some five years or so. A further period or an extension of a lease is known as the 'secondary period' and can be negotiated after the primary period has run its course.

The Consumer Credit Act, 1974, extended the consumer protection available to borrowers on hire purchase, conditional sale, and credit sale to borrowers by way of personal loan. Under this legislation details to be specified include the cash price of the goods or the amount of the loan, the cost of credit, the number and amount of instalments, and the total sum payable.

The greatest change, however, was the requirement for true interest rates to be given for all types of transactions. The object of this was not only to tell borrowers how much their credit is really costing them, but to allow them to compare rates under different contracts. Another safeguard written into the Act was a 'second thoughts' period of three days for the borrower to change his mind if he wants. Once he has undertaken the contract he is entitled to a statutory rebate of charges if he settles the debt before the agreed period.

The finance houses welcomed the Act, which puts every lender, whether a finance house, a bank, or a registered moneylender, on the same footing. Previously the smaller finance houses were obliged to register under the Moneylenders Act if they wished to make personal loans, an Act which was felt to carry a certain stigma. After the passing of the 1974 Act they were free to use whatever type of lending instrument was acceptable to the contracting parties.

Sources of funds

Naturally the proportion of capital and reserves to borrowed funds varies considerably between finance companies, but it is common ground that the greater part of their operating capital is borrowed. There are four main sources of borrowed funds: loan from the parent bank, the inter-bank market, discounted bills, and retail deposits, that is, funds borrowed from the public.

When credit has to be restricted, the bank overdrafts of finance houses are among the first to be limited and even reduced. In normal times, however, the clearing banks are usually quite happy to lend against the security of the hire purchase agreements held by the finance company. These, of course, are continually changing as old agreements run off and new ones are entered upon.

The finance houses also take deposits from accepting houses when the latter have surpluses, usually for quite short periods, and from overseas banks. Such banks hold considerable amounts of sterling and other currencies in connection with the financing of international trade and are substantial investors over a short or medium term.

The second source of borrowing is by way of discount. The finance house draws a bill of exchange which it presents to an accepting house for acceptance. After the bill has been accepted it is offered for discount in the money market. Thus a sum of money is obtained immediately against the need in three or six months' time to put the accepting house in funds to pay the bill on presentment. The accepting house charges a commission for its services.

The third source of borrowing, and much the most important, is by bidding for deposits. A few finance companies advertise for deposits from the public and obtain in this way capital which is a collecting together of many individual sums from small savers, deposited for fixed periods up to one year. Money also comes through the parallel money markets, through which companies, financial institutions and individuals deposit surplus funds with the finance houses for varying periods, sometimes up to six or twelve months.

To get these deposits the finance houses have to compete against banks, building societies and local authorities, all of whom are in constant need of ever more and more deposits from wherever they can obtain them. As a result the finance houses tend to offer a slightly better rate of interest, although this depends in any individual case on the standing of the finance house, the length of time for which the funds are to be deposited, and the amount. If insufficient funds are attracted, then hire purchase contracts will have to be restricted, and profits will drop.

The working capital of the finance houses may seem rather here today and gone tomorrow, and indeed it is thought that some houses have perhaps as much as one-fifth of their funds at call or on seven days' notice. Others have only a very small proportion of their funds deposited at such short periods of notice.

The use made of the funds, however, is also short and constantly changing. A hire purchase contract will be paid off, all being well, in anything from six months to three years, and after the original payment out to the seller has been made, the rest is money coming in all the time at a very good rate of interest. The capital structure is not, therefore, inappropriate. Its inherent strength is derived from the wide spread of customers. The houses write a large number of transactions and in that business the cash inflow of regular payments can be accurately predicted.

The modern view of hire purchase is that it is a useful way of acquiring a capital asset at an early date, provided always that the purchaser is not over extending himself by trying to buy too many things at the same time. The success of hire purchase finance over recent decades shows that there has been a rise in the good financial sense and judgement of people generally, a rise which has gone side by side with a rise in the standard of living. Of course, a check is made in each case from the application form which is nowadays appraised on a credit scoring system or the use of credit-reference agencies. The scoring system allocates points for various aspects of the applicant's lifestyle, e.g. employment, salary, age, marital status, property occupied, etc. The finance house will then decide whether or not to grant the accommodation.

Other financial institutions

Investment in Industry (3i)

This company is an amalgamation of two companies – Finance for Industry and Industrial and Commercial Finance Corporation (ICF). Originally both these companies were established in 1945. The former provided capital for the larger companies in sterling or in comply with his instructions. Such a relationship exists when the customer requires the bank to present cheques drawn in his favour for final payment. This the bank does every single day on behalf of its customers. Other examples of this relationship occur when the bank is asked to either purchase or sell stocks and shares, or to remit funds to a beneficiary abroad.

Mortgagor and mortgagee

With the advent of banks entering into the domestic property
market, there now exists a mortgagor–mortgagee relationship, since
a bank will take the deeds of a house when granting such an advance
to a customer.

While the latter three relationships occur from time to time, the
most important and basic relationship is that of debtor and creditor.
It is encumbent on the bank to repay funds when instructed to do so.
It should also be remembered that any funds paid into the customer's account immediately become the property of the bank
which may utilize the funds as they wish. The courts (Foley v. Hill)
have been asked to say that the banker is a trustee for the customer
or a bailee of the customer's property, but providing a bank is able to
repay funds on demand and fulfils the debtor-creditor relationship,
it is unlikely that the law in this matter will change.

Private customers

The banker, by opening his office(s), issues to everyone an invitation
to treat. It is the would-be customer who makes the offer, which the
banker may accept or refuse as seems good to him. The customer
makes the offer by coming into a branch, or writing to it, or getting
someone else to write in on his or her behalf, requesting that an
account may be opened in his/her name. The bank will normally be
pleased to extend its business and needs only to have its simple
requirements met.

The first of these is that there should be references. Some banks
will accept one, others will require two. It is safer to accept two.
Bank managers will from time to time open an account with no references at all. This will occur when banks are particularly keen to
obtain accounts from a particular sector of society, e.g. students. In
this instance, the banks are quite happy to open an account when
or by a combination of both. Only farm owners can borrow. If a
tenant farmer is granted a loan, therefore, it must be for the purchase
of the farm.

To make these loans the corporation needs funds, which it obtains
partly from the shareholders (clearing banks and the Bank of
England) and partly from the issue of a debenture stock, secured by a

charge on all its property and assets. The decision of the clearing and other banks to increase the amount and length of their term loans to agriculture has had an effect on the corporation's business and the AMC's share of the market has declined.

Revision test 5

Place a tick against the letter you consider is the correct answer.

1 The Stock Exchange dealer who quotes buying and selling prices for stocks and shares is called
  (a) an underwriter
  (b) a factor
  (c) a market maker.
2 'Gilt edged' is a term used to describe
  (a) shares in gold mines
  (b) land and property shares
  (c) government securities.
3 Someone who sells shares which he does not have, in the hope that he can buy them later more cheaply, is
  (a) a bear
  (b) a bull
  (c) a stag.
4 When a customer asks a bank clerk to buy or sell shares for him, the bank clerk will
  (a) contact the broker by telephone
  (b) send the broker a letter
  (c) notify head office.
5 The letters USM mean
  (a) Unlisted Secondary Market
  (b) Unusual Securities Market
  (c) Unlisted Securities Market.
6 A Lloyd's broker is an agent of
  (a) the underwriting syndicate
  (b) the assured
  (c) an insurance company.
7 A finance house is likely to provide finance to individuals for
  (a) purchase of industrial shares
  (b) hire purchase of a consumer durable
  (c) house purchase.

8 The London gold market is a term used to signify
   (a) dealers in gilt edged securities on the London Stock Ex-
       change
   (b) the Bank of England's holding in the 'gold pool' run by
       central bankers
   (c) a number of firms dealing in gold bullion.
9 A television set becomes the property of the purchaser when he
   pays the last instalment under
   (a) a hire purchase agreement
   (b) a credit sale agreement
   (c) an instalment trading agreement.
10 Leasing is a method whereby
   (a) the lessee obtains possession and use of specific asset on
       payment of a rental
   (b) the lessee buys the asset by instalments
   (c) the lessee obtains ownership immediately on delivery of the
       asset.

Questions for discussion

1 Describe the relationships between the banker and a broker and
   the assistance each can give to a personal customer of a bank.
2 Explain how the finance houses obtain the funds which they
   need for their business.
3 Investigate the assistance your bank gives to a small company to
   obtain a loan under the Small Firms Loan Guarantee Scheme.

6

Types of customers

Having dealt at length with banks and other financial organizations our attention must be turned to the *raison d'être* of the operation of all banks, namely to give a service to customers in order to obtain a profit for the shareholders of banks. In order to be a customer of a bank there must be an account opened in the name or names of the persons who have entered into a legal contract with a bank. A person who merely uses a bank, say to change coins for notes each day, or a person who on one occasion only cashes a traveller's cheque, is not by legal definition a customer.

As far back as 1901, in the case of the Great Western Railway Co. v. London and County Banking Co. Ltd, it was stated 'that there must be some sort of account, either a deposit or current account or some similar relation to make a man a customer of a bank'. To re-inforce this, in a later case of Ladbroke v. Todd (1914), the judge declared that, in the contractual relationship between a bank and its customer, time is not of the essence. The relationship commences as soon as the account is opened.

Although this relationship between customer and banker specifies that an account must be in existence, the banking world in 1959 was made to sit up on the judgement in Woods v. Martins Bank Ltd, where the manager gave specific investment advice to a person who was not a customer. The person (Woods) lost his investment. It was decided by the judge that a relationship existed when the bank accepted instructions from Mr Woods to make the investment as recommended by the manager, even though no account was opened until some weeks later.

The usual relationships between a banker and a customer are as follows.

Debtor and creditor

In normal circumstances, when a customer has a credit balance, he is the creditor and the bank the debtor. The bank owes the customer money and the customer has the right to obtain refund of this debt. Under normal commercial circumstances, it is usual for the debtor to seek out the creditor and repay him the debt due within the agreed time limit; however, for a bank to repay every customer immediately funds that are on his account would make nonsense of banking. Again this was confirmed in a case, Joachimson v. Swiss Bank Corporation, which decided that banks hold funds in trust for customers, who may withdraw these funds either in whole or in part during normal business hours, by means of written instructions to the branch of the bank.

This relationship can be reversed when the customer owes the bank money, i.e. when there is an overdraft or loan. In this case there is an agreement that the customer should repay the debt either by regular instalments or by a given date. There is usually an understanding that the bank may at any time request in writing the repayment of the loan.

Bailor and bailee

This relationship occurs when a customer deposits his valuables with the bank. This deposit of items for safe custody requires the bank to take reasonable care of the deposit while in its charge.

It is usual for the customer to put his valuables either in a box or envelope which is received by the bank and recorded in the bank's books as 'contents unknown'. The responsibility for insuring the property rests with the customer. Unless the bank is negligent, the customer cannot make any claim on the bank providing reasonable care has been taken.

As well as holding items in envelopes and boxes, banks are prepared to hold share certificates, wills, building society passbooks, national savings certificates and other documents on open safe custody. A receipt is given to the customer in the usual way, but they are more accessible should the customer require any document quickly.

Principal and agent

This relationship is fundamental to both banker and customer, as in nearly all instances the bank is the agent of the customer and must comply with his instructions. Such a relationship exists when the customer requires the bank to present cheques drawn in his favour for final payment. This the bank does every single day on behalf of its customers. Other examples of this relationship occur when the bank is asked to either purchase or sell stocks and shares, or to remit funds to a beneficiary abroad.

Mortgagor and mortgagee

With the advent of banks entering into the domestic property market, there now exists a mortgagor–mortgagee relationship, since a bank will take the deeds of a house when granting such an advance to a customer.

While the latter three relationships occur from time to time, the most important and basic relationship is that of debtor and creditor. It is encumbent on the bank to repay funds when instructed to do so. It should also be remembered that any funds paid into the customer's account immediately become the property of the bank which may utilize the funds as they wish. The courts (Foley v. Hill) have been asked to say that the banker is a trustee for the customer or a bailee of the customer's property, but providing a bank is able to repay funds on demand and fulfils the debtor-creditor relationship, it is unlikely that the law in this matter will change.

Private customers

The banker, by opening his office(s), issues to everyone an invitation to treat. It is the would-be customer who makes the offer, which the banker may accept or refuse as seems good to him. The customer makes the offer by coming into a branch, or writing to it, or getting someone else to write in on his or her behalf, requesting that an account may be opened in his/her name. The bank will normally be pleased to extend its business and needs only to have its simple requirements met.

The first of these is that there should be references. Some banks will accept one, others will require two. It is safer to accept two. Bank managers will from time to time open an account with no references at all. This will occur when banks are particularly keen to obtain accounts from a particular sector of society, e.g. students. In this instance, the banks are quite happy to open an account when evidence is shown that the person is whom he says he is, and when a grant cheque in his favour is used to open the account. Bank managers are aware of the inherent dangers of this procedure and are taking a considered risk which does not in any way detract from the need to obtain references from somebody unknown to the bank who wishes to open an account.

The references must be carefully checked. The procedure may take a week or more, and during this time no cheque book should be issued. When the references are complete and the funds cleared, the customer should be sent a cheque book, and if his standing is thought to warrant it, a cheque card and possibly a cash card.

The bank must also get a specimen signature to compare with the signature on the cheques which will be presented for payment, and needs to know the address of the customer and his/her occupation. Any connected accounts should be noted. It is not customary to ask for the age of the customer; however, when a young person is introduced to a bank by his/her parents and that person is a minor, i.e. under the age of 18 years, it is necessary to record the date of birth.

The custom of asking a married woman for the details of her husband's occupation has been abandoned since the Sex Discrimination Act, 1975. Originally this was to guard against fraud, but in order for the bank to protect itself there is no reason why a bank should not ask any married person for the name and address of his/her employer, and the name and address of the employer of his/her spouse.

Minors

There is no objection to opening a banking account for a minor, so long as it is kept in credit. Money lent to a minor cannot be recovered if the minor does not wish to pay it back. This is because in the past minors have been exploited, and therefore in 1874 they were given legal protection under the Infants Relief Act, after which year all contracts entered into by infants for repayment of money lent have been absolutely void. However, under the Minors' Contracts Act, 1987, a minor on reaching the age of 18 years may now ratify a contract or a loan made while he/she was still a minor.

A bank, at its discretion, may grant a loan to a minor if it knows that the young person is of honourable character, in receipt of a regular income, perhaps from a family trust, or knows that the minor's parent or guardian would if necessary put matters right. Should a banker lend money to a minor and require a guarantee, the law as amended by the Minors' Contracts Act, 1987, now recognizes that the guarantee is enforecable against the guarantor even though for any reason the original debt is unenforceable against the minor.

A further provision of the Act is to allow the return of the property or the proceeds of the sale of the property acquired by a contract which has been repudiated by the minor.

The Minors' Contracts Act, 1987, has removed a variety of anomalies that have existed since the Infant Relief Act, 1874.

Although it is beyond the scope of this book to go into the full con-tractual relationships of a minor, it should be mentioned that a minor may sign as a witness and he may act as an agent. In the latter capacity the minor may draw and sign cheques on his principal's account, and if the account becomes overdrawn as a result, the principal will be liable, for the agent stands in his place and the acts which he properly does are considered to be the acts of his principal.

A joint account is sometimes opened in the names of a minor and a parent or guardian; the banker will treat this as he would any other joint account, except that he must bear in mind the non-liability of the minor for any overdraft. No minor can give a guarantee.

A minor is bound to pay a reasonable price for necessaries ordered by him and supplied to him. What is a necessary is a question of fact (Nash v. Inman). Likewise contracts of employment are contracts which cannot be considered as voidable. Contracts of tenancy, partnership, or membership of a company, bind a minor unless he expressly repudiates them within a reasonable time after becoming of age. Although he may repudiate them, he cannot recover any money which he has paid.

Joint accounts

Joint accounts may be opened for any number of people more than one, although usually the number is either two or three. Sometimes these may be ordinary people having a joint account for some special reason, perhaps to save for a coming holiday, or where one party is going abroad and sees the joint account as an alternative to giving the bank a mandate to allow another person to sign on his sole account. Very often joint accounts are held by husband and wife, where there are important advantages to the survivor in the event of the death of one (e.g. the wife may continue to have access to a source of money after the death of her husband), or by trustees who hold the money in trust for beneficiaries under some will or settlement or for executors who are winding up an estate.

The first thing the bank will want is the completion of a bank form by both or all parties giving their names, addresses and perhaps their occupations, and telling the bank who is to sign cheques, e.g. 'all to sign', 'both to sign', 'any one to sign' or 'either to sign'. Specimen signatures usually in duplicate will be on this form, and the opportunity will be taken by the bank to establish joint and several liability for any overdraft (see p. 269). It will also give the bank directions as to the disposition of the balance in the event of the death of one or more parties.

The signing instructions for a trustee account must say that ALL trustees are to sign, whereas executors may stipulate that either, or less than all, of the executors are to sign.

The mandate should provide separate sections for signatures on the current account, and signatures for the release of articles on safe custody. It may be 'either to sign' on the current account but 'both to sign' on safe custody articles. Neglect to observe due care may result in a wife, curious to know what provision her husband has made in his will, being allowed to draw it out on her sole signature from safe custody, although the instructions to the bank stipulate 'both to sign'. She may then discover that the husband has left a legacy to a former mistress.

Any joint account holders may fall out with each other, but perhaps this possibility is more real in husband and wife joint accounts. If they separate, or have serious differences which cannot be resolved, there may be trouble over the balance on a joint account opened by them in happier days. Where the instructions to the bank have been 'either to sign', it is possible for either of them to withdraw the whole of the balance, to stop the other from getting it. That other may blame the bank, and while the bank would be in a sound legal position, having acted in accordance with its mandate, an unpleasant situation might arise which would do the bank no good. To avoid all this, therefore, the banker, on learning of a serious dispute from one party, should advise both parties that he can no longer accept the instruction 'either to sign'. Both must sign from that time onwards. This will avoid any difficulty or embarrassment so far as the banker is concerned.

Sole traders

A sole trader is in business by himself, for himself. He may be a shopkeeper, or he may be engaged in manufacture on a small scale, or he may be selling a service, such as repairing electrical equipment or houses.

As long as he is of full age, he is responsible for his debts. If he cannot pay them out of his liquid assets then he may be made bankrupt by his creditors. His house and his car, and nearly everything that he has, can be taken and sold, all by due process of law. If he signs any document he is in general presumed to have read it and understood it, and to be bound by its terms. If he reads it and doesn't understand it he can go to a solicitor and have it explained to him. If it is a bank form then he can ask the bank officer dealing with the matter to explain it to him. A bank officer of some seniority must therefore be able to understand and explain any of the bank forms in general use.

The account of a sole trader will not be very different in any way from the ordinary personal banking account, except that the rhythm of the account will be different. An ordinary individual getting his salary once a month, for example, will spend a lot of it as soon as he gets it, and then try to make the remainder last out the month. His banking account will reflect this procedure, and it will be more or less the same every month. A trader, however, is not paid monthly. He may send out his bills monthly, but they will be paid at any odd times. His account will not present such a regular appearance. Moreover, it will be affected by seasonal factors. To take an extreme case, a man producing Christmas cards will start in February, get orders in May, deliver to the shops in September, and get paid in January. A farmer has a similar annual cycle. On the other hand, hairdressers and undertakers have a steady demand all the year round.

The sole trader must keep accounts of his business – purchases of raw materials, sales of finished product, cost of transport, and so on. He may have a staff – wages and salaries. He must have an office – heating, stationery, telephone. At regular intervals he must meet his VAT commitments, and at the end of the year he will have to pay tax on his profits and the tax authorities have to be satisfied that his return is made on correct figures.

So he needs an accountant, who will produce a balance sheet and final accounts every year. If the sole trader is borrowing from the bank the manager will want to see these figures. We shall see in chapter 14 what lessons can be learned from a study of these figures.

Partnerships

When a sole trader gets tired of doing all the work himself he may take a partner. Alternatively, two or more individuals may start a firm. With a sole trader, the position is governed by common law. There is no act of parliament labelled 'Rules for sole traders'. But there is one labelled 'Rules for partners'. It is actually called the Partnership Act and was passed in 1890.

The definition of a partnership as laid down under this Act is: 'The relationship which subsists between two or more persons carrying on a business in common with a view of profit'. No written agreement or deed between the partners is legally necessary, though it often exists. All that is necessary is either a written, verbal or implied agreement between the partners.

Notice that the definition firmly points to a commercial relationship. Husband and wife are often described as partners, but they do not normally carry on a business in common with a view of profit. (Of course, if they ran a business, they would so far as the business is concerned be partners in a legal sense.)

There can be anything from two to twenty persons in a partnership. However, where the partnership is a group of professional men and women such as accountants, doctors, dentists, solicitors, etc., they are permitted, under the Companies Act, to have more than twenty partners. Otherwise any group of persons in excess of that number wishing to form a business for the purpose of profit must form themselves into a company.

The firm has no separate existence. When people talk about the firm they mean all the partners who compose the firm. Anyone suing the firm is suing all the partners. Anyone making the firm bankrupt is making all the partners bankrupt.

A firm may borrow money. Does this mean that where a firm has eight partners, they all come in to see the bank manager about a loan? In other words, can one, or two, or less than all the partners make an arrangement which will bind the firm (all the partners)?

This is the first really important rule about firms: one partner can bind the firm by any act done in the ordinary course of the firm's business.

So if the firm is engaged in a financial business where it is borrowing and lending all the time, then yes, just one partner can come in to see the manager, arrange for an overdraft, deposit security in support, and sign any papers the bank wants signed; and the firm, not just that partner, will be legally liable to repay and can be sued if it does not.

But most firms are engaged in other types of business and they don't borrow money every day. In fact it is an event that happens occasionally for them. So all of the partners will have to come in and sign the bank's forms. This is very inconvenient. Is there any way in which the bank can get round this?

Yes, there is. When the account is first opened the partners must each give the bank a specimen signature, for the bank wants to know how cheques are going to be signed. For this purpose the bank has a form relevant to partnership accounts, which gives these details and specimen signatures. It is very simple to slip into the form a clause such as: 'We agree that any act done by any partner in relation to the account shall be deemed to be done for carrying out the business of the firm in its ordinary course'. Then any partner can arrange an overdraft and the firm will be liable to repay it. It is perhaps obvious to say that the bank is keen to have all the partners liable for repayment instead of just one, because in that way the bank has a much better chance of recovering the money.

The second important rule concerning firms is, from the bank's point of view, that of the partners' liability for the firm's debts. The law says that all partners are fully liable, but that this liability is joint. If a firm owes a creditor £1,000, and there are four partners, all the partners are jointly responsible to pay £1,000. If they don't pay, and the creditor sues them, he used to have only one right of action: to have the best chance of recovering the debt he had to sue all the partners together; if he sued only one partner, that partner was still liable to pay the £1,000 (there is no question of each partner being liable only for £250 – the liability is a joint one), but should he be unsuccessful he could not after that sue the other partners.

In 1978, however, an Act was passed to lay down that since that year joint debtors can be sued one after another, just as if they are joint and several debtors. This means that each joint account holder, or each partner, is individually liable for the full amount of the debt, as well as being jointly liable. This is in any case established by the bank by the inclusion of another useful clause in the form of application for a partnership account (signed by all the partners): 'We agree that any liability incurred by us in connection with the account or in any other way shall be joint and several'. It might be thought that since the Act of 1978 this clause has no longer been necessary, but has been retained because with joint and several liability contractually established there are important advantages for the bank should the customer(s) go bankrupt.

This useful form also says whether the partners are going to sign in the name of the firm, or on behalf of it. In the first case, suppose the name of the firm is Brown, Robertson, Jenkins & Co. Suppose there are four partners. Then the form shows in the space provided for the specimen signatures the name of the firm written four times, each time in the individual handwriting of each partner. In the second case each partner signs his own name under the words 'on behalf of (or *per pro.*) Brown, Robertson, Jenkins & Co.'

The form also says how many partners are to sign on these occasions. Partners are supposed to trust each other, so there may be only one partner signing on behalf of the firm. On the other hand, it is a useful check if two partners sign. Whatever the firm says, the bank expects to see the signatures as authorized, not only on cheques which come in for payment, but also on any letters sent by the firm to the bank.

That example raises another point. The name of the firm mentioned three partners, but in fact there were four. How can this happen? Well, partners die or retire, and new ones join the firm. This firm did originally consist of the three men whose names still describe the firm, but Brown died, and Benson took his place. Later on the firm ran short of money and Hemmings invested in it in return for a partnership. On both these occasions the name of the firm could have been changed to describe accurately the names of the partners after the change, but by then the name of the firm had begun to get known in the district as people who could be relied upon to do a good job, and it would have been a pity, by changing it, to lose the goodwill attached to the old name.

How then does the bank, or indeed anyone else having business relations with the firm, know with whom they are dealing? One could not lend money to a firm, money for which the partners are jointly and severally liable, without ever knowing who the partners are.

There used to be a system for finding out these things, set up by the Registration of Business Names Act, 1916, but the Department of Trade found it too expensive to administer, and the 1916 Act was abolished by the Companies Act, 1981. The Business Names Register, which used to be maintained at Companies House, has been closed; but the London Chamber of Commerce and Industry Business Registry is doing the job instead.

Partners can be general, dormant or limited. A general partner is one who takes an active part in the management of the firm, while a dormant or sleeping partner, though still having unlimited liability, takes no active part. A limited partner is one whose liability for the firm's debts is limited to the amount of his investment. He has no power to take any active part in the business. Such partnerships are rare.

A minor may be a partner and can do anything an ordinary partner can do (except hold land), but he will not be responsible for the debts of the firm until he has reached his majority.

Limited companies

By far the bulk of business is done by limited companies. Since the first Companies Act in 1862 there have been other Acts, the Companies Act of 1948 being a comprehensive summary of the law at that time, some of whose provisions have been modified by more recent Companies Acts in 1967, 1976, 1980 and 1981, and more recently codified in the 1985 Companies Act.

Limited companies are built around the principle of limited liability. So far, with sole traders and partnerships we have been dealing with people who can lose everything if debts are not paid. Limited liability introduced a new system. The shareholder in a limited company can lose the value of his shares, but beyond that he has no responsibility for the debts of the company. In a partnership, the partners are 'the firm'. In a limited company, the shareholders are not 'the company'. There is one difference of great importance – 'the company' exists in law as being in its own right. This separate legal entity gives the company the same rights as any mature person. That is, it can own assets, it can enter into a contract, buy and sell assets, sue others and in turn it can be sued.

Unlike a human being, a company can continue in perpetuity. That is, it can continue as long as the members wish. The members may die or sell their shares in the company, but the company can go on as long as required. While you and I cannot enter into a legal contract until we reach the age of maturity, which will take some eighteen years, a company from its inception will be able to enter into a contract. However, a company is unable to act for itself, so it has directors and a secretary to act for it.

Types of companies

Companies can be formed in various ways. Before the introduction of the various Companies Acts, the only way in which limited liability could be obtained was from the sovereign. The granting of a Royal Charter was reserved for the organizations that were in favour with the court. Such trading companies as the Hudson Bay Trading Company, the East India Trading Company and many others which went out to various parts of the world to bring back to England the riches of the continent, were encouraged; their leaders were often knighted and given rewards by the sovereign. However, these days the granting of a charter by the sovereign is given rarely and usually only to non-trading organizations, e.g. the Institute of Chartered Accountants, the Football Association, etc. Another method of obtaining limited liability is by statute. By passing a relevant Act of Parliament, the government is able to bring into existence a company whose aims and objectives are written in the Act of Parliament. Usually these Acts are passed when the government of the day wishes to nationalize an industry and therefore will form a company for this purpose. Examples of this are the National Coal Board, electricity boards and gas boards; and even the Bank of England was, under the Bank of England Act, 1946, taken out of private ownership and transferred to public ownership.

However, the majority of trading companies are formed by registration under the Companies Act. We can divide up companies in at least two ways. The first is into public and private companies. A public company is one which gets its capital from the public. When it is floated as a new company, a prospectus is issued by way of advertisement for the company's future (this prospectus is closely regulated by law in case any over-optimistic or downright inaccurate information should creep in), and an issue of shares is offered at a certain price, say £1 each. The shares go out, the money comes in. The underwriters take up or pay for any shares not disposed of.

The company now has capital. Provided all the legal steps have been taken the company can now start to trade. We know it must produce a balance sheet within eighteen months and once every year thereafter. The balance sheet and accounts have to be sent to the shareholders before the annual general meeting. The company may have a stock exchange listing.

A public company must have at least two members and at least two directors. They may be the same. A public company is defined as one

(1) which is limited by shares, or limited by guarantee and has a share capital; in either case the share capital must meet the minimum requirements (£50,000 – all of which must be issued, but need only be one-quarter paid up)

(2) whose Memorandum states that it is public; and

(3) which has been correctly registered as a public company.

All other companies are private companies.

A private company does not appeal to the public for funds, but finds them from private sources. It must have at least two members and at least one director. All companies whose names end with the word 'Limited' are taken to be private companies. A public company will have the letters 'plc' after its name.

In both types of company, the shares are freely transferable, although the transferability of a private company is difficult because there is no market for such transfers to take place. A member of a public company listed on the Stock Exchange can sell his shares without much difficulty. Additionally, the number of shareholders in both types of companies is not limited in any way except by the number of shares the company is authorized to issue.

Powers of the company

The Memorandum of Association of a company is a document drawn up by the founder members. It has six heads:

(1) the name of the company, with 'Public Limited Company' or its abbreviation plc, or in appropriate cases the Welsh equivalent, if it is a public company; or the word 'Limited' if it is a private company

(2) whether the registered office of the company is to be situated in England, Scotland or in Wales

(3) the objects of the company

(4) whether the liability of the members is limited

(5) details of the share capital, and how it is divided

(6) the Association clause: this is a declaration signed by each of the founder members, promising to buy at least one share in the company when it is incorporated.

Under the third heading is listed the objects for which the company was formed, the things it is going to do. Anything listed in those objects, the company can legally do, and be responsible for. Such acts are *intra vires* (within its legal power). Anything else is *ultra vires* the company, outside its powers.

The bank manager will look in the Memorandum under the objects clause to make sure that the power to borrow is mentioned there (it always is), but, equally importantly, to see that any proposed borrowing is for a purpose which is mentioned as one of the company's objects. Banks have lost money over this. As part of the EEC, European law has put an end to the *ultra vires* rule. There the system is that a contract entered into in good faith by a person dealing with a company should not be set aside on the grounds that it is beyond the powers of the company. The directors of the company should be familiar with the objects of the company for which they have a responsibility. Although this seems pretty clear, British bankers are a cautious lot, and until various questions can be answered they will go on checking the objects clause.

The Articles are contained in a document along with the Memorandum. The Articles contain the rules for the internal conduct of the company, dealing with such matters as the issue of shares, notice of general meetings, appointment and duties of directors, etc.

The banker is interested in the powers of the directors, for it is they who usually authorize any borrowing by the company. We must not assume that they necessarily have the required authority to do this; occasionally, where the sum to be borrowed is large, the Articles may say that the company must be called together to discuss the matter first. A motion is put to the company at a general meeting to empower it to borrow £x,000 from Y bank against the security of assets of the company. This has not been authorized by the directors, but by the company. The Articles will say whether the bank needs to see a resolution of the directors, or a copy of the resolution passed by the company.

Shares in a company

The capital structure of the company is set out in the Memorandum. The amount and description of the shares as stated is called 'The Authorized Capital'. This is the maximum amount that is permitted to be issued. The number of shares that can be issued can be altered by a general meeting by increasing the authorized capital.

Ordinary shares

This type of share is often called equity capital. It is the risk capital invested by the numerous shareholders. The amount of shares issued is called 'the issued capital'. Frequently, the amount of issued capital is lower than the authorized capital. It can be the same, but the issued capital can never exceed the authorized capital.

The ordinary shares have a nominal value. Often this is £1, but many shares on the market have a nominal value of 50p, 25p, and so on. This nominal value has little or no relation to the market value of the share. When a company is successful, then the price of the share is often many times greater than the nominal value of the share. Find out the nominal value of your bank's shares and then check the current market value.

Each ordinary shareholder will receive a share certificate stating how many shares in the company are registered in his name. This amount is recorded in the Register of Shareholders and the holder of the shares is entitled to one vote for every share held. The dividends given to the shareholder will depend on the success or otherwise of the company. During years of high profits, the company will give a good return for capital invested, and during bad years the dividend could be small or omitted altogether.

Preference shares

Preference shares carry a fixed rate of interest, which is usually specified in the Articles. Such shares receive their regular interest out of the company's annual profits (assuming profits are available) before the ordinary class of shareholder receives anything. The other form of preference may also extend to repayment of capital if the company should fail.

A non-cumulative preference share has the disadvantage that in a year where profits are not sufficient to pay the whole or any interest on this type of share, the unpaid interest is lost forever.

With a cumulative preference share, however, such lost interest is made up, profits permitting, at a later date, and the total amount of interest due is paid before the ordinary shareholder receives any dividend.

Another form of preference share is a redeemable preference share: that is, at a stated date these shares are redeemed by the company. Frequently preference shares may be quoted as 'cumulative redeemable preference shares', that is, they have all the qualities mentioned above.

A participating preference share is one where the shareholder not only gets his fixed dividend, but should the ordinary shareholder receive a dividend above a certain amount and the profits allow, an additional dividend is then paid.

Deferred shares are rare. They are sometimes issued to the promoters of the company, who usually receive a dividend after payment of a dividend to the ordinary shareholders. They are also known as founder shares.

Unincorporated bodies

There are many associations of people grouped together for the pursuit of a common interest and with no thought of commercial gain, such as sports clubs, social clubs and horticultural societies. Such groups are managed by officers and committees elected from their own number, and they will need a banking account for the receipt of subscriptions of the members, for any grants which they may receive and funds received from any social/cultural activities, and for the payments out which they will have to make.

Such associations have no legal entity that can be sued for repayment of any borrowing. If the society wants to borrow, therefore, someone connected with the society must undertake personal responsibility. Usually a guarantee is taken from such a person in terms which make him directly responsible for the debt. Sometimes a joint and several guarantee will be signed by the members of the committee, and this will be acceptable provided that they are persons of some standing.

Executors and administrators

An executor is a person or persons appointed by a will to carry out the instructions contained in that will. It is the duty of the executor to marshal the assets together, pay what expenses are due, i.e. capital transfer tax, funeral and other expenses, and then distribute these assets in accordance with the deceased's instructions. Normally, before probate – the ability to obtain ownership of the assets – is granted, capital transfer tax must be paid. In practice, a short-term borrowing is arranged with the bank to pay this tax, then on receipt of probate the debt to the bank is repaid either from funds held on a current or deposit account or from the sale of some of the assets.

Where no will is available, that is, the person dies intestate, the court will appoint a relative or close acquaintance as administrator of the estate, by granting Letters of Administration.

Should the estate be very small, i.e. £6,000 or less, it is the practice of bankers to pay funds on current or deposit account direct to the closest relative against personal identification and a signed indemnity.

Trustees

A trustee is a person to whom property is entrusted so that he may deal with it in accordance with the directions given by the creator of the trust. A common example is where a man sets up a trust for the benefit of his children. To do this he has to choose a trustee and give over to him the securities which form the trust property. As the securities produce interest at regular intervals, the trustee pays the money out to the children in accordance with the terms of the trust instrument.

A trustee must take as much care of the trust property as a reasonable man would do of his own property. He is not allowed to make a profit out of the trust. He may or may not be free to vary the investments in the trust as he thinks fit. If he is to have this power, there must be an express authority for it in the instrument setting up the trust.

The person setting up the trust is called the donor. Those who are to benefit under it are called beneficiaries. Trustees are found in many different capacities; perhaps the most familiar is a trustee in bankruptcy, whose task is to take charge of the assets of a bankrupt, turn them into money, and then apply that money as far as it will go in settling the debts. Another is a trustee under a deed of arrangement, which is a kind of alternative to bankruptcy, if the creditors will agree to it. The trustee administers the property of the debtor for the benefit of the creditors.

Banks and other financial institutions have set up trust corporations which administer trusts and wills of customers. The clearing banks have a range of trustee branches which co-operate with the banking branches who find them their business. As trustees cannot make a profit at common law, a special 'charging clause' has to be included in the will or in the instrument setting up the trust. Trusts can arise under a will when all the debts of the deceased have been paid, and all the legacies and bequests discharged. What is left of the deceased's property – the residue – is then paid to the residuary legatee; but if the will has left money to children who are not to have it until they come of age, then a trust will be set up until that time.

Banking accounts for trustees must, in their title, name the trustees, and all trustees must normally sign all cheques, receipts and authorities. It is in order for a single trustee to administer the trust (unless the trust instrument provides otherwise) where he is the only or last surviving trustee, except that, where land is sold, two trustees must sign the receipt for the sale proceeds.

Receiver

When a customer dies, his personal representative carries on for him. A customer may lose his legal powers to look after his own affairs in two other ways: by his bankruptcy, when a trustee is appointed to take over, and by becoming mentally ill, when the Court will appoint a Receiver. A Receiver is a person authorized to receive and administer the assets of a person certified to be mentally incapable, under the direction of the Court.

Where a creditor has petitioned the Court that his debtor should be made bankrupt, as it seems as if this is the only way in which he is likely to get any money at all, the Court will make a receiving order. This means that the Court has appointed one of its own officers, the Official Receiver, to take charge of the debtor's estate as an interim measure. If the debtor is eventually made bankrupt, the estate will be passed to a trustee.

Where members of a firm are in disagreement, a partner may perhaps apply to the Court for dissolution of the firm. For this purpose the Court will appoint a Receiver for Partnership. When a person has deposited the deeds of his house as security for a loan, he has mortgaged them. He is the mortgagor, and the lender is the mortgagee. If the mortgagor fails to repay, the mortgagee can exercise a power of sale over the property. He may choose instead to appoint a Receiver of Rents to collect the rent from the property (say a row of houses) and manage the estate.

Liquidator

An individual is made bankrupt and has a trustee appointed. A limited company goes into liquidation and has a liquidator appointed. A liquidator is a person appointed by the Court (in a compulsory liquidation) or by the creditors of a company (in a creditors' voluntary winding up), or by the members of a company (in a members' voluntary winding up) to get in what is owed to the company, to take charge of the assets and turn them into money, to pay the company's debts and then, if there is anything left, to distribute it amongst the members in proportion to their shareholding.

A compulsory winding up is administered through the Court. It is usually the result of a petition from creditors. A creditors' voluntary winding up does not go through the Court, but is supervised by the creditors.

When the reason for winding up is nothing to do with shortage of money, but is for some amalgamation or merger with another company, or because the purpose for which the company was formed has now been achieved, no supervision by creditors is required, and the winding up is called a members' voluntary winding up.

Revision test 6

Place a tick against the letter you consider is the correct answer.

1 The basic relationship between a banker and a customer is that of
   (a) master and servant
   (b) debtor and creditor
   (c) donor and trustee.

2 A customer who leaves a box for safekeeping with his bank is
   (a) a bailor
   (b) a factor
   (c) a mortgagor.

3 Joint and several liability means that
   (a) only one person can be sued for the debts
   (b) all partners are collectively liable
   (c) each person is personally and collectively liable for the
       debts.

4 When opening an account for a limited company, a Memorandum of Association is shown to the bank. This document is
   (a) a short note from the directors confirming the existence of
       the company
   (b) one that shows the aims and objectives of the company
   (c) a certificate from the Registrar of Companies approving the
       existence of the company.

5 The holder of preference shares has preference over the
   ordinary shareholders under the following circumstances:
   (a) his voting rights are considered more important
   (b) he receives his dividend before the ordinary shareholder
   (c) he has the greater right in choosing the board of directors.

6 When opening a current account for an individual,
   (a) references under all circumstances must be taken
   (b) references need not be taken, if the account is opened with a
       minimum of £10,000 in cash
   (c) students are not required by law to provide references.

7 In which of the following cases is the banker an agent for his
   customer:
   (a) when he cashes a cheque for him at the counter?
   (b) when he receives cash from him over the counter?
   (c) when he credits his account with a cheque drawn on
       another bank?

8 A minor may have an account
   (a) if he wants one
   (b) only if his parents or guardian give permission
   (c) only if he can prove that it is a necessity.

9 An executor is a person
   (a) appointed by a court to take charge of the assets of a company
   (b) appointed by a person in his will to carry out his instructions
   (c) appointed by partners to transact their business.

10 An unincorporated body has
    (a) a legal entity
    (b) an entity as stated in its articles
    (c) no legal entity.

Questions for discussion

1 How does an executor differ from an administrator, and in which cases is the latter appointed?
2 Compare and contrast private limited companies from the point of view of their business advantages and disadvantages.
3 What is a minor? Discuss the reasons why banks treat the accounts of minors with some degree of caution.

7

Accounts of customers

Introduction

You have learnt from previous chapters about the different types of
banks that exist in this country, and the relationships that exist
between them and the various types of corporate and non-corporate
customers. This chapter will be devoted to discussing the various
types of accounts that may be held by customers, and the rights and
responsibilities of both the bank and the customer.

Current accounts

Perhaps the most important and the most popular account held by a
customer of a bank is the current account. From this account stems
the various services that a bank can make available to a customer.
Indeed, in order to have the usual relationship between a bank and a
customer it is vital that an account is held. The current account is
often called the 'cheque account', because money is withdrawn by
the use of a cheque. The current account is an account from which a
customer may withdraw his funds on demand by drawing a cheque,
or by advising the banker to debit his account at regular intervals by
means of a standing order instruction, or by authorizing a bank to
accept debits from certain major organizations for certain debts
incurred on a monthly, quarterly, half-yearly or yearly basis. These
are direct debits which originate from the creditor and are claimed
through the Bankers Automated Clearing Services (BACS) on the
debtor. When the account is opened, the customer is given a cheque
book and paying-in book, free of charge, and he will use these in all
his transactions with the bank. That is, if he receives cheques in his

favour from other people, he may ask the bank to act as his agent for collection and present them for payment to the drawee bank. The cheque or cheques will be listed on the credit slip by the customer, who will pass the paying-in book with the cheques to the cashier, or send them to the bank by post. The bank, on acceptance of the cheques, will tear out the credit slip from the paying-in book, stamp and initial the counterfoil or second copy, then credit the customer's account with the amount and send the cheques for collection via the Clearing House.

The cheque book will of course be used to either draw cash or pay debts due to third parties. It may be used with a cheque card, which guarantees payment up to £50 (in some instances £100), providing certain conditions have been fulfilled.

By far the most important basic service given to any customer with a current account is the despatch of the statement. This indicates the balance due to the customer or, if he has overdrawn, the balance due to the bank. It will also show the debit and credit entries and the balance on the account at the end of each working day. A person may order a statement as often as necessary, either on demand or at regular intervals.

Banks must take extreme care when passing entries to the customer's account, because it is possible to lose considerable sums of money due to carelessness, or breach of secrecy.

Before a statement is despatched, a clerk should verify that the debit entries refer to the account in question, because any errors would mean that the bank would have to refund the amount to the customer no matter when the entry was passed. A customer's account can never be debited without his authority.

Credits which are erroneously passed to the customer's account could also mean a loss to the bank, especially when the customer in all innocence and good faith spends these funds. In the case of Lloyds Bank Ltd v. Brooks (1950), Lady Brooks was credited with a series of dividend warrants to which she was not entitled. The bank attempted to recover these funds, but as she acted in good faith and relied upon the balance, her defence was good.

It is encumbent on all bank staff to ensure that the entries are correct before a statement is despatched; at the same time they must ensure that the statement is sent to the correct person at the correct address. Should the envelope be addressed to another person, and opened by him/her, then there has been a breach of secrecy.

Up till the end of 1988 the current accounts of ordinary customers were free of any charge, providing that the accounts were maintained in credit. Should an account overdraw either officially or unofficially, it was usual for some banks to charge for every entry made in the previous three months.

As competition grew between banks and building societies, so that building societies were offering basic banking facilities and giving interest on the cheque accounts, it was necessary for banks to offer the same service. Since early 1989 banks have offered interest-bearing accounts providing the account remained in credit. Each bank has its own marketing name for the accounts it offers, but basically, the rate of interest offered is equal to that of a seven-day deposit account. This interest is paid net of tax for all customers except non-residents and companies. However, many banks will offer a higher rate of interest with greater credit balances. With corporate customers, charges may be made and are subject to a quarterly or half-yearly levy as agreed between the bank and customer.

Budget accounts

Another type of current account which has some popularity among ordinary men and women is that which assists people to monitor and regulate their cash flow and avoid the peaks and troughs of debt payments.

Each bank gives this type of account a different name, but basically, in consultation with the branch manager or a senior member of staff, the customer calculates his total domestic expenditure, such as rates, electricity, gas, insurance (both house and car) and any other expense that is incurred on a regular basis. The bank adds to this sum its charges, the total is then divided by twelve and the account is opened by a transfer from current account to this 'cash flow' account. This same amount is transferred each month by standing order. The customer is given a cheque book on this account and will then be able to pay his bills as and when they fall due. Obviously there will be periods when this account is in credit and other periods when it is overdrawn, but at the end of twelve months, providing the calculations are correct and there has been no sudden increase or decrease in any item of expenditure, the balance on the account should be nil. The exercise is then recommenced for the following year.

Deposit accounts

It should be noted that, as stated above, interest is now given for holding funds on current/cheque accounts, so that it is quite likely that the ordinary customer, rather than keep transferring funds from one account to another in order to obtain interest on funds that he does not immediately require, will find the operation unnecessary. Whether the number of deposit accounts will reduce can be ascertained only when all banks have for some time been dealing with interest-bearing current accounts. Many customers will keep funds on a deposit account so that they have some form of reserve, should they need funds urgently, without going into an overdraft situation.

Interest is credited either quarterly or half-yearly, depending on bank practice. Withdrawals are subject to seven days' notice; if necessary, withdrawals can be made on demand, but seven days' interest is lost.

As with a current account, statements are sent at regular intervals to the customer.

It should be remembered that no overdrafts are permitted on a deposit account. When cheques are paid in for credit to this account, interest is calculated on the cleared balance; that is, only when the cheque presented for collection is finally paid, normally three days later, will interest start accruing to the account.

The interest available is displayed on the customers' side of the banking hall and is paid to individuals, joint accounts and partnerships, unincorporated societies, executors, trustees, personal representatives, savings clubs and charities, net of tax. That is, tax will have already been deducted by the bank at the Composite Rate of Tax (CRT) for the year, before crediting the customer's account. This system was introduced on 6 April 1985 to all sterling deposits and has applied since 6 April 1986 to deposit account holders of currency funds. It was already in existence for account holders with building societies, and the new ruling merely brought the deposit accounts of non-corporate customers in line with customers of building societies. CRT is not applicable for corporate account customers nor for those persons not ordinarily resident in the UK. Neither is it applied to accounts in the Channel Islands or Isle of Man.

Although deposit account holders are customers of the bank, the normal services of a current account are not available with a deposit account. For example, a cheque book is not issued, nor is a cheque card or cash dispenser card. Standing orders or direct debits are not given. However, the usual advisory services, traveller's cheques, currency, and investment services are all available.

Customers with large amounts at their disposal may consider that a fixed-term deposit account is more attractive to their needs: a sum of money can be put on deposit account for a period of one month upwards and so attract a better rate of interest. The interest given will depend on the amount invested and the length of time that the funds remain on deposit account. The greater the amount and the longer the time, the better will be the rate of interest. Such rates are quoted to customers on request. Should the customer require all or part of these funds before completion of the term, then the bank would be pleased to assist the customer, but a penalty is incurred for early repayment.

Larger amounts, say £10,000 and upwards, may be invested through the bank's treasurer's office, or head office, to attract interest at rates related to those quoted on the London money market. Such large amounts can be placed on the market for short or long periods at the customer's option, but the rates are subject to the fluctuation of the market, so that a rate given one day will not necessarily be the same for the next working day. It may be higher or lower, but once the bank has quoted a rate and a legally binding contract has been made, then the rate quoted is the one in force.

Other types of deposit account are offered to the small saver. In particular the banks are very keen to attract the very young, and therefore offer attractive presents of one form or another to those young people who open a savings account with them. Basically, these are no different from the seven-day deposit account, except the child has a gift or two to take home. Most banks will give a money box into which the child can put his savings. These boxes can normally be opened at home but customers are encouraged to bring the box to the bank where the contents are credited to the appropriate account.

In the past the banks have blown hot and cold on these types of accounts. It was not so long ago that savings accounts of this nature were positively discouraged, but now there is a positive aggressive marketing policy by the large banks to encourage the young and the very young to open an account.

From the bank staff's point of view the emptying of a money box at the counter at the end of the working day, or on a day when the counter staff are extremely busy, cannot be very popular, but it must be accepted.

For the more mature person who perhaps does not want a deposit account but finds a bank a useful place to deposit his money, and who wants to transfer any surplus funds to an interest bearing account, the banks have a 'savings plan' account. This encourages regular savings by transfer from a current account, and it attracts a rate of interest of about $1\frac{1}{2}$ per cent above the normal deposit rate. The only disadvantage is that the banks will only permit withdrawals twice a year. Many customers find this method of saving very attractive as funds are painlessly transferred from one account to another, so that savings for a special purpose, e.g. holidays, Christmas, or a deposit for a house, can be made without effort.

High-interest-earning cheque accounts

This type of account is usually offered by the smaller banks as well as the major banks. The conditions vary between banks, but it is expected that a minimum balance of about £2,000 will be maintained and a condition can be imposed that no more than a certain number of cheques per year may be issued without charges being made; in any case the value of each cheque drawn should generally not be below a stated amount, e.g. £250. Should the customer draw cheques beyond the stipulated number, then a charge may be applied.

Unlike a deposit account, the withdrawals from this interest-earning account do not need notice to be given to the banker, nor is interest lost due to a cash withdrawal or the presentation of a cheque through the clearing system.

Loan accounts

Borrowing funds from a bank by obtaining a loan has its attractions to both the business customer and the private person.

On the agreement with a bank to borrow a given sum of money, a loan account is debited with this sum, and the current account is credited with a similar amount. The loan may be for consumer durables, holidays, or any other acceptable reason. The businessman may require a business loan either to improve or extend his fixed assets, or to purchase additional stock in order to expand his business.

In both instances, the loan can probably be taken for a period of five years and longer if considered necessary. The interest charged is agreed with the customer and will be quoted as x per cent over the base rate. The interest is debited quarterly or half-yearly to the loan account or the current account at the option of the customer. Interest will fluctuate with changes in the bank's base rate.

Personal loans

Another form of borrowing money, particularly for the individual, is the personal loan scheme. It is quite simple to operate, and the customer knows from the start the interest charged for the borrowing, both as a net figure and, as required under the Consumer Credit Act, the Annual Percentage Rate (APR). He can therefore calculate the exact amount he will have to pay each week or each month.

Once the customer knows the item he wishes to purchase or the need for the loan, e.g. a holiday, he can arrange a personal loan with the bank who, on the day the service or goods are purchased, will credit the current account with the required amount, and debit a personal loan account with this amount. The interest on the outstanding amount is calculated on a daily basis, so that as the customer pays off the debt by regular weekly or monthly payments, either in cash or transfer from this current account, the amount of interest is reduced. The interest is charged either quarterly or half yearly. Should interest rates change, then this will affect the interest charged on his loan.

From the customer's point of view, he may go to his retail outlet and purchase the goods for cash or offer a cheque, which could attract a cash discount sufficient to offset any interest paid to the bank. Another attraction of this form of borrowing is the fact that no security is needed and none is in fact asked for by the bank. Finally, there is usually built-in insurance, so that should anything happen to the borrower, the debt is cancelled and the deceased's family is not encumbered with repayment.

Personal loans are perhaps one of the most popular of individual methods of borrowing from a bank. In order to give the customer a speedy reply to his loan application, it is usual for banks to 'credit score' the details of the loan. This may be done by any responsible clerk who will feed the customer's details into the computer and the positive or negative response will be made in minutes. Such details will include age, address, terms of tenancy, occupation, how long in present employment, salary, marital status, etc. Normally the lower the score the better the status.

Currency accounts

Since the suspension of the Exchange Control Act, 1947, it is now possible for residents of this country to own or retain gold and foreign currency either in this country or abroad. Many bank customers, who have business or personal interests abroad, find a currency account, either deposit or current, a very useful and attractive service.

With a currency account, the same conditions apply as to a sterling current account. That is, a cheque book is available and debit entries and credit entries may be passed through the account. Obviously, an account can only be held in one currency. So that if a customer is continually dealing in Deutschmarks and US dollars, he must have two accounts, one for each currency. Should the customer have a surplus of US dollars he may sell a given amount to the bank for either sterling or Deutschmarks, and a simultaneous debit is passed to the US dollar account and a credit passed to the nominated account.

A currency deposit account can be opened, usually with a minimum amount of an equivalent of £1,000 sterling, but this will depend on the policy of the bank. Interest rates are in this case not linked to interest rates in London, but are related to rates in the financial centre of the currency, e.g. US dollars – New York.

The book-keeping and retention of any currency account will vary from bank to bank, but it is not unusual for a currency account to be retained at the local branch of a bank, while all the book-keeping entries, purchase and sale of currencies, and receipt and remittance of funds are dealt with by the overseas branch or international division.

Opening an account

All banks are anxious to expand and increase their business against competition from other banks and financial institutions. One of the

ways of increasing their deposit base, earning funds from investment, lending and offering various services, is by attracting people
who are willing to open accounts.

Notwithstanding this competition, a bank must exercise caution
before an account is opened for any person. The reason for this
caution is simple. The bank can be sued for 'conversion', that is, the
deprivation of the property of a rightful owner to another person. A
bank collects cheques and other instruments every day and can very
easily fall into this trap if it does not take reasonable precautions. In
order to avoid being sued for conversion, it must act in good faith
and without negligence. If it does so, it will receive statutory protection.

Therefore, a bank must always identify the person or persons
wishing to open an account. That is, they must prove that they are
the person(s) they say they are. Time and time again a bank has
opened an account in the name of a person and it transpires that a
false name was given and the account was merely a receptacle for
stolen cheques; after collection and payment, funds were withdrawn from the account and the person(s) disappeared.

Secondly, the person must give proof that he is a fit and proper
person to whom banking services should be given.

Thirdly, has the person authority to open an account in his name?
This may seem strange, but it is possible for a stranger to enter a
bank and request to open an account in the name of a limited
company. If no authority is available, the bank should not open the
account.

Lastly, if the person is in employment, the name of his employer
should be given.

Assuming that a bank has checked the identification of the individual, the next step is to request the person to complete the application
form to open an account and offer the names and addresses of two
people who could act as referees (see the National Westminster Bank
forms reproduced on pp. 146–8).

From time to time banks will dispense with the need to obtain
references, or will leave this to the discretion of the branch manager.
This may be a cost cutting exercise, but the management of the bank
know the risks involved and junior members of staff should not
assume that this is the usual procedure for opening accounts. Management know the law and they have no doubt heard of such cases as
Ladbroke v. Todd (1914), or Hampstead Guardians v. Barclays Bank

Ltd (1923), later the well known case of Lloyds Bank v. Savory & Co. (1932), and finally Marfani & Co. Ltd v. Midland Bank Ltd (1968). These are but a few cases which involved negligence, or possible negligence, by a bank.

Of course, when a branch bank opens an account which has been transferred from another branch, or it has been requested to open an account by another bank, then there is no problem. In the same way, should an existing customer introduce his son or daughter to the bank manager and request that he opens an account in the name of that son or daughter, then an introduction has been made by a customer, and the bank is acting in good faith and without negligence. But at all times the bank, when opening an account, must act with caution.

Having taken the names and addresses of the referees, it is usual for the bank to write to the referees to obtain their confirmation that the person on whose behalf they are writing is a fit and proper person to whom banking facilities should be given. For its own protection the bank will request the referee to give the name and address of his bankers, so that they may, in their turn, confirm that the referee is their customer. It is not beyond the realms of possibility for the potential customer to give a fictitious referee and respond in glowing terms himself to the banker's reference.

Once the references have been proved satisfactory and the funds have been cleared, then the customer can be issued with a cheque book. From the moment the account is opened the banker–customer relationship is in existence.

For a joint account or partnership, it is usual for the bank to take references on all parties. When the application form is being completed, it is not only necessary for the bank to have the signatures of all parties, but to have the signing instructions as well and to ensure that there is joint and several liability.

When opening an account for a limited company, it must be understood that it is a separate legal entity, but being legal fiction, a company must have people acting on its behalf. These people, directors of the company, will meet and pass a resolution appointing a named bank as bankers to the company. This resolution is part of the mandate form of a bank when opening the account. Assuming that the company is newly formed, then the bank official must obtain a copy of the Memorandum and Articles of Association and examine the Certificate of Incorporation to ensure that all is well. Additionally, if the directors are not known to the bank, references will be

Please complete all sections of this form and tick boxes where applicable. Please use block capitals

Branch name

Account number

Type of account required

☐ Current Account ☐ Deposit Account ☐ Savings Account ☐ Current Account and Deposit Account

Personal details (1st Party)	Personal details (2nd Party) (You need only complete details which differ)
Surname (Mr, Mrs, Miss, Ms)	Surname (Mr, Mrs, Miss, Ms)
Forename(s)	Forename(s)
Date of birth	Date of birth
Address	Address
Postcode	Postcode

Telephone: Home	Business	Telephone: Home	Business

Residential status		Residential status	
☐ Owner	☐ In rented accommodation	☐ Owner	☐ In rented accommodation
☐ With parents	☐ Other	☐ With parents	☐ Other

How long have you lived at this address?	How long have you lived at this address?
If under 3 years please give previous address	If under 3 years please give previous address
Postcode	Postcode
Are you ordinarily resident in the UK for tax purposes? Yes/No	Are you ordinarily resident in the UK for tax purposes? Yes/No
If no it will be necessary for you to sign a declaration as to your status.	If no it will be necessary for you to sign a declaration as to your status.

Are you: ☐ Single ☐ Married ☐ Other	Are you: ☐ Single ☐ Married ☐ Other
If Other please specify	If Other please specify
Previous name if changed in the last 3 years	Previous name if changed in the last 3 years
Name and date of birth of children under 18	Name and date of birth of children under 18

National Westminster account application form

1st Party
(Continued)

2nd Party
(Continued)

Your occupation?	Your occupation?

Name and address of employer	Name and address of employer

Postcode	Postcode

Length of service with present employer	Length of service with present employer

Will your company provide you with a pension? Yes/No	Will your company provide you with a pension? Yes/No

Are you: ☐ Self-employed ☐ Retired	Are you: ☐ Self-employed ☐ Retired

How are you paid? ☐ In cash ☐ By cheque ☐ Direct to Bank	How are you paid? ☐ In cash ☐ By cheque ☐ Direct to Bank

Details of income and outgoings
Net income (including overtime) monthly/weekly £

Details of income and outgoings
Net income (including overtime) monthly/weekly £

Gross annual income	£	Gross annual income	£
Regular monthly outgoings		Regular monthly outgoings	
Mortgage/Rent	£ _____	Mortgage/Rent	£ _____
Credit (eg HP)	£ _____	Credit (eg HP)	£ _____
Insurance	£ _____	Insurance	£ _____
Other	£ _____	Other	£ _____

Credit cards held (please specify)	Credit cards held (please specify)

Other Bank/Building Society Accounts held Name	Other Bank/Building Society Accounts held Name

Branch	Branch

Name	Name

Branch	Branch

National Westminster Bank PLC ↻

Please address your reply to the Manager

Your ref

Our ref

Date

Dear

Our prospective customer

whose address is

has given your name as a referee for the purpose of opening a bank account. I shall be grateful if you will answer the questions below and return this letter to me. A stamped envelope is enclosed.

I thank you in anticipation of your reply.

Yours sincerely

Manager

Is he/she, in your opinion, a person to whom the usual banking facilities may be safely afforded? _____

How long have you known him/her? _____

Can you confirm that the specimen signature shown appears to be that of our prospective customer? _____

Please give details below of your Bankers:

Bank: _____

Address: _____

(This information is required by us to conform to accepted banking practice for completion of references and thereby afford us the protection of the Cheques Act.)

Specimen Signature

Please return to:

The Manager
National Westminster Bank PLC
Wembley Branch
520 High Road
Wembley
Middx HA9 7BZ

(Please fold this letter so that the return address appears in the window of the envelope provided)

Please Note:
If you are signing on behalf of a Firm, Company, Public Authority or other Official Body, please give the name and address of the organisation's bankers and arrange for an official stamp to be impressed hereon and add the capacity in which you sign

Signature _____

Date _____

NWB12 Rev Feb 85-2001   Registered Number 929027 England   Registered Office 41 Lothbury, London EC2P 2BP taken out on them, again to ensure that there is no negligence. Providing the references are satisfactory, the mandate completed correctly, and the funds cleared, then an account can be opened and a cheque book, a special one if requested, can be issued.

So far the word 'negligence' has appeared frequently. Negligence is the failure by one person to carry out his duty towards another person to take care of that person's interests. This duty may spring from the terms of a contract between them, or may exist irrespective of any contract. For example, if a banker is careless in dealing with the affairs of his customer, he will be liable, because being negligent is a breach of his contractual duty to take care of the customer's interest.

Conversion, which has also been mentioned, is the tort committed when one person wrongfully interferes with the property of another in such a way as to show that he denies or is indifferent to the title of that other. It is no defence that the tort is committed innocently. Examples in banking are when a box held on safe custody for one customer is mistakenly given out to another, or, more importantly, where a banker collecting a cheque for a customer who has no title to it, or a defective title, renders himself liable to an action for conversion brought against him by the true owner.

The protection a banker has in law is in section 4 of the Cheques Act, 1957. This replaced section 82 of the Bills of Exchange Act, 1882. The section reads:

Where a banker, in good faith and without negligence,
(a) receives payment for a customer of an instrument to which this section applies; or
(b) having credited a customer's account with the amount of such an instrument, receives payment thereof for himself; and the customer has no title, or a defective title, to the instrument, the banker does not incur any liability to the true owner of the instrument by reason only of having received payment thereof.

It is quite clear from the above extract from the Cheques Act that a bank will receive protection in law if it collects a cheque or similar document for a customer whose title may be defective, provided the bank has not acted in a negligent manner. The good faith of any bank has never been questioned.

The responsibilities of a banker

(1) The banker must receive his customer's money on current or deposit account and conduct the account in a proper manner.

(2) He must act as an agent for collection.

(3) He must pay cheques drawn by his customers on himself (assuming always that the account has sufficient funds, or borrowing arrangements have been agreed).

(4) He must keep secret the affairs of his customer except in four cases:

    under compulsion of law

    where there is a duty to the public to disclose

    where the bank's interests demand disclosure

    where the customer has authorized disclosure.

The four rules which breach the rules of secrecy were specified in the case of Tournier v. National Provincial Bank. In this case Tournier had overdrawn his account. The bank manager telephoned Tournier at his place of employment, but, being unable to contact his customer, spoke to his employer. During the conversation, it came out that Tournier had been drawing cheques in favour of a turf accountant and was heavily overdrawn at the bank. The employer, upon hearing this, promptly sacked Tournier. Tournier sued the bank and won.

The rights of a banker

(1) The banker has the right to expect to receive a reasonable commission for services given.

(2) He has the right to expect the customer to maintain adequate funds on his account, or to make proper arrangements to meet any cheques drawn.

(3) He has the right to expect the customer not to mislead him and to notify him should he suspect forgery.

(4) He has the right to close the customer's account, though he must give him reasonable notice of doing so.

In the case of Prosperity Ltd v. Lloyds Bank Ltd, the bank decided to close the customer's account due to publicity involving the company's methods of selling. Prosperity considered that the notice to close the account was inadequate and sued the bank for breach of contract. Prosperity won the case. It is considered that adequate notice for the ordinary customer is 28 days, while a corporate customer should be given 6 months to make other arrangements.

The duties of a customer

(1) The customer must maintain an adequate balance to meet cheques presented for payment.

(2) He must take care when drawing cheques and other mandates, so as to make them difficult to alter.

(3) He must keep the cheque book safe and advise the bank should it be lost.

Closing an account

There are only two parties who can close an account. The first is the customer. All he needs to do is to withdraw his funds whenever he feels it right to so do. Clearly, when a banker is informed that this situation is about to arise, he must ensure that there are no outstanding cheques, either presented in the current day's work or not yet presented for payment. Standing orders and direct debits must be cancelled, and the bank must check up to see that no cash has been withdrawn from its cash dispenser machines. The customer must also confirm that no credits have been paid in at other banks or branches. Next, the bank must obtain the return of any unused cheques, the cheque card or cards that have been issued, and cash dispenser cards. Finally, the bank must take its commission and interest if any is payable, then give the customer his funds in cash, banker's draft or by transfer to another bank or branch.

The bank, on the other hand, cannot close the account of an undesirable customer without giving him reasonable notice. As seen in the Prosperity case a bank must give reasonable notice before effecting closure. However, when a person misuses or abuses the banker–customer relationship, there is no reason why the bank cannot withdraw his cheque or encashment card and refuse to issue a new cheque book.

Supposing a customer to whom due notice has been given refuses to accept the situation and still draws cheques and pays in funds. What can the bank do?

First, the bank can dishonour cheques if insufficient cover is available. Secondly, the bank can refuse to issue new cheque books. Finally, any credits paid in via another bank and branch could be put on a suspense account and repaid to the person when he next enters the bank. In this way the person concerned will realize that the bank is not prepared to co-operate with him, will lose patience and will not trouble the bank any further.

Revision test 7

Place a tick against the letter you consider is the correct answer.

1 The interest rate quoted by banks indicating or affecting their lending and deposit rates is called
   (a) base rate
   (b) modal rate
   (c) transition rate.

2 Disclosure of a customer's affairs may be made under the following circumstances:
   (a) to a parent who wishes to know if his son/daughter at university has sufficient funds
   (b) to a trading company with whom your customer is dealing
   (c) to the executor of a will who has produced a certificate of probate.

3 A person may be asked for the names of two referees if he is opening a
   (a) savings account
   (b) deposit account
   (c) current account.

4 A bank will take up a reference for a new customer because
   (a) he could be liable for conversion – Cheques Act, 1957
   (b) head office instructions say so
   (c) it is required by the Protection of Customers Act.

5 To close the account of a private customer it is necessary to
   (a) give him his balance immediately
   (b) give him at least 28 days' notice
   (c) await his appearance in the bank.

6 A direct debit is
   (a) a commission charged by a banker
   (b) a withdrawal by a deposit account holder
   (c) a claim on a current account by a creditor.

7 When a statement is despatched to a customer, a banker should
   (a) check the details on the account
   (b) not bother to check the details
   (c) it does not really matter either way.
8 Conversion is
   (a) convincing the person the banker is always correct
   (b) denying a person his property
   (c) ensuring that a person will always maintain an account at your bank.
9 The duty of a customer to a banker is to
   (a) maintain an adequate balance and draw cheques carefully
   (b) comply without question with all the requests of a bank
   (c) keep the bank advised about all his personal affairs.
10 Interest is paid on the deposit account of corporate customers
   (a) gross of tax
   (b) net of tax
   (c) at the customer's option.

Questions for discussion

1 A solicitor well known to you introduces two persons for whom he has established a limited company and who now wish to open an account in the name of the company at your branch. Describe the procedures you would adopt.
2 A particularly bad customer is requested to close his current account by your manager. The customer refuses to comply with this request. What action could be taken to deny the customer further banking services without breach of the law?
3 Ascertain from your own bank the cost of the procedures in opening an account, including the issue in the first year of
   (i) one paying-in book
   (ii) one cheque card
   (iii) two cheque books
   (iv) three statements
   (v) four standing orders
   (vi) five direct debits.

Using current notional interest rates, calculate the average balance required on the account to cover these costs and give the bank a 10 per cent profit for its work.

8

The legal background to negotiable instruments

Introduction

The principal statutes relating to negotiable instruments are the Bills of Exchange Act, 1882, and the Cheques Act, 1957.

The first of these was a codification of what was then a mass of legislation on bills of exchange. The Institute of Bankers was instrumental in bringing this about, and the bill was introduced to parliament by Sir John Lubbock, at the time the Institute's president, in the summer of 1881. The bill received the Royal Assent in August 1882. It has since been amended six times, only one of these amending Acts being of major importance, and it has dominated the practice of banking for more than a century. During that time it has regulated every aspect of the issue, negotiation and final discharge of bills of exchange, cheques and promissory notes, with particular attention to the rights of parties and the steps to be taken on dishonour.

In the first half of this century the negotiation of bills had to be authenticated by the endorsement of the payee, and while this is still the case for bills, a point came when the growth of cheques had been so great that the burden on the banks of checking endorsements on all cheques to see that they purported to be in order came to be considered as a waste of time. Only 6 or 7 per cent of cheques were ever negotiated, and the rest went from drawer to payee, then through the collecting bank to the paying bank. Consequently there was only the endorsement of the payee to be checked, but the paying banker still had to turn over every cheque to look at the endorsement, and the customers had to spend much time writing their endorsements on all the cheques they received. Now the only cheques the paying banker has to look at the back of are those he is thinking of sending back unpaid, in case they have a number on them, indicating that they have been taken from a drawer with a cheque guarantee card. It was, and is, the business of the collecting banker to check endorsements where cheques have been negotiated, for only he is in a position to compare the name of the payee on the cheque with the name on the credit slip. (Before 1957 he also had to look at all endorsements, to check that they purported to be correct.) The Cheques Act was not intended to apply to negotiated cheques, which still must have endorsements to authenticate the passing of the title.

Statutory protection for bankers

Since 1957 we have to consider both main statutes together. While the position in respect of a collecting banker is neatly summarized in one section, the legal protection for the paying banker still reflects the hotch-potch of statutes which used to exist, and there are three main sections to consider. The first is section 60 of the Bills of Exchange Act:

> When a bill payable to order on demand is drawn on a banker, and the banker on whom it is drawn pays the bill in good faith and in the ordinary course of business, it is not encumbent on the banker to show that the endorsement of the payee, or any subsequent endorsement, was made by or under the authority of the person whose endorsement it purports to be, and the banker is deemed to have paid the bill in due course, although such endorsement has been forged or made without authority.

The first line here makes it clear that parliament is referring to cheques and not other bills of exchange. This at first appears strange because this section is not included in part III of the Bills of Exchange Act, headed 'Cheques on a Banker', which comprises sections 73–82 (section 82 has now been repealed by the Cheques Act). The reason is an historical one and goes back to the Crossed Cheques Act, 1876 (repealed in 1882 when the Bills of Exchange Act was passed, when it was incorporated into that Act as sections 73–82). Acts of Parliament are not always very logically set out. When they are first passed, as when textbooks are first written, they are fine, but as time passes both get tinkered with.

The purpose of the section, as a careful reading will make clear, is to protect the banker, subject to the conditions mentioned, against paying any cheque (whether open or crossed) which has a forged endorsement. This will only happen when fraudulent negotiation has taken place. Perhaps the payee loses the cheque before he has had a chance to pay it in or even endorse it, and a finder, or thief, comes into possession of it. How to get the money? Obviously, by paying it in to his own banking account (if crossed) or by trying to cash it over the counter (if open). In each case he will have to forge the signature of the payee, to make it appear as though the order cheque has been converted into a bearer cheque payable to the possessor.

The signature cannot be dignified by the name 'endorsement'. It is a forgery and therefore a nullity. It may affect the rights of the endorsers (if there are any after the thief), but it has no effect on the validity of the cheque, title to which still remains with the payee. For *that* to happen there would have to be a forged signature of the drawer.

The section does *not* apply to bills of exchange other than cheques. So if a banker pays a bill of exchange which has a forged endorsement, he has no protection under this section.

Next we come to section 80 of the Bills of Exchange Act. Don't forget we are now in the 'crossed cheques' section of the Act, and therefore any protection that the banker may now get will be for crossed cheques only.

> Where a banker, on whom a crossed cheque is drawn, in good faith and without negligence pays it, if crossed generally, to a banker, and if crossed specially, to the banker to whom it is crossed, or his agent for collection being a banker, the banker paying the cheque, and, if the cheque has come into the hands of the payee, the drawer, shall respectively be entitled to the same rights, and be placed in the same position, as if payment of the cheque has been made to the true owner thereof.

When you have read that through two or three times it should be quite clear to you. Notice that the protection gained by the banker is also extended to the drawer if the cheque has actually reached the payee. The idea is that if that has happened, the drawer's debt must be considered paid, and he must not be held liable for anything that has happened to the cheque between the time when the payee received it, and the time when the payee paid it into his bank for collection.

Notice also that this time the two conditions that the banker has to satisfy are slightly different. In practice they seem much the same, for how could any banker admit that in the ordinary course of his business he was sometimes or often negligent?

Now to the Cheques Act for the third section. First, though, let us summarize the position just before the passing of that Act.

The collecting banker had to check all endorsements when cheques were paid in to see that they purported to be correct. (When we come to section 4 of the Cheques Act, you will see that one of the conditions on which the banker is given statutory protection is that he has acted 'without negligence'. But in those days it was held negligent to pass an endorsement which was irregular, or even non-existent.)

He had to check endorsements (and still has to) where the cheque bore evidence of being negotiated. The cashier, therefore, taking in credits for a particular account, would stop at a cheque which bore not only the endorsement of the customer, but also of a third party. That indicated that the cheque had been negotiated. In this case, of course, the credit would be for the account of the third party.

The *paying* banker had to check all endorsements before paying cheques to see that they purported to be correct. This was because one of the conditions on which he relied for protection was 'in the ordinary course of business' (section 60) or 'without negligence' (section 80). To pass a cheque with no endorsement, or one with an obviously defective endorsement, would not be 'in the ordinary course of business', nor would it be 'without negligence'.

And finally, let's spare a thought for the customer. Really big firms had to spend most of the morning endorsing their cheques before they paid them in. Each endorsement had to be signed by a senior official. Time is money, as someone once said!

The Cheques Act, 1957 (section 1), runs as follows:

S1(1) Where a banker in good faith and in the ordinary course of business pays a cheque drawn on him which is not endorsed or is irregularly endorsed, he does not, in doing so, incur any liability by reason only of the absence of, or irregularity in, endorsement, and he is deemed to have paid it in due course.

(2) Where a banker in good faith and in the ordinary course of business pays any such instrument as the following, namely,

(a) a document issued by a customer of his which, though not a bill of exchange, is intended to enable a person to obtain payment from him of the sum mentioned in the document;

(b) a draft payable on demand drawn by him upon himself, whether payable at the head office or some other office of his bank;

he does not, in doing so, incur any liability by reason only of the absence of, or irregularity in, endorsement, and the payment discharges the instrument.

Points to note here are: that the two conditions are the same as in section 60, Bills of Exchange Act (BEA); that the main purpose of this Act, to eliminate all endorsements except those necessary to transfer title on negotiation, is here effected as far as the paying banker is concerned, in subsection 1; and that the section extends the banker's protection to various instruments, not cheques (which the BEA did *not* do). In the example given in 2(a) the document might be a cheque payable to 'cash' or 'wages'. The definition of a bill of exchange (which includes cheques) includes the stipulation that it 'must be payable to the order of a specified person, or to bearer'. A document payable to 'wages' is neither, and cannot except by courtesy be called a 'cheque'. But it is very common to find a 'cheque' so drawn.

In the case of 2(b) the definition includes the stipulation that the bill must be 'addressed by one person to another'. Here the banker's demand draft is addressed by one person (drawn at a branch) to the same person (paid at head office – both are one in law).

Note finally that this section offers no protection where there is a forged endorsement. That remains the business of section 60, BEA (which only applies to cheques and not to 'instruments', nor to bills of exchange that are not cheques).

There is a school of thought that thinks that a forged endorsement might be brought within this section because it is a nullity and so is equivalent to no endorsement at all. But a quarter-century of experience of the Act has failed to produce a single case on the point.

When we come to consider the legal protection for the collecting banker we are in a happier situation, for we have only one section to worry about, section 4 of the Cheques Act, which is as follows:

S4(1) Where a banker, in good faith and without negligence:
(a) receives payment for a customer of an instrument to which this section applies, or
(b) having credited a customer's account with the amount of such an instrument, receives payment thereof for himself, and the customer has no title, or a defective title, to the instrument, the banker does not incur any liability to the true owner of the instrument by reason only of having received payment thereof.
(2) This section applies to the following instruments, namely:
(a) cheques;
(b) any document issued by a customer of a banker which, though not a bill of exchange, is intended to enable a person to obtain payment from that banker of the sum mentioned in the document;
(c) any document issued by a public officer which is intended to enable a person to obtain payment from the Paymaster General or the Queen's and Lord Treasurer's Remembrancer of the sum mentioned in the document but is not a bill of exchange;
(d) any draft payable on demand drawn by a banker upon himself whether payable at the head office or some other office of his bank.
(3) A banker is not to be treated for the purposes of this section as having been negligent by reason only of his failure to concern himself with the absence of, or irregularity in, endorsement of an instrument.

The collecting banker deals with a great many cheques every day, and he has neither time nor opportunity to confirm that the money he is getting from the paying banker is being credited by him to the account of the person properly entitled to it. Therefore, if he is to carry on his business he must be given statutory protection against actions by true owners. Since 1957, this protection is incorporated in the above-quoted section, but it is given, as always, subject to conditions. This time there are three of them. Not only does the banker have to act in good faith and without negligence, but also he has to collect for a customer. As it has been argued that a banker who normally credits his customer's account with a cheque as soon as it is paid in, which is three to five days before he actually gets the cleared proceeds, is collecting it for himself and not for the customer at all, it was thought necessary to cover this situation by section 4(1)b, and this sets all doubts at rest where the customer's account is in credit; but if it is overdrawn this subsection may not apply.

As with section 1, protection is given in respect of cheques and also in respect of a wider group of instruments not cheques, and these are listed in subsection 2.

Subsection 3 carries out the main purpose of the Act, which was to abolish the necessity for most endorsements.

Negligence of the collecting banker

Of the three conditions described above, the requirement of good faith causes no difficulty. There is no case of a true owner successfully claiming that a collecting banker has acted in bad faith. Whether or not in any particular case a person for whom a cheque is being collected is a customer, has given rise to some litigation, but by far the greater volume of case history has gathered around what is negligence and what is not.

As a result of case law, negligence may be defined in this context as the failure to make enquiry in cases when a reasonably competent cashier would make an enquiry, or, when such an enquiry has been duly made, failure to appreciate that the answer obtained is an unsatisfactory one. Negotiated cheques require special care, particularly where the amount is a large one. The conduct of the account for which the cheque is being collected is a relevant factor; where the account has been giving trouble the banker is expected to look more carefully at the transaction.

The enquiry referred to is that which should be made by the cashier, or perhaps by a more senior officer of the bank, when a cheque being paid in arouses a query in the mind of the cashier, or ought to arouse it. This obligation stems from the duty of the collecting banker to collect the cheque for the person rightfully entitled to it and for no other.

It is negligent not to take up references or to fail to check them properly at the time the account is opened. The negligence does not have to be at the time of the collection of the cheque, or closely connected with it (although it often is).

It is negligent to allow an employee to place to his own account or to his wife's account a cheque drawn by or payable to his employer, without asking for the reason. (Of course, salary cheques call for no query.)

Thus, in one case, cheques were collected without enquiry because they were paid in at another branch. The account-holding branch did not realize that an enquiry was necessary because it did not know that the drawers of the cheques (the plaintiffs) were the employers of the clerk paying in. This was because it never saw the credit and the cheque together, the actual collection being done by the receiving branch.

It is negligent to allow cheques payable to a limited company to be placed without enquiry to the credit of any private account. A similar case would be where a bank collected without enquiry a cheque payable to a firm for the credit of the private account of one of the partners.

It is negligent to collect a cheque crossed 'account payee' for any account other than that of the payee, or to collect without enquiry cheques not consistent with the description given of his occupation by the customer at the time of the opening of the account.

It is not for plaintiff's counsel to prove negligence on the part of the banker; the onus is on the banker. He has to prove that he has not been negligent.

Before leaving the question of negligence and its implications for the collecting banker, some remarks of Lord Diplock in the Court of Appeal in 1967 deserve note. He thought that the facts which ought to be known to the banker must depend on current banking practice, and will change as that practice changes. Cases decided thirty years ago, when the use of banking facilities was less widespread, might not be a reliable guide to what the duty of a careful banker is today. His Lordship also said that a court is entitled to examine current banking practice and to form its own opinion as to whether it meets the standard of care required from a prudent banker. He thought that the Court of Appeal should hesitate before condemning as negligent a practice generally adopted by those engaged in banking business.

Contributory negligence of the plaintiff

This doctrine is well known in the case of collisions between vehicles or ships but, until 1971, it had never been applied to banking cases. The reason for this was that the plaintiff's action against the banker is not for negligence, but for conversion. The provisions

of the relevant statute – the Law Reform (Contributory Negligence)
Act, 1945 – were thought to apply only to actions for negligence.
This view was modified in a case in 1971 when judgment was given
for the plaintiffs in respect of a sum amounting to 90 per cent of their
claim.

Collection for a customer

There are certain occasions when the bank cannot rely on section 4
of the Cheques Act because it is collecting the proceeds of a cheque
not for a customer but for itself. These occasions are:

(1) when the banker is the payee or endorsee of the cheque
(2) when the banker collects a cheque over which it has a lien
(3) when the banker cashes or exchanges a cheque payable elsewhere for his customer
(4) when there is an express or implied agreement between
banker and customer that the latter may draw against uncleared
effects
(5) when the banker collects a cheque paid in by his customer in
specific reduction of his indebtedness.

All these cases are examples where the banker, in one way or
another, has given value beforehand for the cheque which he is now
proceeding to collect. He is, in fact, a holder for value and perhaps a
holder in due course. The pattern here is not that a true owner is
suing a collecting banker for conversion; it is that the collecting
banker has been asked by his customer to give value for the cheque
(in one of the above ways), has done so, and has subsequently found
that on presentation the cheque has been dishonoured. Sometimes
the best way for the banker to get his money back is for him to sue
the drawer of the cheque. If he does this he can be sure of success
only if he can show himself to be a holder in due course; if he is only
a holder for value his title depends on that of his customer, which
can be presumed, in cases where payment of the cheque has been
stopped, to be defective.

Holder

A holder is 'the payee or endorsee of a bill who is in possession of it,
or the bearer thereof' (BEA, section 2). A bearer, according to the
same section, means 'the person in possession of a bill or note which

is payable to bearer'. A bill is payable to bearer which is expressed to be so payable, or on which the only and/or last endorsement is an endorsement in blank (section 8(3)). An endorsement in blank specifies no endorsee, and a bill so endorsed becomes payable to bearer (section 34(1)).

Once a person has established himself as a holder he may go on to claim to be a holder for value or a holder in due course. There has in the past been much judicial confusion over these terms, but it is essential to distinguish between them, because a holder in due course has an indefeasible title, whereas a holder for value has such title, good or bad, as had the person from whom he took the bill (in the banker's case, the customer).

A holder in due course is defined in section 29 of the Act as follows:

> S29 A holder in due course is a holder who has taken a bill, complete and regular on the face of it, under the following conditions, namely:
> (a) that he became the holder of it before it was overdue, and without notice that it had been previously dishonoured, if such was the fact,
> (b) that he took the bill in good faith and for value, and that at the time the bill was negotiated to him he had no notice of any defect in the title of the person who negotiated it.

A holder for value is not specifically defined in the Act, but he is a holder of a bill for which he has given value or a holder of a bill for which value has been given at some stage in the history of the bill. (Section 27(2): 'where value has at any time been given for a bill the holder is deemed to be a holder for value as regards the acceptor and all parties to the bill who became parties prior to such time.')

Similar to the position where value has been given for the bill is that where the holder has a lien. This is therefore treated in another subsection of the same section 27(3): 'where the holder of a bill has a lien on it, arising either from contract or by implication of law, he is deemed to be a holder for value to the extent of the sum for which he has a lien'.

Having a lien on a cheque may come about where a banker lends against a post-dated cheque held for the time being on a short bills account of some kind, or perhaps more usually where a cheque originally received for collection has been returned unpaid and it is then found that the customer's balance is insufficient to meet the unpaid debit.

Also a banker has, by implication of law, a lien on all bills or cheques coming into his hands in the course of his business as a banker, to the extent of the sum owed to him by his customer.

Negotiability

Negotiability is that quality which enables the holder of a bill to claim a good title to it notwithstanding that a previous holder had a defective title. There can be no such indefeasible title where an endorsement has been forged or where the cheque has been crossed 'not negotiable'. This distinction between holder for value and holder in due course is important only where someone at some stage in the history of the cheque had a defective title to it; in the ordinary case where there is no fraud, theft, mistake or misunderstanding it will be just as good to be a holder for value as a holder in due course.

We can now turn once again to the collecting banker and consider his position since 1957. Suppose a drawer sends the cheque to the payee, and the payee pays it in to his banker in specific reduction of his overdraft. Meantime the drawer for some reason changes his mind about paying the cheque and instructs his bank to stop payment. What is the position of the collecting banker? Before 1957 he would have been a holder, being in possession of a cheque endorsed in blank, and might well be able to show himself a holder in due course with a good case against the drawer. Since 1957 he cannot be a holder, for he is not normally either the payee or endorsee, and he cannot be a bearer either because there is no endorsement on the cheque, the payee having paid it in for his account in the usual way.

It was to meet this difficulty that section 2 of the Cheques Act was drafted. By this section the banker is given the same rights as he would have had, had he been a holder, provided that:

(1) he either gave value for the cheque or had a lien on it
(2) he took the cheque from the holder (i.e. the bank's customer must be able to satisfy the definition of a holder)
(3) he took the cheque in order to collect the proceeds of it.

S2 A banker who gives value for, or has a lien on, a cheque payable to order which the holder delivers to him for collection without endorsing it, has such (if any) rights as he would have had if, upon delivery, the holder had endorsed it in blank.

The rights of the holder are summarized in BEA, section 38. The other parties to the bill can be the drawee, who if he accepts the bill becomes the acceptor, any endorser(s) there may be, and of course the drawer. All of these must sign the bill to assume any liability, but of course they have to sign it somewhere, in some capacity, in any case. Two sections of the BEA are relevant here.

S23 No person is liable as drawer, endorser, or acceptor of a bill who has not signed it as such: Provided that,

(1) where a person signs a bill in a trade or assumed name, he is liable thereon as if he had signed it in his own name;

(2) the signature of the name of a firm is equivalent to the signature by the persons so signing of the names of all persons liable as partners in that firm.

S26(1) Where a person signs a bill as drawer, endorser or acceptor, and adds words to his signature, indicating that he signs for or on behalf of a principal, or in a representative character, he is not personally liable thereon; but the mere addition to his signature of words describing him as an agent, or as filling a representative character, does not exempt him from personal liability.

(2) In determining whether a signature on a bill is that of the principal or that of the agent by whose hand it was written, the construction most favourable to the validity of the instrument shall be adopted.

The first subsection can be a little confusing at first reading, so perhaps a couple of examples will help to make it clear. In the first case, an example would be 'J. Jones, *per pro.* W. Walton' (where Jones is the agent of Walton). Jones is not personally liable. In the second case, an example would be 'J. Jones, Agent'. Here Jones is personally liable.

Liabilities of the parties

Now we can go on to the sections dealing in detail with the liabilities of the parties, which also by implication sketch out the rights of other parties. Only in the case of the holder are his rights and duties expressly set out (sections 38 and 39–44).

S54 The acceptor of a bill, by accepting it:

(1) engages that he will pay it according to the tenor of his acceptance;

(2) is precluded from denying to a holder in due course:

(a) the existence of the drawer, the genuineness of his signature, and his capacity and authority to draw the bill;

(b) in the case of a bill payable to drawer's order, the then capacity of the drawer to endorse, but not the genuineness or validity of his endorsement;

(c) in the case of a bill payable to the order of a third person, the existence of the payee and his then capacity to endorse, but not the genuineness or validity of his endorsement.

S55(1) The drawer of a bill by drawing it:

(a) engages that on due presentment it shall be accepted and paid according to its tenor, and that if it be dishonoured he will compensate the holder or any endorser who is compelled to pay it, provided that the requisite proceedings on dishonour be duly taken;

(b) is precluded from denying to a holder in due course the existence of the payee and his then capacity to endorse.

(2) The endorser of a bill by endorsing it;

(a) engages that on due presentment it shall be accepted and paid according to its tenor, and that if it be dishonoured he will compensate the holder or a subsequent endorser who is compelled to pay it, provided that the requisite proceedings on dishonour be duly taken;

(b) is precluded from denying to a holder in due course the genuineness and regularity in all respects of the drawer's signature and all previous endorsements;

(c) is precluded from denying to his immediate or subsequent endorsee that the bill was at the time of his endorsement a valid and subsisting bill, and that he had a good title thereto.

In these two sections the word 'tenor' is used. This means 'the exact purport or meaning' – in the first case, the tenor of the acceptance, and in the second, the tenor of the bill. 'Precluded' means 'estopped' or 'prevented'.

Now you may think that these sections have very little to do with cheques, and you would be right, because they were drafted a century ago to regulate the rights and duties of parties to a bill of exchange, before cheques were of any significance. Don't lose sight of the fact, though, that although cheques are now overwhelmingly important in the field of domestic banking, the bill of exchange is still very important in international trade; also many sections of the Act are still important in their application to cheques, viz. the definition of a holder in due course.

Acceptance and dishonour

In the definition section (section 2) 'acceptance' means an acceptance complete by delivery or notification. The sections dealing with acceptance are sections 17–19.

S17(1) The acceptance of the bill is the signification by the drawee of his assent to the order of the drawer.

(2) An acceptance is invalid unless it complies with the following conditions, namely:

(a) it must be written on the bill and be signed by the drawee. The mere signature of the drawee without additional words is sufficient;

(b) it must not express that the drawee will perform his promise by any other means than the payment of money.

S18 A bill may be accepted:

(1) before it has been signed by the drawer, or while otherwise incomplete;

(2) when it is overdue, or after it has been dishonoured by a previous refusal to accept, or by non-payment;

(3) when a bill payable after sight is dishonoured by non-acceptance, and the drawee subsequently accepts it, the holder, in the absence of any different agreement, is entitled to have the bill accepted as of the date of first presentment to the drawee for acceptance.

S19(1) An acceptance is either (a) general or (b) qualified.

(2) A general acceptance assents without qualifications to the order of the drawer. A qualified acceptance in express terms varies the effect of the bill as drawn. In particular, an acceptance is qualified which is:

(a) conditional, that is to say, which makes payment by the acceptor dependent on the fulfilment of a condition therein stated;

(b) partial, that is to say, an acceptance to pay part only of the amount for which the bill is drawn;

(c) local, that is to say, an acceptance to pay only at a particular specified place. An acceptance to pay at a particular place is a general acceptance, unless it expressly states that the bill is to be paid there only and not elsewhere;

(d) qualified as to time;

(e) the acceptance of some one or more of the drawees, but not of all.

Other rules concerning acceptance are contained in sections 39–44, which come in that section of the Act subtitled 'Duties of the holder'. It is convenient to take them here and you will find that they are all self-explanatory.

S39(1) Where a bill is payable after sight, presentment for acceptance is necessary in order to fix the maturity of the instrument.

(2) Where a bill expressly stipulates that it shall be presented for acceptance, or where a bill is drawn payable elsewhere than at the residence or place of business of the drawee it must be presented for acceptance before it can be presented for payment.

(3) In no other case is presentment for acceptance necessary in order to render liable any party to the bill.

(4) Where the holder of a bill, drawn payable elsewhere than at the place of business or residence of the drawee, has not time, with the exercise of reasonable diligence, to present the bill for acceptance before presenting it for payment on the day that it falls due, the delay caused by presenting the bill for acceptance before presenting it for payment is excused, and does not discharge the drawer and endorsers.

S40(1) Subject to the provisions of this Act, when a bill payable after sight is negotiated, the holder must either present it for acceptance or negotiate it within a reasonable time.

(2) If he does not do so, the drawer and all endorsers prior to that holder are discharged.

(3) In determining what is a reasonable time within the meaning of this section, regard shall be had to the nature of the bill, the usage of trade with respect to similar bills, and the facts of the particular case.

S41(1) A bill is duly presented for acceptance which is presented in accordance with the following rules:

(a) the presentment must be made by or on behalf of the holder to the drawee or to some person authorized to accept or refuse acceptance on his behalf at a reasonable hour on a business day and before the bill is overdue;

(b) where a bill is addressed to two or more drawees, who are not partners, presentment must be made to them all, unless one has authority to accept for all, then presentment may be made to him only;

(c) where the drawee is dead presentment may be made to his personal representative;

(d) where the drawee is bankrupt, presentment may be made to him or to his trustee;

(e) where authorized by agreement or usage, a presentment through the post office is sufficient.

(2) Presentment in accordance with these rules is excused and a bill may be treated as dishonoured by non-acceptance:

(a) where the drawee is dead or bankrupt, or is a fictitious person or a person not having capacity to contract by bill;

(b) where, after the exercise of reasonable diligence, such presentment cannot be effected;

(c) where although the presentment has been irregular, acceptance has been refused on some other ground.

(3) The fact that the holder has reason to believe that the bill on presentment will be dishonoured does not excuse presentment.

S42(1) When a bill is duly presented for acceptance and is not accepted within the customary time, the person presenting it must treat it as dishonoured by non-acceptance. If he does not, the holder shall lose his right of recourse against the drawer and endorsers.

S43(1) A bill is dishonoured by non-acceptance:

(a) when it is duly presented for acceptance, and such an acceptance as is prescribed by this Act is refused or cannot be obtained; or

(b) when presentment for acceptance is excused and the bill is not accepted.

(2) Subject to the provisions of this Act when a bill is dishonoured by non-acceptance, an immediate right of recourse against the drawer and endorsers accrues to the holder, and no presentment for payment is necessary.

S44(1) The holder of a bill may refuse to take a qualified acceptance, and if he does not obtain an unqualified acceptance may treat the bill as dishonoured by non-acceptance.

(2) Where a qualified acceptance is taken, and the drawer or an endorser has expressly or impliedly authorized the holder to take a qualified acceptance, or does not subsequently assent thereto, such drawer or endorser is discharged from his liability on the bill.

The provisions of this subsection do not apply to a partial acceptance, whereof due notice has been given. Where a foreign bill has been accepted as to part, it must be protested as to the balance.

(3) When the drawer or endorser of a bill receives notice of a qualified acceptance, and does not within a reasonable time express his dissent to the holder he shall be deemed to have assented thereto.

Presentation for payment

These rules lead on to the rules for presentation for payment. The sections of the Act dealing with presentation for payment are sections 45 and 46. As before, they are self-explanatory.

S45 Subject to the provisions of this Act a bill must be duly presented for payment. If it be not so presented the drawer and endorsers shall be discharged.

A bill is duly presented for payment which is presented in accordance with the following rules:

(1) Where the bill is not payable on demand, presentment must be made on the day it falls due.

(2) Where the bill is payable on demand, then, subject to the provisions of this Act, presentment must be made within a reasonable time after its issue in order to render the drawer liable, and within a reasonable time after its endorsement, in order to render the endorser liable.

In determining what is a reasonable time, regard shall be had to the nature of the bill, the usage of trade with regard to similar bills, and the facts of the particular case.

(3) Presentment must be made by the holder or by some person authorized to receive payment on his behalf at a reasonable hour on a business day, at the proper place as hereinafter defined, either to the person designated by the bill as payer, or to some person authorized to pay or refuse payment on his behalf if with the exercise of reasonable diligence such person can there be found.

(4) A bill is presented at the proper place:

(a) where a place of payment is specified in the bill and the bill is there presented;

(b) where no place of payment is specified, but the address of the drawee or acceptor is given in the bill, and the bill is there presented;

(c) where no place of payment is specified and no address is given, and the bill is presented at the drawee's or acceptor's place of business if known, and if not, at his ordinary residence if known;

(d) in any other case if presented to the drawee or acceptor wherever he can be found, or if presented at his last known place of business or residence.

(5) Where a bill is presented at the proper place, and after the exercise of reasonable diligence no person authorized to pay or refuse payment can be found there, no further presentment to the drawee or acceptor is required.

(6) Where a bill is drawn upon, or accepted by two or more persons who are not partners, and no place of payment is specified, presentment must be made to them all.

(7) Where the drawee or acceptor of a bill is dead, and no place of payment is specified, presentment must be made to a personal representative, if such there be, and with the exercise of reasonable diligence he can be found.

(8) Where authorized by agreement or usage a presentment through the post office is sufficient.

S46(1) Delay in making presentment for payment is excused when the delay is caused by circumstances beyond the control of the holder, and not imputable to his default, misconduct, or negligence. When the cause of delay ceases to operate presentment must be made with reasonable diligence.

(2) Presentment for payment is dispensed with,

(a) where after the exercise of reasonable diligence presentment, as required by this Act, cannot be effected. The fact that the holder has reason to believe that the bill will, on presentment, be dishonoured, does not dispense with the necessity for presentment;

(b) where the drawee is a fictitious person;

(c) as regards the drawer where the drawee or acceptor is not bound, as between himself and the drawer, to accept or pay the bill, and the drawer has no reason to believe that the bill would be paid if presented;

(d) as regards an endorser, where the bill was accepted or made for the accommodation of that endorser, and he has no reason to expect that the bill would be paid if presented;

(e) by waiver or presentment, express or implied.

(An accommodation bill is a bill to which a person adds his name to oblige or accommodate another person, without receiving any consideration for so doing, i.e. as a surety or guarantor.)

Negligence of the paying banker

We have seen how the collecting banker can be charged with negligence for anything from failing to check the references on a new account, to failing to see that his customer's accepted bill of exchange is presented to the acceptor for payment on the due date (see section 45(1)). The paying banker also has a wide range of opportunities for risking a charge of negligence, some of which have already been mentioned. It may be useful, however, to make a summary here.

He, too, may find a failure to check references when an account is opened, an expensive omission later on. We have seen how his protection under sections 60 and 80 of the BEA depends upon his paying, in the first case, an open or crossed cheque 'in the ordinary course of business' (i.e. without negligence) and, in the second case, a crossed cheque only to the banker to whom it is crossed. We have noted that he would have no protection at all if he paid a bill of exchange, other than a cheque, to a person having no right to it (i.e. the bill has a forged endorsement).

In addition, there is a string of case decisions laying the liability on a paying banker who failed to scrutinize his customer's account properly, i.e. where a cheque which he has carelessly paid is for a purpose quite outside the company customer's Memorandum and Articles. Also, he is likely to be charged with negligence (and certainly with breach of contract) where he has dishonoured his customer's cheque in circumstances where he ought to have paid it.

The BEA does not mention the dishonour of a cheque, but it does have some rules (in sections 47–51) about the dishonour of a bill. In these sections, which follow, only section 47 is given in its entirety.

S47(1) A bill is dishonoured by non-payment (a) when it is duly presented for payment and payment is refused or cannot be obtained, or (b) when presentment is excused and the bill is overdue and unpaid.

(2) Subject to the provisions of this Act, when a bill is dishonoured by non-payment, an immediate right of recourse against the drawer and endorsers accrues to the holder.

S48 Subject to the provisions of this Act, when a bill has been dishonoured by non-acceptance or by non-payment, notice of dishonour must be given to the drawer and each endorser, and any drawer or endorser to whom such notice is not given is discharged; . . .

S49 Notice of dishonour in order to be valid and effectual must be given in accordance with the following rules:

(1) The notice must be given by or on behalf of the holder, or by or on behalf of an endorser who, at the time of giving it, is himself liable on the bill. . . .

(6) The return of a dishonoured bill to the drawer or endorser is . . . . deemed a sufficient notice of dishonour. . . .

S50(1) Delay in giving notice of dishonour is excused where the delay is caused by circumstances beyond the control of the party giving notice, and not imputable to his default, misconduct, or negligence. When the cause of delay ceases to operate the notice must be given with reasonable diligence.

(2) Notice of dishonour is dispensed with:

(a) when, after the exercise of reasonable diligence, notice as required by this Act cannot be given to or does not reach the drawer or endorser sought to be charged;

(b) by waiver express or implied. Notice of dishonour may be waived before the time of giving notice has arrived, or after the omission to give due notice; . . .

S51(1) Where an inland bill has been dishonoured it may, if the holder thinks fit, be noted for non-acceptance or non-payment, as the case may be; but it shall not be necessary to note or protest any such bill in order to preserve the recourse against the drawer or endorser.

(2) Where a foreign bill, appearing on the face of it to be such, has been dishonoured by non-acceptance it must be duly protested for non-acceptance, and where such a bill, which has not been previously dishonoured by non-acceptance, is dishonoured by non-payment it must be duly protested for non-payment. If it be not so protested the drawer and endorsers are discharged. Where a bill does not appear on the face of it to be a foreign bill, protest thereof in case of dishonour is unnecessary. . . .

When a bill has been dishonoured for any reason the holder may wish to sue the acceptor for the sum, and here the terms 'noting' and 'protest' mentioned in section 51 are relevant. When the holder wishes to 'note' a bill, he takes it to a Notary Public who himself presents the bill again and 'notes' the bill for non-acceptance or non-payment. The point about the noting is that it leaves matters open for extending the noting into a protest later, if desired. By section 51(4) (not quoted) this has to be done either on the day of dishonour, or the next succeeding business day.

A 'protest' is a similar proceeding, in that again a Notary Public will represent the bill and on dishonour will draw up a formal Certificate of Protest, testifying as to the facts, and signing it. This Certificate will be accepted in a court of law as proof of dishonour, which will save the plaintiff the trouble of proving that the bill was dishonoured, which he would otherwise have to do.

Now it is understandable why section 51 says, in subsection (1), that an inland bill *may* be noted, whereas in the case of a foreign bill, where an action might have to be brought in a foreign court, protest for non-acceptance is enforced on pain of the drawer and endorsers being discharged from their liability if the protest is not made.

It is not usual to apply these procedures to cheques, where the dishonour is evidenced by the paying banker (in this case refusing to pay) sending the cheque back to the collecting banker by direct post, marked with an 'answer' stating the reason for the refusal to pay. This may be something which can be put right, as where inadvertently the drawer has made out the cheque correctly, but has forgotten to sign it, and no one has noticed the omission until the cheque reaches the paying banker. Or it may be an answer indicative of a lack of funds to cover the cheque, the usual one being 'refer to drawer'.

When the collecting banker gets it, he will send it to his customer (in accordance with BEA, section 49(6), probably with a standard letter). It will then be up to the customer as to what he does to try to get his money.

However, should the customer wish to sue the drawer of the cheque he may do so knowing that the crossing on the cheque by the collecting banker is evidence of presentation, while the answer put on the cheque as the reason for non-payment is evidence of dishonour. The Committee of London and Scottish Clearing Bankers insist that any cheque presented through the clearing system must bear the crossing stamp of the collecting banker, and that any cheque dishonoured must have the reason stated on it.

Revocation of authority

This refers to the occasions on which the paying banker is excused from his duty to honour his customer's cheques. There are quite a number of these, including the mental incapacity of the customer, his bankruptcy, or the service of a garnishee order. These topics will not be dealt with here as they are outside the scope of this book, but we will now look at the more elementary considerations.

The bank would not honour a cheque where it had definite knowledge of a defect in the title of the presenter, which would deprive the bank of its statutory protection under section 60 and/or section 80 of the BEA. Nor would it pay where it had notice that the transaction in question was contrary to law, and again, this is not the place to examine this further. For now, the prime concern is section 75 which is as follows:

S75 The duty and authority of a banker to pay a cheque drawn on him by his customer are determined by:
(1) countermand of payment
(2) notice of customer's death.

Countermand of payment is a notice by the customer to the bank that he wishes payment stopped on a cheque which he has drawn and issued. The customer should ideally state the number, date and amount of the cheque and give the name of the payee. The details may be telephoned in the first instance, but should be confirmed in writing without delay. The banker's first action on receipt of the notice to stop should be to consult the customer's printout or ledger, the day's vouchers and the customer's paid vouchers to ensure that the cheque has not already been paid. Next, the cashiers must be given the details so that the cheque is not paid if it should be presented over the counter. Finally, the computer must be programmed to reject the cheque should it be presented for payment.

After the cheque has been presented and returned unpaid, that is usually the end of the matter unless the customer subsequently removes the stop notice. The bank records should not be allowed to show the stop detail indefinitely, as after six months from the date of the cheque it would be 'stale' and in this case returned.

It is notice of the customer's death and not the death itself which operates to determine the duty to repay. Notice may come from a newspaper or from a letter from a relative. Should the bank pay a cheque after receiving notification of death, the personal representative may challenge that payment has been made without authority. The cheque should either be returned with the answer 'drawer deceased', or, if the authority of the personal representative is obtained, it could be paid. The cheque may be in settlement of an account that is still to be settled; if it is returned the creditor will have to get in touch with the personal representative, who will in due course issue another cheque. This will mean delay and extra work, both of which the bank would normally like to avoid.

Material alteration

The Bills of Exchange Act deals with this in section 64, as follows:

> S64(1) Where a bill or acceptance is materially altered without the assent of all parties liable on the bill, the bill is avoided except as against a party who has himself made, authorized, or assented to the alteration, and subsequent endorsers.
> Provided that,
> Where a bill has been materially altered, but the alteration is not apparent, and the bill is in the hands of a holder in due course, such holder may avail himself of the bill as if it has not been altered, and may enforce payment of it according to its original tenor.
> (2) In particular the following alterations are material, namely, any alteration of the date, the sum payable, the time of payment, the place of payment, and, where a bill has been accepted generally, the addition of a place of payment without the acceptor's assent.

This section is a little vague, in that it does not attempt to specify when an alteration is apparent. But we may perhaps conclude that where the alteration has been carefully done, and would pass a cursory examination, it may be said to be not apparent.

Forgery

Forgery in most people's minds refers to the forging of another's signature. In fact the definition is rather wider than that: forgery is the act of counterfeiting a coin or document, or falsifying a document whether in a material particular or in the copying of another's signature, or illegally using another person's signature.

The BEA confines itself to the question of the forgery of another's signature, and deals with the matter in section 24:

> S24 Subject to the provisions of this Act, where a signature on a bill is forged or placed thereon without the authority of the person whose signature it purports to be, the forged or unauthorized signature is wholly inoperative, and no right to retain the bill or to give a discharge therefor or to enforce payment thereof against any party thereto can be acquired through or under that signature, unless the party against whom it is sought to retain or enforce payment of the bill is precluded from setting up the forgery for want of authority. Provided that nothing in this section shall affect the ratification of an unauthorized signature not amounting to a forgery.

There are two distinctions to be made here. The first is between an unauthorized signature (which can be later ratified) and a forgery (which cannot). The second is between the forgery of the drawer's signature (which renders the cheque or bill completely invalid) and the forgery of an endorser's signature (which has no effect on the validity of the bill, but will affect the rights of the endorsers – if more than one – between themselves).

The effect of a forged endorsement is to halt the legal title to the bill at that point. But if the next holder of a bill himself negotiates it again to a second endorser he is liable on it to his immediate transferee (section 55, BEA).

Revision test 8

Put a tick against the letter you consider is the correct answer.
1 Here is a specimen endorsement: 'Pay Sam Small or order (signed) P. Pitt'. Is this
    (a) an endorsement in blank?
    (b) a restrictive endorsement?
    (c) a special endorsement?
2 A restrictive endorsement destroys the
    (a) negotiability
    (b) transferability
    (c) acceptability of the bill.

3 The Act of Parliament which deals with negotiable instruments is called
   (a) the Act of Negotiability, 1822
   (b) the Bankers Protection Act, 1882
   (c) the Bills of Exchange Act, 1882.

4 When a cheque is paid into a bank account by the payee,
   (a) the payee must endorse it
   (b) he need not endorse it
   (c) it depends if the payee is a company or not.

5 When a banker is requested to collect a cheque to pay off an overdraft or loan,
   (a) he is collecting for the customer
   (b) he is collecting for himself
   (c) the law will decide.

6 A cheque payable to XYZ plc is credited to the personal account of E. F. Gee. The bank
   (a) is correct in crediting the account
   (b) is merely doing what is requested by its customer
   (c) has committed an act of negligence.

7 Negotiability has the quality that will allow
   (a) a person to have a good title to an instrument notwithstanding that the previous holder had a defective title
   (b) a person to transfer an instrument only if he has a good title
   (c) it can only be transferred as authorized by the drawee or drawee banker.

8 A cheque form payable to 'Wages'
   (a) is a cheque as defined by the BEA
   (b) is not a cheque as defined by the BEA
   (c) the bank on whom it is drawn will make that decision.

9 The BEA specifies that an acceptor, by accepting the bill,
   (a) engages that he will pay on the due date
   (b) will only pay to a bank
   (c) will only pay if the goods purchased are in order.

10 In order to retain the liabilities of the other parties, a bill that has been dishonoured must be
   (a) protested
   (b) given to the acceptor
   (c) retained in the files.

Questions for discussion

1 What is the purpose of an endorsement on a bill of exchange? When is it likely that a cheque will be endorsed?
2 Describe the protection given to a collecting banker of cheques presented to him by customers for presentation to other bankers for ultimate payment.
3 Describe negligence with reference to negotiable instruments.

9

Bills of exchange, cheques and promissory notes

The bill of exchange was invented to overcome the movement of gold bars or gold coins from one country in settlement of international debts. It was as long ago as the twelfth century that the bill of exchange was first used in Italy, and the first recorded mention of its use in this country was in 1379.

The basis of the system which the merchants worked out was to 'marry up' as far as possible two separate transactions, that is, the payment to be received for goods going out of a country, with the payment to be made for goods coming into the country. Suppose A in London exported some cotton to B in Paris, and about the same time C in Paris exported some wine to D in London. The cotton was worth £5,000 – B has to pay that to A – and the wine was worth £4,000 – D has to pay that to C. In each case the contract between the two sets of merchants stipulated that payment was to be made three months after the dispatch of the goods.

In due course A would draw a bill on B, and would send it (nowadays with the document of transportation and the insurance policy covering the consignment of cotton) to his agent in Paris. That gentleman would then present the bill to B, and B would accept it by signing his name vertically across the bill. The agent would then hand B the documents.

A's bill of exchange might have looked something like the illustration on p. 181. The date mentioned is the date of the bill, so that payment is due to be made to A on 4 April. C's bill drawn in Paris on D in London would be similarly expressed.

Each bill is accepted by the debtor and returned to the creditor. We now have an accepted bill (now called an acceptance) for £5,000 in the possession of A in London and an acceptance for £4,000 in the possession of C in Paris. (We have supposed for simplicity's sake that C drew up his bill in sterling – more likely, of course, it would be in French francs, £4,000 being the sterling equivalent.)

68, Tooley Street, London.
4 January 1858

£5,000

Three months after date pay to me or to my order the sum of Five Thousand Pounds, value received.

(signed) Alan Andrews

To Bernard Berthold,
14, Place de la Concorde,
Paris.

Now if B in Paris could somehow be put in touch with C in Paris, B could buy from C the bill for £4,000, accepted by D in London, and payable in London. If then B can find another, similar bill for £1,000, and buy this also, he can then pay his debt when the three months are up, simply by sending the accepted bills to A. Once the bills are in A's hand he will have no trouble getting the money, because in each case the bill is payable in sterling in London. If the bills were originally drawn in francs, they would be converted at the time of payment into sterling at the current rate of exchange. B and C have dealt with each other, in francs, in Paris, and A and D similarly, in London, in pounds sterling. No gold or silver has had to be sent either from Paris to London or from London to Paris, but the shipments of cotton to Paris and wine to London have been satisfactorily financed.

Of course, the banks now actually do the work of exchange, which has simplified considerably since the date mentioned on the bill. Today B would not have to worry about finding a French exporter to help him pay his debt for British cotton. He would simply ask his bank to arrange for the bill he had accepted to be met on the due date (the date of payment at the end of the three months) in London. His bank would contact a bank in London and between them they would see that the acceptance was paid in sterling to A (or to A's bank for the credit to his account) in London, the equivalent in francs being debited to B's account with his bank in Paris. Both banks would charge a commission for their services.

The parties to the bill

The bill may be between two parties only, as in the example we have seen, or it may name three parties where the drawer uses the bill to pay off a debt he himself owes to a third party. That is, B owes A money as before, but this time A, when drawing the bill, directs B to pay the money, not to him or his order, but to P or to his order.

68, Tooley Street, London.
7 January 1984.

£5,000

Three months after date pay to Peter Pitt or his order the sum of Five Thousand Pounds, value received.

(signed) Alan Andrews

To Bernard Berthold,
17, Place de la Concorde,
Paris.

As before, the bill once drawn is sent to B, who accepts it and then returns it to A. A sends the accepted bill to P in settlement of his debt to him. When the bill is due P sends it to his agent in Paris who presents it to B for payment. Or P gives it to his bank in London and it is sent by them to another bank in Paris, which presents it for payment. The proceeds are passed back to P.

In this example we have supposed that A and B are the merchants who have agreed to supply goods and to pay for them respectively. A is the seller, B the buyer. A is the creditor, B the debtor. B could have paid in a number of ways. He could have sent gold or silver, or he could have sent a cheque. Instead, the parties to the contract have agreed that payment will be by way of a bill payable at three months. The bill is dated 4 January, and is payable on 4 April. The goods are sent when the bill is drawn, so let's say they arrive in Paris after two weeks and the bill and documents of title are presented to B on

18 January. After he has accepted the bill he then claims the goods from the ship which has taken them from England to France. He then has two months and two weeks in which to resell the cotton. Perhaps he makes the cotton up into shirts and sells them to stores in France. Whatever he does, he hopes to dispose profitably of all the cotton, and have the money for all of his sales in, before he has to meet the bill which he has accepted. This is what the three months are for. It is a period of credit.

A is the drawer of the bill. He is also the seller, and until he is paid, the creditor.

B is the drawee of the bill, the person on whom the bill is drawn. He is the buyer, and until he pays, the debtor. When he accepts the bill he is called the acceptor, and the bill is called an acceptance.

P is the payee of the bill. He is the person who will eventually get the money unless he passes the title on to someone else, i.e. negotiates the bill. He can do this if he wants to, because a bill of exchange is a fully negotiable instrument.

P will pass on the proceeds of this bill by endorsing it, that is by writing his name on the back of the bill. If he simply does that, the bill will become payable to anyone who is in possession of it (the bearer). P is the endorser and he is said to have endorsed it in blank. Then he can send the bill to R. But there is a risk here. If the bill goes astray between P and R anyone can get the money. It would be better for P to endorse the bill specially.

A special endorsement specifies the person to whom, or to whose order, a bill or cheque is to be payable. The special endorsement here would read:

Pay Richard Rowley or order (signed) Peter Pitt.

Then the bill will be payable only to R or to whomever else R chooses to endorse it. Suppose he keeps it and tells his bank to collect the money for it. Before he gives it to his bank he will have to endorse it himself, as a receipt for the money which will be credited to his account. Just his signature will do, under the special endorsement made by P.

Then we shall have P called the first endorser, and R the second endorser. The chain of title to the money will have passed like this:

A ⟶ P ⟶ R
(drawer)   (1st endorser)   (2nd endorser)

If for any reason P did not want R to pass the bill on to anyone else, he could write on the back:

Pay Richard Rowley only (signed) Peter Pitt.

This is called a restrictive endorsement. It destroys the transferability of the bill. A could similarly have drawn the bill restrictively, by substituting for the words 'or his order' on the face of the bill, the word 'only'.

The various parties to the bill, drawer, acceptor and endorser, all have their duties and responsibilities defined in the Bills of Exchange Act as you have read in the previous chapter.

In the above example we looked at a bill that was payable three months 'after date', so that in effect B did not actually get three months' credit, but only two months and two weeks. Since the journey was short, he was able to get the goods in a reasonable time and he still had sufficient time to resell the goods and obtain funds, before presentation of the bill for payment.

But suppose the goods had had to travel not from London to Paris, but half-way round the world, to a place quite some distance from London, say Hong Kong. No one could say exactly how long the journey could take. Therefore to ask a debtor to pay a bill 'x' days from date may seriously reduce the amount of time he has available to pay the bill on presentation, especially if the vessel is delayed on its journey by reason of bad weather, congestion at ports, strikes, etc.

True, an increase in the term of credit, to say six months, could be acceptable to both parties, but a better and more precise way out of the difficulty would be to substitute the words 'after date' for 'after sight'. Then the three months will run not from the date of the bill, but from the date when the importer (drawee, acceptor) first sees the bill.

In this case the drawee will have to add to his signature the date when he sighted the bill, so that the term of the bill may be calculated and the due date ascertained. His acceptance would then look like this:

(signed) Stephen Soames
6 June 1984

So, if this were a case where three months' credit had been agreed, and the bill was dated 31 March 1984, the due date would be 6 September and not 30 June.

A bill of this nature is described as one payable after sight. The word 'after' is important because a bill payable at sight (a sight bill) is one payable immediately, as soon as the drawee sees it.

A term bill, or a bill payable after sight, has to be presented twice, once for acceptance, and once for payment. The bill can be dishonoured at either of these stages; if the bill is dishonoured by non-acceptance there is no point in presenting it for payment. Of course the bill is the visible evidence of the agreement entered into by the parties. A contract (unless under seal) must be accompanied and supported by consideration. (Consideration has been defined as 'some right, interest, profit or benefit, accruing to one party, or some forbearance, detriment, loss or responsibility given, suffered or undertaken by the other'.) That is the point of the words 'value received' which the drawer includes in his form of words. Then when the acceptor signs he is agreeing that he has had the goods and that is proof that the contract was supported by consideration. These words do not have to be included in the wording of the bill, but it is quite usual to see them.

The acceptance is the signification by the drawee of his assent to the order of the drawer. It confirms the original contract. It implies that he is willing to pay the bill in settlement of the contract between buyer and seller.

The acceptor may accept indicating that when the bill is presented for payment it should go to his bank. In this case he would write across the bill 'Accepted payable at the London & Provincial Bank, 12 Throgmorton Street, London', followed by his signature.

Such an acceptance is said to be domiciled at a bank.

Of course any fraudulent person could pick a name and address out of the telephone directory, draw a bill on that person, and send it to him. Such a bill would be neither accepted nor paid. There is no transaction to which the bill refers. There is no consideration for the bill.

Bills which are to go abroad may possibly get lost and so a bill may be written out in a set of two or three and sent by different posts. Such a bill might be worded:

> Thirty days after sight pay this First of Exchange (Second and Third of the same date and tenor being unpaid) to Thomas Trotter or order the sum of Two Thousand Pounds.

This 'first part' will be matched by a second and third part similarly worded. The second part will impose the condition that the first and third parts should be unpaid, and so on.

The debt is only to be paid once, of course, and the drawee must be careful to accept only one of the three parts. If the first part is delayed or lost he may get the second part first, and then he accepts that. Once one part is accepted, the other two are valueless.

All bills drawn abroad and paybable in this country, and all bills drawn in this country and payable abroad, are foreign bills. Bills both drawn and payable in this country are inland bills.

Bills as instruments of credit stand or fall by the reputation of the acceptor and the drawer. The acceptor has promised to pay, by his acceptance; and the drawer, by drawing the bill, has guaranteed that the acceptor will be willing and able to pay on the date, and if he does not, he – the drawer – will.

Very often, therefore, an importer in London would get his bank to accept bills on his behalf. The bank's name would be very much better known than the merchant's, therefore the bill would command more confidence and subsequent negotiation would be more easily effected.

Term bills can be negotiated either before or after they are accepted. Those who take them for value before acceptance by the drawee are relying on the name and reputation of the drawer. Those who take them after acceptance have two names on which to rely.

As banks continued to accept bills on behalf of their customers, there grew up in London firms and merchant banks which specialized in accepting bills on behalf of their merchant customers. These were accepting houses, you will remember. A bill bearing the name of a member of the accepting houses was looked upon all over the world as absolutely good. Such a bill gave rise to the phrase 'the Bill on London', than which there was nothing more reliable. So trade all over the world was financed by undertakings of London bankers. Goods traded between two foreign countries and never going anywhere near London were financed from there. Bills bearing the name of a London accepting house fulfilled the function of an international medium of exchange.

Now let us look at a bill payable on demand (see illustration on p. 187). Here, there is no element of credit in terms of time. The bill is to be paid as soon as it is presented. The bill may perhaps start 'Pay bearer on demand . . .' The words 'at sight' may be used instead of 'on demand'.

As there is no term there is no need for an acceptance, so this bill is presented once only, for payment. It is presented at the usual place

---

4, Tarrant Street, London.
1 January 1984.

£500.60

Pay to my order on demand the sum of Five Hundred Pounds and Sixty Pence, value received.

(signed) Robert Cully

To Charles Freeman,
4, Argyll Street, Durham.

---

of business of the drawee, in this case 4, Argyll Street, Durham. The drawer would not himself make a special trip from London to Durham to get the money, but would give the bill to his London bank, which would send it to their Durham branch (or to another bank in Durham if it did not itself have a branch in Durham) to be presented locally.

The bill of exchange is defined in the Bills of Exchange Act as 'An unconditional order in writing, addressed by one person to another, signed by the person giving it, requiring the person to whom it is addressed to pay on demand, or at a fixed or determinable future time, a sum certain in money to or to the order of a specified person, or to bearer'.

This definition needs some clarification, as to the uninformed reader it can seem quite complicated for a document as simple as a bill of exchange. Remember that the Bills of Exchange Act was an act of codification, so that there are reasons based on custom and case law that brought all these factors together. Going through the definition bit by bit, we can see the points that are being made.

An unconditional order. This means that there must not be any conditions that need to be fulfilled before payment. For example, 'When Concorde lands at London Airport, pay . . . or order. . . .' This would be a conditional payment and not within the definition of a bill of exchange. However, it is quite acceptable that payment should be made on condition that a receipt on the bill or cheque is duly signed and dated. This is in order.

In writing. The Act does not specify the surface that a bill should be written on. Valid bills/cheques have been written on ties, handkerchiefs, hard boiled eggs, champagne bottles, etc. It can be written in ink, typed or printed on indeed any substance of a permanent nature.

Addressed by one person to another. It must be addressed by one person, corporate or not, to another person, corporate or not. A note addressed by one person to himself is not a bill of exchange.

Requiring the person to whom it is addressed. The named person is the drawee and the drawer of the bill guarantees that the drawee will pay, otherwise the drawer is liable.

Pay on demand, or at a fixed or determinable future time. As you have seen, bills are payable at sight (on demand) or at a fixed future time (x days after date) or a determinable future time (x days after sight). All are within the requirements of a bill of exchange.

A sum certain in money. In these days money in this context will mean any acceptable international currency.

To or to the order of a specified person, or to bearer. A bill that is payable to order must have a payee stipulated. It could be 'myself' or 'my order', etc. But a name must be given.

Cheques

A cheque is a special form of bill of exchange, namely one payable on demand and drawn on a banker. It differs from the bill of exchange proper. It does not require acceptance, the drawer is the person whose account will be debited when the bank pays the cheque (although he always has the right to stop payment), and it is always drawn on a banker, never on a person or company.

Cheques first came into use in about 1680. An order cheque (see example on p. 189) was one payable to a named person or his order; a bearer cheque was payable to the bearer, who, as we have seen, was the person in possession of it.

The period of bank expansion was at its height in the middle of the nineteenth century when most cheques were bearer cheques. This was due to the fact that at that time bearer cheques were subject to a stamp duty of 1d per cheque, while order cheques were subject to *ad valorem* stamp duty just like bills. They were charged according to the value of the cheque. The greater the amount the order cheque was made out for, the greater the stamp duty.

Bearer cheques, although cheap, were subject to the drawback that if they were stolen they could be cashed by the thief. So when in 1853 the Stamp Act provided for the issue of a 'draft or order for the payment of any sum of money to the bearer *or to order* subject to stamp duty of one penny' there was a great increase in the use of order cheques.

Stamp duty, later increased to twopence, was abolished altogether in 1971.

Now the order cheque can be said to be one of the main methods of settling debts. The amounts represented annually by the cheques passing through the clearing houses are greatly in excess of the total of all banknotes and coin in circulation. But like the bill of exchange, a cheque is not money. It is a claim to money. When a payee receives a cheque from the drawer, he is no better off in terms of cash until he has paid the cheque in to his bank, and his bank has obtained the money from the drawer's bank and credited the payee's account with it. Sometimes, of course, a cheque can be passed from hand to hand for value (in exchange for cash or for goods), and in that case it does act as a medium of exchange. But although cheques are negotiable instruments, only a small percentage are in fact negotiated (passed from hand to hand for value). The great bulk of them are paid straight into their bank accounts by the payees. The negotiated cheque does not fulfil the function of money long enough to affect the monetary situation in any way.

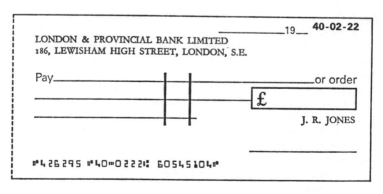

If we look at this form of cheque we shall see that it is an instruction from a customer to the bank, instructing it to pay some of his money away. The drawer's name appears in the bottom right-hand corner. It is printed by the bank before the cheque book is issued to the customer. Its purpose is to assist in the sorting of cheques into alphabetical order. Below the printed name is the space for the drawer's signature. The bank is the drawee, and whatever the name the drawer writes in after the word 'Pay' will be the payee.

In the top right-hand corner is the space for the date, followed by the national number, often called the sorting code number, of the particular branch bank. This number is repeated at the bottom of the cheque in magnetic ink characters which the computer can recognize. To the left of this number is to be found the cheque number and on its right is the number of the customer's account. As soon as the cheque is paid back into the banking system the collecting bank will add a further set of magnetic characters, indicating the amount of the cheque in the amount field situated next to the account number. By use of the account number it is possible to reduce the confusion caused by the existence of customers with similar or the same names and initials.

The two vertical lines constitute a crossing, which will be explained shortly. Cheques can be obtained with or without pre-printed crossings.

It is for the customer to tell the bank what sort of cheque book he wants. If he is likely to send most of his cheques through the post he will ask for a crossed order book. If he is likely to be cashing most of his cheques at the bank, across the counter, he will ask for an open order book.

If the customer has an open book and he wants a crossed cheque, the customer or indeed any holder can add a crossing to the cheque. If he has a crossed book and he wants an open cheque he can write between the vertical lines of the crossing 'Pay cash' and authenticate the alteration with his signature. (Such cheques would only be paid by the bank to the drawer or his known agent, and never, without proper enquiry, to a stranger.) The banks do not encourage any alteration to the line of magnetic ink characters, nor do they encourage customers to use the cheque book for debiting another account. If a customer wishes to debit a particular account at a particular bank branch, he should use the appropriate cheque book.

A cheque has the same definition as a bill of exchange, except that a cheque is a bill of exchange drawn on a banker, payable on demand. In the case of Burnett v. Westminster Bank Ltd, Burnett took a cheque addressed to A branch and altered the address to B branch. Having issued the cheque, he decided to countermand payment. He advised B branch to stop payment. Unfortunately, due to computer sorting, the cheque arrived at A branch, which paid it. Burnett sued the bank for wrongful debit and won his case.

Crossings

Provision for crossings on cheques is made in the Bills of Exchange Act, section 76, which defines a crossing as two parallel transverse lines across the face of the cheque.

Crossings may be general or special.

A general crossing is a crossing with or without the words 'and Company' and with or without the words 'not negotiable'.

A special crossing consists of the name of a bank with or without the addition of two parallel transverse lines and with or without the addition of the words 'not negotiable'.

The words 'and Company' or '& Co.', have no legal significance these days. It was originally put in the crossing to assist either the payee or his collecting banker to cross the cheque specially, e.g. 'Coutts & Co'. Nowadays, all cheques are crossed by the collecting banker either by machine or at the counter by the cashier. There is no need for any crossing to have these words inserted.

The words 'not negotiable' turn the cheque into a non-negotiable instrument, and we shall see presently what negotiability is. The words are not used on a bill of exchange other than a cheque, for a bill of exchange is the supreme example of a negotiable instrument. Where a person takes a crossed cheque which bears on it the words 'not negotiable' he shall not have, and shall not be capable of giving, a better title to the cheque than that which the person from whom he took it had. (A person has a good title to a bill or cheque when he has received it honestly and is entitled to the money which it represents. If he has received it by mistake, or gained it by fraud, he is said to have a defect in his title.)

The effect of crossing a cheque is to oblige the paying banker, when the cheque reaches him, to pay the proceeds only to another banker. If the crossing is a general one, he may pay to any banker; if a special one, only to the banker named on the cheque. (A bill of exchange other than a cheque cannot be crossed.)

So if a cheque is stolen, and the thief forges the endorsement and tries to cash it across a bank counter, he will not be able to do so if the cheque is crossed, for every banker knows that he cashes a crossed cheque over the counter at his own risk.

Now to illustrate the action of a crossed order cheque.

D the drawer owes P the payee £100 and decides to post him a cheque for that sum. P banks at the Northern Bank, Carlisle, and D banks at the Southern Bank, Brighton. D makes out the cheque and posts it. P pays it into his banking account in Carlisle and the Carlisle branch send it to their London office, in with all the other cheques to be cleared, the same evening. The Northern bank, London, transfers it through the clearing house to the London office of the Southern Bank, which sends it to their Brighton office, and they check the signature and other details and then debit it to D's account. We could show this as follows:

D———→P———→Northern Bank, Carlisle———→Northern Bank, London———→Southern Bank, London———→Southern Bank, Brighton

This whole process, from the time of paying in funds at Carlisle to final payment at Brighton, takes three working days. The first day the cheque is processed at the collecting bank's branch; it is received in London and transferred to the paying bank's London office through the clearing system on the second day; while on the third day it is received by the paying banker for ultimate payment and debit to the drawer's account.

The check of the details at the Brighton bank is an essential part of the operation, for the cheque is D's instruction and authority to his bank to pay away some of his money deposited there. If, for example, the signature of D is forged the bank has no authority to pay. If it does, it may have to refund D's account when he finds out about it. It follows that all the staff in the banks must be able to identify correctly the signatures of all their customers. If they are in doubt, they must compare any particular signature with the specimen signature which each customer has to give to the bank at the time when he first opens the account.

If the order cheque is not crossed, and if D and P live in the same town, P may choose to go into D's bank and present the cheque himself across the counter for payment in cash. Then the cheque will not go through the clearing house. In this case P will have to endorse the cheque before presenting it across the counter, partly as a receipt for the money, and partly to identify himself. The cashier at D's bank will not know P's signature, only that of D, but he will check that the endorsement appears to be correct. The idea of this is that if the presenter is not in fact P, but a thief who has stolen the cheque from P, or someone who has found it in the street because P has lost his wallet, then he may be disconcerted at suddenly having to forge P's endorsement, and will perhaps leave the bank without the money because he is afraid of being caught.

Payment of cheques

In every branch bank one of the most important functions of the bank is to honour customers' mandates. The prime mandate given to a bank is the cheque, which is usually presented through the clearing system, or over the counter, or by special presentation, for ultimate payment and debit to the customer's account. The most popular method is presentation through the clearing system, and on every working day one or more people in the office are responsible for ensuring that payment is made. Where there is a technical or other reason, then payment must be refused.

The following are the points that must be considered before payment is made.

(1) The cheque is drawn on your bank and branch.
Remember the case of Burnett v. National Westminster Bank. It is not enough to assume that the cheque is drawn on your office. Quite possibly, some cheques are not drawn on the form you give to customers.

(2) The cheque has the correct date.
A cheque which is postdated is by definition not a cheque, i.e. it is not payable on demand, so that a bank dare not pay it, because it is possible that before the due date the customer may stop the cheque. Alternatively, it is possible for you to pay the cheque, and a day or two later a further cheque is presented and returned unpaid for lack of funds due to payment of the post-dated one. In both cases, the bank has a problem.

Additionally, a cheque which is over six months old, is considered 'stale' and payment is refused. However, over the period of a New Year, cheques bearing the date of the previous year are usually paid if it can be identified that the cheque number is in the current run.

(3) The words and figures agree.
It is essential that the words and figures agree, otherwise the

cheque must be returned. In some instances where there is a difference in the pence, then the lower amount is accepted.

(4) The signatures comply with the authority.
The signature must conform to the one held by the bank; where there is a joint account, then the mandate on the number of persons to sign, or who is to sign, must be observed. The same would apply to a corporate customer's cheque. If in doubt reference should be made to the signing instructions held.

(5) Crossed by two bankers.
Under the BEA, a cheque must not be paid if it bears the crossing of two bankers, that is, two clearing banks. It is quite acceptable where one bank is the clearing agent of another. This situation is quite likely to happen if a cheque is returned to one bank on a technicality then re-presented through another bank. Both are clearing banks. For payment to be made, the collecting banker may endorse the cheque with an indemnity against loss to the paying banker, by virtue of paying the cheque bearing two clearing bank crossings.

(6) Mutilation.
A cheque must be complete and regular. Unless a mutilation has been confirmed by the collecting banker, it should be returned.

(7) Alteration.
This has already been discussed. Any alteration on the cheque must bear the signature(s) of the drawer(s).

(8) Payee.
A cheque must be payable to a specified person or bearer. Most cheques these days are to the order of someone. A cheque without a payee must be returned to the collecting banker.

(9) Countermand of payment.
A customer has the right to stop payment of the cheque before it has been presented for payment. Should the bank receive such notification, it will pay at its peril.

(10) Sufficient funds.
It is usual for customers to either have funds on the account or make arrangements to have an overdraft. But having stated that, it seems the practice, especially before pay day, for customers to

overdraw and for the bank to allow this situation. Where there is an implied agreement, the bank will continue to meet such cheques, but should the situation get out of hand the bank must put any borrowing on a regular basis.

(11) Legal bar.

A legal bar is when the courts impose a stop on the account. This happens when a person either dies, goes bankrupt, or is mentally incapable of controlling his own financial affairs or if a company goes into liquidation. In each case a representative is appointed to look after such affairs. Until an appointment has been made, no cheques must be paid. Occasionally the court will make an order to freeze the funds of an account holder. This is done by issuing either an order of garnishee on the bank or an order of sequestration. In both these instances, payment of cheques must be refused.

All this may seem a long arduous task, but really with practice it takes little or no time at all. Very often a practised eye detects all the technical defects on a cheque very quickly, while the computer will reject stopped cheques and accounts which have legal bars.

Negotiability

Negotiability is that quality which enables the holder of a bill or note to maintain a good title to it even though a previous holder had a bad one. The characteristics of a negotiable instrument are as follows.

(a) Mere delivery of the instrument by one person to another passes the full legal title. In some cases endorsement is necessary before delivery.

(b) No notice of the transfer need be given to the person liable on the instrument.

(c) The title to the instrument passes free from all counter-claims between parties and from defects in the titles of previous parties. The transferee (the person who has received the bill or note) must give value for the instrument and must act in good faith and without any knowledge of any doubt affecting the title of the transferor.

(d) The transferee may sue in his own name if this becomes necessary.

As to (a) we should note that while a bearer cheque passes by simple delivery, an order cheque passes by endorsement and delivery.

With a bearer cheque the legal right to the proceeds of the cheque passes from the drawer to whoever presents it for payment.

With an order cheque the legal right to the proceeds of the cheque passes from the drawer to the payee. If the payee wishes to pass it on to another person he must endorse the cheque to pass the title on. The endorsement may be in blank, in which case it becomes a bearer cheque, or special, in which case the title passes to whoever it was specially endorsed to.

As to (b) there is no need, when a cheque is endorsed over, for either the endorser or the endorsee to inform the drawer. This may seem obvious, but such a characteristic is not true of non-negotiable instruments; for example, when an assurance policy is assigned, say as security to a banker, notice of the assignment must be given to the assurance company.

As to (d) an action at law may become necessary if the cheque or bill is dishonoured when presented for payment. If that happens the holder can sue as a person in his own right; he does not have to claim through the person who transferred the cheque to him.

Instruments which are fully negotiable are banknotes (and other promissory notes), bills of exchange (including cheques – unless crossed 'not negotiable'), bearer bonds, bearer scrip, debentures payable to bearer, share warrants to bearer, treasury bills and certificates of deposits.

Promissory notes

Many of us will perhaps be familiar with the gambler who writes an IOU for his debts. This piece of paper contains an acknowledgement of debt and implies that one day – some time – repayment will be made. It is on this point of the date of repayment that it differs from a promissory note.

A promissory note is an unconditional promise in writing made by one person to another, signed by the maker, engaging to pay, on demand or at a fixed or determinable future time, a sum certain in money to, or to the order of, a specified person, or to bearer.

This definition has many of the words and phrases to be found in the definition of the bill of exchange. Both definitions come from the same Act, the Bills of Exchange Act, 1882. But this is a 'promise', not an 'order'. It is 'made' to another, not 'addressed'.

The writer of a promissory note is a 'maker'. The note is incomplete until it has been delivered to the payee or bearer.

Example of a promissory note payable on demand

> £500
>
>   Liverpool, 30 June 1984.
>
> I promise to pay bearer on demand the sum of
>
> Five Hundred Pounds
>
>   (signed) George Jessel

Example of a promissory note drawn for a term

> £400
>
>   Liverpool, 30 June 1984.
>
> Three months after date I promise to pay William Smith or order the sum of Four Hundred Pounds.
>
>   (signed) George Jessel

Promissory notes issued by private persons are hardly ever seen in banks nowadays, except in the finance of international trade. But this is made up for in the banknotes which banks continually handle. The banknote is the most celebrated promissory note of all. It starts 'I promise to pay'. It is payable on demand, and signed by the Chief Cashier of the Bank of England. Banknotes, like other promissory notes, cheques, and bills of exchange other than cheques, are all governed by the Bills of Exchange Act, 1882.

Promissory notes other than banknotes are not money, although they perform very similar functions. They are like cheques and bills of exchange, sometimes called 'near money'. The bill of exchange finances international trade, the cheque finances nearly all domestic transfers. These two instruments supply nearly all the power to keep the wheels of commerce turning.

Rights of banker, customer and holder

Although chapter 9 has dealt with the different aspects of negotiable instruments, it is worthwhile at this stage to look once again at the rights of the parties when dealing with bills and cheques.

Paying banker

When a banker pays a cheque in good faith and in the ordinary course of business he obtains protection from BEA, section 60, whether he has paid a crossed or an open cheque.

BEA, section 80, refers to crossed cheques only. Here the banker is given protection if he pays in good faith and without negligence to another banker.

Collecting banker

It is the Cheques Act, section 4, that gives the collecting banker all his protection. Providing he has collected a cheque for a customer and has acted in good faith and without negligence the banker has the protection of law.

The customer

The customer can be either the drawer, the payee or a third party who has become the transferee.

The drawer has the right to expect that his cheque, drawn on the banker, will be paid providing there are sufficient funds and that the cheque is complete and regular on the face of it. Under section 80 the drawer has the same rights as the paying banker.

The holder

We have in the previous chapter discussed at some length holders, holders for value and holders in due course, but it is worth reminding oneself of the rights of a holder of a cheque. He can sue on the bill in his own name. If he is a holder in due course, he holds the bill free from any defect which there may be in the title of any prior party to the bill, and he can enforce payment against all parties liable on the bill.

But where he has some defect in his title, he cannot, of course, be a holder in due course. However, if he negotiates the bill to a person who can satisfy the requirements of a holder in due course, he passes on to him a good and complete title to the bill. If he does get payment for the bill, the person who pays him in due course gets a good discharge for the bill.

A holder in due course is one who has taken the bill complete and regular on the face of it under the following conditions:

(1) that he became the holder of it before it was overdue, and

(2) not knowing that it had been previously dishonoured, if such was the fact;

(3) that he took the bill in good faith and for value, and

(4) that, when the bill was negotiated to him, nothing led him to suppose that there was any defect in the title of the person who negotiated it.

Revision test 9

Place a tick against the letter you consider is the correct answer.

1   A bill of exchange begins 'Three months after date. . . .' Is it
    (a) a demand bill?
    (b) a sight bill?
    (c) a term bill?

2   A demand bill
    (a) is one domiciled at a bank
    (b) does not require presentation for acceptance
    (c) is payable immediately after acceptance.

3   The drawee of a cheque is
    (a) the person who gets the value
    (b) a banker
    (c) the person whose account is debited.

4   A special crossing consists of
    (a) the name of the bank
    (b) two parallel transverse lines
    (c) the words 'not negotiable'.

5   The words '& Co.' written in a crossing indicate
    (a) the paying banker must be under enquiry
    (b) the collecting banker is under enquiry
    (c) it has no legal significance.

6   The title to a bearer cheque passes by
    (a) endorsement
    (b) endorsement and delivery
    (c) mere delivery.

7   Which of these is a negotiable instrument
   - (a) a share certificate?
   - (b) a treasury bill?
   - (c) a postal order?

8   A stale cheque is
   - (a) one which bears a date six months ago
   - (b) one which is blank but has an old 2d revenue stamp on it
   - (c) one which has been negotiated a number of times.

9   A 'non-negotiable' crossing on a cheque indicates that
   - (a) it is not transferable
   - (b) it is transferable, but only a good title can be passed on
   - (c) it must be placed to the account of the payee.

10   A cheque may be drawn
   - (a) any day of the week
   - (b) on a working day only
   - (c) only during banking hours.

Questions for discussion

1   List the differences and similarities between a bill of exchange and a cheque.

2   Describe the history of a cheque from the time it is sent by the drawer to the payee until its final payment.

3   In what circumstances might payment of a debt be made by way of a bill of exchange rather than a cheque?

10

The clearing systems

Because of the competition between banks, many branches are now open on Saturday mornings – a few banks are even open on a Sunday – and many have extended opening hours in the week. This competition between banks to attract new customers and retain the loyalty of current ones is fierce. But in one important area, the clearing of cheques and other financial paper, the banks work closely together in order to give the community a most efficient service.

The banks as agents of their customers are duty bound to receive cheques drawn on other banks and branches for the credit of the customer's accounts and then receive reimbursement.

History of the clearing system

The clearing system began some two hundred years ago, when clerks of the various banks in London used to take the cheques paid in by their customers, sort them into bank order, then walk round to each bank presenting these cheques for payment and taking back to their own bank sums of money given in settlement. Like any other commercial activity, the business of banking increased, not only with the number of cheques in circulation but also the number of banks that opened in the City of London and the West End. The clerks, who knew each other, thus decided to short-circuit the system and unofficially agreed to meet at some convenient place – as history tells us, a coffee house – to exchange the cheques drawn on their own banks; any differences in the amounts due could then quickly and easily be settled, often in cash (some banks were not trusted). The employers, who eventually learnt of the system, realized that there were advantages not only to their employees but to themselves as well. Of course, it saved hours of labour, walking the streets of London. In addition, under the new system it was no longer necessary for the banks – which in those days had only one office, perhaps two – to keep large sums of money to meet the presentation of cheques. The surplus cash could be invested to increase profits.

The banks, anxious to improve the system, hired a room for the purpose of exchanging cheques. The system expanded and in 1833, in 10 Lombard Street, the first clearing house was established.

This system continued, but until 1854 the membership of the clearing house was restricted to the private banks only. At that date the joint-stock banks were allowed to have a seat on the Committee of London Clearing Banks. These clearing banks expanded their sphere of operations, so that all towns and cities in the UK had a representative of at least three or four clearing banks. The major cities, of course, had quite a number of branches of all clearing banks.

Until the middle of this century there were the following members of the Clearing House.

Bank of England	Martins Bank
Barclays Bank	Midland Bank
Coutts & Co.	National Bank
District Bank	National Provincial Bank
Glyn, Mills and Co.	Westminster Bank
Lloyds Bank	Williams Deacon's Bank

Added to these were the various banks that were part of the 'walks' system. They consisted of the Scottish and Irish banks, the few foreign banks, merchant banks, and so on. The cheques for each bank were in fact taken by messenger to each bank, who then gave the messenger a banker's payment, in settlement of the total of the cheques presented. The walks system no longer exists as it was a costly and labour-intensive operation. The clearing banks offered the walks banks agency arrangements, giving them a sorting code number from within their own ranges. Thus the cheques are now cleared through the general clearing.

Credits that were paid into a branch for a customer of another branch, or for the credit of a branch of another bank, were actually sent by post. You can imagine the situation. At the end of the day, a clerk sat down and wrote out claim forms for each and every credit, placed them together, wrote out an envelope, then sent them individually to the banks or branches concerned. At times the volume of work was quite substantial, particularly at the end of the month, on quarter days, and so on. There were no automated ways of dealing with these items, nor was there then a credit-clearing system.

The present organization

It was on 1 December 1985 that the organizations responsible for the clearing services in England, Scotland, and Wales were reorganized to oversee all the various forms of clearing.

The former major organizations, the Committee of London Clearing Banks and the Scottish Bankers' Association, were dissolved and the Committee of London and Scottish Bankers (CLSB) was formed as a constituent of the British Bankers' Association. The CLSB concerns itself in dealing with a wide range of issues on behalf of its members, including regulatory, legislative, and fiscal matters.

At the same time as the establishment of the CLSB, the Association of Payment Clearing Services (APACS) became operational and is the body responsible for the clearing systems, which are legally three independent limited companies. They are:

Cheques and Credit Clearing Co. Ltd
CHAPS and Town Clearing Co. Ltd
Bankers Automated Clearing Services Ltd (BACS).

With EFT-POS – Electronic Funds Transfer, Point of Sale – now operational under the marketing names of the various banks, it is quite likely that within a short time a fourth clearing company will be set up.

With the mergers and amalgamations of various banks in the 1960s, a majority of names have disappeared from the original list of clearing banks, while other banks and two building societies have joined one or two clearing companies.

Cheque and Credit Clearing Co. Ltd

The members of this clearing company are as follows:

Bank of England	Barclays Bank
Bank of Scotland	Lloyds Bank

Co-operative Bank	Girobank
Midland Bank	Royal Bank of Scotland
National Westminster Bank	Abbey National
TSB	

The procedure for clearing cheques

When a cheque is presented for the credit of a customer's account, that customer is credited immediately with the amount of the cheque, even though payment has not been received and is considered as 'uncleared effects'. On the day it is received (day 1) the collecting bank will ensure that the amount of the credit equals the amount of the cheques/cash paid in, then it will add the amount in magnetic-ink characters to the code line and then will proceed to sort the credits from the cheques. The cheques may be sorted in bank order, although it is now common practice not to sort cheques, merely to list them as received, bundle the whole lot together, and despatch the cheques received that day to the clearing department.

On day 2, the clearing department will receive bundles of cheques from every branch of the service and with the aid of computers sort the cheques into bank order or, if in bank order already, then present the total received to the appropriate bank, who will present the cheques they have received from their branches to other banks, so that an exchange of all cheques takes place between the banks in the clearing house.

By the third day, the cheques have all been presented to the drawee bank for final payment; then the customers are debited. Should the branch wish to refuse payment for any reason, then it may do so, reversing the entries on the account, despatching the cheque on the same day by first-class mail to the collecting banker with the reason for non-payment, then claiming on that bank for the amount of the unpaid cheque. The whole process should take three working days and the unpaid cheque should be received by the collecting banker on the morning of the next working day. The settlement of the outstanding debt between the banks takes place on this day.

The credit clearing

This clearing system is part of the Cheque and Credit Clearing Co. Ltd, but you may know that in earlier years credits paid in at either another branch or bank were sent on to the named bank and branch by post.

With the expansion in the use of computers and the growth in banking business, it became necessary for this area of operations to be streamlined and an efficient clearing process set up. In 1960 the credit transfer system was introduced. At first the process was rather slow, but as time went on, so the number of items processed through the credit clearing system grew. People began to realize that there was no need to send cheques to a variety of creditors, postal orders for small amounts were unnecessary, and the creditor's account could be credited without any fuss.

At first, all credits that were sent to the clearing house were sorted by hand, but as the Magnetic Ink Character Recognition system (MICR) improved, so all credits contained the magnetic ink characters and are now sorted by computer. The system now known as the Bank Giro system is operated in exactly the same way as the cheque clearing system, except that, instead of debiting a customer, they are credited. It still takes three working days for any credit to go from one bank to another.

Truncation

At this point it is worth mentioning a system which is perhaps in its infancy. Truncation is a means of passing entries to the debit or credit of an account either in another branch or another bank without the movement of paper. It should be emphasized that the system is still relatively new, but the whole point is to assist the reduction in the movement of paper throughout the banking system. As you can see in Tables 10.1 and 10.2, the amount of cheques and credits passed daily through the clearing system is enormous.

An example will help to explain a truncation system. If I wished to draw money from another branch of the bank where my account is being held, then, providing I have either my cheque card, an encashment facility, or other arrangements have been made, then the agent branch will cash my cheque. This cheque, however, will not be sent to the drawee branch, but will be retained in the branch where the encashment was made. The details of my cheque and the amount will be transferred over the branch terminals to the debit of my account. My cheque will not be returned to me with my statement; indeed, it is now the practice not to give cheques to cus-

Table 10.1 Clearing statistics: volume (thousands of items)

| Year | Paper Items | | | | | | Automated Items | | | | | Currency Clearings | |
| | Cheque clearing | | Town clearing | | Credit clearing | | | BACS | | | CHAPS | US dollar | Other currencies |
	Inter bank	Inter branch	Inter bank	Inter branch	Inter bank	Inter branch	Direct debits	Standing orders inter bank	Other credits	Standing orders inter bank			
1978	1,212,161	460,046	4,457	846	180,105	184,838	130,652	137,463	69,884	40,974	–	–	–
1979	1,310,985	462,885	5,098	937	195,940	195,094	152,257	153,238	81,579	43,285	–	–	–
1980	1,453,702	493,625	4,969	945	213,869	208,104	173,417	168,807	96,166	46,829	–	–	–
1981	1,500,888	523,553	4,794	913	202,151	212,253	192,825	181,293	114,749	48,138	–	–	–
1982	1,559,997	545,874	4,848	907	180,823	233,529	220,412	189,598	138,731	48,013	–	–	–
1983	1,672,404	552,193	5,072	929	177,935	249,769	253,983	191,754	167,022	68,884	–	–	–
1984	1,772,439	554,431	4,620	868	167,432	252,561	295,498	218,215	209,562	74,146	1,149	–	–
1985	1,861,649	587,793	4,473	814	164,790	251,358	346,378	235,949	252,203	74,938	2,217	–	–
1986	1,962,143	607,888	4,328	703	174,103	254,742	412,259	243,432	288,504	76,398	3,161	539	–
1987	2,060,707	622,191	3,977	658	183,596	264,597	485,864	249,273	336,095	76,352	4,386	520	175

Source: APACS

Table 10.2 Clearing statistics: value (£ millions)[a]

| Year | Paper Items | | | | | Automated Items | | | | Currency Clearings[b] | |
| | Cheque clearing | Town clearing | | Credit clearing | | Direct debits | BACS | | CHAPS | US dollar | Other currencies |
	Inter bank	Inter bank	Inter branch	Inter bank	Inter branch		Standing orders inter bank	Other credits			
1978	301,647	2,544,254	521,119	36,887	135,204	15,673	6,437	32,925	–	–	–
1979	356,483	3,258,830	585,640	43,497	163,843	19,489	8,762	40,440	–	–	–
1980	405,690	4,051,203	782,172	51,853	193,400	25,916	11,565	53,815	–	–	–
1981	431,620	4,403,794	965,382	61,480	210,532	28,257	13,809	62,274	–	–	–
1982	479,424	5,291,926	1,172,284	62,563	239,395	39,122	17,866	73,420	–	–	–
1983	543,267	6,257,551	1,337,195	67,978	264,030	49,184	18,305	87,004	–	–	–
1984	622,420	6,922,135	1,433,138	69,478	293,257	59,040	24,614	106,063	741,273	–	–
1985	680,207	7,463,677	1,730,196	72,616	331,461	87,017	37,767	128,267	2,355,565	–	–
1986	766,195	8,173,039	2,110,647	80,426	353,505	105,529	45,776	150,073	4,143,877	25,040	–
1987	859,790	8,324,927	2,287,239	91,980	402,910	126,835	52,671	176,838	7,331,906	35,246	810

Source: APACS

(a) No value figures are available for inter-branch cheque clearing or inter-branch standing orders.
(b) The value of Currency Clearings are shown as sterling equivalents.

tomers when despatching statements, except when instructions are given to the contrary. The same applies to credits which can under certain circumstances be truncated, and unpaid claims on other branches have the same treatment. The truncation procedure does not apply to all banks, so you should examine your own banking system to see whether this is in operation. See Jack Committee recommendations Appendix VI.

CHAPS and town clearing

The town clearing system

This is a clearing system that operates in the City of London only and for those banks that are part of the town clearing. These banks will be identified by the fact that the branches within the City of London will have the letter 'T' beside their national code number which can usually be seen on the top right-hand corner of a cheque. The banks are as follows:

Bank of England	Bank of Scotland
Barclays Bank	Citibank
Clydesdale Bank	Coutts & Co.
Co-operative Bank	Midland Bank
Girobank	National Westminster Bank
Lloyds Bank	Standard Chartered Bank
Royal Bank of Scotland	TSB

The purpose of both these clearing systems is to ensure that the large payments between the financial institutions and markets in the City of London are cleared the same day. Large payments are those over £100,000.

In principle, the town clearing system works in the following way. Each working day the cheques that are paid in at the various city branches are sorted and those for the town clearing are sorted specially into the bundles for each of the other clearing banks. When the city branches close at 3 p.m., all the town-clearing cheques are given priority and sorted, listed, and bundled and taken by a messenger to the clearing house, resorted and despatched within minutes to the drawee bank. The cheques, banker's payments, banker's drafts, bills of exchange, and so on, are then paid (or if not paid, returned to the clearing house) by 4.45 p.m.; then messengers return them to the collecting bank.

The CHAPS system

The purpose of the CHAPS system (Clearing House Automated Payments System) is to enable funds to be transmitted quickly and efficiently from one bank to another within the City of London. The system is additional to the town clearing system, but it should be emphasized that, London being a major international financial centre, there must be a means of rapid transmission if London is to retain this position. The system did have a few 'labour pains' before it was finally put into operation in the early 1980s.

The banks in the CHAPS system are the same as those in the town clearing system, but for this purpose are known as settlement banks. These banks have the computer facilities to make and receive the necessary payments. For example, if a company has to make a large payment – say, £200,000 – to another company, and that payment must be made by a certain day, then assuming funds are available, the remitter will request his bank to remit the funds by means of a CHAPS payment. It is assumed that (i) the beneficiary is an account holder of the receiving bank and (ii) the receiving bank is a member of CHAPS. The procedure is as follows:

(1) The bank will process the payment instruction internally.
(2) It will compile a CHAPS payment with authentication.
(3) This will be processed through the remitting banks' 'Gateway' which will send the message via the British Telecom Switching Service. This message will be acknowledged and logged for audit and settlement purposes.
(4) The receiving bank will receive the message, acknowledge, and log the details for settlement and audit.
(5) The message will be checked, the authentication will be confirmed, details of the account, amount, and so on retained and placed on the beneficiary's account by the receiving bank's computer.
(6) The customer will then be advised that his account has been credited and the following details given; the amount, remitter, value, date, references.

Settlement

With the vast volume of payments and amounts being passed through the Gateways of the various banks it is necessary for each bank to keep a record of payments to and payments from a particular bank. To assist the reconciliation, each Gateway has a complete audit trail which can be used if any discrepancies arise, and so any difference can be isolated and rectified. Second, the details of each payment are recorded in the Gateway and, as each payment is executed, a running total can be checked as validation of receipt of payment.

On agreement of each day's business and the agreement between a pair of banks, the bank that owes the outstanding balance will send a CHAPS message to the Bank of England to transfer the amount owed to the bank to whom the balance is due.

Although it has been said that CHAPS is used for payments to and from settlement banks in the City of London, the CHAPS system is nationwide and can be used for:

(1) Urgent payments received from abroad.

(2) Telephonic requests from branches outside the town area to make urgent payments to branches of other banks outside the town area. The recipient bank will on receipt of funds advise the beneficiary branch by the quickest possible means.

(3) Non-settlement banks wishing to pay same-day value to funds of another bank.

(4) Large corporate customers who wish to pay funds to another.

Bankers Automated Clearing Services Ltd (BACS)

This company has the following member banks

Abbey National	Girobank
Bank of England	Lloyds Bank
Bank of Scotland	Midland Bank
Barclays Bank	National Westminster Bank
Clydesdale Bank	Royal Bank of Scotland
Co-operative Bank	TSB
Coutts & Co.	Yorkshire Bank
Halifax Building Society	

It is quite likely that any other financial institution having the criteria necessary would have their application seriously considered.

BACS performs the same function as any clearing department, except that it does not read the MICR numbers at the bottom of a cheque, but reads instructions from a magnetic tape. The importance of BACS is that transmission of funds is carried out without paper and that it can transmit either debits or credits; a branch of any member company can, through its computer system, notify BACS of its standing-order payments in advance so that on the due date the debiting of the bank/customer is made and the crediting of the various creditors is done at the same time.

Very many employees of large companies, government departments, and so on are paid their salaries in this way. The organization will transmit to BACS its authenticated authority to credit its employees with a variety of amounts at a variety of banks and branches. BACS has authority to debit the remitter's account for the total of the payments made. By this method the employees are assured that funds are available on their account on the due date, and the paperwork involved in this operation is almost eliminated. By the same token, companies involved in the direct-debit system can pass one credit to their bank account, and any number of debits to the accounts of their various customers. In this way they are assured of good money on a due date and the administration is reduced. Settlement is made through the Bank of England in the usual way.

Electronic Funds Transfer at Point of Sale (EFT-POS)

EFT-POS is a method whereby a person buying goods in a retail environment is able to hand his 'plastic card' to the cashier in order to pay for the goods obtained. The cashier passes (wipes) the card through the EFT-POS terminal which captures the electronic information contained within the magnetic strips, and this, together with the amount, is then used to debit the consumer's account and credit the retailer's account.

This method of debt settlement was considered by banks in the 1970s, because of the expansion of consumer banking and the need to reduce the paper-clearing systems.

With improvement in technology, and the introduction of BACS and CHAPS, the Committee of London and Scottish Clearing Banks (CLSB) reaffirmed their commitment to develop the EFT-POS system.

At this moment, the system is still in its infancy, but is likely to expand in the not too distant future. The major banks have pilot schemes in existence and have introduced one plastic card for en-cashment of cheques up to £50 and for cash withdrawals at ATMs plus the use of the card for the payment of goods at retail outlets able to use the EFT-POS terminals.

The likely benefits to all parties are:

The retailer

1 The next-day crediting to his account which will improve cash flow, increase interest payable on his/her account, or reduce interest charges
2 Speedier checkout system, with simplified procedures
3 Guaranteed funds not limited to £50
4 Less paper handling
5 Less cash handling, therefore greater security
6 Internal benefits – speedier management information, reduction of staff costs, fewer bank charges.

The customer

1 Convenience in method of payment
2 Speedier service – no writing out of cheques, no £50 limitation, no waiting for authorization for payment by credit card
3 Less risk of loss of cash or cheque book.

Banks

1 Reduction in paper volume and therefore clearing costs
2 Reduction of fraud. A lost card, once it is reported, can immediately be blocked electronically.

While no EFT-POS clearing system is operational at the moment, it is quite likely that, with the speed that this service is being made available, there will be a system operational in the near future.

Special presentations

The special presentation of a cheque for obtaining a speedier settlement of the outstanding debt is both a service to the customer and a means of clearing a cheque. Further details of this as a service to a customer can be found on pages 231–2; it is sufficient to say that, should either the bank or customer wish to obtain cleared funds quickly, then the use of the special presentation is most useful.

Settlement is made by the drawee bank's sending a credit to the collecting bank.

Revision test 10

Place a tick against the letter you consider is the right answer.

1 The origins of the clearing house were in
   (a) a woollen shop
   (b) a coffee shop
   (c) a grocery store.

2 Banks with limited liability were allowed a seat in the clearing house in
   (a) 1854
   (b) 1845
   (c) 1833.

3 The 'walks' system is
   (a) The presentation of cheques to all banks in the City of London
   (b) The presentation of cheques to non-clearing banks in the City of London
   (c) The presentation of cheques to clearing banks only in the City of London.

4 The letters CLSB means
   (a) Council for London and Scottish Bankers
   (b) Compendium from the London and Scottish Bankers
   (c) Committee of London and Scottish Bankers.

5 The time taken for the payment of a cheque presented through the town clearing system is
   (a) one day
   (b) two days
   (c) three days.

6 The town clearing system consists of:
   (a) All banks and branches in the City of London
   (b) Only the branches of the 'Big Five' in the City of London
   (c) All banks and branches which have the letter 'T' against their sorting code number.

7 A 'settlement' bank is one which is
   (a) a member of the CHAPS clearing system
   (b) a bank which has an account at the Bank of England
   (c) a bank whose payments can be received with confidence in settlement of debts.

8 The time taken for payment of a cheque presented through the cheque clearing system will be
   (a) two days
   (b) three days
   (c) four days.

9 The letters BACS means
   (a) British Automated Clearing System
   (b) Bankers Automated Clearing Systems
   (c) Bankers Automated Clearing Services.

10 Truncation is the process of
   (a) passing accountancy entries to another bank/branch via a computer terminal, leaving the paper debit/credit at the office of the remitting bank/branch
   (b) passing accounting entries to another bank/branch, via a computer, then sending a written confirmation to the receiving bank/branch
   (c) passing accounting entries to another bank/branch only with prior authority.

Questions for discussion

1 As the loans officer in your branch, you receive a large cheque payable to a customer who requests you to obtain payment as quickly as possible, using the amount to pay off the outstanding loan. Describe the procedure you would adopt and why.

2 Describe the procedure in your branch when a cheque drawn on another bank is presented over the counter accompanied by a credit in favour of a customer of your branch.

3 A solicitor authorizes you to debit his 'Clients A/c' on a stated day and remit £100,000 value the same day to a solicitor maintaining an account at another bank in another town. Describe the method of payment used in this transaction.

11

Banking services

Banking covers so many services that it is difficult for any one person to comprehend all those available. Yet the modern view is that the cashier on the bank counter – in regular contact with the customers of the bank and the general public – is expected, when taking in credits and/or paying out cheques, to talk to the customer and during conversation find out what opportunities there may be to suggest other appropriate banking services. This of course could make the job of a cashier intolerable, as the tasks entail a heavy load, dealing with the paying out and receiving of funds from customers, and responding to various questions, as well as being aware of the build up of a queue of people waiting to be served. It is almost impossible for a cashier to converse with any customer for more than a moment, so the banks market their services by posters, book-lets, sponsorship, advertisements in newspapers and on TV, etc.

However, the basic services that have always been recognized as the hallmark of the genuine banker are: (i) the receipt of customer's deposits; (ii) the collection of his cheques drawn on other banks; (iii) the payment of the customer's cheques drawn on himself. From this historic foundation has been built a wide variety of services.

Looking at the basic services offered to a customer who has just opened an account, it can be seen that a bank account is not only attractive but need not cost the customer anything for its maintenance.

On opening an account a customer will be given a cheque book containing twenty-five cheques. If the customer is a company, then it may have a larger or different type of cheque book. Paying-in books are available and statements are sent to the customer as and when required, but at least twice a year. It has been established that on average a customer, corporate or not, receives a statement at least every month. These services are free.

Under the Consumer Credit Act, 1974, each party to a joint account must receive a copy of the statement unless a form of dispensation has been signed, allowing the bank to send the statement to one party only. Even though most banks as a matter of good customer relations send a statement at least every six months or so, it is now compulsory under the above Act.

These basic services, plus the collection of cheques for credit to the account, are, for the private customer, made without any charge being effected, providing that he/she is in credit.

Many services offered by banks are available to non-customers and customers alike. Thus banks may charge a commission for such services as sales and purchases of traveller's cheques and foreign currency, use of credit cards, etc. Those services which are available to non-customers should be obvious as you progress through this chapter. These services, with interest being paid on current account, and the availability of the various services described below, make the banking industry very attractive to the 'person in the street'.

Cheque cards

These are plastic cards measuring 85 × 55 mm and are issued to customers by banks. Each card has on it the code number of the branch, a card number, an expiry date, and a strip of special paper on which the card holder must sign his or her name before using it. On the back of the card are the bank's conditions for use, namely that the bank guarantees the payment of one cheque only, not exceeding £50 in any single transaction, if the cheque is signed in the presence of the payee, and the signature on the cheque corresponds with the signature on the card. The cheque has to be one of the bank's own cheque forms, bearing the code number shown on the card, and dated before the expiry date of the card. The cheque must have the card number written on the back by the payee.

If the cheque card is misused by an unscrupulous customer an overdraft will quickly mount up at the bank, and this is also likely to happen if the card and the cheque book are found or stolen by a thief. In such a case the question arises as to who is going to stand the loss, and what the respective rights are of the bank, the customer and the payee.

In the case of an unscrupulous customer, the bank must pay unless it knows that one or more of its conditions have been broken, and the total loss can be 30 × £50 if the cheque book is a new one (£1,500). The payee in each case has a right to expect the bank to honour its guarantee, which it will, and thus the bank is left with a right of recourse only against its customer. This would normally be a civil action for the return of money had and received, and where the sum makes it worth the trouble and legal expenses, this is probably the course which the bank will follow.

In the case where the card is stolen together with the cheque book and is used by a thief, the essential point is that from the first use of the card by the thief there is going to be a forged signature on the cheques. The customer will no doubt inform the bank of the loss, and of the number of the last cheque used in conjunction with the card. All subsequent cheque numbers with the card number on the back will be the subject of intense scrutiny at the paying bank, and will normally be returned unpaid with the answer 'forged signature'. The loss then will fall on the retailer, whose only right will be to bring an action against the thief, if he can find him. The police will be notified and if the thief is caught he will be prosecuted under the Theft Act, 1968. A new card, with a new number, and a new cheque book will be sent by the bank to continue the service to the customer.

If the customer fails to notify the bank of the loss, or is dilatory, some – or even all – of the forgeries may get on to the customer's account. This should not happen in a perfect world, but it does. When the customer finds out he/she may demand the return of the money, represented by payments of the forged cheques, on his/her account. The matter then will perhaps be settled by discussion and compromise, but if it comes before a court, should the amount be large enough to warrant this, the bank will have to admit that they have debited the customer's account without authority. For the bank it may be argued that the reason they have not made a refund is because they feel that the customer is guilty of contributory negligence, by the delay in informing the bank of the loss of the card and cheque book. The court may or may not accept this, but if it does the loss will be apportioned between the bank and the customer as the court decides.

Lastly, we have the case where the cheque card is lost or stolen by itself, and here we might suppose that without the cheque book the cheque card is of little use to a thief, because the retailer on each purchase will check the code number on the card with the code number on the cheque. This is actually the code number indicating the bank and branch, so if the thief could get hold of any cheque book from that particular office he could surmount this difficulty.

Unfortunately, fraud is so rampant with these cards that banks are regularly considering various ways in which security can be improved.

Having looked at the illicit side of cheque cards, it should be remembered that they are most useful to people who wish to purchase goods from shops, settle hotel bills, etc., without the need to carry cash around. Should customers require cash, then the card will allow them to withdraw funds from all major British and Irish banks up to a maximum of £50 in any one day, although customers of Barclays Bank may withdraw at Barclays branches up to £100 per day.

The three-in-one card

For want of a better name, the writer has given the above title to a card that performs three functions: cheque card, cash dispenser card, EFTPOS card. Each bank will have its own marketing name for this type of card and it would be wrong to describe this service using the name given by any particular bank, but with the introduction of EFTPOS it is possible to introduce into the magnetic strip all the necessary details that are on the cash guarantee card and cheque card, so that the customer need keep only one card instead of three. This service, introduced only a short time ago, will take some time to percolate through the system so that it may be a year, or longer, before the cheque guarantee card and cash dispenser card are withdrawn from circulation and only the above card is available to all customers of a bank.

Cash dispensers

A bank opening an account for a customer undertakes to repay on demand. Certain legal limitations have been placed on the repayment. It must be sought at the branch where the account is, and during business hours.

The banks are closed at what the business community regards as an early hour. Sometimes they have fixed their closing time at 3 p.m. and sometimes at 3.30 p.m. To overcome part of the problem, most banks open some major branches on a Saturday morning for limited personal services only. This extended service was pioneered by Barclays Bank.

Another way to assist customers to obtain funds has been the introduction of cash dispensers. There are different designs of this machine, but one of the earliest consisted of a safe let into the outer wall of the bank and containing packets of £10 in £1 notes. The customer was issued with a cash card having punched holes, which was fed into the machine for electronic checking. If this was satisfactory the customer was then given access to a keyboard of ten numbered buttons on which he tapped out his personal code number. The machine then delivered the £10 packet. It retained the cash card, which initiated a debit to the customer's account and was then returned to him for further use.

This first generation of cash dispensers is now obsolete. They no longer meet the demands of customers who have become more sophisticated and who have to cope with the ravages of inflation. They had no link with a central computer and therefore there was no check against the customer's account to see that he actually had the funds. Because of this the maximum sum fixed by the banks was very limited.

More recent developments involve the use of cash dispensers both inside and outside branches, to supplement the cashier's work. A computerized cash dispenser – given different names by the different banks – is capable of dispensing variable amounts of cash. Not only are these dispensers capable of giving cash, but they can inform the customer of his balance, accept orders for statement despatch and order a cheque book. With progress, the services offered by these automatic teller machines (ATMs) will expand to offer paying-in services not only to current accounts but to deposit accounts as well. No doubt in the not-too-distant future it will be possible not only to order a statement, but to obtain directly from the computer a printout of the more recent entries and the final balance.

The card which is used by the machine has a strip on the back of it which contains the personal identification number (PIN) of the individual, who is the only person who actually knows this number. Having been fed into the machine to obtain the required funds and/or give the bank the required instructions, the card is returned to the holder. In all cases there is a maximum that can be drawn from the ATM: this can either be a maximum weekly amount agreed between the bank and customer, or it can be the amount standing to the credit of the customer's account. These days the ATMs will only issue cash in either £5, £10 or £20 notes. £1 notes have not been available from these machine for some years, and since 1 January 1985 they have been withdrawn from circulation.

Credit cards

Credit cards are similar in size and general appearance to cheque guarantee cards and are embossed with the cardholder's name, the account number and an expiry date. The best known cards in this country are Access and Barclaycard, the latter being part of the VISA group. American Express and Diners Club, also well known cards, are often known as leisure cards or debit cards, and can be used for the same purpose, but there are slight differences between the two types as will be discussed later on.

With a credit card, goods can be bought in shops, petrol obtained at a service station, hotel bills paid and air fares met, and many other uses are available in many parts of the world. The retailer obtains reimbursement from the card-issuing organization either by paying in the sales vouchers at the bank branch or by sending them to the credit card company.

As mentioned, the cards are divided into two categories. With the first category, Access and VISA, the cardholder receives his monthly statement and he has the choice of paying the balance in full, in which case no interest is charged, or spreading repayments over a number of months. The only requirement is that a minimum repayment of at least 5 per cent or £5, whichever is the greater, should be paid. This has to be paid within twenty-five days of the date of dispatch on the statement, after which interest is charged at a given percentage per month on the outstanding balance. The percentage charged will vary depending on the current rates of interest in operation in the country.

Diners Club and American Express, variously called leisure, debit, travel or entertainment cards, levy an entrance fee and an annual membership charge to their cardholders. It is claimed that unlimited purchases are allowed. Cardholders are expected to repay their account in full each month, again within twenty-five days of the statement date. The cards issued by Access and VISA are sent to the cardholder free of any charge, but in each case the cardholder is granted a credit limit which can be increased or decreased as agreed between the credit card company and the cardholder. Holders of these cards need not necessarily have accounts with the banks which own the credit card companies. Indeed, it is possible to have a credit card and not have a bank account at all.

Credit cards have been criticized for making borrowing too easy. If they are used to create or stimulate a burst of consumer spending it could be argued that they are inflationary, but no more so than the use of other forms of consumer credit.

From the point of view of the retailer, business is attracted to his premises when he is permitted to accept payment for his goods by the customer's signature on a sales voucher specifically printed by the credit card company. It is usual for the retailer to display either on the shop window, door or wall the logos of the credit card companies whose cards are acceptable to him.

The credit card company, as well as giving the cardholder a credit limit, will also give the retailer a limit available for each sale. Should any particular sale go over that limit then authority to make the sale must be obtained by telephone.

The advantage to the retailer is that as he is not dealing in cash any theft from his premises of these vouchers is useless to the thief. Additionally, the copy vouchers paid in to the bank for credit to his account are considered good money, so that these funds can be used immediately. However, the credit card company will charge between $2\frac{1}{2}$ and 5 per cent of the turnover for use of the credit card system. This charge is made at regular intervals by means of a direct debit.

On 1 July 1977 a section of the Consumer Credit Act came into force which gave additional rights to those cardholders who received their first Access or VISA card (not American Express and Diners Club) after that date. It deals with the situation where goods or services (costing at least £30 and less than £10,000) are purchased with the use of a credit card and a dispute arises between the cardholder and the supplier, usually over the quality of the goods and service. The section in question allows cardholders to include the credit card company in any proceedings which they may bring against the supplier concerned in such a dispute, or to bring a separate action against the bank. The result of this legislation has been to divide cardholders into two groups according to whether they took out their cards before or after 1 July 1977. The first group have a limited recourse to the credit card company; they are allowed to claim only up to the amount charged to the credit card account. But the second group are able to claim not only on the basis of the amount borrowed to purchase the product, but also for any consequential damage arising from the use of faulty goods. So if a gas cooker explodes and demolishes a house, both the gas company and the card company might be liable, not only for the cost of the replacement cooker, but also for the cost of building a new house.

Recent developments in credit cards have brought about an increase in their use. For example, Barclays Bank has combined the cheque card and credit card so that, instead of carrying three cards, the customer needs only to carry two. Both Access and VISA have arranged that each cardholder is given a personal identification number so that funds may be withdrawn from a cash dispenser machine.

Credit cards are also acceptable for settlement of debts in very many countries. The conversion from foreign currency to sterling takes place on the day the voucher is received in the UK and the sterling equivalent is then shown on the customer's statement.

Safe custody

Articles of value, locked boxes, wills and many other things are left by customers in banks' strong rooms for safety. Boxes should be locked and parcels sealed by the customer before handing them in to the bank. The banker will issue a receipt and will at the same time inform the customer that he is responsible for insuring all items deposited.

The contract between customer and banker is one of bailment, and, whether a charge is made or not, it is expected that the banker will take the same care of the customer's property as he does of his own.

Banks must take great care when accepting boxes, parcels or other items from partnerships, companies, trustees, etc., as the acceptance and withdrawal must comply with the mandate held. The risk here is that of conversion, which briefly means that the delivery of the property belonging to one person is handed to another. The other risk is that of negligence. Banks must ensure that the property of customers does not lie unguarded in areas such as waiting rooms or the banking hall, so that theft is not possible.

Safe deposits

Some banks maintain a safe deposit service whereby the customer is taken into a strong room and he himself puts his documents or articles of value into his box or compartment, to which he alone has the key. The strong room is available to customers during normal business hours when the customer can put in or withdraw any items he so wishes.

The banks keep duplicate keys in case of an emergency, but do not use them except in the presence of the customer or by his express authority.

Night safes

A customer wishing to pay in regularly at a time when the bank is shut may be offered a night safe wallet. The service is particularly suitable for a shop keeper wishing to bank his day's takings rather than leave them in the shop overnight or take them home. He puts his credit and cash in the leather wallet supplied, locks it, and then 'posts' it down a chute through the bank's exterior wall into the bank's night safe. The entrance to the chute has a locked cover to prevent undesirable items being inserted, but the customer has a key to this.

In the morning the bank staff clear all the wallets out of the night safe and list them in the record book. Wallets are of two kinds, one to be opened by the bank's staff and the proceeds credited to the customer's account, and the other to be handed back to the customer, or his agent, during banking hours, because he prefers to open the wallet and pay in himself.

The customer who can combine this service with the use of a cash dispenser can make an entirely automatic use of his bank.

Encashment facilities

A customer who may wish to draw money at a branch other than the one where he keeps his account, may, of course, use his cheque card, which is limited to £50 a time. If, however, he anticipates requiring more than this, perhaps while he is on a holiday, he may arrange with his branch to have money made available at the bank's branch in the town where he is going to be or, if the bank does not have a branch there, at the branch of another bank.

His own branch will need to know the dates between which he

will be drawing, the amount that he expects to want, and the town where he wants it. The account-holding branch will then send these details, together with a specimen signature of the customer, to the branch bank which is going to pay the cheques, and the customer can then draw his money there.

This service is particularly useful for business customers who have officials staying in a particular town for some length of time and wish to reimburse them for expenses involved. Similarly, if they have a branch office, shop, warehouse, etc., in a particular town, arrangements can be made for the collection of wages and/or petty cash by the branch manager or clerk. In each case adequate identification must be provided by the business customer.

Standing orders

This useful service is available to corporate and non-corporate customers alike. Should a customer wish to make regular payments such as mortgage instalments, club subscriptions, or monthly rate instalments, he must notify the bank of the name of the beneficiary, his bank and branch address, the amount of the standing order, the date of the first payment and the frequency with which the payments should be made, e.g. weekly, monthly, quarterly, etc. The customer gives the authority to make the payments on his behalf, as and when they fall due. The customer must see that on the due date there is sufficient money on the account to meet the transfer, and if the customer is persistently careless in this respect the bank will be justified in notifying him that it has cancelled his standing order arrangement and that in future he should make his own arrangements.

In practice, the beneficiary company will give the debtor its own form for completion which they (the company) will remit to the paying bank. Alternatively, all banks will have their own standing order forms that customers can complete to authorize regular payments.

Direct debits

Direct debiting is yet another method whereby regular payments may be made by a debtor to a creditor, but by this method the creditor is authorized to pass a debit to the bank account of the debtor.

At first glance this seems rather a risky affair, but in practice the banks will only allow approved organizations to operate the direct debit system, the debtor must be notified of any changes in the amount of the debit, and lastly, any incorrect debit is repayable without question by the debtor's bank who will immediately reclaim these funds from the creditor.

In order to operate this system, the company, be it a building society, insurance company, local authority, etc., must give its bankers an indemnity should any errors occur. On receipt of this, they will be able to ask their clients/customers to complete a direct debit form authorizing the debtor's bank to accept a debit at regular intervals – monthly, quarterly, etc. The amount of this debit can if necessary vary, as very often club subscriptions, mortgage repayments and other payments can vary either with the change of interest rates or due to inflation. Should this happen, the debtor is notified.

The method of debiting the account is usually through the Bankers Automated Clearing System (BACS), so that the amount of paper transmitted through the banking system is kept to the minimum. However, should the customer not have sufficient funds on his account, or the account be debited in error, then the debit can be returned unpaid to the collecting bank.

Both parties have advantages. From the payer's point of view, once having given the instruction he need not amend the amount each time there is a change in the charge. He can also be assured that any changes will be notified to him and that any wrong payments will be refunded to him without delay.

From the beneficiary's point of view, he has a cheap and efficient method of collecting funds due to him: by using his computer system and BACS, his account can be credited with good money on the day it is due. His records are kept straight and it of course reduces time and expense in chasing outstanding debts.

Purchase and sale of stocks and shares

Under the Financial Services Act, 1986, banks as investment managers must be members of the Investment Management Regulatory Organization (IMRO). In fact, branch managers and others involved in investment services will have on their personal business card their name, name and address of bank, and 'Member of IMRO', (see Appendix IV).

It is a criminal offence to give investment advice if the adviser or his employee is not authorized.

In order to allow a bank to give a customer a service to buy or sell stocks and shares on his behalf, a customer must complete a comprehensive form in order to comply with the Financial Services Act. It is only when such a form has been completed that a bank may take instructions regarding this service.

When a customer wishes to deal in stocks and shares, he may in the first instance request the bank to find out the present buying or selling price of shares of a specific company. This the bank will do by telephoning the broker and will advise the customer accordingly. The customer will, on noting the price, give the bank instructions to buy or sell a stated number of shares in a named company. Alternatively the customer may request the bank to invest a given amount in the shares of a company, or buy/sell at best. Whatever the instructions are, the bank must scrupulously note the instructions and deal accordingly. If the instructions from the customer are given over the telephone, then such instructions must be confirmed in writing. The information given over the telephone must be checked with the written confirmation.

The bank often receives no commission from the customer for the transaction, but receives a percentage of the broker's commission. When a banker is asked for advice as to investment, he will not give this advice himself, except of a general nature, but will pass the request on to a broker for his recommendations. At the same time the banker must give the broker some idea of the circumstances of the customer, and whether he is looking principally for security, or is willing to take some degree of risk in the hope of a quick capital profit. The broker should be informed, if necessary, of any existing investments which the customer has already made, and whether the sum in question is to be invested in one amount, or spread over a number of stocks and shares. The customer's age, occupation and tax position will also be relevant.

When the recommendations are to hand the banker will pass the information to the customer, so that the latter may make the actual choice.

At this point it is worth discussing the difference in UK terminology between a stock and a share. Basically a stock is a lending of funds to a company, local authority or government. The largest borrower of funds is the government. The funds they borrow are called 'gilts'. As funds are borrowed, they are usually repaid, so that on the majority of gilts there is a redemption date, e.g. 1992/96. The government will at its discretion repay the funds any time between the two dates. The borrowing will attract interest which is usually paid twice a year. With companies, the borrowing can either be secured or unsecured and the interest paid is a 'charge' to profits. Stocks are usually bought in units of £100.

Shares, on the other hand, are investments in the capital of a company which are not repaid, but can be sold in the market at the price appertaining at that time. Interest is not paid, but instead a dividend is paid usually twice yearly. If profits are good the dividends could be high, but if profits are low, then dividends are low or can be omitted altogether during a depressed period. Dividends that are paid are an 'appropriation' from the profits. That is, once all expenses have been paid, some of the residue is paid in the form of dividends to the shareholders. Shares have nominal amounts, e.g. 10p, 50p, £1, etc., and, subject to market availability, any number can be purchased. Confusingly, in the US shares are called common stocks or more simply stocks, while what we in Britain would know as a stock is a bond in the US.

Unit trusts

Banks are permitted to sell unit trusts only if they are members of the Life Assurances and Unit Trust Regulatory Organization (LAUTRO). Under the regulations of the Financial Services Act the banks must be very careful when they are approached by a customer who wishes to buy unit trusts. Banks, building societies, etc., may sell either their own unit trusts, or all others available on the market. They cannot sell both. National Westminster Bank has elected not to sell its own unit trusts but all others. The other major banks have elected to be tied to selling their own products.

However, to overcome the situation, the investment subsidiaries of banks have elected to sell all other unit trusts, so that should a customer of Lloyds Bank for example, wish to buy a unit trust owned by Lloyds Bank, then the branch would oblige and fulfil the service.

Should the customer wish to buy a unit trust of another company, then the subsidiary of that bank will perform the service.

Unit trusts vary widely in the type of shares included in the share portfolio and in the proportion of money invested in any given organization. They may also specialize either according to commodities, geographical areas, capital appreciation, income, etc. Some unit trusts specializing in a narrow range of relatively speculative activities may carry a high risk but, primarily, unit trusts are designed to sell to individuals who consider safety as their prime objective.

Generally, they are very suitable for people of limited means who cannot afford to accept large risks or who don't understand the operations of the stock market. Such people can be absolutely sure that the strict control exercised over all unit trusts by the Department of Trade, coupled with the name and reputation of the bank, means that their unit trust investment will be handled with scrupulous care and absolute honesty, although this is no guarantee that the price of the unit will not fluctuate up or down.

Purchase and sale of gold coins

The purchase and sale of gold coins is a fairly recent service offered by banks to customers. The type of service offered will vary from one bank to another. The price of coins will vary according to market fluctuations, but banks will purchase coins on behalf of customers, who are requested not only to pay the current price but VAT as well. These coins may be given to the customer or held for safe keeping, by the bank in the customer's name. Merchant banks will readily agree to buy and sell coins via their offices in the Channel Islands where the tax payable is less than the mainland.

Insurance

The bank's insurance subsidiary or department will arrange cover for almost any insurable contingency. The most usual requests are for marine insurance, fire insurance, comprehensive house insurance, car insurance, goods in transit, and holidays. Increasingly with banks expanding loans for residential property, mortgage protection policies and life assurance are being requested.

Holiday insurance would cover against the risk of air travel, loss of baggage or personal effects, illness while abroad, and personal injury.

Additionally the bank will assist customers, particularly the self-employed, in dealing with problems of life assurance, pensions and annuities. Advice on investment plans is also available, and the bank is happy to advise customers on any aspect of insurance.

With the advent of the Financial Services Act, 1985, the banks, with the exception of National Westminster Bank, will sell only their own life assurance products. However, if the customer wishes to receive independent advice, then the bank will put that person in touch with a subsidiary that is not tied by the decision to sell the bank's own products.

Banks will either set up an insurance broking department or a subsidiary company specializing in this type of work.

Income tax management

The bank's income tax department will handle the tax affairs of any private customer, and for this purpose may be supplied with duplicate copies of the customer's account by the banking branch. The work consists of preparing the customer's annual statement of income and expenditure, claiming allowances as permitted and generally seeing that the customer pays no more tax than necessary, and claiming any rebate to which he may be entitled. The income tax department will also advise on how the customer's affairs could be arranged in order to minimize tax, possibly through setting up trusts for the benefit of children, or in other ways.

For the sole trader or partnership, the bank, in addition to undertaking income tax work, will also be prepared to undertake the maintenance of the accountancy records of the business, so as to leave the owner or owners free to concentrate on other business matters.

Investment management

The bank's investment department will manage the portfolios of customers, attending to registrations, rights issues, or bonus issues. The investments are transferred into the bank's name and thereafter the bank will collect dividends and interest, crediting them to the customer's account, review the securities from time to time, make any sales or purchases as seem desirable, and maintain a valuation of the portfolio. According to the type of agreement with the customer, any changes made may be after prior consultation with and approval of the customer, or entirely at the bank's discretion. If the customer is working or spending time abroad, or is unskilled in investment, or uninterested, he will probably find it convenient to leave matters entirely in the hands of the bank.

Banks will charge an annual fee based on the market value of the portfolio for the service rendered.

Executor and trustee business

The clearing banks and some other banks maintain special trustee branches to handle executor and trustee business. The work consists of handling the estates of deceased persons, agreeing and paying the capital transfer tax, and supervising and carrying through the administration of trusts and settlements for the benefit of beneficiaries.

The bank may be appointed in a will, or it may be approached to act on a death. If a will is being drawn up it should contain a charging clause empowering the bank to pass its fees to the debit of the estate. Without such an express clause the bank could not pass any charge unless it could obtain the permission of all the beneficiaries, for the bank in this business is a trustee, and trustees are not allowed to make a profit from their trust unless so expressly authorized.

The bank charges an acceptance fee on a percentage basis on the value of the estate as ascertained for capital transfer tax purposes, an annual fee for administration, which may well include the judicious investment of trust funds, and a vacating fee on termination. It may act alone or jointly with a named executor.

Banker's drafts

A banker's draft is an instrument rather similar to a cheque, but instead of being drawn by a customer on his banker, a banker's draft is drawn by a branch of a bank on its head office. As it is certain to be paid on presentation, it commands much greater acceptability than an ordinary cheque. A person completing the purchase of land, or wishing to pay for a car, or engaged in any large transaction where the other party refuses to accept his cheque for a large amount, may ask his banker for a draft, authorizing him at the same time to debit his current account accordingly. A charge is made for this service.

Banker's drafts are also used as a means for settling debts abroad, and in this capacity may be issued either in sterling or in foreign currency.

Emergency payments

Circumstances may arise whereby a customer urgently wishes a sum of money to be paid out in a distant town as soon as possible. An example might be where a weekly salaries and wages cheque sent out from a head office in London by post has failed to reach a factory in the provinces, so that they cannot take it to their local branch.

In such a case the payment would be authorized by telephone from the company's London bank. Banks have a code system whereby they can identify calls between branches as genuine.

Where a payment is required at another bank the request will have to go through both head offices, because each bank has its own code. The customer's bank will therefore telephone a coded message to its head office, where a typed request will be prepared and signed by authorized officers. The letter is taken to the head office of the paying bank, which has copies of all signatures of signing officials of all head office banks. The signatures are checked and a coded telephone call is then made to the paying branch. The customer later authorizes this payment in writing.

In addition to this, there has now developed a system in London which is gradually taking the place of the town clearing. This system is the Clearing House Automated Payment System (CHAPS). Through this, it is possible for a branch outside the City to communicate with its head office, to transmit a large sum of money – usually over £10,000 – to a beneficiary in another bank outside the City of London. The sum is transmitted between the head offices of the banks through the CHAPS system by a computer network. The recipient head office will then transmit the funds urgently to the beneficiary's branch.

Special clearance

A customer who pays in a cheque for collection will normally get it cleared in three to five days. However, if he is in a hurry to know whether a particular cheque is paid he can find out by paying it in separately, marking the credit boldly at the top 'Special Clearance'. The bank will then present the cheque directly by first-class post to the paying banker, telephoning next morning to enquire as to its fate.

The result is then telephoned to the customer, who learns the fate of the cheque the next day. The system does not speed up the receipt of funds. It simply tells a customer that a cheque is paid, and that the drawee bank will be sending funds through the credit clearing system, which will be received two days hence (or four if a weekend intervenes). If the paying bank is within messenger distance, the cheque can be presented and paid the same day.

A charge is normally made for this service.

Credits may also be dealt with in a similar way. In the absence of postal delays or other exceptional circumstances, credits should reach their destination on the second business day after receipt. In the case of need, however, a credit can be sent direct to the recipient's bank, so that it arrives earlier than it would through the clearing. A charge is made for this service.

Guarantees and indemnities

A customer who has lost a share certificate may obtain a duplicate certificate from the company concerned, but it will want a banker to add his guarantee to the application as a check on the genuineness of the request.

Similarly, a customer wishing to make application for payment of money to him from a deceased person's estate may request the banker's assistance. This would arise where the estate is too small to attract estate duty and therefore no probate or letters of administration have been applied for. Without such authority, however, no money can be paid over, however small the sum, unless a banker certifies that the facts are as stated and that the application is a genuine one.

In these cases a banker covers himself against the risk of loss by taking a counter indemnity from his customer.

Status enquiries

The bank will answer status enquiries about its customers and will make similar enquiries about other people's financial position on its customers' behalf. For exporters it will obtain reports on traders abroad.

To preserve the secrecy about the customer's affairs which banks must maintain, certain rules have to be made. The bank will only answer enquiries which are put to it by other banks at home and abroad or by reputable trade organizations. It will not answer private enquiries, nor disclose addresses. Recent legislation has imposed a duty on a creditor or hirer to disclose on request the name and address of the credit reference agency consulted, and a subsequent duty on the credit reference agency to furnish the consumer with a copy of the file relating to him kept by the agency. It does not appear, however, that a bank comes within the definition of a 'credit reference agency', and therefore it seems that the present system whereby one bank answers in confidence to another will continue for some time. The practice of giving a confidential report on a customer to an organization established for the protection of trade has been discontinued.

The replies to all enquiries must be carefully considered and tactfully phrased. If a favourable reply cannot be given, a form of words must be used which conveys the right impression but does not harm the customer's credit. In any case it is always the practice for a bank responding to an enquiry to insert a disclaimer clause on behalf of the bank and the bank official.

When the customer has requested that enquiry shall be made, he must give the name, address and bank account of the person or company which is the subject of the enquiry, and the amount and purpose of the credit involved, e.g. 'whether good for £500 in the normal course of business over a period of twenty-four months'; 'whether good for £250 in one sum'; 'whether suitable as a tenant paying £100 per week', etc.

Attention has been focused on the banks' procedures. In the course of business certain enquiries may be received and answered for customers who do not know that an enquiry has been made. The banks have always considered that it is to the benefit of the customer to have a reference given when properly requested on a business matter, and that the customer gives his implied authority to what is a normal banking custom by the act of opening his account.

From time to time it has been recorded in the press that private enquiry agents, and occasionally journalists, have been able by some form of deception to build up a financial dossier on a person. It is possible for an inexperienced clerk to be tricked, but the remedy in all cases is to request the enquirer to give the code number. It should be remembered that every person on joining a bank signs an oath of secrecy, and if it were found that any clerk had broken this oath he would be dismissed.

In addition to the above services which are available to all customers of a bank, there are many which are only likely to be used by corporate customers. They are as follows.

Special cheque books

Many businesses will accept the offer from its bank to have a special cheque book. Most banks will have specimens of the cheques that can be purchased by the customer and, generally, the customer is willing to accept any one of these. But should the customer wish to have his own cheques made, then the banks would be willing to accept any reasonable design, providing the quality of the paper, the size of the cheque and other standards conform to those laid down by the Committee of London and Scottish Bankers.

Business advisory service

All banks have strenuously marketed their services to small businesses. The banks are most willing to send an executive to the offices of the customer, to discuss accounting procedures, methods of invoicing, debt collecting, and forecasting of cash flow; he will analyse the budgeting, costing, stock control, and assessment of overhead costs. His recommendations, which are confidential, will suggest how the customer can save money, improve the efficiency of his business, or use additional capital.

Cash management service

This is a service to enable corporate treasurers to obtain speedily from a single source details of their company's bank accounts in the UK and worldwide. The service is derived from computer-based modules, available through the subscriber's own terminal linked by telephone to the worldwide time-sharing network of Automatic Data

Processing Network Services. The balance reporting module collects, consolidates and reports the data of the customer's bank account in any location or currency. Transaction reporting can show either the total of the debits and credits, or details of all transactions passing through an account. Balance history reports are also available to give a trend of the account activity. The service will be extended to include electronic funds transfer.

Computer services

The bank may sell time on one of its computers to a customer who has no computer of his own but really has a need for the use of one at certain times. An example might occur where the customer is a big employer of a labour force which has to be paid once a week. The computer, given the necessary details, will quickly produce a list showing what each man or woman should get after allowing for deductions for tax, holiday pay, insurance, short-time working, and so on. At every payrun the employer is supplied with a detailed summary of tax, National Insurance stamps, pension contributions, and all allowances and deductions.

Other possible uses of the computer would be to produce figures for the purchase and sales ledgers, supply stock control reports as required, and management information.

It is possible for a customer to have a terminal in his own office which is connected to one of the bank's computers through the telephone network. The terminal will normally consist of a visual display unit (VDU) and a printer. Security is assured by the use of various codes.

Certificates of deposit

These certificates may be purchased by a customer who wishes to deposit, for a specified period, a sum of money with the bank to earn interest, but at the same time may consider that before the certificate matures he may need these funds for business purposes. This certificate is a negotiable instrument which can be sold by the depositor at any time to another investor. From the bank's point of view, it is assured of the deposit for the whole of the specified time.

Factoring

Factoring has its seeds in the Industrial Revolution, when the textile mills in the north of England, exporting to North America, appointed agents, or 'factors', to sell their product and to get the money for them and send it back. In time these factors became more involved with their clients in America than with their principals in England. Commission on sales made became less than the profits to be made in providing collection, credit insurance and other services for American businessmen.

As their profits increased they were able to finance the long debt collection period involved in Anglo-American trade by offering British suppliers payment on export.

During the development of US industries the factors specialized more and more in 'home' trade rather than import trade and the business grew, although, in view of their origins, activity was still mostly concentrated in the textile trade. During the last two decades, however, there has been a mounting diversification and a growing volume of industries using factoring services.

The first factor in Britain started business in 1960. After an uncertain start the major clearing banks became interested, and then involved through either their own subsidiaries or associated companies. 'Factoring' is a term sometimes used rather loosely. There are in reality three kinds of factoring services.

Non-recourse factoring

The factor operates by buying from his client, a trading company, their invoiced debts. The client has fulfilled an order, dispatched the goods, and now awaits payment. Some debtors are slow to pay up, some may never pay at all. The credit control in the trading company may be lax. The factor becomes responsible for all credit control, sales accounting and debt collection. If a debtor fails to pay, the factor accepts the loss (he has no recourse against his client). Thus companies are able to sell their outstanding book debts for cash. The selling company receives payment for debts purchased on a calculated 'average settlement day' instead of haphazardly. The company passes copies of its invoices to the factor as soon as it has made them out, and sends the originals directly to the customers.

The full factoring service has four elements: the maintenance of the company's sales ledger (including the dispatch of statements to debtors and any necessary follow-up procedures); credit control over the customers of the company exercised by the factor, who incorporates in his service the giving of credit advice and guidance based on his very considerable knowledge of existing and potential customers of the company; 100 per cent protection for the client company against bad debts due to insolvency, providing the client does not exceed the credit limit imposed by the factor; and collection from the customers of money they owe, paid by the factor to the client on the average settlement day (the 'maturity date').

Each factoring house has conditions under which it will accept a client. Some will impose a minimum annual turnover, others a minimum invoice value. The factoring house will make a charge of up to about 5 per cent, depending on the complexity of the sales ledger to be administered and the likely incidence of bad debts.

The benefits to clients of the full factoring service are considerable. The expenses of, and management time involved in, running a sales ledger section is saved; no provision need be made for bad and doubtful debts; detailed information in relation to a company's progress is made available; cash flow (the money coming in and available for the company's use and to provide profits) in respect of factored sales is accurately established and is often improved; and heavy involvement with slow payers and doubtful customers is avoided. It all adds up to a very much easier life for the company's managers.

The benefits to a factoring house are:

(1) they obtain a commission from the client
(2) the status enquiries made on clients' customers can be used for other clients
(3) by having a large number of clients they can economize in expenses by maintaining standardized accounting procedures for sales ledgers
(4) funds received from debtors before the due date may be put on the money market to obtain interest for the factor.

Recourse factoring

Recourse factoring is similar to non-recourse factoring with the important exception that the factor does not extend to the supplier any credit protection. All indebtedness is handled by the factor with full recourse to the supplier in the event of the insolvency of the customer.

Both recourse and non-recourse factoring used to be either disclosed or undisclosed. The former, which was by far the most common arrangement, involved notification by the supplier to his customers that payment had to be made to the factor; the latter involved some form of arrangement that disguised the factor in order that customers should believe they were still paying direct to their supplier. This stemmed from the belief that factoring was not quite reputable, a belief which died when the major clearing banks took an interest, bringing with them backing and respectability. A better understanding now prevails of factoring's value in strengthening the businesses using such services. These companies are in a firmer position in respect of both their suppliers and their customers. As a result, nowadays factoring is always disclosed.

Invoice discounting

The purpose of invoice discounting is to enable a supplier to get his money earlier, so as to improve his cash flow, or to use the money for obtaining discounts, or for any other reason useful in his business. Invoice discounting agreements are nearly always based upon the purchase by the discounter of the debts (receivables) which are yet to be settled, in much the same way as a factor would buy debts. There must be a good status rating and regular orders on the part of the buyers. The discounter then appoints the client as his agent to administer the sales ledger and collect the money. Strictly speaking, therefore, it is not a lending/borrowing arrangement at all, but rather a principal/agent relationship.

The discount houses' approach to the prospective customer is a strictly banking one. At least three years' audited balance sheets are required for analysis, and these must show acceptable ratios of borrowing to shareholders' funds. The maximum figure agreed for an advance is always smaller than the total of shareholders' funds. There is no credit control and none of the other factoring services. The client pays a charge rather in excess of a bank overdraft rate. Invoice discounting is almost always undisclosed, the supplier's customers knowing nothing of the arrangements, but there are variations which involve disclosure.

Export factoring

Export factoring provides for British exporters, when selling on short-term credit, all those services that are available in the domestic market, plus the ability to invoice customers in their own currencies. The factor looks after the exchange risks and the collection from customers overseas. The factor's client enjoys an immediate sterling equivalent, has no problems dealing with difficult payers in a foreign language, and is not concerned with fluctuating exchange values between date of invoice and date of payment. Customer collections are made by local staff in the factor's own office, or through correspondent factors. Where the factor has his own overseas offices, it is possible for the client company to arrange for factoring services to be provided for its overseas sales subsidiaries by overseas offices of the factor.

The factor can account to his client, if so desired, in the currency of invoice, and can provide, if necessary, a financial facility in that currency. This offers advantages to certain exporters.

A few of these factors are members of the British Export Houses Association (BEHA), which includes also confirming houses and finance houses interested in export finance. The Association of British Factors has members which provide full factoring services as their main business, as opposed to those interested only in invoice discounting.

There is little doubt that factoring is not only here to stay, but is expanding, giving solid administrative and financial support for growing companies. The company using the full range of services regularizes and speeds up its cash flow, and in place of a wide range of assorted customers has only one undoubted debtor – the factor.

Hire purchase

Clearing banks and others have subsidiaries and associated companies which deal in hire purchase, and banking branches will put business their way when they can.

The investment by banks in hire purchase finance companies has led to new forms of lending. Normal instalment finance was largely provided for the private consumer and covered such goods as cars and commercial vehicles, household and other goods. In addition, these companies now provide services to meet the needs of modern business enterprises.

Hire purchase for the consumer means that when he wishes to purchase a household commodity he will undertake to pay a fixed weekly/monthly amount over a given period. The property does not belong to the consumer until he has paid the last instalment of the contract. The commercial or industrial purchaser is in the same position, i.e. that the property only becomes his when the last instalment is paid.

Leasing

This is a particularly important area and should not be confused with hire purchase. Under leasing arrangements, companies will lease from a finance house a major capital asset which is necessary for the business, e.g. buildings, computers, fleet of cars, etc. The asset is leased to the company by the finance house, to which a predetermined amount is paid at regular intervals. From the lessee's point of view, he is merely paying prescribed sums – deductable for tax purposes – to the lessor. No initial deposit is payable since it is not an agreement of hire purchase, nor is it an outright purchase, so it improves the user's cash liquidity. The lessor – the bank's subsidiary or associated company – can, as the purchaser of the asset, claim a tax allowance in the year of purchase.

It is usual that the asset at the end of its life is sold to a party who has no connection either with the lessee or the lessor.

Merchant banking services

Since 1970 the clearing banks have no longer been content to leave to the merchant banks that business in which they had always traditionally excelled. Instead, the clearing banks formed their own merchant banks, or took over an existing merchant bank, and are now able to offer many new services.

A complete registration service is provided for companies, local authorities and public boards. Modern computer techniques are employed. A registrar's and new issues department acts as receiving banker for public issues, offers for sale, rights issues and local authority bonds. The merchant banking services developed include corporate financial advice, loan syndication and acceptance credits. The banks represent companies in mergers, amalgamations and takeovers. They manage the investment of pension and similar funds, whatever their size or diversity. In fact the banks now offer all the services usually associated with the accepting houses and other leading merchant banks.

Foreign services

These services can be provided to corporate and non-corporate customers alike. Indeed many of the services are marketed to non-customers as well, as it is usual for the bank to make some charge for providing them.

Foreign currency

Any branch bank will obtain foreign notes needed for a holiday. It will also purchase notes on return from that holiday. It is doubtful whether a bank will purchase foreign coin from a customer; if it did, then the rate of exchange would be unfavourable to the customer as coins take up space, need packing, involve the bank in remittance costs, etc. On the other hand should you, by coincidence, wish to buy coins that a bank has in its possession, then you will probably get them at an attractive rate.

Not all branches keep stocks of foreign currencies, but they can get them fairly quickly. Many large branches will keep stocks of some currencies, but it will be only the very large branches that are likely to have all the major international currencies. The bank remunerates itself, buying the foreign currencies at a high rate and selling at a low rate of exchange in relation to the domestic currency.

In addition to this, where a country has foreign exchange regulations, then the foreign cashier should warn the customer that he cannot purchase more than a given amount of foreign currency, e.g. Portuguese escudos, or take out of a particular country more than a certain sum of local currency.

Travel cheques

Travel cheques are issued in sterling or in most major international currencies by banks to their customers and others wishing to travel abroad. In sterling they can be obtained in denominations of £10, £20, £50 and £100. Each cheque has a space for the customer to sign immediately he gets the cheques. This he must do in the presence of the issuing agent as it is a prevention against fraud. There is another space provided for him to sign in the presence of the paying agent at the time he is cashing the cheque. In this way he identifies himself as the correct and proper person to receive the money. The cheques take the form of drafts drawn on the head office of the issuing bank. The person pays for them in full, plus commission, when they are issued to him. He is also given a small book containing the name of the bank's various foreign correspondents, and which contains instructions on the care of the travel cheques and instructions in case of loss. Should the customer lose them, then he must report the matter to the local police and to the nearest correspondent bank. The latter will refund him the equivalent of the amount lost against identification and signing a form of indemnity.

Travel cheques, due to present custom, easy recognition and negotiability, can be used in shops, hotels, casinos and many other places. Payment is made in local currency.

Most banks will be able to arrange for the supply of travel cheques of any international currency, by way of either their own travel cheques or those of another international bank.

Eurocheque scheme

British banks now provide a service whereby customers can obtain a cheque guarantee card for use with a special cheque book which a customer can use and be guaranteed payment by any bank abroad which displays the EC symbols. The cheque will be drawn payable to the customer and in local currency on London. The local bank will remit the cheque to London and the customer will be debited in sterling at the current rate of exchange.

Cash cards

A service is now beginning whereby the cash cards of some banks can be used in banks abroad to obtain funds from a cash dispenser. Obviously the drawback for the customer is not being able to read the instructions that appear on the cash dispenser, but in his favour he will be able to obtain funds as and when required and be debited a short while after the transaction.

Passport service

A service seldom used by customers is the ability of a bank to obtain or renew a passport for a customer who wishes to travel abroad. The bank will obtain the customer's signature on the application form, request him to obtain two passport photographs, and the bank manager will countersign the form and certify on the reverse of one of the photographs that it is a true likeness of the applicant. The bank remits the documents with the fee to the Passport Office, and on receipt of the passport will give or send it to the customer.

Foreign exchange

In order to fulfil international contracts of various types, it is often necessary for merchants and others to be able to purchase/sell foreign currency. The intermediaries that could and do fulfil the function of buying and selling foreign currency are of course banks.

You have read a short time ago that foreign currency can be purchased and sold over the bank counter. For international trade actual cash is unnecessary, but some instrument evidencing the movement of funds from one person to another must be used. Before dealing with such matters it is necessary to mention, be it only briefly, the availability of foreign exchange to those who need it.

When a person wishes to remit currency abroad, or is in receipt of currency from abroad, it is usual for funds to be exchanged at a bank. The bank will quote the rate of exchange applicable to the currency. Currency can be exchanged on the day needed and this is regarded as a 'spot' transaction, i.e. the customer is debited or credited on a given day. The rate of exchange will fluctuate, so that it is impossible to say that because £ = $1.70 then it will remain so. Within 1988, for example, the £ moved from $1.40 to $1.80. Many thought that this rate was rather high as it affected the cost of our exports to the USA.

Should a merchant know that he will need to purchase foreign currency at some date in the future, he can arrange a contract called a 'fixed forward exchange contract' for that particular day. By doing this he can eliminate the exchange risk. True the rate may go in his favour, but it can also go against him and then he would lose all his profit. Once a person knows how much he will have to pay in sterling terms he can calculate his profit and know that will be so. An exporter expecting to receive funds on a future given day can arrange a fixed forward contract to sell the currency to the bank. He knows how much the goods cost him to produce, he knows how much he will receive in sterling terms, he will therefore know his profit.

The bank will cover itself in any forward exchange contract by matching it with another.

Forward exchange rates are quoted in terms of premiums and discounts on the spot rates. The currency which is at a premium is dearer, so that fewer units will be received for £1. Conversely, a discount will show that a currency will be cheaper so that more units will be received for £1.

It is quite likely that a person will know approximately, but not exactly, when he will want a forward foreign exchange contract. In this case, the bank will quote him a rate for a contract that will be completed between two given dates. This is called a 'forward option contract'. The option is NOT whether the customer will perform the contract, but when he will perform it within the specified dates.

The bank may also offer the opportunity of having a currency option contract. In this situation the customer may, for a small premium, select a currency that he may wish to buy or sell by a given date, but should the rate of exchange move against him/her, then the customer in this situation would have the option to cancel the contract. If however, the rate stipulated in the contract is more attractive than the current spot rate, then he may request the performance of the contract.

In the major trading currencies such as US dollars, Deutschmarks, etc., forward exchange cover may be obtained for periods of up to five years and even beyond. In other less important currencies, cover may be restricted to a maximum of one year, or not obtainable at all. At any time facilities for cover in any currency may be suspended or curtailed by exchange control regulations, but it is usual that existing contracts will not be affected.

Mail and cable transfers

A customer wishing to make a payment to a person abroad may instruct his bank to transmit equivalent sterling from his account to a foreign bank which will notify the beneficiary, who can then go in and get the sum authorized in the currency of the country, or have his account credited. Normally this advice will be sent by mail, but in cases of urgency a cable or telex message will be sent. The customer usually pays a commission plus charges for the service, or should he wish the beneficiary to pay the remitting bank charges, this amount will be deducted from the funds transferred. The foreign bank will be remunerated by a credit to the sterling account which it keeps with the remitting bank in London.

Should the customer require a foreign currency amount to be remitted abroad, then the UK bank will debit his account with the sterling equivalent and request the overseas bank to debit the account of the UK bank (held in their books) with the currency amount.

Since 1977 the time taken to transmit both mail and cable transfers has been reduced by the use of the facilities afforded by the Society for Worldwide Interbank Financial Telecommunications (SWIFT). This is a co-operative society under Belgian law, registered in Brussels. It is wholly owned by the user banks situated in Europe, Japan and North America. The aims of SWIFT are to enable members to transmit between themselves international payments, statements, and other messages connected with international banking.

The system offers both urgent and ordinary methods of transmission, but in both cases the method offered is usually faster than cable or mail. The banks that are connected to the SWIFT system do not, with the exception of Barclays Bank, advertise this service. The cost for a SWIFT is much lower than a mail or cable transfer, but most banks will still offer a mail or cable transfer service, even if the message goes faster by SWIFT.

Banker's drafts

Although they have been mentioned previously, banker's drafts are also so named when they are drawn by a bank on the head office of another bank. For example, should a customer wish to have a banker's draft payable to a beneficiary in the USA, then he could request a dollar banker's draft. This would mean that the draft would be in cheque form but addressed to a bank in New York or some other US financial centre and in US dollars. It would be presented through a US clearing system and debited to the account in the US of the London bank.

Sterling banker's drafts are of course available and many drawn on UK banks are sent abroad, but they need to be presented for collection and final payment in London.

Trade introductions

At regular intervals banks will issue bulletins in which they will give updated information regarding international trade, showing any change in documentary procedures and, more important, details of companies abroad that would like to contact UK exporters in order to purchase specific goods. Additionally, both importers and exporters may contact their bank in order to find buyers and sellers abroad for the various products in which they have an interest.

Status enquiries

Before a buyer or seller completes a contract with an overseas company, he is advised to obtain the credit rating of that company. The procedure is exactly the same as obtaining a status report on a person in this country.

Economic reports

The economic intelligence departments issue reports on all the countries of the world. These are regularly updated and are available free from the bank. They give general information about the country, economic and political facts, trade restrictions, documentary procedures and any other information likely to be of use to firms dealing in international trade.

Bills for collection

Where a bank's customer is an exporter, he is dispatching goods to a buyer abroad. Usually the exporter will draw a bill of exchange at a term on the importer, and ask his bank to collect the proceeds. The bank sends the bill to its agent in the foreign town where the importer lives, and has the bill presented for acceptance, and, at the end of the term, for payment. It then brings back the proceeds, if necessary converts them into sterling, and credits the customer's account.

There are many variations on this. The customer may himself get the bill accepted by the importer through the post, and later bring it to the bank, with the documents of title to the goods attached, for presentation for payment. If a bill has documents attached it is called a documentary bill; if there are no documents it is a clean bill. The customer must instruct the bank whether documents are to be released against acceptance by the importer (D/A) or against payment (D/P).

The bank remuneration for this service is a small charge on the sum involved, plus costs of mail and/or other transmission charges.

Bills for negotiation

The customer may not wish to wait for the proceeds of a collection to reach his account. As an alternative he may ask his bank to negotiate the bill, i.e. he sells the bill to the bank. If the bank agrees it will pay the customer the face value of the bill, less discount and charges. This part of the procedure is exactly the same as if the bank were discounting a bill, but as far as foreign bills are concerned the practice is termed 'negotiation'. In many cases, of course, the bill will be drawn in a foreign currency, and probably has not yet been accepted.

The banker is naturally concerned to safeguard his position if the bill should be dishonoured on presentation for acceptance or on payment. He therefore negotiates 'with recourse'. This means that the customer agrees to pay the banker if the acceptor does not. The banker may ask for security to be deposited to back up the customer's promise, and if the bill is a documentary bill the banker will certainly regard the documents as part of his security. Once he has bought the bill he is collecting the proceeds on his own behalf.

Documentary credits

With a documentary collection, the exporter has control of the goods and documents until acceptance. After acceptance he has no guarantee that payment will be made. On the other hand, the importer who has to pay against the documents cannot be sure that he is paying for goods of the quality and quantity specified in the contract. Both parties have their problems. The exporter does not want to part with the documents (i.e. lose control of the goods) until he has been paid for them. The importer does not want to pay until he has had a chance to look at the documents to make sure that the description, cost and quantity of the goods are in accordance with the contract between the parties.

The banker solves the difficulty by offering a documentary credit.

Assuming that within the terms of the contract both parties agree that a documentary credit should be opened, the importer will instruct his bank to open a documentary credit in favour of the exporter. In his instructions to the bank he must list all the details which must be shown on the documents which he requires the exporter to present before he is given payment. The importer, who gave the instructions, is content to know that the issuing bank – his bank – will only honour the documents presented under the letter of credit if they strictly conform to the terms and conditions he specified.

The issuing bank will remit this letter of credit to its correspondent bank or branch in the country/town of the exporter (the beneficiary), who will send it to the exporter. The exporter, knowing that the letter of credit has been issued by an international bank stating that it will honour his drafts if presented in accordance with the terms and conditions, is therefore confident that payment will be made, because a bank had said so. Should he doubt the word of the issuing bank he may request that the advising bank adds its confirmation to the credit, i.e. its own undertaking that the payment against the documents will be duly fulfilled (a confirmed credit).

The credit may also be revocable or irrevocable. Once the latter has been opened, it cannot have any of its terms altered without the agreement of all parties.

Once the exporter has received this notification, he can feel easy in his mind that he is going to be paid, and will prepare his goods for dispatch. The credit should be opened for a period of time which will give the exporter adequate opportunity to ship the goods, plus a margin for unforeseen delays. It will, however, name a certain date as the last day for shipment and the expiry date of the credit.

Before this day the exporter ships the goods and presents the documents to the agent bank for payment. That bank checks the documents carefully against the terms and conditions specified in the credit, and if all is in order, pays the exporter.

The agent bank forwards the documents, which are usually in duplicate, by two separate air mails (a precaution against the accidental loss of one set), and debits the importer's bank with the cost plus charges. There will be an extra charge if it has itself confirmed the credit.

The importer's bank checks the documents again, reimburses the agent bank, sends the documents to the importer, and debits the importer's account with the total plus its own charges.

Both parties are satisfied. The exporter receives prompt payment and the importer obtains the documents that he specified in the credit.

There are many variations of the documentary credit, but the main one used in international trade is the irrevocable credit.

Performance bonds

A customer engaged in the building or construction industry may tender for a contract and be asked to supply a performance bond or tender guarantee. Such a requirement is often found in contracts for work overseas. The authority inviting tenders is really asking to be reassured that the builder or contractor who gets the job will be able to finish within the contract terms and is not likely to go bankrupt or into liquidation before the project has been completed.

The bank, if satisfied that its customer is technically capable of handling the job, and financially strong enough to see it through, will issue a bond for due performance. The bank will take a counter indemnity from the customer to cover its own position. This counter indemnity may be backed by some form of security given by the customer.

Eurobond sales and purchases

Banks have always been willing to purchase Eurobonds for clients for a small commission. The minimum investment in these bonds is usually denominated in thousands, that is, a bond for US $1,000 or a bond for Deutschmarks 1,000, and so on.

Investors who are not prepared to hold Eurobonds until maturity may sell them on a secondary market. The attraction of Eurobonds to the investor is, of course, that interest is paid gross without deduction of tax. For the issuing companies the attraction is that they qualify for tax relief.

Postscript

Having described in broad detail the main services offered by a bank it must be realized that it is impossible to describe in detail all the services of all banks. These are growing every day.

The hallmarks of a genuine banker are the receipt of customer's funds, the collection of cheques drawn on other banks, and the payment and honouring of customers' mandates. From this foundation the following are a wide variety of services offered by most banks. These have been arranged under eight heads, as follows.

Advances

Overdraft
Loan
Personal loan
Bridging loan
Farming advance
Probate advance
Business development loan

Business expansion loan
Business start loan
Farm development loan
Home improvement loan
House mortgage loan
Small firms guarantee scheme
Personal credit plan

Deposits

Current account
Deposit account
Safe custody

Safe deposit
Statements
Stops

Financial services

Acceptance credit facility
Bills discounted
Business advisory service
Cash management service
Computer services
Dollar certificates of deposit
Executor and Trustee business
Factoring
Hire purchase
Income tax management
Insurance

Investment management
Leasing
Purchase or sale of gold and
  gold coin
Merchant bank services
Money Doctor
Personal banker
Purchase or sale of stocks and
  shares
Sterling certificates of deposit

Foreign services

Bills for collection
Bills discounted (see under
  Financial services)
Bills for negotiation
Documentary credits
Eurobonds – sales and
  purchases
Eurocheque scheme
Foreign currency

Insurance (see under
  Financial services)
International money order
Letter of credit
Letter of introduction
Mail and cable transfers
Passport service
Performance bond (see under
  Status)

Forward exchange
Guarantees and indemnities
(see under *Status*)

Produce loan
Status enquiries (see under
Status)
Travel cheques

Money transmission

Banker's draft
Collection of cheques
Direct debiting

Emergency payments
Standing orders
SWIFT

Savings

Bonus savings account
Budget scheme
Budget travel plan

Investment account
Savings account
Unit trusts

Services of place or time

Cash dispenser
Cheque card
Encashment facilities
Drive-in bank

Mobile bank
Night safes
Special clearance

Status

Credit card
Guarantees and indemnities
Leisure card

Letter of introduction (see
under *Foreign services*)
Performance bond
Status enquiries

Revision test 11

Place a tick against the letter you consider is the correct answer.

1 A person on holiday in Wales was able to draw £50 at a local
   bank by showing a card. Was it his
   (a) cheque card?
   (b) credit card?
   (c) cash card?

2 A bank customer asks the bank to buy a documentary bill. Is
   this
   (a) a collection?
   (b) a documentary credit?
   (c) a negotiation?

3 A credit card can be used
   (a) at any shop
   (b) at any organization offering goods and/or services
   (c) at any place displaying the credit card logo.

4 To be a holder of a credit card
   (a) you need not have a bank account
   (b) you must have a bank account
   (c) you must have a bank account at a specified bank.

5 A customer who leaves a parcel with his bank for safe custody is
   (a) a debtor
   (b) a bailor
   (c) a factor.

6 A banker who wishes to buy or sell shares on behalf of a customer will contact
   (a) a broker
   (b) a jobber
   (c) an underwriter.

7 A forward option foreign exchange contract must be performed
   (a) any time at the customer's option
   (b) between two specified dates
   (c) the customer has the option not to perform the contract.

8 A premium on a foreign exchange rate means
   (a) the foreign currency is dearer
   (b) the foreign currency is cheaper
   (c) it has no relevance at all.

9 When responding to a status enquiry a bank
   (a) must give all the details it knows about a customer
   (b) protect a customer and answer deceitfully
   (c) respond directly to the enquiry, taking care not to harm the customer's credit.

10 The letters CHAPS mean
   (a) Cheque Handling Automated Payment Services
   (b) Clearing House Automated Payment System
   (c) Computer House Automated Personal Services.

Questions for discussion

1 Describe the banking services likely to be needed by (a) a person who has just left school and has got his first job; and (b) a person,

middle-aged, married with two children, just appointed as a senior executive of a company.

2 What are the methods of payment available to a UK importer for settling transactions with a foreign supplier through his UK bank? Discuss their relative merits with regard to speed, safety and convenience.

3 List and briefly describe the services available to the two directors of a company, and to the company itself, from your bank.

12

The balance sheet of a bank

Having discussed the activities and services of a bank it is now time to look at the balance sheet of a bank. The figures given on pp. 256–7 are of one of the large clearing banks, and if we are able to read the figures, that is, know what they mean, we should be able to come to some conclusions as to how the bank is doing, how strong it is financially, how it is affected by any monetary restrictions in force at the time of the balance sheet, and what use it is making of the money it has.

Some people have a gift for figures and take naturally to the understanding of balance sheets. Others feel at a disadvantage when looking at an indigestible array of information which means nothing to them. In fact, of course, like everything else, it is quite easy when you know something about it. Let us start by answering the question: what is a balance sheet?

A balance sheet has been described as a photograph of a company's business at a moment in time. Every business needs money for something it does, and this at once raises two points: where is it going to get the money from, and what is it going to do with it when it has got it?

A public company gets its money by advertising itself to the public (by a prospectus, when it is just beginning) and selling shares in return for money subscribed. This money is a liability from the company to its shareholders, and by tradition appears on the left-hand side of the balance sheet.

It will spend the money on things it needs to do and have, and so will acquire assets. These appear on the right-hand side of the balance sheet. (Some people remember which is right and which is left by thinking that liabilities begins with an L and goes on the left.)

The bank balance sheet will show how much it has obtained from the public in this way and also what money it has obtained from other sources, such as customers opening accounts with it and depositing money in them. From the bank's point of view these are all debts, or liabilities, to go on the left-hand side of the balance sheet.

On the right-hand side we shall see what has been done with all this money. Some has been lent out, some may have been invested in subsidiary companies, some is with the Bank of England. Because we are dealing with one total sum of money, but looking at it from two points of view, we expect to find that the figures on each side of the balance sheet add up to the same total.

The figures present only a momentary glimpse of the business, for naturally most of the details specified in the balance sheet are continuously changing. Nor does it matter what point in time is chosen, as long as once it is fixed the same date is kept year after year, so that when we compare this year's figures with last year's figures we are comparing like with like, and can draw valid conclusions.

For many companies 31 December seems a logical time to present a balance sheet; others have theirs at the end of their financial year, whenever that may be.

It is stipulated by the Companies Act that alongside each year's figures must be stated the corresponding figure for the year before. For the sake of simplicity the notes attached to this balance sheet have been omitted.

We will start with the liabilities.

Shareholders' funds

The first group of figures is subtotalled. This is to give the exact amount of how much of this money belongs to the shareholders.

Preference share capital refers to those shares which carry a fixed rate of interest and which are entitled to receive this interest before any other payments out of profits to ordinary shareholders are made. If in any year the profits made by the company are only just sufficient to pay the preference shareholders, no other class of shareholders will get anything.

The ordinary share capital refers to the money put in by the ordinary shareholders, who have no preference at all. They are paid a dividend after the preferential shareholders have been looked after,

National Westminster Bank plc
Consolidated balance sheet
at 31 December 1988

	1988 £m	1987 £m
Ordinary shareholders' funds:		
Ordinary share capital	778	*754*
Reserves	3,664	*2,699*
	4,442	*3,453*
Preference share capital	14	*14*
Undated loan capital	1,302	*1,068*
Dated loan capital	1,581	*775*
Deferred taxation	8	*28*
Amounts due to subsidiary companies	1,624	*1,702*
Current, deposit and other accounts	45,293	*41,378*
Other liabilities	700	*554*
	54,964	*48,972*

	1988 £m	1987 £m
Coin, bank notes and balances with the Bank of England and with State banks abroad	782	686
Items in course of collection on other banks	671	1,373
Money at call and short notice	2,763	3,049
Bills discounted	1,393	1,687
Dealing assets	46	68
Certificates of deposit	592	502
Investments	334	855
Advances and other accounts	33,194	27,561
Amounts due from subsidiary companies	10,645	10,003
Investments in associated companies and trade investments	155	122
Investments in subsidiary companies	2,205	1,565
Premises and equipment	2,184	1,501
	54,964	48,972

and only if profits permit. In a bad year the ordinary shareholders may get nothing by way of dividend, whereas in a good year they will probably do very well. There is no fixed rate at which their dividend will be calculated, as there is with preference shares. The ordinary shares are often called the 'equity' of the company. Their holders take the main risks (in banks of this standing this risk is so small one couldn't even guess what it might be).

Although within the balance sheet the actual number of shares issued are quoted, the notes to the accounts must show the authorized capital, that is, the maximum number in any class that can be issued. Often the authorized capital is greater than the issued capital, but it can never be exceeded. Should the bank require any additional capital, it may be necessary to require the approval of a general meeting to increase the authorized capital.

The reserves are the total of those amounts which have over the years been prudently set aside for a rainy day, before the dividends were paid. They come, as do the dividends, out of past profit, which is why we say they belong to the shareholders, the risk takers who are entitled to any profit there may be. We can see these reserves have reached a pretty hefty total, more in fact than the ordinary share capital. This is due to the fact that in any major bank only about 25 per cent of the declared profits are in fact distributed to ordinary shareholders. The remainder is retained in the reserves. The reserves give some indication of the strength of the bank. This is reflected in the Stock Exchange quotation of the shares. The value of the shares of any quoted bank can be seen on the financial page of any daily newspaper. Look at the value of the shares of the bank in which you work or maintain an account.

In the report and accounts of each publicly quoted bank, you will see somewhere in the booklet the number of shares held by different types of corporate and non-corporate members. One of the biggest groups of shareholders is women. This applies particularly to the 'Big Five'. The shareholdings of the directors are also as shown.

Loan capital

This item consists of loans made to the bank in various currencies, under various conditions and at various times. The banks will borrow, more often than not on an unsecured basis, not only sterling funds but Deutschmarks, US dollars and other currencies. The repayment of these funds may extend from the short term to the very long term. The loan capital is frequently larger than the equity.

Deferred taxation

Here is seen the bank's provision for its potential liability for deferred taxation in respect of short-term timing differences and capital allowances, principally on equipment held for leasing.

Current, deposit and other accounts

This is the total of the depositors' money. The different accounts on which customers can keep money are not specified here, but are all totalled together for the purposes of the balance sheet. Certificates of deposit issued by the bank come under this heading as deposits. They are not separately specified here, though some of the smaller banks differentiate between funds held on customers' accounts and certificates of deposit issued. By comparing the total for deposits with that of last year we can get a good idea as to whether the bank is expanding its business. An adjustment for inflation must be taken into consideration. More important is the figure of funds held on behalf of customers as a percentage of the total of the balance sheet, which as you can see is about 90 per cent. Of the amount deposited you can also observe that a large proportion of these funds is loaned to customers. We shall return to this figure a little later on.

Now let us turn to the assets.

Coin, banknotes and balances with the Bank of England

We know that the banks have to keep a certain amount of banknotes and coin in their tills to meet the demands of their customers, and that they keep balances with the Bank of England so that the daily adjustments with other banks on the debit and credit clearings can be settled by a book transfer.

As none of this money earns any interest, indeed money kept in tills costs money to keep it there, i.e. insurance, transport costs, etc., banks are naturally keen to keep this cash as low as possible consistent with good management. There is no official requirement now to keep any minimum cash in tills, and it is no longer anything more than a stock in trade; only enough is needed to service customers' demands. There are other controls now to ensure prudence. Although it is possible to consider the total of coin, banknotes and balances with the Bank of England as a percentage of funds held on current, deposit and other accounts, this will not give us a breakdown between the amount held at the Bank of England and cash in tills.

Cheques in course of collection on other banks

We have seen how customers paying in cheques for the credit of their accounts get their accounts credited the same day, but that the clearing of those cheques takes three (or five) days to effect. During this time the total of money represented by all these cheques is said to be in the clearing pipeline. While it is in this pipeline it earns no money, so if it were possible to cut this time down the banks would be very pleased, even though some of it would reduce debit balances earning interest.

So on any day a proportion of current, deposit and other accounts is somewhere in the clearing pipeline. The figure varies with seasonal and other factors, but is normally about 2–3 per cent.

If we add together these two items – coin, banknotes, and balances with the Bank of England, *and* cheques in course of collection on other banks – we can see the amount of customers' money that earns no interest.

The remainder is carefully invested in many ways. The balance sheet will tell us how this has been done. The general principles which the bank will keep in mind here are that investments must be spread so that not too much is lent in any one direction. Also, the bank should be able to get at the money, or some of it, quickly and without losses on realization, should the need arise. There must be liquidity. Some investments, therefore, will be in government stock (which can be quickly sold, but at market price) and in the very short-term money markets (which will repay on demand or at a few days' notice). Other investments will be less liquid, such as money lent to other customers of the bank. Such loans will be technically repayable on demand, but will usually prove more difficult to recover than those already mentioned.

The greater the element of risk, the higher is the interest rate which can be obtained. The bank has to remember not to lend too much at high rates of interest because if it did it would be taking unacceptable risks in the hope of greater profits.

Money at call and short notice

The bulk of these loans are mostly on a day-to-day basis or at most seven days' term or notice. For some time such funds were lent only to the London discount market; however, with the availability of other markets, particularly the inter-bank market, funds are made available to institutions other than the discount houses. This item represents the bank's most liquid item, after cash, and if the bank itself were short of cash this is where it would turn to first to get some, by recalling money at call.

As a result of Competition and Credit Control, overseas, merchant and foreign banks had to start maintaining reserve assets as soon as they were brought into the system. This gave the discount houses more of a choice in where to go for their daily loans. The overseas, merchant and foreign banks were quite willing to lend to them because money at call with the market qualified as a reserve asset.

The discount houses can as a last resort borrow from the Bank of England, but this must mean that none of the banks has any money to lend. There is a shortage of cash in the system as a whole. If this persists interest rates will rise. The Bank of England can engineer such a shortage (by open market operations) if it thinks short-term interest rates should go up, and can relieve it by feeding a fresh supply of money into the system by lending to the discount houses.

We have therefore a system through which the ebb and flow of cash in the banking system can be evened out.

Bills discounted

The figure for bills discounted by the bank is shown in the notes to the accounts to be made up of British government Treasury bills and other bills. Banks keep a supply of Treasury bills for their own account, as a safe way of investing money, and they increase or reduce these quickly as their liquidity requirements vary. Other bills discounted reflect the bills which the bank has discounted for its own customers and those which it has purchased from bill brokers. When anticipating requiring a certain sum at a certain date, the bank may buy first-class bills from brokers which will mature at the time it will be likely to want funds. On the other hand it is important to remember that it is a requirement that each bank must keep the equivalent of 5 per cent of its eligible liabilities in bills with the discount market, so that the Bank of England may control the money markets by re-discounting these bills via the discount houses.

The concept of liquidity is still important. If a bank locks up in medium- or long-term loans more than is prudent, it may find that it does not have enough ready cash to meet all its obligations. Although a bank can now borrow funds on the inter-bank market, and consequently the maxim that those who borrow short must never lend long has lost some of its force, it is still necessary to keep a reasonably liquid position.

Since the suspension of Competition and Credit Control, the liquidity ratio of any bank is only known by that bank and the Bank of England. This liquidity percentage must have a tolerance as the demands of personal customers can vary during the year depending on such factors as tax payments, holiday spending, etc., while the needs of business customers are continually changing.

Other ratios neglect the effect of inflation. The first is the relationship between capital and deposits. As the capital of any concern is the 'buffer' between the creditors and any possible loss, it is important to see that it is increased in line with inflation, otherwise the figure for deposits will go up while the capital remains the same. To guard against this risk banks have from time to time issued loan stock, bearer bonds, capital bonds and capital notes, in sterling and various other international currencies. This means that in the event of the liquidation of a bank the claims of the holders of these various issues to repayment would be subordinated to the claims of the shareholders of the bank, and this is why it is possible to add this figure to the total of capital. In a commercial issue of loan stock this clause imposing subordination would not appear, because the lenders would not agree to it. In the case, however, of an immensely strong organization such as a bank, the risk of liquidation is so small as to be practically non-existent.

Another important ratio concerns the effect of inflation on working capital. This is the 'free' capital (i.e. capital minus fixed assets) to deposits. Insufficient working capital means that the business is obliged to rely on trade creditors, or borrowing, or both, to keep the floating assets moving. As a result there is a danger that creditors necessarily unpaid may press to the point of forcing the company into liquidation. Here we come up against the difference between a bank and another type of commercial organization, where the fixed assets may include factory, plant and machinery, vehicles, office equipment and furniture. In a bank the fixed assets are premises, office equipment, vehicles and computers. These are aggregated under the heading 'premises and equipment'.

Dealing assets

These are investments made by the bank on its own account, mostly in purchases and sales of foreign currencies.

Certificates of deposit

'Negotiable certificates of deposit' describes a way in which banks take deposits for large sums. Unlike other forms of deposit, the depositor receives a certificate, which is a negotiable instrument, transferable by delivery. Certificates are issued for a minimum period of three months, up to a maximum of five years. The minimum denomination of a certificate is £50,000 and the maximum is £500,000. They are readily realizable at current market rates in London, where the discount houses provide a secondary market in them. On the balance sheet this figure represents the total of the certificates of deposit issued by other banks which this bank has purchased from the market and is holding.

Investments

The notes to the balance sheet show that practically the whole amount under this heading is invested in securities of, or guaranteed by, the government. These securities can be sold when the bank needs money or when it is decided to switch into a higher yielding stock. But generally the intention when the stock is purchased is that it shall be held until maturity, that is, until the government repays it. For this reason only dated stocks are taken up, that is, stocks which quote the year in which they will be repaid. Usually the banks buy 'shorts' (five years or less to maturity) rather than the longer dated issues. The value of these stocks may vary during their lifetime, but the value must adjust up or down in the final stages to what they are going to be worth when repayment is made. Holdings are planned so that a proportion of them mature each year, thus lessening the risk of loss if the bank has to realize any of these investments.

Advances and other accounts

Now we come to the biggest item on the assets side – the loans and overdrafts made by the bank to its customers. Here the risk is much higher than on money lent to the money market or to the government, and therefore the interest rate obtained will be much higher. In normal times this money will be lent to anyone who, being a customer, can satisfy the bank that the sum borrowed is within the borrower's capacity to repay (always provided that the purpose for which the money is going to be used is acceptable to the bank), but in times of restriction the Bank of England has directed the banks as to the classes of borrowers who should receive favourable consideration. These priority categories usually comprise exporters (whose efforts tend to reduce the unfavourable trade balance with other countries), those producing equipment for national defence (who add to the safety of the country), farmers (who produce some of the country's food), and those engaged in projects assisting regional policy, particularly in areas of high unemployment.

These are called qualitative restrictions and in practice the banks have complied with these official 'requests' even though they have not had statutory backing.

Banks traditionally lend for short periods and prefer to lend working capital for business and to provide bridging finance, that is, short-term loans, pending the provision of longer term finance from some other source. Of recent years, however, a willingness to lend for longer terms has been noticeable. Banks are becoming increasingly involved in house purchase mortgage loans and property improvement schemes, business expansion schemes and in long-term loans to industry.

In this section of the balance sheet we find the source of the banks' greatest profit. At times when interest rates are raised to high levels the banks' profits go up automatically.

In an attempt to maintain a fiction of liquidity all advances under this head are legally repayable on demand, but the ordinary borrower is not usually able to repay on demand.

It is accepted that these loans are the riskiest form of lending, and that the percentage of advances to deposits is quite high. But bankers, being sound business people, make a provision for possible doubtful debts and this is shown in the accounts. When a bank suspects that a loan or overdraft is bad, it is not unusual for the bank to have some security available to cover all or some of the possible bad debt.

'Other debtors' need no explanation. 'Prepaid expenses' are expenses paid earlier than they need have been. Anything paid in advance entitles the bank or any company to show it as an asset until such time as the goods or services for which payment has been made are duly delivered or performed.

Trade investments

These include the bank's investments in affiliated banks and associated companies, and may be seen in the report and accounts of any major bank. For quoted investments a middle market valuation is taken, half-way between the buying and selling price. Where the investment has no quotation the directors of the bank place a valuation on it according to what they think it is worth.

Investments in associated companies

Under this part of the heading is shown the value of the bank's share holdings in such companies as BACS, Joint Credit Card Company, and others. A study of the various names serves to remind us that this is a very big banking group.

Premises and equipment

Bank premises used to be shown at a very conservative figure indeed, thus building a hidden reserve in the assets. However, most banks have recently revalued their premises and National Westminster has been one of these. It would be wrong to say, however, that the current figure represents the full market value, only that the figure now is less conservatively valued than it used to be. The National Westminster, whose figures we are looking at here, was formed by merger of the Westminster, National Provincial and District Banks in 1968. Of course it was found that in some places the new bank had too many branches and some had to be closed down and sold. This process has been going steadily on, and indeed this rationalization is part of merger benefits, which ought to include operating economies. However, the figure for premises is lumped in with equipment, and equipment not only includes plant and machinery in the giant office centres which have been built, but also the bank's computers.

So much for the balance sheet. Note the importance of the current, deposit and other accounts figure. Everything flows from that. The percentage in the clearing pipeline, the proportion of funds reinvested at interest, the liquidity ratio, the cash ratio, the lending ratio; to work out any of them we have to go to the total deposits. This total is the mainspring of any bank. The bank must advertise for these funds, some of which it gets quite cheaply (in the case of current accounts, for nothing), and must face fierce competition from other banks, building societies, etc.

As well as getting new deposits, however, the bank must do its best to keep the deposits it already has. This is equally important. To do this it must see that its staff understand what good service is and then give it to customers. It is ultimately in the opinion of its customers that a bank will succeed or fail.

A balance sheet is to give information. But in order to give additional information and to market the services of the bank, the balance sheet is put into a smart presentable booklet which gives further information relevant to the accounts. Most importantly, the statement of the chairman of the bank is included. This looks at the bank, its past activities both in the domestic and international fields, assesses the future and discusses the bank in the context of UK and international economic affairs. For the student of banking the reports of the chairmen of the major banks are important reading in order to understand the relationship between the banks and the outside world.

The other reports are of significance in as much as they will provide information about the various operational areas of the bank, the services offered and the areas of contraction and expansion. These latter reports are particularly important for, year after year, they will emphasize the areas that are of importance to the bank and how the bank regards its policy for the future.

Other critical eyes will be looking at the reports and accounts of the bank. For example, all banks are competitors to each other and will read what they will into these figures. The bank staff and their unions are for obvious reasons also interested.

The Companies Act says a balance sheet and other accounts must be presented to the shareholders yearly. Copies must be registered at Companies House, where anyone may ask to see them on payment of a small fee. However, the report and accounts of any bank are available from its head office, free of charge.

The balance sheet of a bank is drawn up by its chief accountant and his staff. When the figures are ready they are checked by an independent firm of chartered accountants who can and do ask any questions they wish, and, if there is a need, make any necessary investigations into the bank's affairs. The large banks often have two or more firms of accountants to audit the accounts.

When the accountants are satisfied that all is in order they add their report. They will state that they have examined the balance sheet and accounts together with the notes associated with it. They go on to certify that in their opinion the balance sheet and the associated accounts comply with the requirements of the Companies Act and give a true and fair view of the state of the bank's affairs at the balance sheet date.

This report by qualified auditors is a guarantee to all reading the balance sheet that the figures are fair. Should the auditors be unable to obtain all the information they require, or disagree with the company's treatment of some of the figures, they must say so in their report.

Revision test 12

Place a tick against the letter you consider has the correct answer.
  1 The item 'reserves' refers to
      (a) money kept at the Bank of England
      (b) money belonging to the shareholders
      (c) money put aside to meet bad debts.
  2 The cash ratio is found by comparing deposits with
      (a) liquid assets
      (b) money in tills and at the Bank of England
      (c) advances to customers.
  3 The equity of a company is
      (a) the sum set aside to pay pensions
      (b) the preference share capital
      (c) the ordinary share capital.

4 Much the largest figure on the assets side of a bank's balance sheet consists of
 (a) advances to customers
 (b) money at call and short notice
 (c) balances with the Bank of England.

5 Certificates of deposit are
 (a) given by the bank to deposit account holders
 (b) negotiable securities issued by banks
 (c) issued for a minimum period of one month.

6 Trade investments are
 (a) investments in associated companies
 (b) investments in local authorities
 (c) investments in government securities.

7 A balance sheet may be produced
 (a) once in twelve months
 (b) once in eighteen months
 (c) once in twenty-four months.

8 The auditors' report will state that the balance sheet shows
 (a) the correct valuations of all assets
 (b) the cost price of all assets
 (c) a true and fair view of all assets.

9 The item 'current, deposit and other accounts' is
 (a) usually smaller than the issued capital
 (b) the largest item on the liabilities side of the balance sheet
 (c) an asset to a bank.

10 The asset side of a bank balance sheet is usually shown in order of
 (a) profitability
 (b) liquidity
 (c) repayment.

Questions for discussion

1 Describe the main liabilities and assets of a bank. To what extent do these reflect the banking services provided by that bank?

2 What criteria govern the use that a bank makes of the deposits entrusted to it?

3 What are the ratios usually connected with the 'current, deposit and other accounts' figure, and what is their purpose?

13

Lending against security

Looking at the balance sheet of any bank, you will see that a major part of the deposits, shown on the liabilities side, is utilized for advances to customers. These advances are in the forms of overdrafts and loans and discounted bills of exchange.

Overdrafts

An overdraft occurs when, with the permission of the bank, a customer is able to borrow on current account; that is, he will be permitted to have a debit balance up to an agreed limit. Interest is payable on the overdraft amount at a given percentage above the bank's base rate. This is a relatively cheap form of borrowing as the interest charged is calculated on a daily basis, so that as funds are paid into the account, the overdraft balance is reduced, while the withdrawal of funds will increase the overdrawn balance. From the bank's point of view the authority given can be quite informal and, providing the overdraft limit is not exceeded and repayment is made within the stipulated period, all is well. However, with a minority of customers it can be difficult to monitor the situation, and should the bank consider that the overdraft situation is 'hardening' it may be necessary to demand repayment. In any case the bank will periodically review all overdrafts to ensure that repayment is taking place within the agreed terms.

From time to time banks will have an unauthorized overdraft to contend with. In this situation they may permit the occasional overdrawn balance, but will charge the customer a penal rate of interest. If this continues, then the bank will request the customer to regularize the position.

Loans

Loans are granted when the bank wishes to ensure that an agreed amount is borrowed. The amount is recorded by the debit entry in a loan account opened in the customer's name, and a credit entry in his current account. An agreement will be drawn up between the banker and customer for repayment by instalments which are made by transfer from current account to loan account. Interest is charged on the reducing balance and debited to the loan account or the current account of the customer, as agreed.

Personal loans

These loans are perhaps the most common, but not necessarily the most popular. The reason for calling them 'personal loans' is because they are normally granted to enable individuals to purchase consumer durable goods, e.g. motor cars, television sets, washing machines, etc.

Usually security is not required for this type of loan as frequently there is built into the loan agreement an insurance against non-payment should the borrower die before repayment.

Interest is charged 'up front', that is, when the loan is granted. Thus interest is added to the total amount which is repayable. In practice this means that the interest is charged on the full amount over the total period. As a result the customer is repaying the capital by regular instalments, which means that each month or so the debt due to the bank is being reduced, yet the interest charged is on the full amount for the whole period which makes the interest charged penal.

Once interest is fixed, the customer can be at a disadvantage if interest rates are reduced nationally; alternatively, if during the life of the loan interest rates are increased, he may benefit.

Discounting of bills

This is a useful facility for large companies who receive term bills of exchange in settlement of commercial debts. The banks, as well as other financial institutions, are willing to discount term bills of exchange. They will do so providing that:

(a) the bill has been accepted
(b) the parties to the bill – acceptor, drawer, payee and endorsers – are good names

(c) should the bill be dishonoured for any reason, there is recourse to the customer.

The bank will discount a bill by reference to the current base rate, the term of the bill and the risk involved. For example, assuming that a bill has a value of £1,000, has a term of 90 days and that the current rate for discounting bills is 10 per cent, the customer's account will be credited with £975. That is, 10 per cent of the face value of the bill is £100, and one-quarter of this sum (90 days) is £25. This amount is deducted from £1,000 and the net figure is credited to the customer. On the due date, the bank will present the bill on the acceptor. For the purpose of this example, bank charges have been omitted.

Types/reasons for borrowing

Seasonal shortages – personal

From time to time the individual requires funds to see him over a period when his expenditure exceeds his income. This short-term borrowing, often on an overdraft basis, is frequently granted with what may appear to be undue formality. It could be argued, however, that some customers consider seasonal shortages as justifiable towards the end of each month. Somehow they are unable to control their expenditure. They can be troublesome to banks.

Temporary requirements – business

Often businesses require funds between seasons for a variety of reasons, which could be to pay wages during off-season periods, renew fittings, purchase stock, etc. These funds are repaid when the season begins and funds come in from sales of goods. This seasonal cycle can happen in agriculture, retail trade, hotels, etc.

Bridging loans

When house-owners require temporary finance in order to purchase a property at the same time as selling the house in which they live, it is often the bank that provides finance to purchase the new property and receives repayment when the old property has been sold. When this type of loan is required, the bank likes to see that the completion dates of the sale and purchase contracts are known and they have a solicitor's undertaking that the proceeds of sale will be delivered to the bank. It is on rare occasions that the bank will give an 'open-ended' bridging loan, which is a loan to cover the purchase of a property before the first property is sold.

Bridging loans are, from the bank's point of view, simple, profitable, and self-liquidating.

Probate loans

Briefly, a probate loan is granted to an executor of a will when, in order to obtain probate (i.e. the transfer of the deceased's assets to the executors), capital transfer tax must be paid. The executor needing funds will go the bank, show the manager evidence of his right to the executorship and, providing this evidence is satisfactory, a loan is granted and the tax paid. Probate is then granted. The loan is either repaid from the deceased's current/deposit account, or if this is insufficient, an asset – say stocks and shares – is sold to repay the loan.

Purchase of consumer durables

It is usual to offer the individual a personal loan for the purchase of such items. The period of the loan tends to be up to about three years, depending upon the customer, bank policy and the item purchased.

Sundry personal reasons

It is quite customary to borrow money from a bank for a variety of reasons which may range from payment for a wedding, holidays, school fees, medical expenses, tax, etc. There is no end to the reasons why customers might require an advance. These are but a few.

Business development loans

These loans are used for the expansion or development of a business. The funds are used to purchase fixed assets and provide working capital. Often the loan is for a period of five years or more. Security may be taken by the bank.

Business start-up loans

Start-up loans, particularly for small businesses, are a fairly recent phenomena. Due to the unemployment situation, the government has encouraged banks to provide funds for those men and women who are sufficiently enterprising to start their own businesses.

The banks are only too willing to provide these funds to the right applicants.

As with business development loans the funds are lent for medium- to long-term periods.

Foreign trade

Both importers and exporters look to banks to finance their purchases and sales. Such finance is available by means of overdrafts, loans, negotiation of bills of exchange, discounting of bills, documentary credits and documentary collections. Often the security offered is the goods themselves, so that the banks will look to the ultimate buyer for reimbursement.

Agricultural loans

The farming community plays an important part in the British economy, and funds are lent on both a short-term and a long-term basis for the purchase of seed, fertilisers, machinery, cattle, etc. As with other advances the banks ensure that repayments can be made within the agreed time. If necessary some form of security will be obtained.

Canons of lending

When a bank is approached for a loan, a borrower is asked four questions:

(1) How much is required?
(2) What is the purpose of the loan?
(3) For how long are the funds required?
(4) What is the source of repayment?

When all these have been answered satisfactorily, it is time to think about security. No advance is to be made just because it is secured. The banker's decision will be influenced by many factors, of which the most important are the character of the borrower, the risk involved, the profitability of the transaction to the bank, the lending policy of the bank (which may be influenced or determined by government policy), the best interests of the borrower and of the community generally, and of course the answers to the four questions.

The perfect advance will be safe, liquid and profitable. It will be for a suitable and legal purpose. Needless to say, these qualities will not always be present at the same time and the banker will therefore search for an acceptable compromise.

Security is taken as a kind of insurance. The real security is the character of the borrower. Unsecured borrowing, in the shape of balance sheet advances to big established limited companies, may account for nearly half of the bank's lending in any particular year. These advances, made to trusted borrowers, are usually far less trouble than the secured advances, which require a certain amount of work before the advance is taken, to ensure that the security is perfected and that the bank has control over it.

It is a golden rule of banking that if the banker cannot see how the customer can repay an advance, he must not lend even if adequate security is available.

We can work out some simple rules by asking ourselves some simple questions:

(1) Why does the bank take security (in those cases where it does)?

Obviously, to sell it if the borrower defaults.

(2) How does the bank know it could sell, if it wanted?

There are two answers to this one:

(a) Only an owner can sell. Therefore the bank must either be the owner of the security, or be in a position to get the ownership if it wants.

(b) There must be a market in the security taken, from which it follows that a bank must only take marketable securities.

(3) How does the bank know how much the security is worth?

It must not only be possible, but easy, to value the security. The bank should try to take only those securities for which there are current valuations.

Security can come from the borrower himself or be provided by another person: in banking terminology, either first-party or third-party security. Secondly, security can be something tangible or intangible. But whether the security is from a third party or tangible or intangible, the golden rules of securities are repeated in more obvious form:

(1) The bank must be able to obtain OWNERSHIP.

(2) VALUE must be easily obtainable.

(3) It must be MARKETABLE without difficulty.

Applying these rules, we can write out a list of suitable types of securities, which are both easy to value and easy to sell.

Bearer bonds	Stock exchange securities
Life policies	Guarantees
Land	Debentures
Others	

Over the centuries various types of security have been known by various names. Thus land is mortgaged, assurance moneys are assigned, bearer bonds are pledged. A pawnbroker takes the actual article by way of security – this is a pledge, too – and keeps it until his loan has been repaid. The banker does not take the actual article, but he takes some kind of paper which shows the customer's title to the security – a share certificate, a life policy, deeds, etc. These are 'valuable paper'.

Lien

A lien is the right to retain the property belonging to another person, until the debt due from the owner of the property to the possessor of the property is paid. The lien has nuisance value, in that the owner of it cannot get it back until he has paid up. The possessor of the property cannot sell it, and so get the money owing to him, because he is not the owner, although sometimes a right of sale is given by some statute.

There are different sorts of liens, but basically they all have one thing in common. A is doing some service for B. B owes for the service. During the course of the service, property of B comes into the possession of A as a result of the service. A has a lien over the property.

A carrier has a carrier's lien over the goods transported.

An innkeeper or hotel owner has an innkeeper's lien over the luggage of the traveller or guest.

A warehouse keeper has a warehouse keeper's lien over the goods he stores in his warehouse.

A banker has a lien (if the customer is overdrawn) on any property of the customer coming into his hands in the ordinary course of his business as a banker. Cheques for collection would fall into this category, but articles deposited for safe custody would not. There is a certain lack of logic here. Taking articles on safe custody is really just as much in the ordinary course of the banker's business now as is collecting the proceeds of cheques, but the argument is that the article has been deposited by the customer for a specific purpose and that this is enough to destroy any claim to a lien.

Any person having any sort of lien over any kind of property should never part with it (unless he is paid). He cannot claim a lien until he is in possession of the property and he will lose it if he parts with the property, even temporarily.

Pledge

A pledge is a delivery of goods or documents of title to goods by a debtor to his creditor as security for a debt, or for any other obligation. The subject of the pledge will be returned to the debtor when he has paid his debt.

The pledgee (the creditor) can sell the goods if the debt is not repaid.

The lender should not part with his pledge before he is paid, or he will lose his remedy.

The banker takes bearer bonds by way of pledge, and also documents of title to goods.

It should be recorded that where the loan is considered a regulated agreement under the Consumer Credit Act, no such security can be given.

Hypothecation

In Roman law a hypothecation was an advance to a farmer against the security of his agricultural implements, to be repaid out of the proceeds of sale of his crops. The hypothecation has come to be a name for that type of security where neither ownership nor possession passes to the lender, but the word is imprecisely used. In maritime law it refers to the charging of a ship's cargo, or the ship itself, as security in certain circumstances; in banking a hypothecation is an agreement to give a charge over goods, or over the document of title to goods, in circumstances which make it impossible to give the banker possession. If this were possible the banker would take a pledge. In recognition of this fact the agreement may undertake to give a pledge when the goods or documents become available.

At the same time, however, a 'trust release' or a 'trust letter' signed by a customer (who has already given a pledge over goods to a lending banker, and who now wishes to obtain the documents of title for the purpose of obtaining the goods, selling them, and repaying his debt out of the proceeds), is sometimes loosely and inaccurately called a letter of hypothecation.

A hypothecation has the disadvantage that the banker has very little, if any, control over the security. This makes his estimate of the customer's integrity vitally important, for there is often considerable scope for fraud. A further disadvantage is that the line of division between an agreement to hypothecate and a bill of sale requiring registration is not very clearly defined.

Mortgage

A mortgage is the conveyance of a legal or equitable interest in real or personal property as security for a debt. Deeds are mortgaged (real property) and so are share certificates (personal property).

The distinction between legal and equitable rights or interests stems from the historical development of our law in the common law courts and in the courts of equity. A legal right is where a person has the ownership of property. He can do what he likes with it, sell it, destroy it if he wants – he is the owner. A person having an equitable interest does not have anything more than a claim on the property. He cannot sell it, for he is not the owner. Moreover, other people may have similar claims on the same property.

Real property is freehold land. Everything else (including leasehold land) is personal property. The distinction is again an historical one. An action *in rem* was an action for the land itself, nothing else would do. An action *in personam* was an action against an individual, a person, who might have to pay damages or make restitution in some way.

Assignment

An assignment is a transfer by a creditor to an assignee of the right to receive a sum of money, or some other benefit, from a debtor.

A contract between two people raises rights and duties for each of them. These rights and duties can be enforced at law. A right is often to receive money. One party to the contract renders a service, the other pays for it. In our earlier history the law courts refused to recognize that the right to receive a payment under a contract could be passed by the contracting party to someone else – the assignee. They would only hear an action by one of the contracting parties, not by an assignee.

Thus if A and B make a contract under which A owes money when B has rendered a service, then the sequence of events might be:

B renders the service
B assigns the benefit of payment to C
A does not pay
C wants to bring an action against A.

No, said the law courts, we can only hear B in this court. B must obtain a judgement, get the money, and then give it to C. There is no legal assignment.

To fill this gap, equity gave an equitable remedy to C. So there was an equitable assignment.

The common law was modified in 1873 and confirmed in 1925. A legal assignment could after 1873 be obtained, on conditions; notice of assignment itself must be in writing, and it must be unconditional.

The bank is interested in the assignment of book debts (so are factors) and of life policies.

Charging the security

Now we look briefly at the charging of security against an advance. The customer has requested accommodation and answered the four questions to the satisfaction of the banker, who has then stipulated for security to be deposited. It is for the customer to say what security he has got, if any. Sometimes the security may be whatever he is going to buy with the money the bank is to lend him.

The customer may be an individual, which includes sole traders, partnerships, married women, minors, unincorporated associations, executors, trustees, solicitors, and many more; or a limited company which exists independently of the members who compose it. The banker has to know in each of these cases whether the borrower has legal power to borrow, and whether there are any obstacles in the way of getting his money back.

Bearer bonds

Bearer bonds are negotiable instruments. Ownership is passed from hand to hand and that act, as long as it is coupled with intention, will be enough to give the transferee a right to sell.

Contrast:

(1) A customer hands bearer bonds to his bank with the intention that they are to be security for a loan which the bank is granting the customer. This is acceptable, providing it is not a regulated agreement under the Consumer Credit Act. The bank has a right to sell the bearer bonds if the customer does not repay.

(2) A customer hands bearer bonds to his bank with the intention that the bank shall keep them in safe custody. The banker has no right of sale. The bearer bonds do not belong to him.

The bearer bond meets all three attributes of negotiability. These are:

(a) mere delivery transfers a legal title to the transferee

(b) no notice of the transfer need be given to the debtor

(c) the title passes free from equities (the transferee must give value and act in good faith).

Equities are counterclaims. Suppose company A issued a series of bearer bonds, and B possessed some of them. A is the debtor, B the creditor. But B also owes company A some money for work which the company has done for him.

B transfers the bonds for value to C, who receives them free of equities. He is not concerned with company A's claim against B, that is between the two of them. The existence of the counterclaim does not reduce the value of the bonds which he now holds.

Bearer bonds pay interest quarterly, half-yearly, or from time to time. In the latter case the company will advertise the next date of payment.

The company which issues the bonds has no idea who is holding them. There is no register or list of names of bond holders. As they are negotiable, and keep passing from hand to hand, it would be impossible to keep such a list. Therefore there has to be a system whereby the company knows to whom to send the interest each time it falls due. So each bearer bond has attached to it a number of tear-off coupons, rather like a sheet of stamps. The coupons are numbered.

The holder of the bonds sends to the company the correct coupon, just before interest is to be paid, and this is proof that he is entitled to receive the interest.

When borrowing from the bank against the security of bearer bonds, the customer will be asked to sign a memorandum of deposit, which in this case is mainly important because it is evidence of the intention of the customer. Then the customer can take his loan. The security has been perfected. It can be valued, from the Stock Exchange List, and it can be sold by the bank if necessary. The bank has the power of sale, and there is a ready market on the Stock Exchange.

While the bank holds the bearer bonds for the customer, the bank will tear off the coupons when they become due, submitting the coupons on the right date to the paying authority, collecting the proceeds, and crediting them to the customer's account.

Registered stocks and shares

Where the security offered is a registered stock or share certificate, the banker must think how he is going to put himself in a position to sell, if need be.

Stocks and shares are transferred from one person to another by completion of a stock transfer form, signed by the transferor, which is sent, together with the registered certificate which has on it the name of the transferor as owner of the shares, to the registrar of the company which has issued the shares. The transfer is registered in the books of the company and a new certificate is issued to the new owner, the old one being cancelled.

In effect then, the registered share certificate not being a negotiable instrument (the certificate does not pass from hand to hand on a change of ownership), the company concerned knows where the owners of all the shares are, and it keeps a list of the names. On receipt of the stock transfer form (comprising a request to transfer, a proof of intention, and an authority to the company) the company registrar simply crosses out one name against the numbers of the shares being sold or transferred, and writes in another.

The banker could get his customer to complete a stock transfer form in favour of the bank, take the registered share certificate, send both to the company registrar, and get the bank registered as owner. Then the banker could sell, if necessary. He would have taken a legal mortgage or charge over the shares. The customer would have lost his ownership and have left as his only interest in the shares a right to have them re-transferred to him when he has repaid the loan.

The banker may be content to take an equitable mortgage or charge. This would leave the customer as owner. Something, therefore, will have to be done about acquiring the right to sell, if necessary.

In each case, legal or equitable, the banker will take the customer's share certificate and will get the customer to sign a memorandum of deposit. In the case of a legal charge the banker will, as we have seen, send the certificate to the registrar of the company. In the case of an equitable charge he will just keep it. Having possession of it, the banker effectively stops the customer from charging it elsewhere; not that he would, of course, but it's part of banking to take no avoidable risks.

The memorandum of deposit has several clauses and does several things. We have seen that it establishes the intention of the customer to charge the named security – otherwise, of course, he wouldn't have signed the form. Another clause opens the door for the banker to acquire ownership later on, if need be, as a preliminary to selling the security. This clause extracts a promise from the customer that he will later sign anything which the bank wants in order to perfect its security. This would be a stock transfer form. A disadvantage is that the customer might refuse when the time comes, in which case the bank would have the trouble and expense of taking him to court. Another solution is to get the customer to sign a blank undated stock transfer form at the same time that he signs the memorandum of deposit, i.e. before he takes the borrowing. This blank stock transfer form can be held by the banker together with the share certificate against the possible day of need.

This leads us to the second rule of lending against security – always get the customer to sign anything or do anything that is necessary *before* any borrowing is taken. He may not be so willing afterwards.

In the preliminary negotiations the customer should be given to understand that the bank will let him know when the security has been perfected, and therefore when he is free to start taking the accommodation.

One danger with an equitable mortgage is that, unknown to the bank, a prior equitable interest may already exist. An example would be where the customer is in fact holding the shares as a trustee. If he does not disclose this, and if the share certificate does not describe him thereon as a trustee, the bank has no way of knowing. In such a case the earlier equitable interest (which would here belong to the beneficiaries under the trust) would take priority, to the detriment of the bank.

The only way to guard against this risk – which is negligible in the case of an honest customer – is to take a legal mortgage. If the customer is not honest he should not be an account holder.

Life policies

The bank must take from the customer his life policy, and get him to sign a form of assignment over the policy moneys. A life policy is not a negotiable instrument; it does not pass free from prior equities, and it is necessary to give notice to the debtor (the assurance company) in order to get a legal assignment. Only the latter will give the banker the right to sue the assurance company, in the (highly unlikely) event of its refusing to pay, in his own name.

The form of assignment is a notification by the creditor (the borrowing customer) to the debtor (the insurance company) that the debt (the policy moneys) is to be paid, if necessary, not to him but to a third party (the banker). This may be by payment of the surrender value on demand by the banker (the usual case where a borrowing is not repaid and the banker has to enforce his security), or by payment of the policy moneys on maturity, that is, when all the premiums have been paid. If then the policy moneys are still assigned to the lending banker, they will be paid to him and not to the policy holder (the customer).

Valuation is obtained by asking the company to state the surrender value of the life policy; saleability is assured by surrendering the policy to the company in return for payment to the bank of its value.

In the case of a life policy, prior equities are likely to be a previous loan from the company to the policy holder which is still outstanding. So the bank will enquire of the company if there are any prior assignments still outstanding, and at the same time ask the company to acknowledge the bank's interest.

The surrender value of a policy is its surrender value now – what the company would pay for it now if the policy were cashed in. The policy may be for £5,000 in twenty years' time, but its surrender value now may be only £100. It depends on how many premiums have been paid.

The banker must read the policy carefully. Not all types of policy are suitable as bank security, but the endowment policy, with or without profits, is excellent, as is a whole-life policy payable on the death of the assured person.

The assurance company should be reputable, and should the policy be expressed in a foreign currency, or payable abroad, extreme caution must be exercised to ensure that the currency is an international one. A margin must be allowed for exchange fluctuations. Additionally, it is possible that the country of origin of the policy has exchange control regulations that do not permit the transfer of funds without authority. Whenever the banker is offered a policy expressed in foreign currency, or payable abroad, some investigation must be made and each case considered on its merits.

Finally, to ensure that the surrender value of the policy increases, the banker would require proof that the premiums are paid on time. In order to do this, it would be usual for the banker to arrange payment either by standing order or by direct debit.

Guarantees

A guarantee is an undertaking to be responsible for the debt of another. The guarantor is to be called upon only if the principal debtor (the customer) fails to repay. The guarantee is an example of collateral security. To be collaterally responsible is to be responsible as a third party, as someone other than the person actually borrowing money. If that person – the principal debtor – were himself depositing security that would be direct security. If the security is collateral the third party cannot be made responsible if for any reason the principal debtor cannot legally be made to repay. If a limited company having no legal power to borrow nevertheless did so, against a guarantee given by a third party, the company could not be forced to repay because a court would hold that there was no (legal) debt, no debt that could be enforced in a court of law. So neither could the guarantor be made to pay.

To avoid this, the usual bank form of guarantee has an indemnity clause and in fact should be called an indemnity and not a guarantee. The indemnifier is responsible whatever happens. He says to the lender, 'lend my friend £100 and I will personally see that you suffer no loss, whatever the circumstances that may arise'. The guarantor says only, 'lend my friend £100 and if he does not repay you, I will'.

It is for the borrowing customer to name a person who is willing to stand as a guarantor for him. The two tests for any security – valuation and saleability – still apply. The valuation to be made by the manager is an assessment of the status of the proposed guarantor, who must be considered both able and willing to pay if called upon. If the manager has any doubts he can call upon the guarantor to deposit security in support of his guarantee.

Once the guarantor has been named the bank manager must confirm, by seeing him or writing to him, that he is willing to undertake the responsibility. The guarantor's bank must be written to for a report on his standing. This is the status enquiry. The answer should state that the guarantor is considered 'good' for the sum mentioned. Anything less positive than that will not do for an unsupported guarantee.

If the reply is satisfactory the guarantor will be invited to call at the branch, or at another branch more convenient to him, to sign the guarantee. His signature must be witnessed, and he has to come to the bank so that the bank can be quite certain that the signature they are getting is genuine and not forged. The person standing to benefit is the principal debtor, so the form of guarantee must never be given to him, although he may offer to get it signed for the bank. If a form of guarantee has to leave the branch it should go for signature to one of three places only: another branch, another bank (where there is no convenient branch of the lending bank), or to a solicitor known to be reliable (where there is no branch of any bank). If the solicitor is not known the bank must make a status enquiry on him before using him.

The signing of the guarantee initiates a contract of guarantee between the banker and the guarantor. Of course a contract of banking already exists between the banker and the principal debtor, his customer. The banker has duties in each case: a duty of care and secrecy towards his customer, and a duty not to mislead the guarantor. If the guarantor should sign the guarantee under a serious misapprehension of any kind he may later be able to get out of it, so the banker has to take great care that the guarantor is treated absolutely fairly before he signs. This means answering any relevant questions about the principal debtor and his account which the guarantor may ask. The guarantor is entitled to inform himself of any fact which is important in helping him to make up his mind whether to sign the guarantee or not. However, the bank manager does not have to volunteer information. His duty is only to answer truthfully any relevant questions which the guarantor may ask. Any more, and he might breach the duty of secrecy to his customer.

The guarantee is the easiest of all 'securities' to take – only a status enquiry to make and a form to be signed. The difficulty is always to impress on the guarantor the seriousness of the guarantee – he usually thinks it is just a temporary formality. If he does get called upon he seldom pays up immediately and without fuss.

The status enquiry should be repeated every six months during the currency of the loan, for a person's financial position may deteriorate.

If the banker has been unable to get a satisfactory status report from the guarantor's banker, and has therefore insisted on having security lodged in support, he must see that the guarantor also signs the appropriate form of charge for whatever the security may be – a memorandum of deposit, a form of assignment or mortgage – in addition to signing the form of guarantee. The security should be effected as though it were security for a direct borrowing by the guarantor.

Land

The proof of ownership of land is called the title to land.

Because of its peculiar importance, the person who owns land has to be able to prove that it came to him in a proper manner, and he has to show what has happened to the land for the last fifteen years, or even longer. Everyone has to have some interest in land, because they have got to live somewhere. If they own their own house, or if they are buying it on mortgage, or if they are renting it from someone else, or even if they have only one room in an apartment block, everyone has some claim on a piece of land.

The definition of land includes anything on it, principally, of course, houses, but trees and ponds and mines as well.

Land is state registered and the title to registered land is evidenced by a registered land certificate. The work of registering land titles has been going on for many years, and is nearly complete. There is some land still not registered, and the title to unregistered land is evidenced by a bundle of deeds. This system is a very old one and has to be understood as a preliminary to studying the rules for registered land.

Deeds

The borrower who offers title deeds as security must deposit them with the lending bank. The banker sends the deeds to a solicitor, who will check the title of the customer. The solicitor has to read all the deeds through, seeing that the titles of the various people who have held the land link up with each other for at least the last fifteen years. This is called the 'chain of title'. The deeds may include conveyances, mortgages, or assents. A conveyance is the deed whereby the ownership of the land passes from one person to another, usually when a house is sold. A mortgage is the deed which is signed by the parties when the land is used as security. An assent is the written authority of a personal representative passing the ownership of the land to the person to whom it has been left by the deceased, or to whom it passes, or descends, on his death. The title is said to 'vest' in the new owner if it has been properly passed to him.

The solicitor has to demonstrate a good chain of title for at least fifteen years, starting with what is called a 'good root' of title. The bank taking the title from the customer needs to be sure that the customer has a good right to it. The customer's title in turn depends on the title of the person who sold or passed the land to him, and so on. One cannot go back for ever, so the state has fixed this period of fifteen years, and a conveyance or mortgage at least fifteen years old will be the good root – the starting point for proving the title. A conveyance or mortgage is accepted as a good root because in either case money passed and therefore it is reasonably certain that the title was carefully checked then. The title is checked through the chain from the good root to the holding deed. The holding deed is the deed which vests the land in the present holder, who must be the bank's customer.

The solicitor has to make various searches, against the customer's name on the Land Charges Register (set up by act of parliament to record claims against land), to see if anyone has registered a claim there which would constitute a prior charge; and against the address of the property on the Town and Country Planning registers, to see if the property will be affected by the plans drawn up by the local authority for the future development of the area. These latter are called the 'local' searches.

All these searches must show that there is no claim registered against the property which can in any way detract from its value to the lending banker. Then the solicitor must see that the property is adequately insured against fire, and that notice of the bank's interest is given to the fire insurance company. In some cases banks will see to the insurance themselves.

Then the solicitor can write to the bank saying that as a result of the checks he has made he is satisfied that the bank will have a good and marketable title to the property. This is called his report on title.

The bank manager must look at the property and value it. If it is a long way from his branch he can get another manager, whose branch is near, to do it for him. The customer must sign another of the bank's forms, this time a mortgage of the property to the bank. The mortgage can be either legal, or equitable, just as in the case of stock exchange security. If it is legal, then the bank's form of charge is a conveyance, which is defined as the act of conveying real property (freehold land) from one person to another, or the deed by which it is transferred. The actual ownership of the land is transferred to the bank (or, for convenience, to its nominee company), and, if and when the customer repays his loan, the property will have to be reconveyed back again. If it is equitable, then the effect is that the borrowing customer retains the ownership but gives the bank certain rights over it which will enable the bank to sell the property, if this should prove necessary.

Obligations of mortgagor and mortgagee

As the object of a mortgage is merely to afford security to the mortgagee, any provision in the agreement between the parties which prevents the recovery of his property by the mortgagor after he has duly repaid his loan is normally repugnant to the law, for when performance is completed there is no longer any justification for the retention of the security by the mortgagee. The mortgagor therefore gives rights over his land, but he is always entitled to what is called 'the equity of redemption'. This right is lost by any of the following events:

(1) the release of the right by the mortgagor to the mortgagee, as long as this is the result of an independent bargain made subsequent to the mortgage deed
(2) the lapse of time under the Limitation Act, 1980
(3) a foreclosure decree obtained by the mortgagee.

It is therefore an obligation of the mortgagee to reconvey the property promptly as soon as repayment has been effected, and the bank mortgage forms have such a form of reconveyance printed on the back of the mortgage.

There is another obligation of the mortgagee, which comes at the beginning of the contract, and not, like the equity of redemption, at the end. It is to make the advance once he has agreed to do so.

The obligations of the mortgagor are, to pay the instalments of capital and interest promptly on the due dates, and to keep the property insured against fire and the usual other risks during the term of the mortgage.

The property may be freehold or leasehold. The land owner is said to own an estate in the land. An estate is the length of time for which an interest will exist or endure. A freehold estate is the best title to land that anyone can get, and is the nearest approach to absolute ownership.

A leasehold estate is created by a freeholder when he grants for a fixed number of years a right to another person to use and enjoy the land. The leaseholder may have a house on the land, and he may sell it in due course. The house may be sold several times, involving each time a new occupant. So a chain of title develops on the leasehold side, springing from the head lease, which is the document by which the original lease was granted. When the lease reaches the end of the fixed number of years the leaseholder then in possession has to hand back the land to the descendants in title of the original freeholder, and the lease is extinguished. (Arrangements may be made in some cases to renew the lease for a further period.)

When the security consists of leasehold deeds the solicitor will make the same checks as before, with one more. He must see that the ground rent is promptly paid, otherwise the freeholder can bring the lease to an end even though the full term has not been taken. This would mean the abrupt disappearance of the bank's security. Ground rent is paid annually. All the solicitor has to do, therefore, is to see the last receipt. Thereafter the bank must ask to see each one as it becomes available. Ground rent is rent which is payable to the freeholder by the person to whom the land has been leased.

Registered land

The system of deeds as evidence of title has disadvantages. The most serious is that the constant checking and re-checking of chains of title, as land continually changes hands, makes for a great deal of duplication of work, all of which has to be paid for.

Surely, people said, we can have a system of registration of title, like shares. The evidence of title can be a registered land certificate. Let the state investigate each title once more, for the last time. Let it then issue a certificate and guarantee it as correct. Then when land is sold all that need happen is that the state can call in the old certificate and issue a new one, just like a company does with share certificates.

This process of registering titles has been going on since 1925, and it is just about completed now. What the banker usually sees now, when his customer offers land as security, is a registered land certificate. Land is graded into two types of freehold land, and four types of leasehold. The most usual titles encountered are called absolute freehold and good leasehold.

The certificate is a copy of the entries concerning the land at the Land Registry, which is kept up to date with changes as they occur. When the certificate is issued it is up to date with the Register, but thereafter it will get out of date as fresh entries are put on the Register. Therefore there is provision for the certificate to be sent back to the Registrar at any time to be written up to date. Only titles to legal estates can be registered.

There are two ways of taking a registered land certificate as security, corresponding to the equitable mortgage and the legal mortgage. They are called 'deposit of the certificate protected by the notice of deposit' and 'registered' charge.

Deposit of the certificate protected by notice of deposit

The banker takes the certificate from the customer and inspects it. Like the register of which it is a copy, it is in three parts.

The Property Register gives the index letters and numbers assigned to the land (like a car number), a short description of the property (its address), states whether it is freehold or leasehold, and gives a reference to the official Land Registry general map for purposes of identification. That part of the map which includes the particular property is copied into the back of the land certificate as a scale plan.

The Proprietorship Register gives the name, address and the description of the proprietor, the date of registration, the consideration paid for the land last time it was sold, and the type of freehold or leasehold title.

The Charges Register gives details of charges affecting the land, such as mortgages.

The customer signs a form of legal charge containing provisions very similar to those found in a form of legal mortgage over deeds.

The banker must make a search to ensure that there are no prior claims against the land. He does this by sending the land certificate to the Registrar to have it written up to date. At the same time the banker completes and sends a special Land Registry form called Notice of Deposit. This form notifies the Registrar that the land holder has deposited the land certificate with the bank (as security for a loan) and therefore that the bank has an equitable claim against the land.

The Registrar puts this entry in the Charges section of the Register, writes the certificate up to date, to include the bank's charge, and sends the certificate back to the bank, where it is kept. The banker will see, by looking at the copy of the Charges section in the land certificate, whether his title is clear. His own notice of deposit should be entered therein, and this should be the only charge outstanding. The inside cover, where there is provision for a number of date stamps, will show the date up to which the land certificate has been made to correspond with the Register.

Thus the creation of an equitable mortgage is simple and easy, needing no solicitor's investigation. Local searches, fire insurance and valuation are attended to as with deed security. If the land is leasehold, the last ground rent receipt must be seen.

Registered charge

The customer signs a form of legal mortgage. The banker takes the customer's land certificate and makes a search on the Land Register, using a special Land Registry form for this purpose. He does not now search by having the land certificate written up to date because, as will be seen in a moment, he will send it to the Land Registrar and won't get it back.

A duplicate of the Land Registry search form is returned to the banker, and should show that there are no prior claims against the land on the Register. If this is so, the banker will take the form of mortgage, prepare an office copy of it, and send both to the Registrar together with the land certificate and the appropriate fee for registration.

The registrar will keep the land certificate and the copy mortgage. He will make the appropriate entry in the Register, and then issue to the banker a document called a Charge Certificate, which will have the original form of mortgage stitched inside. This is the evidence of the bank's legal mortgage. The evidence of the customer's land holding – the registered land certificate – is withdrawn from circulation and kept at the Land Registry. The Charge Certificate has taken its place. When the customer has repaid, the bank will notify the Registrar that the Charge Certificate can be cancelled and the land certificate returned to the customer.

As before, the banker must attend to the local searches, the valuation, the fire insurance, and (if the land is leasehold) the ground rent receipts.

The work of the Land Registry has been decentralized and there are several District Land Registries, each handling the registration of titles within its own district.

Limited companies

Although it is not possible in a work of this nature to go minutely through every detail which must be seen to where the borrower is in a special class, such as executors, solicitors, unincorporated associations, and so on, something should be said about limited companies as borrowers because of their importance.

Limited companies exist as separate entities, and it is this entity which in law is borrowing from the banker, although the negotiations will be carried out by the company's agents, the directors, as it cannot speak for itself.

In all cases the first step for the banker is to check from the Memorandum of Association that the company has power to borrow, and that the declared purpose for which the loan moneys are required is within the objects of the company. Then he must check from the Articles of Association that the directors are empowered to commit the company and that no general meeting of the company to consider and authorize the borrowing is required. This is in spite of the protection given to lenders advancing money to companies which is afforded by legislation passed consequent upon the entry of this country into the European Economic Community. That legislation appears to make some of the checks mentioned unnecessary, but it is thought that until some experience has been gained of the working of the new law it is best to play safe and stick to the old routines.

In the case of a guarantee to be given by the company, the banker must check from the Memorandum of Association that the company has power to give guarantees. A company is in general forbidden to give a guarantee to secure any loan to any person or body for the purpose of buying that company's shares or stock, nor may it, except in special circumstances, guarantee a loan to one of its own directors.

Most shares of private companies are unsuitable security because they cannot be easily valued. The Companies Act, 1985, has allowed the transfer or sale of shares of private companies, but for all practical purposes it would be difficult to find a buyer.

With the introduction of the Unlisted Securities Market, the smaller companies have taken the opportunity of having their shares quoted in this area of the Stock Exchange, so that a valuation is readily available on a growing sector of limited companies.

Nearly all charges given by a limited company require registration within twenty-one days at the Companies Registry at Companies House. The exceptions are charges on stocks and shares, on negotiable instruments, on a life policy, on documents of title to goods, or on a policy issued by the Export Credits Guarantee Department.

It may be thought strange that an artificial entity such as a company can offer a life policy as security, but it is quite possible, though rare. Some companies maintain policies on the lives of the company directors, because of the special importance to the company of the work which the directors are doing. It is one of these policies which the company may offer.

The Companies House Register will contain for any company not only details of charges given by the company, but also copies of any special resolutions passed, copies of the last profit and loss accounts and balance sheet – anything which is of real importance, in fact. Any person thinking of lending to a company should, therefore, 'make a search' against it at Companies House. This is done by making a personal visit to the Registry and paying a small fee. On request one is then given access to the company's file and from that one can see what charges, if any, it has already given and what its balance sheet position is. From this a prospective lender can check that any security offered has not already been charged, and, in general, what the prospects of repayment are.

The administration and registration of limited companies, which used to be in City Road, London EC1, moved to Cardiff in 1976. In that year microfilm reading was introduced: in return for the standard search fee copies of the original documents are supplied on microfiche, which can be taken away. Full-sized copies of the filmed documents are available from microfilm printers which the searcher can operate himself. A reading room is provided at Companies House in City Road and facilities are available there and at Cardiff.

The most usual security offered by a company is its land. Every company has to have a headquarters. Land is one of those securities where a charge has to be registered at Companies House. Once on the file there, a charge is available for anyone to see. Certain charges are regularly noted in certain trade journals, and some publicity is unavoidable. Most companies strongly resent this publicity, because it allows their trade competitors to see that the company has had to borrow money. For this reason a borrowing company may well ask its banker to lend on terms that will not necessitate registration.

Such requests take the form of a proposed deposit by the company with the bank of the registered land certificate with a written undertaking to execute a formal mortgage over the land if the bank ever so requires, or a proposed deposit of the land certificate with a completed form of mortgage accompanied by a request not to register it.

The effect of the relevant section of the Companies Act is that failure to register such a charge has no penalties unless the company should go into liquidation. In such an event, however, the lending banker who has acquiesced in non-registration would have to give up his security to the liquidator for the benefit of the company creditors generally. He would become an unsecured creditor.

The banker knows this, yet he wants to oblige his customer. If the company is a strong one and most unlikely ever to go into liquidation the banker will probably be happy to accept an undertaking to charge if ever required to do so, plus a deposit of the land certificate.

Debentures

A debenture is a type of security which can be given only by a limited company. A debenture in itself is merely an acknowledgement of an indebtedness. The usual type of debenture found in banking business is a mortgage debenture, that is, a debenture accompanied by a charge over the assets of the borrowing company. A fixed charge covers the fixed assets of the company, such as its land, and a floating charge covers the floating assets of the company, such as its raw materials in store, or stock in hand. Where the mortgage debenture is worded to provide security for any sums owing by the company to the bank, on any account, at any time, it is called an 'all moneys' debenture. This is the usual banking security. It is taken under seal and makes the entire assets of the company subject to the charge. Its terms will specify that the debenture shall be a first charge on the undertaking and property of the company. It will be drawn in favour of the bank and will stipulate that the loan is repayable on demand. It should include a legal mortgage over the company's real property, and the relative deeds should be deposited at the bank. Where land is concerned the bank will take all the steps it would take if it were taking a specific charge over land, including the completion of the bank's form of mortgage to supplement the debenture. This form of mortgage will have to be produced to the Chief Land Registrar when the charge is registered with him. He will not act on the debenture, in which the land is not described in detail.

This is the fixed charge. Thereafter the company cannot deal in any way with any of the fixed assets without prior consent of the bank.

The debenture deed then proceeds to give a floating charge on the other company assets, but the company must be left free to deal with these, for this is necessary in its business. One cannot take a fixed charge on the company's stock, and forbid the company to deal with it. On the contrary, repayment can only be hoped for if the company does deal with its stock, that is sells it. A manufacturing company buys raw materials, converts them into work-in-progress, and then into finished stock. It then sells this stock, at a profit. With the proceeds it buys more raw materials, and starts the process all over again. The raw materials come under the 'umbrella' of the floating charge as soon as they are bought, and finished stock passes out from under it as soon as it is sold. As long as the company continues to trade normally, and as long as it continues to meet the repayments on its loan satisfactorily, and pays the interest, this process will continue. But if anything happens to cause the bank to demand repayment and to put a receiver in, the floating charge will 'solidify' or 'crystallize' and catch the floating assets which happen to be there on the day the receiver is appointed. The same thing will happen if the company ceases business, or goes into liquidation.

The bank is given power by the debenture to put in its own receiver where the company has defaulted, and he will administer the assets so as to apply them towards repayment of the bank advance. The debenture will list the events which will force the bank to take this step. These usually include failure to respond to a formal demand for repayment made by the bank, default in payment of interest by the company for a specified number of months, the cessation of business by the company, the commencement of winding up, the attempted alteration of the company's Memorandum or Articles of Association in a manner which would be harmful to the bank's interest, or the appointment of a receiver by some other creditor or by the court.

The power to give a debenture is limited to a company. A trader with a hotel business might wish to borrow, and could suggest as part security the stock of furniture, etc. – beds, carpets, linen, everything wanted for running a hotel – which he possessed. The bank would refuse as this is not a type of security in which it is interested. But if the trader turns his business into a limited company, and gives the bank a debenture, the furniture is included along with all other assets.

Other forms of security

Frequently, a bank is offered a building society passbook, a book containing National Savings Certificates, National Savings Bank passbook, or any other form of savings from the Department of National Savings.

Banks are reluctant to take these items as security as it is not often possible to register their interest with the financial institution concerned. Thereby the charge that they would like to register could or would be ignored.

For example, a person may wish to borrow a sum of money from a bank for the purchase of a consumer durable item, but does not wish to use funds he holds in a building society. However, in order to show good faith with the bank he is willing to offer the book and the balance of funds as security. The bank manager will use his discretion and, if he is willing to sanction the loan, he will accept the building society passbook with a signed but undated withdrawal form under cover of a memorandum of deposit. He might even notify the building society that he is holding the passbook, which may be recorded or not depending on the policy of the building society.

Any item of deposit representing savings with the Department of National Savings cannot be registered with that department. Again, at the manager's discretion, a passbook or certificate may be held as possible security, with a withdrawal form in case of need.

These items are of little use to the manager, but give an indication to the bank that the customer is honest and willing to repay the loan in accordance with the arrangements. Should he default, the bank can but try to obtain repayment of the capital and interest due, by presenting the withdrawal form and passbook to the building society or Department of National Savings and obtaining funds from this quarter.

Farming advances

Country banks may find their business predominantly agricultural, for in general banks are both able and willing to meet all applications by credit-worthy farmers for short-, medium- and long-term credit. The nature of the farming to be followed will determine the picture presented by the farmer's banking account. Arable farming will show a yearly cycle as the crops are sown and harvested; sheep farming produces lambs annually and shearing too is done annually. At the other extreme eggs are laid daily and quickly sold, milk sold to the Milk Marketing Board will be paid for by monthly cheque, and so on.

Long-term lending must be for the purchase of a farm (an expensive operation in view of the price of good farming land) or for major long-term improvements to the farm, i.e. irrigation. The security must be the deeds or the land certificate relating to the farm, and will be perfected like any other land security.

However, the valuation of such land, done either professionally or by the bank manager visiting the farm, presents a number of features which would be quite strange to a city manager accustomed to valuing houses. Although there must be a farm house on the property, this will not normally be so important; what matters is the quality of the land and the acreage involved. The visiting manager will assess the quality of the soil. Heavy clay is difficult to break up for cultivation, on the other hand light soil dries out quickly in drought or hot weather and starves root crops of water. A good, deep, easily-worked loam is ideal.

He hopes to find that the farmland is reasonably level, with good drainage. On steep slopes water will run off before it can sink in to nourish the crops. He looks for roads which will be needed to bring manure and fertilizer in, and harvested crops out. The site should be near a source of labour if many hands are required. Farm buildings should be adequate for the type of farming intended to be pursued. A large arable farm, for example, should have grain drying and storage facilities if the farmer is to be free to sell his product at the time most advantageous to him. The farm should be a compact unit, easily worked. It should generally be in a good state of cultivation and repair, with hedges and ditches properly maintained.

Such advances are technically subject to annual review, but repayment would not normally be expected until the farm was sold.

Medium- and short-term or seasonal lending is usually unsecured, and normally granted by way of overdraft. The farmer is basically an honest person and the banker knows this and places reliance on it. Farming is more than an occupation – it is a way of life. The bank manager has to commit himself fully to what is a specialized situation; he must judge his borrower as a man and meet him on his farm and in the marketplace rather than in his own office. The manager, when examining the statement of assets and liabilities or balance sheet, should know enough about farming and agriculture to check the farmer's book values. This will be done by visual inspection when he 'walks' the farm.

The valuation of growing crops varies as the season progresses, so it is essential to obtain the statement at the same time each year, otherwise the figures cannot meaningfully be compared. This will be easier if a time is chosen when the growing crops are at a minimum. The valuation of farm animals will be governed by market prices, but may be difficult where pedigree animals are concerned. The bank manager must keep in touch by reading the farming journals, keeping up with the local press, visiting the markets to note the prices obtained, and by nurturing frequent contacts with local farmers. He will have the advantage of having many farms and farmers on his books, so that he can compare the performance of one with another.

When the bank manager has arrived at what he is satisfied is a fair figure for the total assets of his farming customer, he can check that the overdraft is a reasonable one. The annual assets and liabilities figures, or audited accounts if the farmer uses a professional accountant, will indicate whether the borrowing situation is improving or deteriorating, and may suggest measures which should be taken for the future.

The vast majority of farming advances are to owner-occupiers. Farms can be let, however, and the tenant farmer is protected to the extent that he cannot be evicted unless he is judged to be farming badly, or unless he is not paying his rent. He should make improvements to the land as he farms, for instance by sowing seed and digging in manure, and if he has to leave the farm he is entitled to an allowance for such improvements, to be paid by the owner of the land. This is called 'tenant right', the compensation for the unexhausted manure and the crops left to be harvested by his successor. On the other hand, the outgoing tenant has a liability for dilapidations and this liability forms a set off to his tenant right.

Agricultural charges

An Act of 1928 provided for the setting up of the Agricultural Mortgage Corporation. It also dealt with agricultural short-term credits. It provided for any farmer to create an agricultural charge in favour of a bank on the farming stock and agricultural assets belonging to the farmer, as security for any money lent to him. This wording covered, and the security was appropriate to, either a tenant farmer or the owner of the holding. The agricultural charge was to be a fixed charge upon the farming stock and other agricultural assets belonging to the farmer at the date of the charge and specified in the charge, or a floating charge upon the farming stock and other agricultural assets from time to time belonging to the farmer, or both.

The sum secured was to be either a specified sum, or a fluctuating amount advanced on current account.

The floating charge would crystallize over the various assets in such circumstances as the death of the farmer, or the making of a receiving order against him, and the banker would then be entitled to put in a receiver to collect his assets.

The agricultural charge was therefore very similar to a debenture given by a limited company.

Neither the farmer nor the banker has looked upon this system with very much favour. The farmer objects to signing away his assets, as he sees it, and prefers his banker to trust him. The banker finds from experience that the cases where the security has had to be claimed show that, by the time the receiver gets there, the floating assets have all gone anyway. Pressing creditors have caused the farmer to dissipate these assets in an effort to satisfy them.

Agricultural charges have to be registered within seven days with the Agricultural Credits Superintendent at the Land Registry. Very few are now registered each year.

Other sources of finance for farmers

The government recognizes the importance of the farmers' worth to the nation and gives a degree of preferential treatment by way of grants and in other ways. One company sponsored by the National Farmers' Union, the Agricultural Credit Corporation, assists farmers to obtain bank credit by offering to guarantee advances made to finance a programme of agreed improvements on the farm. A condition is that the farmer shall accept specialist advice cn the best way of carrying out these improvements. The government will meet part of any sums which this company has to pay to banks in cases where its guarantees are called upon.

Another national institution is the Lands Improvement Company, which was formed more than a century ago and is still in operation. It makes loans for up to twenty years to farmers for land purchase, including bridging advances; improvements to farms and estates, including buildings, houses, cottages, fencing, drainage, tree planting, roads, etc; repayment of other borrowings; purchase of machinery and equipment; taxation, including Capital Transfer Tax; and any item eligible for a grant under the Farm and Horticulture Development scheme and the Farm Capital Grant scheme. Specialist intensive livestock and horticultural proposals will not normally be approved unless supported by a reasonable amount of ordinary agricultural land. Loans are for a minimum of £25,000 and are normally limited to a maximum of two-thirds of the value of the security offered.

Variable rate loans carry an interest charge related to the company's base rate. Fixed rate loans may also be negotiated. Repayment is in full at the end of the term, or by annual or half-yearly instalments.

The Land Improvement group may also buy on leaseback farms requiring improvement.

Syndicates and co-operatives

Modern conditions in farming are still putting the small man out of business. Syndicates of up to twenty farmers are formed for joint ownership and use of farm machinery and equipment, such as a combine harvester which is expensive but only needed for a period once a year. A system of syndicate credit has grown up, financed by county central organizations, registered as limited companies and themselves borrowing most of the required funds from the banks.

Another co-operative activity concerns the buying of farming requirements in bulk, and therefore at cheaper rates and the selling of produce to the markets in bulk.

Revision test 13

Place a tick against the letter you consider is the correct answer.

1 The valuation of some securities can fluctuate from day to day. Does this apply to:
   (a) stock exchange securities?
   (b) life policies?
   (c) land?

2 Assurance policy moneys are
   (a) mortgaged by way of security
   (b) assigned by way of security
   (c) pledged by way of security.

3 No right of sale accrues to the creditor who has
   (a) a mortgage
   (b) a pledge
   (c) a lien.

4 The lending banker takes a pledge when the customer charges
   (a) bearer bonds
   (b) a life policy
   (c) shares in a limited company.

5 Negotiable instruments include
   (a) bills of lading
   (b) certificates of deposit
   (c) registered land certificates.

6 An advance is always granted when
   (a) the customer has more than adequate security
   (b) the customer has the ability to repay
   (c) the customer has a good safe job.

7 When the bank requires a guarantor to sign the form of guarantee it will
   (a) hand it to the customer requesting him to obtain the guaran-
       tor's signature
   (b) send it by post direct to the guarantor
   (c) request the guarantor to come to the bank.
8 A mortgage debenture is
   (a) a promise from the board of directors of a company to repay
       a loan within the agreed time
   (b) the charge over the personal assets of a company director
       when lending to a company
   (c) the charge taken over the assets of a company.
9 A bridging loan from the bank's point of view is often
   (a) simple, profitable, and self-liquidating
   (b) profitable, self-liquidating, but needs registering
   (c) simple, profitable, but is usually repayable in the long term.
10 One of the first questions asked by a banker when confronted
   by a request for a loan is:
   (a) how much security is available?
   (b) do you own your own house or business?
   (c) what is the source of repayment?

Questions for discussion

1 Discuss the acceptability of the following items as security for
   an advance to an individual:
   (a) guarantees
   (b) life policies
   (c) krugerrands.
2 Discuss the advantages and disadvantages from (a) the customer's point of view and (b) the banker's point of view of
   (i) a personal loan
   (ii) a loan.
3 You have been asked by a person to accept his National Savings
   Certificates worth £1,000 and his building society passbook
   with a balance of £3,000 as security for a loan of £3,500 for the
   purchase of a motor car for personal and social purposes. What
   particular points would you take into consideration regarding
   the loan and the security offered?

14

The balance sheets of customers

The final accounts of a business, so called because they are made up only at the end of each trading year, consist of a manufacturing account, if this is appropriate to the business, the trading account, the profit and loss account, and, except in the accounts of a sole trader, the profit and loss appropriation account.

Manufacturing account

The manufacturing account shows the direct cost of the production of the goods, starting with the cost of the raw materials used, and of their transport into the factory, then those items which comprise the direct cost of production, e.g. fuel, power, direct labour costs, etc. Other indirect factory costs are included such as depreciation of factory and machines, indirect labour, etc. In order to arrive at the manufacturing costs, it is essential that only those items relevant to the factory and production should be included. Other costs such as administration, selling and distribution are shown in the profit and loss account.

From time to time a business will have a considerable amount of work which has passed from the raw materials stage but has not, by the date of the account, reached the status of finished stock. The work-in-progress or partly finished goods are valued at cost of raw materials plus an element of labour and are shown as a credit item in the manufacturing account.

Trading account

The trading account is compiled to show the gross profit or loss of the trading period under review. In the case of a manufacturing company

Example of a manufacturing account

	£		£
Opening stock of raw materials	4,000	Cost of production	75,000
Purchases	20,000		
Carriage inwards	400		
	24,400		
Less			
Closing stock of raw material	2,000		
Raw materials used	22,400		
Manufacturing wages	48,000		
Prime cost	70,400		
Factory lighting and heating	800		
Power	400		
Depreciation of plant	2,400		
	74,000		
Add work in progress at start	2,000		
Less work in progress at end	1,000		
	£75,000		£75,000

Example of a trading account

	£	£
Sales		162,000
Stock: balance 1 January	56,000	
Manufacturing account	75,000	
	131,000	
Less stock 31 December	51,000	
Cost of goods sold		80,000
Gross profit to profit and loss account		£82,000

the stock will come from the factory, and the amount coming into the trading account will be the same as that shown as going out in the manufacturing account. In a trading company, as opposed to a manufacturing company, the item which will replace the cost of manufacture will be shown as purchases less any returns, plus the cost of any carriage and other expenses to bring the goods to the shop or warehouse.

Profit and loss account

The gross profit from the trading account is credited to this account together with any unusual or non-recurring items of gains from sources other than normal trading – for example, a profit from the sale of an asset. The debit side will show the overhead and administrative charges incurred during the year, plus financial charges, e.g.

Example of a profit and loss account

	£	£
Balance of gross profit		82,000
Discounts received		4,960
		86,960
Rent and rates	1,360	
Office salaries	41,840	
Insurance	840	
Printing and stationery	1,960	
Office expenses	12,360	
Discount allowed	6,800	
Bad debts	3,360	
Provision for bad debts	360	
Depreciation: fixtures and fittings	280	
		69,160
Net profit to capital account		£17,800

Example of a profit and loss appropriation account

	£	£
Net profit for the year		48,600
Taxation		20,800
Net profit after tax		27,800
Balance from previous year		7,400
		35,200
Proposed dividend	19,200	
Reserves	8,000	
		27,200
Balance carried forward		£8,000

interest on bank loans/overdrafts and any depreciation of fixed assets and the amount of provisions for bad and doubtful debts. The balance of this account is the net profit, which forms the basis for the calculation made for charge of tax on the firm. The profit or loss to the business of a sole trader is usually transferred to his capital account, which will in the case of a profit increase the amount he has in the business, or in the case of a loss reduce his capital in the business. A limited company will open an appropriation account which will show what actually happened to the net profit. The opening balance from the previous year is brought forward, added to the current profit. The distribution of the total amount is then decided by the directors of the company, and must include the corporation tax and proposed dividends, and the remainder is retained in the business and shown as reserves. Any remaining balance in the profit and loss account is shown in the balance sheet.

Balance sheets of sole traders, partnerships and limited companies

When summing up a balance sheet it is important to distinguish between the figures of a sole trader, a partnership and a limited company. The balance sheet of a sole trader will disclose only those assets which are being used in the business and will not mention the assets and liabilities which the trader may have in his private life. Thus he may own a house and a car, and perhaps have a life policy with a good surrender value. He may also have mortgage payments and hire purchase commitments to meet.

As he is fully liable for the debts of his business his creditors would in case of need have recourse against all his private assets as well as those shown in the balance sheet. Usually, therefore, the position is rather stronger than it appears to be from the balance sheet.

The basic accounts of a partnership are very similar to those of a sole trader, but with two or more partners interested in the business the final accounts must show figures denoting their respective rights as to capital and profit. The firm's balance sheet will show all the partnership liabilities and all the assets of the firm available to meet them, but, as with the balance sheet of the sole trader, it will not show the private assets and liabilities of the parties.

Only the balance sheet of a company shows the complete position. Creditors have no claim beyond the assets there shown, unless a company is unlimited, or limited by guarantee. Only the balance sheet of a company must have attached the certificate of a qualified auditor. This gives a real protection to both creditors and shareholders.

Structure of a company balance sheet

The structure of a balance sheet is not laid down in any act of parliament, but the information contained therein is subject to the Companies Act, 1985. It would be true to say that you will find many balance sheets presented in horizontal form, rather like that of the balance sheet of a bank, showing the liabilities on the left-hand side and the assets on the right-hand side. But having said that, there is a slow movement towards continental and American presentation, showing the assets on the left-hand side (the same side as debit balances in a ledger) and the liabilities and capital on the right-hand side (the same side as credit balances in a ledger).

Most public companies – these are companies that have the letters plc after their name – present the balance sheet in vertical form. That is showing the capital and its structure, and how that capital is utilized in fixed assets and working capital. Due to the legal requirements, large public companies will set out the information required in the form of notes, so that the balance sheet itself will merely specify the asset or liability and the appropriate note will set out the information that is legally required.

Balance sheet terms defined

Capital

The capital of a company is shown in two forms. The first is the authorized capital, that is, the maximum amount of shares that can be issued as laid down in the Memorandum of Association. The issued capital is the actual number of shares issued to shareholders. The issued capital can be the same as the authorized capital, or less, but it can never exceed the authorized capital. The issued capital is

Example of a vertical balance sheet of a limited company

		£	£
Capital employed	Preference capital		1,740
	Ordinary capital		33,719
	Reserves and retained profits		46,263
	Shareholders' funds		81,722
	Loan capital		63,542
			£145,264
Employment of capital	Land, buildings, plant and equipment		49,345
	Investments in subsidiaries		72,275
	Other investments		3,897
	Fixed assets		125,517
Current assets	Stocks	16,009	
	Debtors	13,089	
	Deposits	9,835	
	Cash	876	
		39,809	
Current liabilities	Creditors	11,788	
	Overdraft	2,054	
	Dividends	6,220	
		20,062	
Net current assets			19,747
			£145,264

shown as an integral part of the balance sheet, showing not only the number of shares issued but the nominal value of each share and the type, e.g. ordinary and/or preference share.

The ordinary shares, often called the risk capital or equity, are the most common type of share. The ordinary shareholder will buy these shares knowing that in years of good profits he will receive high dividends and possibly an increase in the value of his shares, i.e. £1 share can be worth more than £1 in the market; while in bad years he will receive a lower dividend, or perhaps no dividend, and the value of his investment can drop substantially.

However, the ordinary shareholder has the right to vote at the annual general meeting and usually has one vote for every share he possesses.

The preference shareholder has preference over the ordinary shareholder to the extent that he will receive his dividend before the ordinary shareholder, and should the company go into liquidation he will receive the return of his capital first. As the dividend of the preference shareholder is fixed, the share is quoted as a percentage of the nominal amount, e.g. 10% Preference Shares £1 fully paid. That is, he will receive 10 per cent each year, paid in two instalments.

Another type of preference share is the cumulative preference share. With this type of share, if no dividend is paid one year then double is paid the second year, and so on. Until the dividends due to the preference shareholder are paid, no dividend is paid to the ordinary shareholder.

The third type of preference share is the redeemable share. That is, at some future date, the shares will be repaid by the company. This is shown as follows: 10% Redeemable Preference Shares 1999.

Finally, there can be a combination of all three types: 10% Cumulative Redeemable Preference Shares 1999.

To this paid-up capital must be added any retention of profits either made from normal business or from the sale of an asset. This profit retention is shown as a reserve, either capital or revenue. The total of capital and reserves belong to the owners of the company and is shown in the balance sheet as 'shareholders' funds'. Should the reserves grow beyond a reasonable amount, it is customary to issue bonus shares to members; this is called a scrip issue.

Long-term liabilities

Under this heading come liabilities which are not repayable at short notice. This will include such items as secured or unsecured loans obtained either from the public, banks, or other concerns.

Current liabilities

Current liabilities are debts arising in the normal course of business, such as debts due to trade and hire purchase creditors, or sums owing to the bank. All these debts have to be paid in the next twelve months, i.e. before the next balance sheet can be expected.

Fixed assets

Fixed assets are those which have been acquired for the purpose of carrying on the business of the company, and which will not be resold, but kept in permanent use until they wear out. They will make production possible. A manufacturing company must have a factory, plant and machinery, and vehicles. The office staff must have furniture and office equipment. These are fixed assets. Without them no production would be possible. All these assets are shown in the balance sheet at cost less aggregate depreciation, i.e. at the current book value.

Floating assets

Floating or current assets are those bought so that they may pass through the normal business cycle and then be sold for cash. Floating assets do not stay with the company long. They are sometimes called quick, liquid or circulating assets.

Fictitious assets

Under this heading we speak of intangible assets such as patents, trademarks or goodwill; and fictitious assets such as preliminary expenses when a company is being formed. The money has been spent and therefore has to appear somewhere, but the fictitious asset has no value and will be written out of the balance sheet as soon as the company has made sufficient profits. Intangible assets, on the other hand, have a real value, sometimes considerable value.

Working capital

The sum which must finance the day-to-day operations of the company is called the working capital. This can be thought of as the money which is left over after the fixed capital has been brought in and the fixed assets bought and paid for. Another way of arriving at the same result is to subtract the current liabilities from the current assets. The layout of the balance sheet is designed to make it easy to do this quickly.

If the company has insufficient working capital, it has spent too much on buying fixed assets and as a result will be permanently short of ready cash. It will be obliged to rely on trade debtors paying up promptly, or on the bank letting it go over the top of the overdraft limit. This condition is called 'overtrading'. There is no cure, except an injection of fresh cash into the company. If creditors, who have of necessity been left unpaid too long, press their legal rights against the company there is a danger that the company will be forced into liquidation.

What a sufficiency of working capital is will depend on the type of company and its financial policy.

Lending against a balance sheet

The question for the lending banker is whether the company's position, as disclosed by the balance sheet, is sufficiently strong to justify an advance unsecured in another way, or whether, should the advance be granted, it be on the condition that security be lodged in support. One balance sheet on its own is useful, but gives only a picture at one moment in time; it is better to have balance sheets for the last three years, so that the trend of the company's business can be estimated. Three years' profit figures will show whether profits are increasing or the reverse; three years' turnover figures will show the general progress or otherwise of the company.

The banker will look first for a satisfactory liquid position. Floating assets less current liabilities will show, amongst other things, whether the company has adequate working capital. Can it pay all its creditors without difficulty and go on with its business in the normal manner? Other points will be whether the balance is properly certified by a qualified auditor, what the distribution of the debtors is (well spread, rather than a few big debts), whether proper provision has been made for tax, and what claims there might be against the company which would have priority over the bank. Machinery, plant and similar assets should be regularly written down to provide for depreciation and a reserve fund established for their replacement. Reserves, whether for specific purposes such as future tax, or for the purpose of providing a fund for general unforeseen expenditure or loss, should be invested outside the business in sound securities bearing interest, and not left in the business as part of the working capital. If the latter is the case it is possible that the money may be difficult to get at when it is wanted.

Interpretation of balance sheets

In order to assist the bank official to interpret the trends of the business and understand the accounts presented, it is necessary not only to be able to calculate certain ratios and percentages and examine the trends, but to apply this useful information so that the lending risk is reduced to the minimum.

The basic ratios and percentages to be examined are as follows.

Gross profit as a percentage of turnover

$$\frac{\text{Gross profit} \times 100}{\text{Turnover}} = \text{per cent}$$

The gross profit which is found in the trading account is compared with the turnover, and the percentage figure can be compared, first, against the corresponding figures of the years before, and, secondly, with those of similar businesses in the same area. Where market conditions are uniform similar businesses should show similar percentages.

If the value of the percentage is low it would indicate that the cost of the purchases and/or production costs have risen and these costs have not been passed on to the customers. On the other hand, the volume of sales may be the same, but there may have been a deliberate policy of management to reduce the selling price in order to attract custom, which is taking some time to pay off. Alternatively, if the percentage of gross profit to sales is high, this could mean perhaps an overvaluation of the closing stock or an increase in the selling price of the goods.

Many factors should be considered if the trend of this percentage radically alters.

Net profit as a percentage of sales

$$\frac{\text{Net profit} \times 100}{\text{Turnover}} = \text{per cent}$$

Where this percentage is a falling one, the explanation must lie in the profit and loss account. A survey of the main charges to the account and a comparison with previous years will suggest possible further enquiries. A large figure for bad and doubtful debts may indicate slack credit control. Unduly high figures for expenses or entertainment may indicate extravagance on the part of the management. The total of administrative costs may appear to be out of all proportion to the turnover figure.

Net profit to shareholders' funds

'Shareholders' funds' includes not only the share capital issued but must include the reserves, which after all belong to the shareholders. The regular increase of the reserves indicates to the lending banker that a given percentage of the profits has been retained in the business for expansion purposes and therefore implies that the management of the company are prudent. The bank would probably be more willing to lend under these circumstances. The formula for ascertaining this percentage is as follows:

$$\frac{\text{Net profit before tax} \times 100}{\text{Shareholders' funds}} = \text{per cent}$$

For the sole trader, he must compare his return from the business with the possibility of being a wage/salary earner in a similar trade or profession and investing his capital in some relatively risk-free venture, e.g. building society, or gilts. Should it be possible to earn a larger gross amount by obtaining employment elsewhere, the sole trader might be tempted to do just that.

Credit given by creditors and credit given to debtors

$$\frac{\text{Creditors} \times 52}{\text{Purchases}} = \text{weeks} \qquad \frac{\text{Debtors} \times 52}{\text{Turnover}} = \text{weeks}$$

A comparison between the average length of time which is taken by the company before paying its suppliers, and the average period of credit which the company allows its customers, may show that the creditors are waiting a long time for their money but that the debtors are being pressed to pay more quickly. This would suggest that the company is short of working capital and showing the first signs of overtrading.

Again, each ratio considered on its own may give valuable indications.

Credit periods differ in different trades, but normally there should be about one month's creditors outstanding. If the creditors appear excessive in comparison with purchases, enquiry should be made of the customer to ascertain the reason. It may be that the company has spent too much on acquiring stock and left itself with insufficient working capital to pay creditors at the right time. This test should show that the total of trade creditors is reasonable, and that payment is being made to them out of normal trading receipts in the normal working of the business cycle.

The comparison of debtors with sales turnover should confirm that the customer is allowing that period of credit which is normal for the business and no more. If the period of credit is greater than it should be, it may mean that there is slackness in the collection of debts, of which debtors are naturally taking advantage; or it may mean, more seriously, that some debtors are finding it difficult to pay. Slow payment for goods supplied points to a risk of bad debts. Reference to previous profit and loss accounts will show the customer's previous experience with bad debts, and it may be that outstanding items are being retained on the books long after they should have been written off. This in turn will raise the questions of whether the reserve for bad debts is reasonable, and whether the customer is making proper status enquiries through his banker before accepting new orders. In general, debtors should be well spread. Unduly large debtors may attract special enquiry as to whether payment is reasonably certain. If goods are sold on hire purchase terms, cash debtors and hire purchase debtors should be shown separately in the balance sheet, so that the extent of the credit allowed to the hire purchasers may be seen. If too much working capital is engaged in this way there may be less than sufficient to sustain the remainder of the business.

Working capital

The working capital is calculated by deducting the current liabilities (creditors, taxation and other expenses due to be paid) from current assets (stock, debtors and cash balances). This amount – often calculated as a ratio – indicates the sum that must be available to meet payments of expenses as and when they fall due. It is not correct to state precisely how much money should be needed, or to quote a given ratio, i.e. 2:1; in practice the amount or ratio will depend entirely on the efficacy of the business management and the type of business.

Liquidity ratio

This ratio, often called the acid test, refers to the ratio of debtors and cash to current liabilities. It indicates the amount of cash or 'near cash' that is available to the business to meet its everyday expenses. You will notice that stock is not mentioned as in many businesses it is often necessary to convert raw materials to finished goods, which could take some time, then these goods must be transferred from factory to warehouse or shop, then sold. After sale, a period of credit must be given to the customer, so that the whole process, from commencement of manufacture to receipt of funds from the debtor, may take several months. Hence the 'near cash' test cannot in this case include stock. Again, the perfect ratio will depend on the business. Too much cash will indicate funds not being put to effective use, while an insufficiency of funds will indicate that the company cannot take advantage of discounts and may from time to time resort to borrowing from the bank, which means payment of interest on loan or overdraft, and a consequent lowering of profits.

The overriding rule is whether the company can pay its bills as they fall due.

Rate of stock turnover

$$\frac{\text{Average stock} \times 52}{\text{Cost of goods sold}} = \text{weeks}$$

'Average stock' is the sum of the opening and closing stock figures for the trading year divided by two. 'Cost of goods sold' is the sales turnover less the gross profit.

Money invested in stock is money locked up. Of course, it is necessary that adequate stocks should be held if orders are to be met promptly and good profits made. On the other hand, an over-investment in stock means that a certain proportion of working capital is being under-employed and money is lying idle. The speed of turnover of stock naturally depends upon the nature of the business and seasonal factors (for example, the Christmas trade). However, in general an increase in the time taken to turn stock over suggests that some of it has become unsaleable at normal prices, perhaps because of a change in fashion or in buying habits. In time, a hard core of stock may be built up. This will be a drag on the business for two reasons: first, it is not earning the profit expected; and secondly, it is taking up storage space which should have been made available for other, more disposable items. A sale at reduced prices, perhaps preceded by a special advertising campaign, may be necessary to clear it.

A well run company will know within limits what its stock figure should be at any given time. On the basis of its past experience it will link its stock level with the current turnover and with its order book. A loose relationship will be seen which links creditors, debtors, stock and turnover. If the trading account shows that the turnover has increased since the last year by one-quarter, then the same order of increase ought roughly to be seen in debtors, creditors and stock. Any pronounced discrepancy may prompt an enquiry which will yield further information. If stock has increased disproportionately, this may, as before, be due to a proportion of stock having become unsaleable; or it may turn out that the company has taken the opportunity to buy a bulk lot cheaply.

If creditors show a disproportionate increase, the inference is that the company is not paying as promptly as it did. This may be because it is finding working capital tighter, or it may be because fresh credit terms have been negotiated.

If it is the debtors' figure which calls for attention, the reason may be that the company's arrangements for collecting the money due to it have become laxer; or it may mean that some of the debtors are finding it more difficult to pay promptly.

All these indications are there as early warning signs for those who can read. This may very often be anybody but the customer, who frequently manifests an almost total ignorance of accounts. It will be the duty of his bank manager to give guidance.

The cash flow

A customer seeking a loan from his bank should be able to convince the manager that he has carefully thought out the proposition from all angles. He will certainly have to satisfy the manager that he has done a forward budget and a cash flow projection.

A cash budget is prepared to exercise control over cash flow. The budget is intended to ensure that adequate cash will be available to meet the company's needs as and when necessary. It is prepared by estimating the expected receipts for the period in question (one month, one year) in the light of the trading conditions and prospects of the company, and then subtracting an estimated total in respect of expected payments. There should be a balance in hand to be carried forward to the next period.

Receipts come from sales, so credit periods allowed and trade and cash discounts must be reckoned with here. Short-term loans may come from the bank on a seasonal basis, long-term funds would follow a debenture or share issue. Other income may come on a regular or occasional basis such as rents or proceeds of sale of a capital asset.

Payments are estimated in much the same way. Wages, salaries and overtime can be forecast on the basis of what has been paid out in the recent past, allowing for any increases in wage rates or any upsurge in the work to be done.

If there is a forecast shortage of cash, the cash budget will show how it proposes to overcome the shortage.

The cash flow is gross or net. Gross cash flow is the sum of the net profit after taxation and directors' remuneration, and the provision for depreciation which rests on an estimate made by the company's directors. It is a book entry only, and does not affect cash coming in to the company, but it operates to reduce the published profit figure and thus affects any disposition made of those profits, especially dividends, which represent a cash outflow.

Net cash flow is the gross cash flow less dividends paid, plus the depreciation charge.

A properly executed cash flow projection will ensure that the business is never likely to run out of working capital.

Each balance sheet must be scrutinized in the light of the trade in which the company is engaged, but in general the amount of book debts and stock disclosed by the balance sheet would have to be considerably marked down to arrive at a reasonable estimate of what would be realized if the debts were suddenly called in or the stock sold by a forced sale. In other words, the balance sheet figures are those of a company which is a going concern. There are times, as we shall see, when it is necessary for the banker to think of the company in 'gone concern' terms, and so convert the balance sheet valuations to 'break up' figures.

The valuations of any land and stock have usually to be taken on trust. Sometimes a professional valuation may have been available for the land, or part of it may have been sold, or bought recently, which will give a guide. The stock valuation is usually done by the directors and the figure there is likely to be an undervaluation because this reduces the profits and thus the tax to be paid. The nature of the stock must be kept in mind; some articles deteriorate if kept too long, others go out of fashion. Some businesses, such as the manufacture of ladies' clothing, must maintain a rapid turnover which must be based on an accurate forecast of the market.Other businesses demand long and careful preparation, so turnover is slow, e.g. the manufacture of aircraft engines. The way in which the money is going to be used is important. The banker prefers to lend money for use in the business, on a short-term basis. He does not want to see it used in the purchase of a fixed asset, because that will lock it up. He does not want to see it used to pay off pressing creditors, because that will take it out of the business altogether. In any case, of course, the purpose of the advance must be covered in the objects clause of the Memorandum of Association.

The effect of borrowing

The effect of any borrowing must be either to reduce the outstanding liabilities of the business or to increase its assets, either current or fixed.

Advance to reduce an outstanding current liability

The banker asks himself, if I grant this advance, what will be its effect on the company's balance sheet? Will it have the result that the company's working capital is reduced? An advance to reduce a current outstanding liability will not affect the liquid position, because the increase in 'bank overdraft' will be offset by a reduction in 'creditors', both items being in the liquid section of the balance sheet. However, the banker will not be very keen to lend money to pay someone else off, perhaps only one of the many pressing creditors. He could keep on doing this, each time lending more to the company to pay off creditors and so avoid its being put into liquidation by one of them. In the end the banker would wind up by having to put the company into liquidation himself as the only way of getting even part of his money back.

Advance to increase fixed assets

Advances for the purpose of investing in, say, new plant or machinery are advances for capital expenditure. The current liabilities are increased as the item 'bank overdraft' or 'bank loan' goes up, but there is no corresponding increase in the current assets. The increase is in the fixed assets. So the liquid position is worse and the company's working capital has been decreased.

Advance to increase current assets

In this case the liquid position is unchanged, for current assets and current liabilities will both increase by the same amount. An advance to buy stock would be an example under this head. A request for an advance of this nature would be more likely to receive favourable consideration.

Now we can take two examples, remembering that the banker never wants to be asked to advance the whole of the sum required, but thinks that his customer ought to put something into the kitty himself as well. We must remember also that we are coming to conclusions on one balance sheet only, whereas the banker prefers to have some previous experience of the company's business and for this purpose will copy out the balance sheet figures year by year on to a comparative form of some kind which will permit a detailed analysis.

The company is a private one, operating as a builders' merchants in a suburb of London. They have a busy shop which is always full, with stock all over the floor and very little room to move. There is a display floor upstairs showing various layouts for kitchens and bathrooms. Space at the rear allows builders to come in to get their supplies, load them up, and drive off with them. The shop is used also by do-it-yourself individuals who are making their own improvements at home. The firm has been in account at the bank for a number of years, and has a good reputation both with the bank and in the town. There is an unsecured overdraft limit of £16,000, which is fully used at times, but the account swings well and occasionally goes into credit.

The bank is asked to increase the limit to £50,000. The increase of £34,000 will finance an extension to the shop which will take in part of the space at the rear. Repayment out of profits is promised over four years.

The directors' capital in the balance sheet is £90,000. All this money must be lost before the settlement to creditors becomes endangered. There is a liquid surplus of £39,128. A comparison of stock and sales figures suggests a brisk turnover.

ABC Company Ltd

	£	£		£	£
Capital		40,000	Land and buildings		42,680
Reserves		21,000	Fixtures and fittings		4,080
Profit and loss account		29,000	Vehicles		4,112
		90,000			50,872
Trade creditors	45,120		Stock	41,680	
Tax – current	13,840		Trade debtors	78,444	
Tax – future	14,400		Cash	4,280	
Bank	11,916				
		85,276			124,404
		£175,276			£175,276

Profit for the year (after tax) £13,276. Sales £372,000.

What will the balance sheet look like if this advance is granted? The figure for land and buildings will rise by £34,000, as will the total of current liabilities (the bank overdraft will rise by £34,000 as well).

The liquid surplus has dropped to a mere £5,128 (£124,404 minus £119,276), and the current tax has to be paid. Once the extension to the shop has been completed, there will be room for more stock, which will in turn increase the sales and therefore the profit. But the working capital which is required to pay for this increased stock is not there, so it is apparent that the bank advance of £50,000 is not going to be enough.

However, many practising bankers will take the view that, since the borrowing is over a period of four years only, part of this sum should be a current liability (i.e. one-quarter), and the remainder, not being repayable in the next trading year, must be considered a long-term liability. Consequently, this approach would mean that the liquid surplus, instead of being £5,128, would be increased by £25,500, that is, three-quarters of £34,000.

The situation should be discussed with them. Obviously the question of granting an unsecured advance should be carefully considered – should a debenture be suggested? Is the overall situation marginal, or does the bank consider that given reasonable trading conditions the customer will repay the loan in accordance with the terms agreed?

Balance sheet of ABC Company Ltd showing the effect of a £34,000 advance

	£	£		£	£
Capital		40,000	Land and buildings		76,680
Reserves		21,000	Fixtures and fittings		4,080
Profit and loss account		29,000	Vehicles		4,112
		90,000			84,872
Trade creditors	45,120		Stock	41,680	
Tax – current	13,840		Trade debtors	78,444	
Tax – future	14,400		Cash	4,280	
Bank	45,916				
		119,276			124,404
		£209,276			£209,276

These are the immediate reactions to this single balance sheet. In a real life situation, the account of the customer will be carefully monitored and returns of debtors and creditors will be expected by the bank at regular intervals, while the final accounts and balance sheets, at quarterly and/or half-yearly intervals, will be closely scrutinized by bank officials to ensure that their lending is in no way endangered.

Now another proposition, from a similarly sized company. This is a small private company, engaged in light engineering, which was founded some eight years ago in rented premises. The directors are young and energetic, and have built up the business by hard work and by remunerating themselves modestly so as to leave as much of the profit in the company as possible. A bank overdraft was agreed over the first five years of the company's life, since when it has been able to operate in credit. Business has continued to increase and the directors now find that the rented space is inadequate for their requirements and they judge that the time has come to build their own works. The estimated cost of this is £56,000. The directors can arrange for half of this to be found informally from family sources, and ask the bank to lend £28,000. The freehold deeds of the new workshop are offered as security. Repayment out of profits is promised over four years.

The history of the company and the quality of its management will tend to inspire confidence within the bank, together with the fact that half of the sum required is to be found elsewhere. The request is reasonable, one which every small company making progress will

DEF Company Ltd

	£	£		£	£
Capital		32,000	Plant and machinery		23,520
Reserves		6,008			
Profit and loss account		34,000			
		72,008			23,520
Current tax	12,880		Stock	73,880	
Trade creditors	137,656		Trade debtors	106,448	
			Cash and bank	18,696	
		150,536			199,024
		£222,544			£222,544

Profit for the year (after tax) £33,760. Sales £410,320.

have to make at some stage or other. On the figures supplied there is a good liquid surplus of £48,488. However, the advance is again to be used to acquire a fixed asset, and therefore working capital will be cut down.

Rewriting the balance sheet to see the position after the loan has been taken, one sees that the liquid surplus will then be £20,488. Tax is to be paid, but there are enough funds in hand for this. Good security is offered. Trade creditors are rather higher than one would like to see, bearing in mind the trade debtor figure, and it may again be the case that the company should have asked for rather more, say another £8,000 or £10,000, to give them more elbow room with their working capital position. Also the bank manager will want to know whether in the new building the business is expected to require more in the way of stock, or whether the present stock will be adequate for the immediate future. Details of contracts on hand will help in assessing this. Subject to satisfactory information from the directors on these points, the bank would probably be prepared to help. Repayment will be from profits, and these, we may take it, have been increasing year by year up to this point. A forward budget, although by necessity only an estimate, will give some guidance on whether the annual repayments are feasible, and whether the number of years over which repayment is to be made is satisfactory to the bank.

Going concern and gone concern

The appraisals made so far have all been on the supposition that the balance sheet figures are those of a going concern, that the sums recorded are in fact of that worth to the continued progress of the company. If it is anticipated that the company may fail, a very different interpretation must be placed on the figures. On a gone concern footing the liabilities side of the balance sheet will remain the same, but on the assets side there will be a drastic scaling down. Figures for goodwill will disappear. Property will be conservatively written down, plant and machinery, office furniture and the like will be written in at scrap value only. Vehicles will usually come out of it reasonably well, provided they have been well maintained, for there is nearly always a ready sale. Stock will usually have to be marked down, work in progress will be of little value, being neither one thing nor another. Raw materials will keep their value reasonably well.

Let us take a look at an example.

XYZ Company Ltd

	£	£		£	£
Capital		12,000	Freehold		
			property	20,500	
Reserves		3,500	*Less* mortgage	16,000	
					4,500
Profit and loss account		2,000	Plant and machinery		3,500
			Fixtures and fittings		2,200
			Vehicles		3,400
					13,600
		17,500			
Trade creditors	13,800		Sundry debtors	9,400	
Hire purchase			Stock	21,800	
creditors	4,000		Cash in hand	900	
Taxation	4,000				
Bank	6,400				
		28,200			32,100
		£45,700			£45,700

XYZ Company Ltd is an old established customer of the bank which has for some years enjoyed temporary and fluctuating unsecured overdraft limits up to £6,000 to finance normal trade needs. Recently the advance has become much more solid, that is, the overdrawn balance seems to have been going up all the time, and the manager has had to write to the company calling their attention to the overdraft and asking for a reduction. The company manufactures transistor radios, high fidelity equipment, and electric clocks.

Use to be made of the bank's advance

	£
Settlement of overdue tax	4,000
Settlement of certain pressing creditors	3,000
Advertising costs	2,000

Analysis of balance sheet

	£	£		£	£
Capital		12,000	Freehold property	nil	
Reserves		3,500	Plant and machinery		350
Profit and loss account		2,000	Fixtures and fittings		220
			Vehicles		2,000
		17,500			2,570
Sundry trade			Sundry debtors	3,960	
creditors	10,800		Stock	10,900	
Hire purchase					
creditors	4,000				
Bank	15,400				
		30,200			14,860
		£47,700			£17,430

Its business has suffered recently from competition from abroad. The bank has been asked to increase the overdraft limit to £15,000 to finance an advertising campaign stressing the company's after-sales service (£2,000), settle pressing creditors (£3,000), and pay overdue tax (£4,000). A fixed and floating debenture on the company's assets is offered as security.

The company's liquid surplus is poor for a manufacturing concern of this size, and unduly dependent upon stock, which stands at rather a high figure. The bank's records show that turnover at £79,000 is well down on the previous year (£108,000), while profits before tax have dropped from £11,000 to £2,000. The directors admit that the company is suffering from a temporary financial stringency, but expect trade to recover as a result of the advertising campaign. Repayments are to be out of profits over the next four years.

Further enquiry of the directors reveals that two large debtors totalling £5,000 are six months overdue, and that one-half of the stock of high fidelity equipment has been in store for eighteen months. The question of a reduction in price to clear them is being discussed.

It is now clear that current assets could not raise enough to clear current liabilities, and that the bank's existing loan is in danger. Would the taking of a debenture, together with the granting of the fresh limit required, improve the bank's position? The manager decides to apply the gone-concern test to estimate the position in the event of liquidation. He estimates the break up value of the assets and analyses the creditors as shown below.

The manager considers the freehold factory to be well sited, but specialized and difficult to adapt. He thinks there will be little if any money left over after the mortgage is paid off. Plant and machinery, and fixtures and fittings, he values as scrap. Vehicles are in reasonably good condition, but five or more years old. He values sundry debtors by writing off the two doubtful cases and allowing 10 per cent loss on the remainder. He puts the stock in at half price, and makes no allowance for cash, which will all have disappeared by the time it is most wanted.

On this estimate the business will produce £17,430 cash assets to satisfy the creditors. This sum would all fall under the debenture, if taken, and so be available for the bank (supposing the company continued in business for twelve months after the taking of the debenture), which would in this way secure repayment in full, leaving about £2,000 over for the other creditors, who would thus get about 13p in the £.

The requirement for the company to continue in business for twelve months after the taking of the debenture results from a section of the Companies Act which makes floating charges taken from a company within the twelve months before its liquidation void and of no effect in certain conditions. The intention is to stop certain creditors of a failing company improving their position at the expense of other creditors, as indeed the bank would be doing here.

A similar exercise to show the position if the company were to go into liquidation now shows that the £17,430 expected would first go to pay the £4,000 owed in tax. Certain creditors are by law 'preferred', that is, they are paid in full first, before anyone else gets anything. The Inland Revenue is such a preferred creditor in respect of any one year's tax owing. (We will suppose that the £4,000 is in respect of the last year's tax.) The remainder, £13,430, would be available for all other unsecured creditors including the bank. They total £24,200, so the company would pay 55p in the £ and on its advance of £6,400 the bank would lose £2,880.

These figures are of course very rough. An exercise of this nature is merely to indicate the broad choices open to the bank, and to try to assess the bank's position in the worst of all possible cases.

Revision test 14

Place a tick against the letter you consider is the correct answer.

1 Interest charged on an overdraft paid for the year will be shown in
  (a) the trading account
  (b) the profit and loss account
  (c) the profit and loss appropriation account.

2 Goodwill is
  (a) a fixed asset
  (b) a floating asset
  (c) a fictitious asset.

3 A bank overdraft appears in a company's balance sheet as
  (a) a long-term liability
  (b) a current asset
  (c) a current liability.

4 Working capital is
  (a) fixed assets minus current liabilities
  (b) current assets minus long-term liabilities
  (c) current assets minus current liabilities.

5 Part of the profits retained in the business for expansion is
  (a) a reserve
  (b) a provision
  (c) an asset.

6 A bank advance to purchase stock will
  (a) reduce the outstanding liabilities of the business
  (b) increase the fixed assets of the business
  (c) increase the current assets of the business.

7 The balance sheet of a business is likely to be drawn up
  (a) monthly
  (b) annually
  (c) at the request of the tax inspector.

8 The profit and loss account will show
  (a) the profit/loss
  (b) cash receipts/payments
  (c) liabilities/assets.

9 The auditor will certify that the accounts and balance sheet show
   (a) an accurate statement of income and expenditure
   (b) that the figures stated are accurate and correct
   (c) a true and fair view of the business.
10 The manufacturing account of a business will show
   (a) the total cost of manufacture
   (b) the total cost of manufacture, administrative costs and sales costs
   (c) the total cost of manufacture plus financial costs and director's fees.

Questions for discussion

1 List and describe at least six ratios and percentages that a lending banker would calculate for the final accounts and balance sheets of a company.
2 What are the principles involved in assessing a company's balance sheet on a 'gone-concern basis'?
3 List the items that make up the 'shareholders' funds' of a well known public company and compare them with the 'shareholders' funds' of a major bank.

15

The savings media

Introduction

This chapter lists the various types of savings. Before we go into this, however, we should ask ourselves what savings really are, how they are arrived at, what types of people save, and what is the effect of such savings.

Savings are defined as income less consumption. Consumption may be curtailed in order to save, or income may be so high that saving is effortless. Factors which affect the amount of saving actually achieved are, rather obviously, the amount of income coupled with the desire to save. The rate of interest obtainable at any time should, one would think, be a factor of some importance, and yet it does not seem to be of primary importance. People seem to react to bad economic conditions by tending to save more as if, in response to some deep-seated urge, they wish to establish around them a little oasis of security in an uncertain world. The amount of income received, out of which savings must be made, is clearly linked with the level of unemployment, and where this is high, again rather obviously, savings will tend to be less. Again, where one is living in an inflationary age, one would expect savings to be less, on the principle that it is better to spend one's money as soon as one gets it, rather than save it and see the real value of one's savings slowly diminish as time passes. This is not the case with the ordinary worker, who does not have the necessary expertise to understand the principles involved, although more expert savers, such as trustees of pension funds, are well aware of the danger and have the necessary knowledge and time to switch their funds around periodically to take advantage of fluctuating conditions.

Savings are made (i) by individuals for their own personal reasons, such as to make provision for old age, to have a little something in reserve, to finance the education of their children, or to make it possible to pay for some expensive goods or services, such as a foreign holiday; (ii) by corporations ploughing back profits into the business and so reducing the amount of dividends paid to shareholders. These are voluntary savings. Enforced savings occur when the state increases taxation, or at a time of rising inflation when the earner's income won't go round as far as it did before, with the result that spending has to be cut down.

The effect of savings is to channel some of the money saved into productive investment, which will result in an increase in real capital. Thus, where money is saved on bank deposit accounts the bank will use it to lend to industry, and this will tend to create more jobs and lead to the production of more goods, some of which can be sold abroad. Where money is saved in government securities such as National Savings Certificates or balances with the National Savings Bank, this will mean that the Chancellor, when calculating his requirements for the following year's Public Sector Borrowing Requirement, can afford to reduce his borrowing (necessary to meet expenditure) which he would otherwise have to arrange – mostly by the issue of Treasury bills and gilt-edged securities – or to reduce the rate of income tax, or to postpone a projected rise in income tax.

The words 'savings' and 'investment are often used synonymously. The meaning of each can be a little vague. Savings as mentioned in the second paragraph is money put away often on a regular basis into some fund that has the least possible risk element. Investment is usually a sum of money, often savings, invested in some enterprise for the purpose of making capital gains or income, or perhaps a combination of both, with some degree of risk involved.

The Department of National Savings

This government department offers savers a variety of securities which are available mainly from post offices but some can be purchased from banks.

National Savings Bank

The National Savings Bank was originally called the Post Office Savings Bank and under that name was established in 1861. It is now probably the largest organization of its kind in the world. There are two sorts of accounts: ordinary and investment. An account may be opened at any of the 20,000 post offices. Ordinary accounts are subject to a condition that on opening the account the minimum is £5 while the maximum is £10,000.

Ordinary accounts carry interest, the rate varying from time to time in accordance with the general money rate level. There are two interest rates for the Ordinary Account which are fixed for the whole of each year. For 1989 they are 2½ and 5 per cent per annum. If the account is open for the whole year, then 5 per cent will be paid for each complete calendar month that the account balance is at least £500. For other months 2½ per cent applies. Interest is calculated on whole pounds for each complete calendar month and is automatically added to the accounts on 31 December each year. Interest is calculated on whole pounds for each complete calendar month and is automatically added to the accounts on 31 December each year. The first £70 of interest each year is exempt from income tax. Husbands and wives are each entitled to the exemption. Deposits and withdrawals must be recorded in the depositor's passbook and may be made at any post office where savings business is transacted.

Withdrawals on demand are limited to £100 per day, but if you have a Regular Customer Account at a chosen post office it is possible to withdraw up to £250 on demand. On the Ordinary Account it is possible to purchase Thomas Cook Traveller's Cheques. Standing orders for payment of life assurance, hire purchase, mortgages, etc., can be arranged free of charge. A Paybill service enables the account holder to pay normal household bills up to the value of £250 by the simple expediency of filling in a form for the amount, and the post office will deal with the transaction. No money needs to be handled.

Investment accounts were introduced in 1966. These accounts carry a higher rate of interest. Like the Ordinary Account this will vary from time to time, but at the moment it is 10 per cent per annum which is calculated on a daily basis and is earned on each pound for each day it is held on deposit. The interest is credited annually on 31 December. This interest is not taxable at source, which is an advantage for those who are not liable for tax, but must be declared on the tax return.

The minimum deposit is £5, while the maximum balance is £10,000.

One month's notice of withdrawal is required.

Unlike the Ordinary Account which is only available to individuals, joint accounts, clubs, societies and formally constituted trusts, the Investment Account is available to registered companies and other corporate bodies.

National Savings Bank deposits are lodged with the National Debt Commissioners and are invested in government securities. The government guarantees the repayment of the sums invested, with accrued interest, when required. The interest earned by these investments is set against the interest due to depositors and management expenses.

National Savings Certificates

The first issue was offered in 1916 as 'War Savings Certificates' (the name was changed in 1920). Since then there have been many fresh issues offering various rates of interest. Interest is by way of accruals to the capital value and is paid out only when the certificates are cashed. In early 1989, the 34th issue is offering a return of 7.8% per annum compound, if held for the full five years. If the certificates are cashed earlier, the return is less and, if repaid in the first year, no interest at all is earned. Units are priced at £25 and a maximum of 40 (£1,000) may be purchased. However, if you are reinvesting from earlier certificates held for at least five years, an additional £5,000 may be bought. The certificates are available at post offices and banks, and, although intended to attract the small savers because they are free of income tax and capital gains tax, they are also particularly attractive to the higher tax payers.

Holders of previous issues that have run their full five years may retain the certificates and earn a tax-free extension interest which can vary. Fixed at 9.51 per cent from 1 April to 30 September 1985 it was then lowered to 8.52 per cent. Currently it stands at 5.01 per cent.

Index-linked National Savings Certificates

Originally these were only available to persons of pensionable age, were given the name 'Granny Bonds', and were intended to be a means of keeping a proportion of people's savings in line with any subsequent rise in the cost of living. They are now available to everybody no matter what age, in minimum units of £25 up to a maximum holding of £5,000 in addition to holdings of all other issues of savings certificates.

No interest is paid, but after a certificate has been held for one year its value is adjusted monthly as from the date of purchase in accordance with the general index of retail prices plus an extra interest rate on a sliding scale each year. Over the five years this additional interest gives an overall return of 4.04 per cent compound each year on top of the inflation proofing. Repayments are free of income tax and capital gains tax.

Apart from the general public, trustees, registered friendly societies and eligible charitable and other bodies are all able to hold National Savings Certificates.

Save As You Earn

This method of saving was withdrawn in May 1984 as it was felt that it was no longer competitive with other forms of savings, as many persons could not, due to the present economic climate, commit themselves to a contract of payment over five years. In its place the Department of National Savings has introduced the Yearly Plan which is discussed below.

Yearly Plan

This scheme enables a person to make regular savings over a minimum period of one year. By this scheme, the saver is able to purchase certificates carrying an interest rate at the beginning of 1989 of 7.5 per cent per annum if held over a five-year period.

The investor will pay between £20 and £200 a month by standing order for twelve months and he will then be given a Yearly Plan Certificate which he should hold for a further four years. The interest stated on the certificate is guaranteed, even if other interest rates change. All interest is tax free. The certificates can be held for longer than four years, but the extension rate will be varied. This rate – the same as for National Savings Certificates – will be publicized through the national press and post offices.

Deposit Bonds

These bonds are no longer available as they have been replaced by Capital Bonds. They were originally designed for those persons who had a lump sum to invest. The minimum purchase was £100, while the maximum holding was £50,000. They were available to individuals, companies, and trustees.

Income Bonds

These bonds give the investor the opportunity of obtaining a regular monthly income. The initial investment must be for £2,000 which may be increased in multiples of £1,000 up to a maximum of £100,000. The bonds begin to earn interest from the date the investment is received at the Bonds and Stock Office, and the interest is paid monthly on the fifth of each month either direct to the holder's bank account or National Savings Account or by crossed warrant sent through the post.

The interest rate is subject to change at six weeks' notice. It is currently 10.75 per cent. Interest is taxable but paid without deduction of tax. Three months' notice is required for repayment and, if this occurs during the first year of the investment, interest will be paid at only half the usual rate.

Capital Bonds

This new type of National Savings investment was launched on 1 January 1989 and is the first new National Savings product in three years. It is designed to attract savings from those persons who are willing to lock up their funds for at least five years and, in so doing, the government are offering what can only be considered, at this time, a most competitive rate of 12 per cent per annum.

For the non-tax-payer, it is a useful investment as interest is paid gross, while for those that pay standard rate or higher rate of tax, the government has guaranteed that the rate of interest will be fixed for five years. This compares well with National Savings Certificates which pay only 7.5 per cent. The minimum purchase is £100 and there is no maximum.

The unusual feature of this bond is that the investor is liable for tax each year of the life of the bond, even though he does not in fact receive such interest. This may prove a burden to some investors who pay the standard rate of tax, but attractive to the non-tax-payer.

Should the bond be surrendered in the first year, then the investor only receives his/her money back. If the surrender take place in the early years, then the interest received is low.

Premium Bonds

Investors in these bonds, which are issued in £1 units in multiples of £5, with the minimum purchase of £10 up to a maximum holding of £10,000, enjoy no interest, but have the chance of a prize. The bonds can be purchased at either post offices or banks.

Premium Bonds are, in fact, a national lottery with security for the investor's money built in. A bond must be held for three calendar months before it qualifies for the draw, made by the computer 'ERNIE'. From time to time the amounts of the prizes are altered. At the moment the top monthly prize is £250,000, with one weekly prize of £100,000, one of £50,000 and one for £25,000. Other monthly prizes range from £10,000 down to £50. All prizes are free of income tax and capital gains tax.

In order to obtain funds to distribute as prizes, the government will allow the Department of National Savings interest at the rate of 6.5 per cent on the amount invested in Premium Bonds. Even with the large numbers of prizes available it has been calculated that the chance of winning is 1 in 11,000 for each bond.

Government stock

Through the National Savings Stock Register it is possible to purchase around sixty government stocks. This is an alternative to buying stock through a stockbroker. The rates of commission charged for buying and selling are usually lower than those charged by a stockbroker, especially for small amounts. The maximum that can be invested by any individual is limited to £10,000 in any one stock in any one day.

This stock can be purchased by anyone. The price is quoted for each £100 nominal stock and will be as on the day the order is received at the Bonds and Stock Office. In order to purchase the investor may state a specific amount of nominal stock, or he could send a cheque for, say, £1,000 and this will be invested in the named stock at the price of the day less commission.

The interest is specified in the title of the government stock and this would be earned for each £100 of nominal stock held. This interest is paid without deduction of tax, but the holder is liable to tax and the interest must be included in the tax return. Such interest may be credited to a bank account, National Savings Account or by a warrant sent by post.

A list of the stock available can be obtained from the Bonds and Stock Office, Blackpool, Lancs., or at major post offices.

Building societies

Building societies are the major source of funds for the provision of long-term loans (home loans) on the security of houses and land. In this capacity they are non-profit-making bodies and their interest rates are strictly linked with money rates, although they are slower to respond to any change than, say, the banks' base rates. To gather the funds which they lend out, the societies must offer an attractive rate, sufficient to bring in the funds they need. If money is difficult to get, interest rates offered will have to be raised, and this in turn will mean that mortgage rates will also have to go up.

Building societies thus have two faces. The first is as a savings medium, the second as a lender. Here we are interested in the societies from the savings opportunities point of view. They form an important channel for the investment of small personal savings.

The first building society is said to have been established in Birmingham in 1775. A century later they were to be found in the industrial areas of the country. They were small groups of people, called members, who paid fixed monthly sums, gradually accumulating funds which could then be used to buy land and build houses on it. As the houses slowly became ready for occupation they were allotted to members by ballot or perhaps by payment a premium. When everyone had eventually acquired a house the society was dissolved. They therefore became known as terminating building societies. They were able in the end to provide the houses, and they did show that regular saving by people working together for mutual benefit could achieve objectives beyond the reach of individuals. But the disadvantage was that members could wait many years for a house. The society did not borrow, and therefore had only the funds which its members paid in.

About 1850 a relaxation of this rigid link between the investing and borrowing aspects of membership permitted the emergence of a new and more efficient type of building society, the permanent building society. Funds were now borrowed not only from those who were saving for the express purpose of buying a house but also from those who had savings to invest but did not wish to take anything out. So the societies were able to make loans to borrowing members so that they could build or purchase a house quite quickly. The members got into their houses much sooner. There was no longer any need to dissolve the society when each of the original members had got his loan.

The development of these societies led to the grant of the right of incorporation under an Act of 1874, and a firm base was secured for the rapid growth which has occurred in more recent times. An Act of 1962, consolidating earlier measures, now imposes conditions affecting the functions, operation and management of societies, provides for audit and the publication of detailed yearly accounts, restricts borrowing and lending powers, and confers certain privileges, such as the limitation of liability of members. It also regulates the way in which the societies can advertise for funds, and the way in which any surplus funds may be invested. The 1962 Act did nothing to stop the expansion of building societies. The numbers of depositors increased, so did the total amounts of deposits, as did mortgages. With competition from banks, the Building Societies Act, 1986, which came into force on 1 January 1987, recognized this fact and allowed them to offer the following services:

1 Unsecured loans up to £5,000
2 Estate agency and surveying services. Note that banks also offer this comparatively new service
3 Cheque guarantee cards and overdrafts
4 Insurance services
5 The purchase and sale of shares
6 Index-linked or equity mortgage loans
7 Participation in ownership schemes and the development and management of residential land
8 Own subsidiary companies
9 Lend in the EEC and other approved countries
10 Building societies can become public companies and become banks providing that at least 20 per cent of the membership vote and that 75 per cent of votes are in favour of the change.

Now that these various new services can now be offered, the competition between banks and building societies will intensify.

The Chief Registrar of Friendly Societies is by virtue of his office Registrar of Building Societies. He has powers to investigate the affairs of societies in the interests of depositors or investors and, if he thinks fit, to prohibit particular societies from advertising for additional funds.

Nearly all the bigger societies are members of the Building Societies Association, which imposes certain conditions of membership, such as the maintenance of minimum liquid resources in cash and securities, and makes recommendations to members on interest rates to be charged to borrowers and offered to investors.

Share accounts

Shares in a building society are not dealt in on the Stock Exchange, but may be withdrawn at par in cash, on giving notice if necessary. They carry a rate of interest which is usually fixed by the directors of the society and is varied from time to time in accordance with changes in monetary conditions. The period of notice required for the withdrawal of shares varies according to the rules of the society.

Building society interest is deducted at a composite rate, which at the moment is 25¼ per cent, because the societies have come to an arrangement with the Inland Revenue to pay the tax at a rate which is supposed to be the average rate which the investors would have paid if they had been taxed on the income instead of the societies. Non-tax payers who maintain building society accounts will not be able to reclaim the tax deducted.

The amount of share capital in a building society is not fixed, as in a public limited company, but may be regulated in accordance with the amount lent on mortgage.

Shares in an established building society offer a reasonably good rate of interest, coupled with security and the ability to withdraw capital at short notice.

Some societies offer a slightly higher rate of interest on some types of share accounts. To take advantage of this it may be necessary for the depositor to leave his money in for a definite length of time and/or maintain a specified minimum balance in the account. The terms of such accounts vary according to the society.

For people who need their income from their building society more frequently than six monthly, some societies run monthly income shares where, as the name implies, interest is paid monthly in return for specified conditions which may include up to three months' notice of withdrawal, earlier withdrawal subject to loss of interest, and the holding of a minimum balance in the account.

Cheque accounts

One of the great attractions for the personal customer is the ability to deposit funds in the building society and not only obtain interest on the deposit, but also to use that account in exactly the same way as a current account in a bank. That is, he is able to deposit funds over the counter, have his/her monthly salary credited automatically, pay or receive standing orders. The customer is able to draw cheques, and use an Automated Teller Machine. Abbey National and the Halifax are both members of BACS and, to improve customer service, building societies will build up their relationships with banks for the greater provision of these types of services.

Subscription schemes

Regular savings accounts are offered by most societies. Under such schemes a shareholder agrees to save a regular weekly or monthly amount over a period of years. A slightly higher rate of interest is usually paid on these savings provided that there is no interruption to the regularity of the payments. Some societies have introduced a little flexibility by allowing one withdrawal a year, or one withdrawal after two years. The penalty for any variance from the conditions is a lowering of the special interest rate to that of an ordinary share account.

Details of these schemes will vary between societies, but most will offer an attractive rate of interest, depending on the amount deposited and the length of time the funds remain in the account.

The societies as bankers

We saw earlier some of the ways in which the building societies are encroaching on the traditional business areas of the banks. In a recent survey it was estimated that the clearing banks' share of the deposit market had fallen to about 35 per cent, while the deposits of building societies are growing greater each year.

Suppose we now look at this question from the building societies' point of view. If we do that we will find at once that the banks are encroaching into the business of house mortgages. Building societies are encroaching into the business of banking. Some building societies have now made available Automatic Teller Machines to

Building societies: progress

Year	Number of societies	Number of branches	Number of share-holders 000's	Number of depositors 000's	Number of borrowers 000's	Share balances £m	Deposit balances £m	Mortgage balances £m	Total assets £m	Advances during year Number 000's	Advances during year Amount £m	Average mortgage rate %	Average share rate %
1900	2,286		585					46	60		9		
1910	1,723		626					60	76		9		
1920	1,271		748			64	19	69	87		25		
1930	1,026		1,449	428	720	303	45	316	371	159	89		4.65
1940	952		2,088	771	1,503	552	142	678	756	43	21	4.76	3.27
1950	819		2,256	654	1,508	962	205	1,060	1,256	302	270	4.18	2.22
1960	726		3,910	571	2,349	2,721	222	2,647	3,166	387	560	5.89	3.37
1970	481	2,016	10,265	618	3,655	9,788	382	8,752	10,819	624	1,954	8.58	4.94
1980	273	5,684	30,636	915	5,383	48,915	1,762	42,437	53,793	936	9,503	14.92	10.34
1981	253	6,162	33,388	995	5,490	55,463	2,577	48,875	61,815	1,096	12,005	14.01	9.19
1982	227	6,480	36,607	1,094	5,645	64,968	3,532	56,696	73,033	1,322	15,036	13.30	8.80
1983	206	6,643	37,711	1,200	5,928	75,197	5,601	67,474	85,869	1,511	19,347	11.03	7.27
1984	190	6,816	39,380	1,550	6,314	88,087	8,426	81,882	102,689	1,658	23,771	11.84	7.74
1985	167	6,926	39,997	2,150	6,659	102,331	10,751	96,751	120,764	1,678	26,508	13.47	8.69
1986	152	6,954	40,559	2,850	7,023	115,538	16,862	115,669	140,603	2,062	35,913	12.07	7.75
1987	138	6,962	41,953	3,648	7,182	129,948	20,575	130,905	160,098	1,889	35,848	11.64	7.42

Source: Annual Reports of the Chief Registrar of Friendly Societies, *Annual Report of the Building Societies Commission 1986–87* for 1986, BSA estimates for 1987.

Notes: 1. The figures until 1985 are based on annual returns provided by all building societies in Great Britain. From 1986 the figures include information from the four societies based in Northern Ireland. At the end of 1986 these societies had total assets of £113 million.

2. The figures are the aggregation of figures for societies' financial years ending between 1 February in the year in question and 31 January of the following year.

3. The average mortgage rate shows the gross rate charged in the year while the average rate indicates the net rate paid.

allow customers to withdraw funds by the use of a plastic card and a Personal Identification Number (PIN). There are also available from many of the large societies such services as cheque books, standing orders, monthly statements and travel cheques.

Many building societies are working in conjunction with banks, so that a person having an account with a linked bank and building society can maintain a free account with the bank by having funds automatically transferred from the building society account to the bank, or, where a maximum balance is reached, a transfer the other way is automatically made.

Additionally, people may borrow from a building society funds which do not just cover the purchase of a house. Money may be borrowed for extensions and improvements, and it is possible to obtain a lending package that allows people to borrow money to purchase various household furniture and fittings, so the total loan for the purchase and refurbishing of a house can be obtained from one institution.

While building societies are gradually encroaching on the services of banks, banks in their turn are now offering attractive interest on current accounts, a greater number of ATMs and certainly a wider range of personal and corporate services. While building societies are expanding the numbers of personal customers, they have not yet been able to obtain the corporate business, nor have they the inherent knowledge and skills to lend on an unsecured basis. The banks still have a greater efficiency in the transmission of funds.

Registered provident societies

Registered provident societies take in a group of varied institutions registered under the Friendly Societies Act and other legislation which give them certain privileges, such as limited liability, and imposes upon them various limitations and obligations.

Friendly societies are mutual insurance societies in which the members subscribe for provident benefits: in particular, sickness, death, endowment, and old age benefits, and provisions for widows and orphans. They first appeared in the sixteenth century as local organizations which by three hundred years later had developed into centralized bodies with branches throughout the country. Although the National Health Service now meets most of the needs for which the original friendly societies were set up, they still continue to operate and have diversified to include industrial insurance; industrial, provident and building societies; trade unions' certified loan societies; and some superannuation and pension schemes. All are closely controlled by various Acts.

Industrial assurance business is the effecting of life insurance by means of premiums which are paid to collectors, who make house-to-house calls for this purpose, at intervals of less than two months. Only friendly societies registered under the Friendly Societies Act or authorized assurance companies may engage in this business. Registered friendly societies and insurance companies which effect industrial assurance business are known as 'collecting societies' and 'industrial assurance companies' respectively.

Industrial and provident societies are incorporated with limited liability. The shareholding of any member, except another registered society, is limited to £1,000. Important under this heading are the wholesale and retail co-operative societies.

As we have seen, investment in building societies is in the form of deposits or shares. By contrast trade unions receive contributions from members, and some provide sickness and accident, superannuation, funeral and various benefits.

Credit unions

The credit union system, popular in North America, is a system whereby people with a common bond – membership of the same club, church, tenants' association or trade union – may collaborate to put their savings into a joint fund in a kind of money co-operative. A dividend is paid to savers. Members can then apply to borrow from the fund and make repayments at an annual interest rate of no more than 12 per cent. Northern Ireland, where there are more than 400 credit unions, has laws providing for them, but until 1979 there was no legal provision in Great Britain, although the National Consumer Council had been pressing parliament for three years to pass appropriate legislation.

Credit unions were started in this country by West Indian and Irish immigrants who had left flourishing unions behind them. The first credit union was founded in 1964 by the West Indian community in Hornsey, London; there are now some seventy unions, varying in size from 30 to 1,000 members. Members share in all decision making, and an elected committee from the ranks decides who is to have loans. These may be for any reasonable purpose; hefty fuel bills and holidays are typical examples. Credit unions are of invaluable help in providing credit for low income borrowers, many of whom have no bank account and would otherwise be driven into the expensive arms of tallymen, money lenders or pawn-brokers.

The Credit Union Act was passed in 1979. It provides for the regis-tration of a society subject to conditions, defines the objects of a credit union (promotion of thrift, creation of sources of credit, use and control of savings, training and education of members in the wise use of money), and sets out the qualifications for membership.

The minimum number of members is to be 21 and the maximum 5,000. The title is to contain the words 'credit union'. Any surplus funds are to be kept with a bank on current or deposit account, such a bank being one authorized to hold the funds of credit unions. The Chief Registrar designates the authorized banks. Interest on members' deposits is tax free for the first six years, then taxed at the standard rate.

Growth is expected to come through associations at work and through clubs and trade unions. There are thought to be at least 36,000 social clubs, 84,000 manufacturing establishments and well over 12 million trade unionists in the UK. Progress so far, however, has been slow.

Assurance companies

Insurance companies in this country began in the middle of the sixteenth century with marine risk insurance. We have seen how the association of underwriters known as Lloyd's developed. About the same time, round about the turn of the seventeenth century, the first fire and life offices were founded.

Insurance may now be said to fall into the following main groups: life; property; marine, aviation and transport; motor vehicle; third-party liability; and personal accident and sickness. The first and last of these are means of saving, but life assurance is much the more important.

A certain amount of insurance is provided by friendly societies, but this is a small proportion of the total business, which is looked after by Lloyd's or by mutual or joint stock companies.

All types of insurance companies are closely regulated by various Acts so as to protect the interests of those insured, and the Department of Trade is given power to supervise and to grant or withhold authority for new companies to act, or for an existing company to take on additional classes of business. Authority will be withheld if the Department is not satisfied as to the company's financial resources, its internal administration, and the fitness of the people who control and manage the business. A minimum paid-up share capital is required, as is a certain solvency margin, that is, a certain excess of assets over liabilities.

The Department also has a number of powers relating to the annual returns of any company, and in certain circumstances may petition for the winding up of a company, or may intervene at an earlier stage if it appears that a company's business is being so conducted that there is a risk of it becoming insolvent.

Companies carrying on life business are not required to have any specific solvency margin, but there must be an actuarial valuation of their assets and liabilities at least once in every three years, and this must make it clear that prudent margins have been allowed in the calculations.

All types of risk other than life are 'insured' against, but a person's life is 'assured'. An assurance company, therefore, is one dealing with life risks. Life assurance has three characteristics which are peculiar to it: it is essentially long term; it deals with something certain to happen (e.g. death or the attainment of a specified age); and an annual premium agreed at the beginning of the contract continues throughout the contractual duration.

Most of the companies are members of the Life Offices' Association and the Associated Scottish Life Offices, or the Industrial Life Offices' Association. There are about fifteen industrial life assurance companies and some seventy or eighty collecting societies.

Life assurance companies have very large sums for investment at their disposal and this form of insurance has become the largest single regular saving medium in the country. Over the last quarter of a century the growth of occupational pension schemes (not all administered by assurance companies) has greatly increased the rate of accumulation of funds for investment. Roughly half of these funds are invested in government and industrial fixed interest stocks, and the other half in shares and property.

Over the past fifteen years or so many life companies have introduced new forms of policies linked to groups of property and equity investments, in order to meet the demand for equity and property shares as a hedge against inflation. The variety of policies is now quite bewildering, but the basic forms are five in number: term policies, whole life policies, endowment policies, endowment or whole life with profits policies, and annuities.

Term policies insure your life over a certain period. If you wanted to insure yourself against the risk of an aircraft crash when you were flying on holiday you would take out a term policy for a few weeks. Term policies can, however, last for thirty years; it depends on the term. If you die during the term your heirs get the benefit. If you survive the term there is no benefit. These are purely protective policies, with no investment element.

Whole life policies yield a lump sum on your death, consequently they are strictly for your heirs or dependants. As no one knows when you are going to die, no one can say what the exactly correct premium ought to be. But although the assurance company does not know when you are going to die it does know how many people die at what age all over the country, and from these statistics the actuaries of the company will fix the premium so as to show a profit for the company, while the same time offering a competitive proposition to the proposer.

Endowment policies offer a lump sum at a certain age, often 60 or 65, provided you live that long. Otherwise they will pay the lump sum on your death. These have the attraction that if you live to the age stipulated you will get the money yourself. It will then be up to you to provide for your heirs.

Either whole life or endowment policies may be obtained 'with profits' for an extra premium, and this means that the policies will share in the fortunes of the company by having bonuses declared every so often (usually every three years) added to the eventual sum to be paid. The bonuses are not the amounts you could get now if you drew them out, but the amounts you will get provided you leave the money in. If all bonuses are left in and the policy is allowed to lie undisturbed, the with-profits policy will represent a very good investment, partly because the funds of a big assurance company are expertly managed.

Some companies offer life assurance linked with the purchase of unit trusts. Here a percentage of the premiums paid is invested in a particular unit trust and the remainder goes to provide term insurance. At the end of the term the assured is entitled either to the units purchased, or their sale proceeds. If he should die during the term, his estate would benefit by the value of the units at the date of death, or a guaranteed sum of money, whichever is the greater.

Index-linked policies began to appear in 1974. Under such a policy both the periodic premium payments and the benefits from the contract are adjusted in line with the movement of the General Index of Retail Prices. In this way compensation is made for the falling value of money in an inflationary era.

At first these concerned house buildings insurance and house contents insurance. Such policies contained an 'automatic escalation factor', which is a polite way of saying that the premium will go up by 4 or 5 per cent every year – but so does the cover. By the end of 1975 you could also get index-linked policies for family income benefit, flexible endowment assurance and renewable term assurance.

But it took more than a decade of inflation for life assurance companies to come to terms with declining money values. Until 1981 only a handful of companies offered life policies with defences against inflation in the form of regular increases in the sum involved. Early in 1981, however, more than a dozen companies brought forward new schemes. The majority of these were term policies, usually for an initial period of five to nine years, with various built-in rights.

Among them are the right to take out a policy for another term of the same length, and to repeat this up to some ultimate date (usually to terminate at 65 or 70), the right to convert into a permanent policy such as a whole life or endowment, with a sum assured equal to that on the term assurance, and the right to increase the sum assured at regular intervals.

With an annuity you pay a lump sum and the assurance company pay you an income for the rest of your life whether it be short or long. The later you leave the payment, the greater the income. If you come from a long lived family you have the chance of making a good profit, but this will be balanced, as far as the company is concerned, by those who die earlier than the average. It is wise, however, to think carefully before committing capital in this way because the fixed income provided by an annuity can very soon lose much of its real value in times of high inflation. It is possible to defend against inflation to some extent with an increasing annuity. But most companies will quote only at modest escalation rates of 5 per cent a year. This also reduces the initial annuity substantially.

The annuity can be made payable for a fixed number of years or only during the lifetime of a named individual. Part of the purchased life annuity will be considered by the tax authorities as return of capital and thus non-taxable. The balance is classified as unearned income and is subject to income tax and investment income surcharge if applicable. Obviously the larger the capital content, the greater the net return of annuity after tax. At lower ages the capital content becomes such a small proportion of the annuity payable that it is generally not considered advisable to take out an annuity before the age of 65.

Life policies in general are aimed at men. The old fashioned idea that a woman does not need protection from death or illness if she has a husband to fend for her still persists. This attitude is based on the supposition that the worst thing that could happen financially to a family would be the death of the husband, but a few companies advertise a form of life cover and savings policy for women. Others consider that what they offer can be adapted equally well to men and women, and choose to offer assurance for both husband and wife under one policy, i.e. joint life contracts. Joint life mortgage protection policies are actively marketed by a few companies.

Everyone who can should take out an endowment with profits policy. It represents a genuine saving, for it gives cover for dependants against the premature death of the wage earner, it provides a lump sum on retirement, and it is a hedge against inflation. Furthermore, as its value increases over the years it becomes an acceptable security for a lender. A bank in particular will be reassured to find the prospective borrower has demonstrated a saving disposition earlier in his or her life. This makes it more likely that repayment of any loan they grant will be duly made, and this in turn makes the bank more disposed to grant the loan.

Investment and unit trusts

The function of investment trusts and unit trusts is to raise collective capital from the public and to direct it into profitable investment channels. The two different types of organization enable the small investor with limited capital to spread his risks over a wide range of securities under full-time specialist management.

Investment trust companies

Founded soon after the introduction of the principle of limited liability for joint stock companies, investment trusts are public corporate bodies registered under the Companies Act. Their capital is derived mainly from public issues of debentures, preference and ordinary stock which are quoted and dealt with on the Stock Exchange. They are companies formed for the purpose of holding investments. The amount of the company's stock is fixed until any further issue of capital, and new investors can obtain holdings only by buying stock from existing holders.

The management of an investment trust is often carried out by a professional management company, which will take the policy decisions on what investments should be held, look after the actual buying and selling of the securities, and make the interest and dividend payments to the shareholders. Such management companies may come from firms of solicitors or accountants, or from merchant banks, or from specialized trust management organizations.

The debenture, preference, and ordinary stock commonly associated with a corporate body serve to raise the capital which the company needs in the first place, to buy the investments which it is going to hold. If it needs any more capital later on it can float a loan at a fixed rate of interest or issue a further series of debentures. Investment trust companies also like to build up a stock of foreign currencies so that they can include in their securities (portfolios) stock of US, Japanese, Australian, etc., investments. This has led to the raising of loans in dollars and other currencies, so that the assets of the company may consist of both sterling and foreign securities.

In the past, English and Scottish investment trusts have played an important part in overseas development by mobilizing private capital for employment in the Commonwealth countries, the British dependencies, and in several foreign countries. In the 1870s Scottish investors were able to invest quite heavily in American shares at a time when the US dollar was weak following the Civil War. These movements of capital contributed much to the development of the United States in the period before the outbreak of the First World War, and the holdings now show an advantage when sterling is weak against the dollar. The end of exchange control restrictions in October 1979 left the trusts free to invest abroad as they wished.

The Association of Investment Trust Companies was formed in 1932 for the 'protection, promotion and advancement of the common interests of members'.

The provision by the Companies Act, 1981, giving companies the right to buy back their own shares, was of great benefit to investment trust companies and solved the industry's problems of oversupply and the large variations on the underlying assets of trusts reflected in share prices.

Also, the lifting of exchange controls and changes in capital gains tax have made the investment trusts more attractive to institutions and will eventually be more decisive for the industry. The advantages of investment trusts are not generally appreciated by small investors, as the trusts are not allowed to advertise. The advantages are, however, that they provide an investment medium for shareholders to spread their risks and buy an interest in first-class companies on the Stock Exchange which otherwise they could not afford; they direct funds into industrial expansion, which is of general benefit to all in the long run; and through their earnings on their overseas investments they contribute to the country's invisible earnings, which is good for the country's balance of trade.

Unit trusts

A unit trust is a method of investment whereby money subscribed by many people is pooled in a fund, the investment and management of which is subject to the legal provisions of a trust deed. The fund is invested in securities on behalf of the subscribers by a management company. The investments so acquired are held by a trustee, usually a bank or insurance company. The management company and the trustee must be quite independent of each other. They are parties to the trust deed, which defines their collective responsibilities toward the subscribers to the trust fund and sets out the rules for the operation of the trust.

The earliest unit trust in this country was formed in 1931, and the idea caught on rapidly, although control over new capital issues restricted the offering of new units for much of the post-war period.

The advantages claimed for the unit trust idea of investment are security, regular income distribution, and, above all, spread of risk. A few unit trusts have obtained a stock exchange quotation, but the majority are not quoted but are bought and sold by the management company, which works out purchase and sale prices ('bid' and 'offer') based on the market value of the underlying securities. The management company undertakes to purchase all sub-units offered to it; thus there is an assured market for those wishing to realize their investment.

The portfolio of securities is the unit. This is divided into some thousands of sub-units, which are sold to the public, the investor being given a sub-unit certificate. The value of this is based on the market price of the unit portfolio.

Before the units are offered for sale to the public a unit trust must be authorized by the Department of Trade. The Department will not issue a certificate of authorization unless it is satisfied that the trust deed is drawn up in a way to satisfy the Department's requirements.

The trust deed must provide for the provision of funds for future management expenses; for the audit and circulation to sub-unit holders of the accounts of the managers in relation to the trust; for the manner in which the sale and re-purchase prices of sub-units and the advertised yield is calculated; for the examination by the trustee of all advertisements; and for changes in management if the trustee certifies that this is necessary in the interests of the sub-unit holders.

Through his subscription to the trust fund each subscriber acquires a fraction of interest in the block of securities in which the fund is invested, while the dividends received from the investments form the income of the trust. The net income is paid to all investors in the trust fund in proportion to the size of their holdings.

The primary functions of the trustee are to make sure that the terms of the trust deed are observed; to act as custodian of the capital and income of the trust; to hold in its name the securities in which money subscribed by the public to the trust fund has been invested by the managers; to take responsibility for the register of sub-unit holders; and to ensure that advertising details are correct and not misleading.

The trustee company's remuneration comes from an agreed part of the loading charge, shared with the managers, and commission on stock orders. (The loading charge is the charge made for the administration of the trust, spread over the life of the trust.)

The managers are responsible for the administration of the unit trust, for the calculation of the unit offered and its price, for preparing income distributions, for managing the investment portfolio of the trust fund, and for maintaining a market in the units of the trust.

The remuneration of the management company comes from a portion of the loading charge and from the 'turn' or difference between transactions at offer and bid prices.

The costs of running the trust are met partly by an initial charge which forms part of the price of the sub-unit, and partly by a semi-annual service charge which is taken out of the income of the trust. The level of both charges is controlled by the Department of Trade.

Some unit trusts accept holdings as small as £25. The trusts differ considerably in character: some aim at securing a high income while others aim at capital appreciation. Some invest widely over all classes of ordinary shares, while some specialize in, for example, bank, insurance, or investment trust shares, or put a high proportion of their money in specific overseas securities.

Local authority loans

Local authorities are usually in need of money, being government on a smaller scale. They need to borrow money in advance of the yearly rates influx. To find large sums quickly they operate on the money markets, where they obtain quite large amounts for anything from seven days to a year. For more permanent borrowing they may issue loan stock, which is quoted on the Stock Exchange. They also adver-tise for loans from the general public, and the amounts which they are prepared to take can vary with each authority. These will be for fixed periods of between one and seven years, with no withdrawal facilities. The rates of interest will be competitive when the loan is made, but it will be fixed, so that the investor will do better if interest rates fall subsequently. Interest is paid with tax deducted, but investors paying a low rate of tax can reclaim the tax involved. Smaller councils may offer a slightly higher rate of interest, though all local authority loans are equally secure. Full details of the various offers available can be obtained from one of the information bureaux run by the Chartered Institute of Public Finance and Accountancy, and it usually pays to shop around a bit.

An example of the various types of loans and bonds available is the yearling bond, normally issued for periods of one year. An issue of bonds is placed weekly on Tuesdays for settlement the following day. The bonds are registered securities and are listed on the Stock Exchange. Dealings are in multiples of £1,000.

Finance company deposits

Some of the highest interest rates of all are offered by commercial companies who used to describe themselves as 'banks', by finance houses, or by hire purchase companies. Many of these should be treated with caution. The three points where difficulty may be expected are: Are there any facilities for withdrawal? Is the deposit for a long term of years? Is the sum to be invested fixed at a large minimum?

Stocks and shares

Though the majority of shares are still held by institutions such as pension funds and insurance companies, share ownership by individuals has recently become more widespread with the increased privatization by the government of such companies as British Telecom, and more firms issuing shares to employees.

People buy shares for different reasons. Some, short-term speculators, look for quick gains by trying to spot anomalies in share prices, following rumours such as takeovers or significant oil finds, or dealing just before the results are published in the hope that market expectations are wrong. Most investors prefer to take a longer view, selecting companies whose profits will grow and whose dividends will increase and so make share ownership more attractive and therefore increasing the share price.

To ascertain whether any particular company is likely to show profit growth requires a close look at the company, the sector of industry in which it is involved, the economy as a whole, and many other factors.

Stockbrokers and other financial institutions employ expert analysts who examine a company's profitability, trying to establish whether the shares are relatively cheap or expensive. Most stockbrokers' recommendations are based on this research, which is called fundamental analysis. However, there are other ways of trying to predict share prices. Some people use charts, or graphs, of share price movements, saying that future prices can be predicted from these by spotting particular patterns. The success of these methods is still the subject of much debate.

The risks involved in buying shares should not be underestimated. Even large, well established companies have been known to have a sharp terminal reversal in fortunes. For this reason many advisers will not consider recommending this form of investment unless the individual concerned can afford to suffer losses without hardship.

A portfolio of a dozen or so equities is normally regarded as sufficient to spread the risk without diluting it too much. An essential part of most stock exchange portfolios is fixed interest stock.

Fixed interest stock

The most secure are government securities or gilt-edged stocks. There are about 100 in existence, with maturity dates ranging from a few weeks or months to well into the next century, and even some undated stocks.

Coupons, the amount of interest paid each year per £100 of stock, go from $2\frac{1}{2}$ per cent to $15\frac{1}{2}$ per cent. There are also index linked stocks whose coupon and repayment value are dependent on the movement of the Retail Price Index.

Similarly there are corporation loans, and 'bulldogs' which are sterling bonds issued by overseas governments.

Less secure, and therefore offering better returns, are corporate debentures and unsecured loans.

Obviously, with such a large choice selections can be made to suit most investor needs, either for capital growth or income. For capital growth, investors are likely to choose a low coupon stock whose price is below par, giving a low yield. On most of these stocks, growth will be exempt from Capital Gains Tax. Income seekers will select high coupon securities usually standing near the par value and offering a yield which reflects current interest rates.

Pension schemes

Pensions are often the only form of saving for retirement which a person will make. They are part of the remuneration of the employee, deferred until he has finished active work, to which he has a right.

The 1973 Social Security Act stated conditions for the recognition of a private pension scheme. Formerly these schemes were of two basic kinds, both shaped by the tax concessions which the authorities were willing to give. The first gave less tax allowance, but allowed part of the pension to be converted into a cash payment – commutation – on retirement. The second gave a greater tax allowance, but no right of commutation.

Some limit to pension benefits has to be set if these tax concessions are not to be abused, and therefore the maximum yearly pension amount under the rules is one-sixtieth of final year's salary multiplied by the years of service, being not less than ten nor more than forty. In other words, provided an employee has served at least forty years with the same company he can get two-thirds of his final salary by way of pension. This figure may be exceeded because in 1974 the government ruled that pensions could be based on what the salary would have been, but for pay restraint. The yield of many schemes is less than this.

An employee leaving one job and taking up another has only two options. The choice he is confronted with is either to accept a deferred pension based on salary at the time of leaving, or to take a transfer value to his new employer's scheme. In either case a loss of pension rights results. The deferred pension, which becomes payable only on retirement, is based on the frozen salary at the time of leaving and takes no account of future salary increases. Inflation gradually erodes its value so that on retirement the deferred pension may be worth only a pittance.

The alternative is to take a transfer value, if that is allowed, and purchase back years of service. However, because of the conservative assumptions of the actuaries of both sets of employers, the number of years' service that the transfer value is deemed to purchase generally falls short of pensionable years actually served, and it is not uncommon to find that, by taking transfer value, the employee can lose as much as two-thirds of his previous pensionable service.

All employers use pension fund contributions from 'early leavers' to subsidize the cost of providing pensions for those who stay. This can be done either by the failure of the employer to credit the former employee with the full value of the interest earned by his contributions, or, if the former employee was in a private pension scheme which has been contracted out, by the use of the former employee's preserved benefits to pay for the inflation proofing which the employer is bound by law to provide for the former employee's 'guaranteed minimum pension' (a practice known as franking).

Self-employed people

The self-employed man or woman, or anyone else who wishes to provide for retirement, can take out an endowment assurance policy to provide a pension or lump sum on retirement which can be invested; or can contract with an insurance company for an Individual Retirement Annuity.

Endowment assurance carries the same tax relief as for any other policy, but the Individual Retirement Annuities get the same tax relief as is granted to an approved employer's scheme, a much better proposition. Any annuity is subject to the disadvantage that if you die soon after you have retired you have made a bad bargain. To cover this the annuitant should see that the annuity payments are guaranteed for five or ten years after retirement. If then the annuitant is dead there will be something to be passed to his dependants.

All pensions and annuities should have built-in provision for cost of living rises; otherwise continuing inflation will progressively eat away the real value of the payments at a time when the recipient is least likely to be able to do anything to supplement them.

The state pension

Under legislation which came into force in 1961 a 'graduated' element was added to the basic flat rate pension. This was meant to provide a higher level of pension, which would be more in proportion to the income earned during working years, for those earning more than the national average. This system ended in April 1975. From 6 April the Social Security Act, 1973, came into operation. From that date flat rate and graduated contributions ceased to be payable for employees and were replaced by wholly earnings-related contributions. Stamp cards for employees were abolished at the same time, and the earnings-related national insurance contributions are now collected with income tax under the PAYE procedure.

The 1973 Social Security Act established a two-tier pensions scheme, a basic scheme plus a state reserve scheme. The basic scheme is available for everyone at 65 (60 for women) provided that they in fact retire at that age. This part of the pension is guaranteed by the state.

On 8 May 1974 the government announced modifications of the 1973 Social Security Act. The state reserve pensions scheme was scrapped, for the reason that it would leave thousands of people dependent for years to come on means-tested supplementary pensions. Also, it made particularly poor provision for widows and other women. At the same time, the government was in favour of good private pensions schemes. Apart from the state reserve scheme, the basic provisions of the 1973 Social Security Act would remain.

This would include the change from the then graduated pension scheme, which would be wound up, to a system which would be fully related to earnings. Provisions to preserve existing occupational pension rights would also come into force as planned.

Those who since 1961 have been earning more than the national average will be entitled to a graduated pension if they did not contract out at the time. Those who did contract out have had to make contributions since 1966 and will receive some extra pension on this account when they retire. Although the graduated scheme was terminated in 1975, benefits that have accrued under it are preserved, although without interest. For most people these benefits are likely to be very small.

A Social Security Pensions Act was passed in August 1975; its provisions came into effect in May 1978.

The new pensions system is financed by increased National Insurance contributions and by a Treasury supplement coming from direct taxation. Benefits are of two kinds: a basic pension, corresponding to the existing flat-rate pension, and an earnings-related pension, which will build up over twenty years and by 1998 will equal 25 per cent of each persons' average yearly earnings between a lower and an upper limit. To get this maximum benefit a person has to work for twenty years after 1978.

By 1998 the objective of the Act will have been fulfilled. From then on, there will be guaranteed pensions of up to 54 per cent of national average earnings. This should take the poverty out of old age. Unfortunately, very few people can understand the new system, which has been the subject of one White Paper, three Acts of Parliament, twenty-one occupational pension board memoranda and nine sets of regulations totalling 167,000 words.

Miscellaneous investments

Finally, one must remember that there are very many people who save part of their income not in building societies, banks, insurance policies or stocks and shares, but buy other things as a hedge against inflation.

Often the purchase of material things is bound up with a hobby, but the intention is not only the interest in the hobby, but also the love of items possessed, and the eventual accumulation of wealth. Whether the accumulation of wealth or the pursuit of a hobby predominates will depend entirely on the person concerned.

These collections have obvious drawbacks. They provide no income, often need to be insured and need adequate storage, which could involve considerable expense. Often a precise valuation cannot be obtained, and when the time comes to sell a ready market might not always be available.

A lot of items are subject to fashion so that predicting future trends can be very difficult. For most people this means that collecting must be a pleasure, and only as a secondary consideration, a hedge against inflation.

Revision test 15

Place a tick against the letter you consider is the correct answer.
1 A suitable investment of £5,000 for an elderly widow paying no tax would be
   (a) shares in a building society
   (b) premium bonds
   (c) gilt-edged stock on the National Savings Register.
2 Interest on Deposit Bonds is paid
   (a) by accrual to capital
   (b) twice yearly without deduction of tax
   (c) quarterly, tax paid.
3 A person participating in the National Savings Yearly Plan pays his contributions for
   (a) five years
   (b) three years
   (c) one year.
4 Which of these can be bought and sold on the Stock Exchange:
   (a) building society shares?
   (b) investment trust stock?
   (c) unit trusts?
5 Protection against inflation is incorporated in
   (a) a with-profits endowment life policy
   (b) a bank deposit account
   (c) a finance house deposit account.

6 Life assurance policies can be linked to
   (a) unit trusts
   (b) Premium Bonds
   (c) investment trusts.
7 Survival to a stated age will give a lump sum under a
   (a) whole life policy
   (b) term policy
   (c) endowment policy.
8 A 'yearling' bond is issued by
   (a) a bank
   (b) a local authority
   (c) a stockbroker.
9 A person who has just been given a redundancy payment of
   £25,000 will be able to obtain from his bank
   (a) specific investment advice
   (b) general investment advice
   (c) no investment advice at all.
10 Fixed-interest return on an investment is available from
   (a) a gilt-edged investment
   (b) Premium Bonds
   (c) equities.

Questions for discussion

1 Discuss the difference between investment and saving.
2 Explain the difference between a unit trust and an investment
   trust.
3 When a movement in interest rates is expected, describe how
   this is likely to affect the price of government stock.

16

The banking environment

Pre-automation

In the lifetime of the author and no doubt in the lifetime of some older bankers, the banking system has seen remarkable changes in procedures, law, expansion of services, and attitudes of customers to banking and to the deposit and withdrawal functions in particular.

It was some time after the Second World War that any form of automation was introduced. Many branches and departments of banks had little or no machinery with which to do their daily work. In the small- to average-sized branch the cashiers took in credits, which consisted of cash and/or cheques, and these were listed and agreed by hand on 'waste sheets' or 'control sheets'. The junior clerks, by listing the amounts, had to prove the accuracy of the customer's credit and at the same time write the details against each item, so that should a query arise sometime in the future the cheque or credit could be identified.

The cashier had no machine or calculator to assist him with his work, and the cashier's book identified to some considerable extent the items cashed, whether they were house debits or other cheques. Money paid in was recorded by the name of the customer or the named person and his bank/branch.

Having agreed the waste or control sheet, the next procedure was to sort the items and then list them on either debit batch sheets or credit batch sheets. Often, for quick identification and to reduce errors, these sheets were of different colours. For example, on the debit batch sheets there were columns for house debits, impersonal debits, unpaids, and claims on other banks and branches. Cheques drawn on other banks and branches – comprising the majority of debits – were listed on clearing sheets, totalled, and, before despatch to the clearing house, agreed with the day's work.

The credit batch sheets consisted of columns for house credits, other bank credits, branch credits, impersonal credits, unpaids, etc. At the end of the day the summary totals of the credit batch sheets had to agree with the summary totals of the debit batch sheets.

The ledgers were usually large leather-bound books, and all entries were hand posted. Each sheet or sheets had the name of the customer written in neat, often copperplate, lettering, and any instructions regarding signatures, limits, stops, etc., were usually written in spaces provided on the sheets; every time a balance was transferred from one sheet to another, the details were also transferred. As all entries were made by hand, and the balances calculated by mental arithmetic, it was necessary to check not only that the items were posted to the correct account, but that the balances were also correct. For this purpose a check ledger system was imposed, and this list of entries was called by the manager or his deputy each morning for the previous day's work.

Statements made their appearance in the late 1930s, but even after the Second World War there existed a mixture of statements and passbooks. These were all written up by hand and checked daily, and when customers required either their passbooks or statements these were given out over the counter – complete up to the previous day's work and checked with the ledger balance by two people before delivery.

Just for the record, passbooks were rather bulky items, quite unlike the present type of passbook issued by the building societies. The debits were listed on one side and credits on the other, so either the customer had to add up both columns and deduct one from the other to obtain a balance, or the bank clerk added up the amounts and showed the total of each column in pencil. The figures were of course reconciled with the ledger before issue. Many junior clerks complained when customers bought in their passbooks, say, every quarter or so, to be made up and returned there and then at the counter. The customer waited for this to be done and would complain if the service was slow. All vouchers were returned with the passbook, and the passbook cover often had a pocket to hold the vouchers.

The accounting machine

Adding machines made a slow introduction at the turn of this century. They were, in comparison with present machines, very cumbersome things and merely used in large offices for listings only or ledger extracts.

Much later on the accounting machine was introduced. The use of accounting machines came in easy stages. First they were manual, that is, on pressing the appropriate keys a handle had to be pulled to put the amount into the machine memory to add to the previous total. Later, with the growth in the use of electricity, a bar was introduced on to the machine, which meant that instead of pulling a handle, rather like pulling a pint of beer, a bar could be lightly pressed to produce the same result.

The accounting machines, if they were good, had two registers and often included a swinging carriage, whereby the waste/control sheets could be inserted and the operator could record in distinct columns the debit and credit items and show either a sub-total or a full total, depending upon the time of day or whether the machine was going to be used for another purpose, e.g. to list the out clearing.

Not only was the machine used for the purposes of the waste, but the check ledger system could operate as well. With the introduction of a typewriter into a branch, the check ledger system did not need to be handwritten, the amounts were recorded by the accounting machine, and a typist, or a clerk who could type, would type the customer's name against each debit or credit entry.

From this emerged the machine that could be used for ledgers and statements. These machines could not only record debits and credits, but could produce a balance on the press of a button, so that, rather gradually, every branch of a bank had loose-leaf statements and loose-leaf ledger systems. As a result the internal audit check on entries and balances became much easier. The passbook system was beginning to disappear: although some customers of long standing insisted on retaining the system, new customers were not offered a choice – it was statements only.

Although the use of accounting machines was revolutionary, it brought in its wake problems of noise, boredom and, more important, problems of a bottleneck in the flow of work. Whereas under the old hand-written systems additional clerks could move into areas of crisis, now with the machine the progress of the office could only be as fast and as accurate as the machine operator.

Within a short space of time further refinements were added to these machines. The first was the use of a magnetic strip which enabled the operator to place correctly into the machine the ledger or statement sheet so that figures were not overprinted on others. Secondly came the introduction onto the machines of a typewriter keyboard, so that the particulars of the entry as well as the amount could be recorded onto the waste sheet in one operation. Eventually the posting of the ledger and statement sheets became one operation.

Further progress was made in the 1940s by the introduction of microfilm to banks. In branches this was particularly important as it did away with the tedious procedure of writing up the details of every credit and cheque. Instead, after listing the items on the waste/control sheet, every item went through a microfilm process so that it was photographed. The processing of the film usually took about forty-eight hours or so. Queries then had to be looked up on the roll of film representing the particular day's work.

Punched cards

The beginnings of the automation process in banking procedures commenced with the introduction of punched cards and punched paper tape. These were the original methods of feeding information into computers, which in those days were large cumbersome machines, taking up a lot of space and certainly working at a much slower pace than those functioning today.

Paper tape was used to transfer the day's work from the branch bank to the central computer system. The system in general worked as follows. The work was processed on an accounting machine which not only gave information on paper, but from its side or at the back it produced paper tape on which was recorded the same information. This tape was carefully kept so that, at the end of the day, the tape was either fed into a terminal connected directly to a computer, or a member of the staff took the tape to a larger branch, or to a central point in the town or city, for the staff there to process the information on to the terminal. This as you will no doubt be aware is the beginnings of a centralized accounting system. Before this time each branch kept ledgers, on either a hand-written system or an accounting machine system, so that access to balances was available within the branch. From this time a computer some miles away had to be contacted and information received by the branch for its daily use.

Not only were the accounting records put on computer, but customer records were on punched cards which had to be amended as and when customer information changed. Many readers will recall the use of punched cards for the production of personalized cheque books which showed the customer's name, account number and branch code. These items were printed from the punch card, and other information such as cheque numbers were added sometime during the production of the cheque book.

Automation of the clearing systems

With the production of Magnetic Ink Character Recognition symbols (MICR symbols) on each cheque, the main area of automation was in the clearing departments of the various banks, which used these processes to sort cheques into bank and branch order, and finally to debit the customer's account which was held in a central system. Very gradually all branches of the major banks were placed on direct line to a central computer system; but it should be realized that it took quite a number of years from the time it was decided to put a branch on to an automated system until final accomplishment.

At the time there were no plans to place credits on to a computer system. In fact the credit clearing system was in its infancy, and many small branches, on receipt of a credit for another bank or branch, still remitted this credit with a banker's payment to the beneficiary branch/bank by mail.

At the same time as all this was taking place, the local clearings, which were a daily occurrence in many small towns, ended. The procedure had been labour intensive and too expensive.

Cash dispensers

Then came the gradual introduction of the cash dispenser. The dispenser in those days merely gave out an envelope containing £10. Although a card was used this was retained by the machine, which meant that on the following business day a bank clerk had to send the card back to customer and raise a debit manually to pass to the account. This of course was time consuming and expensive. The present cash dispensers, Automated Teller Machines (ATMs), are much faster and return the card to the user, but above all they allow the customer to obtain a balance, order a cheque book or statement, and obtain cash, usually in round amounts of £5, up to an agreed daily or weekly amount. Individual banks give the ATMs other names such as Cashpoint, Autobank and Service Till.

Expansion of services

The expansion in the use of computers meant that standing orders could be computerized and that the introduction of a direct debit system would mean that a cheaper method of remittance of funds could be introduced, placing the onus of originating the debit with the creditor company. The use of direct debits, standing orders and the present system of cash dispensing has meant a reduction in the use of staff in the more menial tasks in the bank.

Looking at the system as a whole, what aid does automation give to banks?

Computerization gives the banks the ability to store, produce, obtain and dispatch information to any section of the bank. This information can be sent in words, numbers, and even in picture form if necessary, in a reliable, quick and economical way.

The information can cover such operations as customers' accounts showing the number of debit/credit items, turnover, average balances, charges, interest to be given/charged, statement despatch, etc.

As a means of money transmission the automation of banks has meant that the quick, safe and easy method of dispatch and receipt of funds has worked well, not only in the banks' favour but for customers as well. It should be remembered that such organizations as the Society for World Wide Interbank Financial Transactions (SWIFT), Banks Automated Clearing Services (BACS) and, more recently, Cheque Handling Clearing Processes (CHAPS) have been brought into existence specifically to ensure that a cheap, safe method of dispatch and receipt of funds, in the shortest possible time, is available for use by banks and their customers.

Not only is automation used for the benefit of customers, but the bank will use the computer for its own needs as well. The records of banks are kept on computer: bank staff salaries, staff records, branch and central costs are on computer, so that the bank has this information at its immediate disposal. Of course in the banks' roles as financial advisers and lenders the computer is used for research and the interpretation of accounts, etc.

In the specialized areas of trustee work, share registration, new issues, foreign exchange, etc., the use of computers has been invaluable, and it seems that no branch or area of a bank can be without a computer system of one sort or another.

Automation in banks is of course expanding. Word processors are now in greater use, cash dispensers are getting more sophisticated, the automation of credit clearing operations is spreading, and the truncation of cheques and other items between branches is now clearly used in certain instances, e.g. unpaid items.

The future

For the future, we shall see facilities in home banking for personal customers. For treasurers of corporate customers the ability to link to the computers of banks will enable them to obtain balances daily or when needed, to authorize the transfer of funds from one place to another and to authorize the purchase of assets or the deposit of funds anywhere in the world.

For banks this will mean that more and more banking will be effected away from the hall of the branch bank. For example EFTPOS (Electronic Funds Transfer Point of Sale) is already in existence, although banks are giving this service their own market names, e.g. Connect, Switch, etc. With the introduction of this service, banks are already combining their cash cards and cheque guarantee cards with the EFTPOS card.

Eventually we will have the paperless, cashierless bank. All that will be required by a customer will be a plastic card, knowledge of his or her Personal Identification Number (PIN), and the ability to use a simple processing system situated at some strategic place, such as home, a store, place of work, or a bank. This will allow the customer to withdraw or transfer funds, obtain information or statement print-outs, authorize the purchase of stocks, shares, etc., and do all manner of things – now undertaken at a counter – without seeing a member of the bank's staff. The same thing would apply if a customer wished to have a loan or overdraft, he would use his plastic card, punch in the required personal details, and the authorization for a loan would, if necessary, be granted showing interest rates, terms of repayment, etc.

Banks themselves realize that they not only compete with each other for customers, but also with other financial institutions, so that the banks are not only spending hundreds of millions of pounds on improved technology, but making the branch bank 'customer friendly'. That is, they are changing the fabric of the building, to make it less imposing and more attractive – perhaps with window displays – making the interior more inviting and providing a warm, friendly atmosphere in order to provide caring and efficient services. Very slowly, the long counters are being scrapped, so that customers who wish to discuss personal financial matters may do so with members of staff seated at desks in the banking hall, and the necessity for persons to shout at each other through quarter-inch glass plate will be a thing of the past.

Banks will also be places where persons can go to look for leaflets, VDUs, posters, and other advertisements showing the various services offered by banks.

Whereas in the past banks earned most of their income from interest and other account charges, they are now not charging for any personal current account that is in credit, no matter how many entries are passed each month or quarter. Indeed banks are now offering interest on current accounts. So in order to obtain an income, banks are charging fees for all the various services offered. To sell these services, clerks must not be movers of paper from one point to another. They must spend more time providing customers with advice and service. 'Tellers must be Sellers'.

The internal workings of a bank will also be revolutionized by the eventual withdrawal of the many and varied books of head office instructions, and the circulars sent down with regular monotony by regional and area offices. Instead information will be available on VDU which will be accessible to all bank staff. For example, when a clerk has to verify the procedure for the collection of a foreign draft, rather than having to search for such information in a book, he will merely touch the VDU screen and the information will appear. Training of staff at all levels can be computer assisted. Will this mean that large numbers of personnel used in conducting courses will be made redundant? Already banks are making extensive use of video equipment for in-branch training.

The scope for the use of computers in banks and for communication purposes are limitless. Already work is proceeding on voice and facsimile transmission of data. Changes will be more frequent in order to increase efficiency and standardize procedures. We live in interesting times. With each area of a bank there will again be a division, often quite a sharp one, between those offices serving corporate customers and those giving service to non-corporate customers. There are organisations that will have 'satellite' offices that offer the basic banking services, leaving the main office in town to offer the more specialist services, e.g. foreign, investment, loans, etc.

Banking services

It is now reckoned that all the major banks offer two hundred or more services. The sharp end of banking is the branch. How can the branch manager or any of his staff be competent to deal with the intricate problems involved with any particular service? Obviously they cannot. Instead, the problem is passed to a department of the bank that specializes in that particular area.

Long before automation the major banks offered specialized services in trustee and executor work, then taxation followed by insurance. Again, in each of these areas additional services were offered; for example, within the insurance field, pension schemes were introduced and now form an important part of the insurance services offered by banks.

Banks found that in order to keep ahead of their rivals, and also their competitors in other fields, they had to offer a wider range of services. This meant that in order to become efficient it was necessary to form subsidiary companies or take over existing specialist companies. Areas such as leasing, factoring, and company registration work that were not part of any bank's service just after the Second World War, are now as much a part of the banking scene as any other activity.

Each major bank is not just one company but a group of companies answerable to a holding company. Indeed, it is quite possible to see from an organization chart that many banking subsidiaries own subsidiaries. This has meant that the organization is large and complex, so that banks are divided up into operational divisions and areas. Each area or division is responsible for its activities and profitability. In order to use the funds deposited with the banking groups, there are now sterling and foreign exchange dealers, treasurers and accountants in the head offices of banks and their subsidiary companies. They use sophisticated techniques to handle vast sums of money to maximize profits yet maintain the liquidity necessary to meet the demands of a financial institution taking deposits on terms varying from demand to long term.

The international or overseas divisions of banks have expanded enormously over the last decade or so, and have seen tremendous advancement and profitability. It was not only the suspension of the Exchange Control Act, which obviously had some effect on overseas services, but the competitiveness of British banks and overseas banks which expanded these services, encouraged foreign banks to open offices in London and caused the major UK banks to open offices in the USA, Europe and elsewhere. In fact many banks not only opened branches abroad but bought out foreign banks to complement their own services.

With the 'Big Bang', banks have acquired broking and jobbing firms, so we now have banks directly involved in the stock market. If one can call this fringe banking, then the acquisition of large firms of estate agents must be even more on the fringe of banking services. This expansion into areas remote from the basic essentials of a bank is unlikely to stop. As time goes on, there is no doubt in the mind of the author that some sort of banker/building society relationship will emerge to offer a total financial package to any non-corporate or corporate customer.

Staff

With all this continual change in banking services, automation, and of course with the economies imposed on all businesses, including banks, what is the effect on bank employees?

First, bank staff, particularly at branch level, are receiving regular training that in the past was never even thought of. An interest is shown by management in the development of all bank staff so that they may reach their potential as quickly as possible. Those members of staff destined for managerial positions are further encouraged by allowing them either day release or half-day release from work to attend classes to obtain The Chartered Institute of Bankers' Diploma.

However, it is a well known fact that banks are continuously looking not only for profitable services but the expansion of services to attract new customers. One major service recently given to the general public is the re-opening of selected branches on a

Saturday morning. True, it is only personal services that are offered, but nevertheless those banks that first started Saturday morning banking found that the numbers of people opening accounts with them were growing steadily. This has meant that an additional burden is placed on staff, because the bank is committed to maintaining opening hours once Saturday arrangements have been advertised.

The additional hours of work are on top of the usual five-day week, which in many branches and departments is frequently an 8.30 a.m. start and a 5.30 p.m. finish.

Banks are proud of the personal service that they can give customers. It is not just the manager who is consulted, but the security clerk, standing order clerk, etc., are also at the forefront, giving advice and reassurance to customers. In addition to this, there is now the delegation of lending authority to non-supervisory staff. Whereas not so long ago the authority to lend to customers was vested in supervisory and managerial staff, it is now possible for grade 4 and possibly grade 3 unappointed members of staff to authorize small loans to customers.

With all the automation, expansion of services, pressure of work and so on, the bank clerk must of course ensure that he is fully conversant with current affairs. He must ensure that there is, for example, no breach of the Consumer Credit Act, nor any breach of secrecy when, in an unguarded moment, he may reveal to an unauthorized person some details of a customer's account. He must be constantly vigilant in maintaining a good service and ensuring that his knowledge is up to date.

With all these pressures, the bank clerk often has the opportunity of moving out of branch banking into some area which he may find more interesting or which will give him more job satisfaction. Indeed there are more bank clerks involved in departmental jobs and servicing branches than actually serve in branches. The banking environment has changed and will continue to change.

Questions for discussion

1 Describe the advantages of the automation of banking services to
   (a) the bank
   (b) the bank's staff
   (c) the bank's customers.

2 In the near future, it could be possible to have a 'paperless branch'. Discuss how you consider the use of computers will do away with customers' paper files in areas of
   (i) interview notes
   (ii) personal records
   (iii) advances.

3 To what extent do you consider that the computer has made the work of a bank clerk more interesting and less routine than the work of the previous generation? To what extent do you consider that the present bank clerk needs greater skills and knowledge of banking than his predecessor?

Appendix I

The Chartered Institute of Bankers

The Chartered Institute of Bankers is a professional body whose members are men and women engaged in banking of every sort all over the world. It was founded in 1879, and its two main objects have always been:

    (i)   to provide an education in banking
    (ii) to maintain the standard of the profession.

There are four grades of membership: student members who are not eligible for any of the other grades; ordinary members who must be employed in banking or other relevant occupations and who must also:

    (i)   have at least 3 years in such employment; or
    (ii)   have passed or been exempted from the Stage 1 examinations; or
    (iii) be at least 25 years old.

Associates, who have completed the banking, trustee or international banking diploma examinations; and Fellows, normally elected from Associates who have had at least five years' managerial experience and have given service to the Institute. The total of all four grades of membership is now about 135,000.

For members in their early years, the main part of their formal banking education (apart, that is, from their working experience) is provided through courses of study for the associateship examinations. For the vast majority, the Banking Diploma is the qualification which they are encouraged to obtain by their employers; for the much smaller numbers on the executor and trustee side, a separate route is available – the Trustee Diploma. A Credit Card Certificate, for staff employed by the credit card companies, has been introduced, and more recently an International Banking Diploma has been launched.

As a prelude to their studies for the Associateship examinations, members other than those who already hold a degree acceptable to the Institute will be expected to complete Stage 1 of the Institute's educational structure. There are two main courses, the Banking Certificate, which is primarily a qualification in its own right leading to the award of a Certificate, and catering for senior supervisory grades and the staff who aspire to them, and the Foundation Course, which is designed specifically as a route to Stage 2 for 'A' Level holders.

Both courses provide a basic commercial background in Economics, Law and Accountancy, as well as the subject of this book 'Elements of Banking'.

The Banking Diploma leading to the award of ACIB (Associate of The Chartered Institute of Bankers) forms Stage 2 of the Institute's educational structure. Its object is to provide a knowledge of technical banking and applied business studies and it is the basic qualification for the majority of career bankers. Subjects covered in Parts A and B of the Banking Diploma include accountancy, monetary economics, law relating to banking, finance of international trade, investment, and the nature of management. Part C of the Banking Diploma entails study for two compulsory Institute papers in the practice of banking.

Full details of Stages 1 and 2 of the Institute's educational structure are given in the respective syllabuses. These are obtainable from the Registrar's Department, The Chartered Institute of Bankers, Emmanuel House, Canterbury, Kent CT1 2XJ.

Financial Studies Diploma

Completing the educational structure is the Financial Studies Diploma, the Institute's premier qualification in banking and management subjects for those who are expected to achieve senior management appointments. The diploma covers subjects such as human resource management, marketing and business planning, as well as advanced banking practice. Entry is restricted to (i) Associates of The Chartered Institute of Bankers, and (ii) holders of acceptable degrees or professional qualifications. Students of the Financial Studies Diploma receive a *Newsletter* three times a year. A wide-ranging programme of revision seminars and workshops takes place throughout the academic year.

Details of the syllabus and regulations for the Financial Studies Diploma are obtainable from the Registrar's Department (see address above). There are now over 250 holders, who are entitled to use the letters 'DipFS'.

Tuition

Students have a choice of methods of study for the examinations: they can attend college classes, take correspondence courses, or rely entirely on private study. For the majority, good oral tuition is likely to be the most effective method of study.

A system of recognition, for correspondence courses, was started in 1968 to ensure that material for the final subjects of the Banking Diploma is kept up to date, and that the marking of test papers corresponds with the standards expected by the Institute in the examinations. A considerable number of courses, offered by five commercial correspondence colleges, are now recognized under this scheme.

Revision courses

In the UK, the Institute runs an extensive revision course programme in London and through the local centres (see below). Similarly, to assist candidates overseas, the Institute has arranged a number of courses locally, sending tutors from the UK to help students revise and generally prepare for the examinations.

The banks themselves offer a great deal of encouragement to their staff to complete the examinations. In some cases candidates are given study leave – a half day or a full day per week – and some of the larger banks run their own revision courses.

The Institute also provides a comprehensive service to banking teachers through regular education bulletins containing up-to-date information about the subjects they teach, and short courses for those who are teaching banking subjects (including teachers in overseas institutes and local centres).

An important feature of the Institute's examinations is that they are not 'competitive': an objective standard is set, and those who reach it pass, those who do not, fail. This means that the percentage of those passing can fluctuate from one examination to the next.

Local centres

It is vital that any sort of vocational education should be kept up to date, and the Institute sets out to provide the banker with the means of doing this throughout his career. To cater mainly for the qualified members it has encouraged the formation of local centres of which there are now more than 100, including those overseas. These centres each have honorary education officers, whose task is to deal with the problems of students in their areas. The main work of the centres, however, is in arranging programmes of lectures, discussions, seminars, industrial visits and social events for its qualified members. Over 1,250 meetings are arranged annually, attended each year by over 40,000 members and their colleagues in allied professions.

Local centres also compete each year in two national competitions run from Institute headquarters. In the computer-based Banking Game, teams entering are each responsible for managing a fictional branch bank for profit and the team making the largest profit wins. The Debating Competition runs throughout the winter, with regional heats and the final held in London.

Other facilities

The main medium of communication with the members is a monthly magazine, *Banking World*, which provides information on all major new developments in banking and in the Institute. The Institute also publishes a wide range of other publications including many specially commissioned to meet the needs of those studying for the new subjects in the qualifications. In 1987, the Institute opened its own bookshop, Bankers Books at 17 St Swithins Lane, London EC4. The shop has a very comprehensive stock of financial literature including all the books recommended in the syllabus. A mail-order service is available for those who cannot visit the shop.

The Institute's library, with over 30,000 volumes, is well known in the financial world, and in addition to the usual services provides members with excellent postal borrowing facilities and a wide-ranging information service.

At national level, the Institute runs regular management seminars which enable managers and potential managers from every kind of bank to widen their outlook on professional problems. Short management development courses and an evening lecture series on a wide range of banking topics are now an established part of the Institute's work.

The annual International Banking Summer School attracts senior bankers from more than fifty countries to discuss topics of professional importance. Started by the Institute in 1948, it is now held all over the world, returning periodically to its original home in England.

For young Associates, the Institute arranges banking study tours which enable these members to study at first hand the banking systems of other countries.

In short the Institute aims to provide something for everyone at every stage of his or her career in banking. In the long term the services which it offers should help its members in their careers, the banks with their profits, and, perhaps most important, improve the standard of service enjoyed by their customers.

Appendix II

The Financial Services Act, 1986

In various parts of this book you have seen reference to the Financial Services Act, 1986. This Act is perhaps one of the most important acts which has attempted to regulate the business of investment, so that readers should understand that all financial institutions, including banks, are affected in some way. It is particularly important to those who sell either the investment services of their own institution, or the services of other institutions; whether they are working from a branch level or departmental level, they should be aware of the legal consequences of any action they take.

Following the collapse of some financial institutions, Professor Gower was asked by the government in 1982 to review the whole area of investor protection. This report was published in 1984 (Cmnd 9125, 1984) and was subject to a lot of discussion both in and out of parliament. At the same time the Stock Exchange was realizing that its trading conditions were beginning to change. Other than the normal traditional types of investments available, there was a growing number of new types of investments and instruments available to the investor. The abolition of fixed rates of commission was being considered as well as the need to dispense with the dual-capacity trading procedures (i.e. stockbroker and jobber). Further, it was necessary to consider that information technology was an important element to bring the investment industry into the twentieth century.

The Act is primarily concerned with the protection of the private investor and, in order to achieve this, it is necessary to have some form of supervision of the investment business.

What exactly is the investment business? In general, it is:

(1) Dealing in investments: buying, selling, subscribing for or underwriting investments or offering or agreeing to offer invest-

ments either as a principal or agent. A person dealing in investments for his own account is excluded.

(2) Arranging deals in investments; making, offering or agreeing to make arrangements with a view to another person's buying selling, subscribing for or underwriting a particular investment.

(3) Managing investments; managing offering, or agreeing to manage assets belonging to another person if those assets consist of or include investments, or may do so at the discretion of the person managing, offering, or agreeing to manage them.

(4) Advising on investments; giving or offering or agreeing to give advice to investors on the merits of the purchase, sale, subscription for, or underwriting of investments, or on the exercise of rights conferred by investments to acquire, dispose of, underwrite or convert an investment. (Schedule 1).

Under the Act it is a criminal offence for an unauthorized person to carry on an investment business.

The Act is not intended to cover those who give advice regarding the tax or legal consequences in the purchase/sale of an investment, nor is the Act meant to cover those who may give general advice about different types of investments. For example, in a classroom a tutor is able to explain the advantages and disadvantages of perhaps a unit trust and compare it with an endowment policy.

Having discussed an investment business, we now need to discuss what exactly an investment is.

Under Schedule 1 of the Act, it is any right, interest, or asset within the following:

(1) Shares/stock in a company: this covers not only companies registered in the UK but includes unincorporated companies and foreign companies. It does not include 'open ended' investments such as investments in building societies, credit unions, and provident societies.

(2) Debentures: this includes debenture stock, loan stock, bonds, certificates of deposit and any other instrument creating or acknowledging a debt. It excludes notes of indebtedness for a contract to supply goods or services, e.g. bills of exchange, cheques, banker's drafts, and letters of credit, statements of account.

(3) Government, local authority, or other public authority securities: this includes the UK government and foreign governments.

(4) Warrants or other instruments entitling the holder to subscribe for investments in categories (1) to (3): these give the holder the right to purchase these securities at a stated price. This regulation does not cover contracts dealing with 'Options' or 'Futures'; these are dealt with elsewhere in the Act.

(5) Certificates or other instruments conferring rights to acquire, dispose of, underwrite, or convert any investments falling within the above categories. This includes such instruments as depository receipts, e.g. American Depositary Receipt.

(6) Units in collective investment schemes: such schemes are unit trusts or any securities in open-ended investments.

(7) Options to acquire or dispose of investments: within this category, LIFFE (London International Financial Futures Exchange) contracts are included as well as options on commodities such as gold, silver, and currencies. However, it is strange that options on other metals, e.g. platinum, are not included under paragraph 7 of this schedule but may be included below.

(h) Futures for investment purposes: these contracts are rights under a sale of a commodity or property for delivery at some future date. For simplicity, it is considered as an investment if a contract has been arranged for a member of the public, but where the contract is for trading or commercial purposes as distinct from investment, then the latter are excluded from the regulations. This seems an area of possible dispute. When is such a contract for example, an investment or a speculation, a hedge or a commercial contract? Only time will tell.

Authorization and exemptions

The basic requirement in the Financial Services Act is that anyone doing investment business must be authorized. The function of preparing the groundwork for recognizing persons and companies is in the hands of an institution established by the Act called the Securities and Investment Board (usually known as the SIB). The members of this board are appointed jointly by the Secretary of State and the Bank of England.

Briefly, the SIB is the City 'watchdog'. Its power comes from the Act, but it also has the authority to transfer its power to a designated body or bodies.

The functions of the SIB are as follows:

(i) to recognize or withdraw recognition of a self-regulating body (SRO)

(ii) to recognize or withdraw recognition from a professional body

(iii) to grant direct authorization to an investment business or refuse or suspend authorization if necessary

(iv) to recognize an investment exchange and clearing house

(v) to request information

(vi) to make rules regulating the conduct of investment business by those so authorized

(vii) to make rules concerning compensation funds and insurance requirements

(viii) to make regulations which will apply to authorized persons on unsolicited calls, cancellation, and segregation of clients' money

(ix) to intervene in the interests of investors and seek injunctions and restitution orders where necessary

(x) to approve collective schemes for promotion to the public generally

(xi) to investigate anyone carrying on investment business, either unauthorized or authorized and to prosecute offenders.

Exempted persons

The following are exempted from the Financial Services Act:

(1) The Bank of England

(2) Lloyd's – those who are permitted by the Lloyd's Council to act as underwriting agents are exempt in respect of investment business carried on in connection for the purpose of insurance business at Lloyds

(3) Appointed persons: these are persons who are representatives or employees of insurance and other companies involved in selling investment services or giving advice to persons who may wish to enter into investment transactions. The principals must be authorized or exempt under the act

(4) Money market institutions: it is usual for such institutions to be supervised by the Bank of England who ensure, amongst other

things, adequate capital, liquidity, and the rules of conduct. The list of such institutions will include banks, building societies, and others that have approval to operate in the money markets
(5) Others: there are a variety of other persons that are exempted including: liquidators, the Public Trustee, Official Solicitor, etc.

Delegation by the SIB

Although the authority of the Financial Services Act gives power to the SIB to act independently, it has authorized others to act on its behalf. These organizations are as follows:

(1) Self-regulating organizations (SROs)
(2) Professional bodies
(3) Clearing houses and investment exchanges.

Self-regulating organizations

The following are SROs that have been recognized:

The Securities Association (TSA)

They authorize firms who deal as brokers in securities, international money-markets instruments, and related futures and options, investment management and advice which is incidental to their business.

Association of Futures Brokers and Dealers (AFBD)

Deals with firms and brokers dealing and giving investment advice in connection with futures and options.

Financial Intermediaries, Managers and Brokers' Regulatory Association (FIMBRA)

This body covers firms that deal in securities and investment products; investment management and advisers and those who act as intermediaries for insurance and unit trust business.

Investment Management Regulatory Organization (IMRO)

This covers investment managers and advisers, trustees of collective investment schemes and of house pension funds. By the very nature of their business, banks are members of IMRO and often this is stated on banks' notepaper, personal cards of bank representatives, etc.

Life and Unit Trust Regulatory Organisation (LAUTRO)

Assurance companies and unit trusts are members of this organization. Their representatives sell insurance-linked investments and unit trusts.

These SROs are given their statutory powers by the SIB, providing their rules and procedures are up to the standard set down in the Act. The rules of an SRO usually cover:

(1) Fit and proper persons to carry out the investment work of the organization
(2) Rules and practices of an organization, the admission, expulsion and discipline of members
(3) Investor protection
(4) Powers to intervene in the affairs of a member if necessary
(5) Power to monitor and ensure enforcements of its rules

Recognized professional bodies

In investment terms this would include accountants and solicitors whose members become involved in giving investment advice. Each professional body so recognized will be able to give a certificate to its members to enable them to carry on an investment business without seeking authorization from any other body. The professional body will impose its own standards and regulations on its members and, in practical terms, the investment business will be incidental to the professional practice of the members.

The following have been considered as likely to seek recognition:

Law Society of England and Wales
Law Society of Scotland
Law Society of Northern Ireland
Institute of Chartered Accountants in England and Wales
Institute of Chartered Accountants in Ireland
Chartered Association of Certified Accountants
Institute of Cost and Management Accountants
Institute of Consulting Actuaries

Faculty of Actuaries
Royal Institute of Chartered Surveyors
Institute of Chartered Secretaries and Administrators.

Clearing houses and investment exchanges

Those institutions which run a market or exchange need authorization from the SIB. In order to be eligible for such recognition the following must be observed:

(1) Sufficient financial resources must be available for the performance of its functions
(2) Its rules and practices must ensure orderly conduct of its business and protection for its investors
(3) It must permit dealings only in a proper market
(4) Information regarding current values must be available
(5) Arrangements must exist for ensuring proper performance of transactions either direct or through a clearing house
(6) Ensure proper arrangements for recording transactions
(7) Have effective arrangements to investigate complaints
(8) Able to promote a high standard of integrity and fair dealing.

Clearing houses and investment exchanges could include:

International Stock Exchange
London Commodities Exchange
London International Final Futures Exchange (LIFFE)
London Metal Exchange
Association of International Bond Dealers.

Banks and their subsidiary companies would, where necessary, seek to become members of one or possibly more SROs. Their business and profits depend on their ability to market and sell a variety of financial services, whether as principals or agents.

Appendix III

The Banking Act, 1987

History

Before 1979 there was no formal system of supervision of the banking sector. It was possible for anyone to take deposits, provide banking services, and call themselves a 'bank'. Any supervision of the operations of these organizations was undertaken informally by the Bank of England as part of its role as the Central Bank.

By 1979 a formal system was needed for the following reasons:

(1) The EEC required that we fall into line with our EEC partners.

(2) The 'secondary banking crisis' in the 1970s had meant the collapse of many of the small 'fringe' banks with a loss of confidence in the system, both nationally and internationally.

(3) There was public confusion about what banks were. Particularly in the 1960s and 1970s all sorts of institutions were being established calling themselves banks, and using titles which seemed to indicate that they were large and well-established financial institutions. Bureaux de change at that time often had the word 'bank' in neon lights outside their premises. The ordinary man in the street could not readily identify one type of institution from another.

The Banking Act, 1979, provided a statutory framework for the authorization and supervision of the banking sector. While the Act worked well on the whole, a number of changes were considered necessary, in particular, the distinction between 'banks' and other 'licensed deposit takers'. The separate requirements for each category, were found to cause difficulties and were abolished by the 1987 Act.

The Banking Act, 1987

The Banking Act, 1987, replaces the 1979 Act which now has only a place in history. The Act became law on 15 May 1987, but most of the provisions only came into force on 1 October 1987 and some not until 1 January 1988.

The system of supervision

The supervision of the banking sector is by the Board of Banking Supervision which meets monthly and consists of the Governor and the Deputy Governor of the Bank of England, the Executive Director in the Bank of England responsible for banking supervision, and six external members.

Any institution which takes deposits in the UK must be authorized by the Bank of England. Once authorization is given, then supervision commences immediately. The Bank has the power to investigate any illegal deposit taking and to order the early repayments of deposits.

A deposit is a sum of money paid on terms that it will be repaid:

(1) with or without interest, and

(2) on demand, at an agreed time or on the occurrence of an agreed event.

Authorization

The Act lays down four minimum criteria for authorization of an institution:

(1) Every director, controller, and manager must be a fit and proper person to hold his position

(2) The business must be conducted in a prudent manner. This covers, *inter alia*, adequate capital, liquidity, provisions for bad debts, accounting, and other records and internal controls

(3) The business must be carried on with integrity and with the appropriate professional skills

(4) The paid-up capital and reserves must be of £1 million (£5 million if called a 'bank').

The Bank of England may at its discretion refuse authorization. Anyone taking deposits illegally may be fined or imprisoned.

Certain institutions, particularly those controlled by other Acts, such as the National Savings Bank, building societies, and local authorities do not have to be authorized.

Changes in control, takeovers and mergers

The Bank must be notified of changes in directors, controllers, and managers. Any person who can be classified as a significant shareholder (i.e. holding between 5 and 15 per cent of the voting rights) must notify the Bank. Any person who is proposing to hold more than 15 per cent of the voting rights of an authorized institution must give *advanced* notice to the Bank. Failure to do so is a criminal offence.

Information and investigations

It will be a criminal offence to provide false or misleading information to the Board of Banking Supervision. No institution must withold information and the Bank has powers to obtain information and documents. While such information is strictly confidential, provision has been made for the exchange of information with other regulatory bodies and government departments.

Auditors

Any changes in auditors or their resignations must be notified to the Bank. Auditors should give notice if they intend to qualify their opinion of the institutions's accounts. The bank may require auditors to disclose information obtained in the course of their audit, provided such disclosure is made in good faith and is relevant to the Bank's supervision.

Depositors' Protection Scheme

All institutions are covered by this scheme and the cover is 75 per cent of the first £20,000 of a customer's sterling deposits.

Appendix IV

Institutions under the Banking Act, 1987

Authorized institutions

*UK-incorporated (including partnerships formed under the law
of any part of the UK)*

ANZ McCaughan Merchant Bank
  Ltd
Adam & Company plc
Afghan National Credit & Finance
  Ltd
Airdrie Savings Bank
Aitken Hume Ltd
Ak International Bank Ltd
Albaraka International Bank Ltd
Alliance Trust (Finance) Ltd
Allied Arab Bank Ltd
Anglo-Romanian Bank Ltd
Anglo Yugoslav Bank Ltd
Henry Ansbacher & Co. Ltd
Arbuthnot Latham Bank Ltd
Argonaut Securities Ltd
Assemblies of God Property Trust
Associated Credits Ltd
Associated Japanese Bank
  (International) Ltd
Associates Capital Corporation Ltd
Atlanta Trust Ltd
Authority Bank Ltd
Avco Trust Ltd

BC Finance Ltd
BNL Investment Bank plc

Banco Hispano Americano Ltd
Bank in Liechtenstein (UK) Ltd
Bank Leumi (UK) Ltd
Bank of America International Ltd
Bank of Boston Ltd
Bank of Cyprus (London) Ltd
Bank of Scotland
Bank of Tokyo International Ltd
Bank of Wales plc
Bankers Trust International Ltd
Banque Belge Ltd
Banque de la Méditerranée (UK)
  Ltd
Banque Nationale de Paris plc
The Baptist Union Corporation Ltd
Barclays Bank plc
Barclays de Zoete Wedd Ltd
Barclays Bank Trust Company Ltd
Baring Brothers & Co. Ltd
Benchmark Bank plc
Beneficial Bank plc
Boston Safe Deposit and Trust
  Company (UK) Ltd
British & Commonwealth
  Merchant Bank plc
The British Bank of the Middle
  East

British Credit Trust Ltd
The British Linen Bank Ltd
British Railways Savings Company
    Ltd
Brown, Shipley & Co. Ltd
Bunge Finance Ltd
Burns-Anderson Trust Company
    Ltd
Business Mortgages Trust plc

CL-Alexanders Discount plc
Canadian Laurentian Bank Ltd
James Capel Bankers Ltd
Cater Allen Ltd
Central Capital Mortgage
    Corporation Ltd
Chancery plc
The Charities Aid Foundation
    Money Management Company
    Ltd
Charter Consolidated Financial
    Services Ltd
Chartered Trust plc
Charterhouse Bank Ltd
Chase Investment Bank Ltd
Chesterfield Street Trust Ltd
Citibank Trust Ltd
Citicorp Investment Bank Ltd
City Merchants Bank Ltd
City Trust Ltd
Clive Discount Company Ltd
Close Brothers Ltd
Clydesdale Bank plc
Clydesdale Bank Finance
    Corporation Ltd
Combined Capital Ltd
The Commercial Bank of the Near
    East plc
Consolidated Credits Bank Ltd
Co-operative Bank plc
Coutts & Co.
Coutts Finance Co.
Craneheath Securities Ltd
Credito Italiano International Ltd
Credit Suisse First Boston Ltd

Daiwa Europe Bank plc
Dalbeattie Finance Co. Ltd
Darlington Merchant Credits Ltd

Dartington & Co. Ltd
Deacon Hoare & Co. Ltd
Den norske Creditbank plc
The Dorset, Somerset & Wilts
    Investment Society Ltd
Dryfield Finance Ltd
Dunbar Bank plc
Duncan Lewis Ltd

EBC Amro Bank Ltd
E T Trust Ltd
Eagil Trust Co. Ltd
East Trust Ltd
Eccles Savings and Loans Ltd
Edington plc
Enskilda Securities-Skandinaviska
    Enskilda Ltd
Equatorial Bank plc
Euro-Latinamerican Bank plc
Everett Chettle Associates
Exeter Trust Ltd

FIBI Bank (UK) Ltd
Fairmount Trust Ltd
Family Finance Ltd
Federated Trust Corporation Ltd
FennoScandia Bank Ltd
Financial & General Bank plc
James Finlay Bank Ltd
First Indemnity Credit Ltd
First Interstate Capital Markets Ltd
First National Bank plc
First National Commercial Bank plc
Robert Fleming & Co. Ltd
Ford Financial Trust Ltd
Ford Motor Credit Co. Ltd
Foreign & Colonial Management
    Ltd
Forward Trust Ltd
Robert Fraser & Partners Ltd
Frizzell Banking Services Ltd

Gartmore Money Management Ltd
Gerrard & National Ltd
Girobank plc
Goldman Sachs Ltd
Goode Durrant Bank plc
Granville Trust Ltd
Gresham Trust plc
Greyhound Bank Ltd

Grindlays Bank plc
Guinness Mahon & Co. Ltd
Gulf Guarantee Bank plc

HFC Bank plc
Habibsons Bank Ltd
Hambros Bank Ltd
Hampshire Trust plc
The Hardware Federation Finance
   Co. Ltd
Harrods Bank Ltd
Harton Securities Ltd
Havana International Bank Ltd
The Heritable & General
   Investment Bank Ltd
Hill Samuel Bank Ltd
Hill Samuel Personal Finance Ltd
C Hoare & Co.
Julian Hodge Bank Ltd
Holdenhurst Securities plc
Humberclyde Finance Group Ltd
Hungarian International Bank Ltd
3i plc
3i Group plc
IBJ International Ltd
Industrial Funding Trust Ltd
International Commercial Bank plc
International Mexican Bank Ltd
International Westminster Bank plc
Iran Overseas Investment Bank Ltd
Itab Bank Ltd
Italian International Bank plc

Jabac Finances Ltd
Japan International Bank Ltd
Jordan International Bank plc
Leopold Joseph & Sons Ltd

King & Shaxson Ltd
Kleinwort Benson Ltd

Lazard Brothers & Co. Ltd
Libra Bank plc
Little Lakes Finance Ltd
Lloyds Bank plc
Lloyds Bank (BLSA) Ltd
Lloyds Bank (France) Ltd
Lloyds Bowmaker Ltd
Lloyds Merchant Bank Ltd
Lombard Bank Ltd

Lombard & Ulster Ltd
Lombard North Central plc
London Arab Investment Bank Ltd
London & Continental Bankers Ltd
London Law Securities Ltd
London Scottish Bank plc
Lordsvale Finance plc

MLA Bank Ltd
McDonnell Douglas Bank Ltd
McNeill Pearson Ltd
Manchester Exchange and
   Investment Bank Ltd
W M Mann & Co. (Investments) Ltd
Manufacturers Hanover Ltd
The Mardun Investment Co. Ltd
Marks and Spencer Financial
   Services Ltd
Mase Westpac Ltd
Matheson Bank Ltd
Medens Trust Ltd
Meghraj Bank Ltd
Mercantile Credit Company Ltd
Mercury Provident plc
Merrill Lynch International Bank
   Ltd
The Methodist Chapel Aid
   Association Ltd
Midland Bank plc
Midland Bank Finance Corporation
   Ltd
Midland Bank Trust Company Ltd
Minories Finance Ltd
Minster Trust Ltd
Moneycare Ltd
Samuel Montagu & Co. Ltd
Moorgate Mercantile Holdings plc
Morgan Grenfell & Co. Ltd
Moscow Narodny Bank Ltd
Mount Banking Corporation Ltd
Mutual Trust and Savings Ltd
Mynshul Bank Ltd

NIIB Group Ltd
National Guardian Mortgage
   Corporation Ltd
National Westminster Bank plc
NatWest Bank Ltd
The Nikko Bank (UK) plc

Noble Grossart Ltd
Nomura Bank International plc
Northern Bank Ltd
Northern Bank Executor & Trustee
    Company Ltd
North West Securities Ltd
Norwich General Trust Ltd

Omega Trust Co. Ltd
Orion Royal Bank Ltd

PK English Trust Company Ltd
PaineWebber International Bank
    Ltd
Panmure Gordon Bankers Ltd
The People's Bank Ltd
Philadelphia National Ltd
Pointon York Ltd
Postipankki (UK) Ltd
Prestwick Investment Trust plc
Privatbanken Ltd
Provincial Bank plc

Quin Cope Ltd

Ralli Investment Company Ltd
R Raphael & Sons plc
Rathbone Bros & Co. Ltd
Rea Brothers Ltd
Reliance Bank Ltd
Riggs A P Bank Ltd
N M Rothschild & Sons Ltd
Roxburghe Guarantee Corporation
    Ltd
The Royal Bank of Scotland plc
Royal Trust Bank
RoyScot Trust plc

SDS Bank Ltd
SFE Bank Ltd
SP Finance Ltd
Sangster Trust Corporation
Saudi International Bank (Al-Bank,
    Al-Saudi Al-Alami Ltd)
Scandinavian Bank Group plc
Schroder Leasing Ltd
J Henry Schroder Wagg & Co. Ltd
Scotiabank (UK) Ltd
Scottish Amicable Money Managers
    Ltd

Seccombe Marshall & Campion plc
Secure Homes Ltd
Security Pacific Trust Ltd
Shire Trust Ltd
Singer & Friedlander Ltd
Smith & Williamson Securities
Société Générale Merchant Bank
    plc
Southsea Mortgage & Investment
    Co Ltd
Spry Finance Ltd
Standard Chartered Bank
Standard Chartered Bank Africa plc
Standard Chartered Merchant Bank
    Ltd
Standard Property Investment plc
Sterling Bank & Trust Ltd
Svenska International plc

TSB England & Wales plc
TSB Northern Ireland plc
TSB Scotland plc
Treloan Ltd
Trucanda Trusts Ltd
Tyndall & Co. Ltd

UBAF Bank Ltd
UCB Bank plc
Ulster Bank Ltd
Ulster Bank Trust Company
Union Discount Company Ltd
The United Bank of Kuwait plc
United Dominions Trust Ltd
Unity Trust Bank plc

Wagon Finance Ltd
Wallace, Smith Trust Co. Ltd
S G Warburg & Co. Ltd
S G Warburg Discount Ltd
Welbeck Finance plc
Western Trust & Savings Ltd
Whiteaway Laidlaw Bank Ltd
Wimbledon & South West Finance
    Co. Ltd
Wintrust Securities Ltd

Yamaichi Bank (UK) plc
Yorkshire Bank plc
H F Young & Co. Ltd

Incorporated outside the UK (includes partnerships or other unincorporated assocations formed under the law of any member State of the European community other than the UK.)

African Continental Bank Ltd
Algemene Bank Nederland NV
Allied Bank of Pakistan Ltd
Allied Banking Corporation
Allied Irish Banks plc
Allied Irish Finance Co. Ltd
Allied Irish Investment Bank plc
Al Saudi Banque SA
American Express Bank Ltd
Amsterdam-Rotterdam Bank NV
Arab African International Bank
Arab Bank Ltd
Arab Banking Corporation BSC
Australia & New Zealand Banking
  Group Ltd

Banca Commerciale Italiana
Banca della Svizzera Italiana
Banca Nazionale dell'Agricoltura
  SpA
Banca Nazionale del Lavoro
Banca Serfin SNC
Banco Bilbao-Vizcaya
Banco Central, SA
Banco de la Nación Argentina
Banco de Sabadell
Banco de Santander, SA
Banco di Napoli
Banco di Roma SpA
Banco di Santo Spirito
Banco di Sicilia
Banco do Brasil SA
Banco do Estado de São Paulo SA
Banco Espirito Santo e Comercial
  de Lisboa
Banco Exterior – UK SA
Banco Mercantil de São Paulo SA
Banco Nacional de México SNC
Banco Português do Atlantico
Banco Real SA
Banco Totta & Açores SA
Bancomer SNC
Bangkok Bank Ltd

Bank Julius Baer & Co. Ltd
Bank Bumiputra Malaysia Berhad
Bank für Gemeinwirtschaft AG
Bank Handlowy w Warszawie SA
· Bank Hapoalim BM
Bank Mees & Hope NV
Bank Mellat
Bank Melli Iran
Bank Negara Indonesia 1946
Bank of America NT & SA
Bank of Baroda
The Bank of California NA
Bank of Ceylon
Bank of China
Bank of Credit and Commerce
  International SA
Bank of India
The Bank of Ireland
Bank of Montreal
Bank of New England NA
The Bank of New York
Bank of New Zealand
The Bank of Nova Scotia
Bank of Oman Ltd
Bank of Seoul
The Bank of Tokyo, Ltd
The Bank of Yokohama, Ltd
Bank Saderat Iran
Bank Sepah-Iran
Bank Tejarat
Bankers Trust Company
Banque Arabe et Internationale
  d'Investissement
Banque Belgo-Zairoise SA
Banque Bruxelles Lambert SA
Banque du Liban et d'Outre-Mer
  SAL
Banque Française du Commerce
  Extérieur

Banque Indosuez
Banque Internationale à
  Luxembourg SA
Banque Internationale pour
  L'Afrique Occidentale SA
Banque Nationale de Paris
Banque Paribas
Banque Worms
Barbados National Bank
Bayerische Hypotheken – und
  Wechsel – Bank AG
Bayerische Landesbank
  Girozentrale
Bayerische Vereinsbank
Beirut Riyad Bank SAL
Bergen Bank A/S
Berliner Bank AG
Berliner Handels-und Frankfurter
  Bank
Byblos Bank SAL

CIC –Union Européenne,
  International et Cie
Caisse Nationale de Crédit Agricole
Canadian Imperial Bank of
  Commerce
Canara Bank
Cassa di Risparmio delle Provincie
  Lombarde
The Chase Manhattan Bank, NA
Chemical Bank
Cho-Hung Bank
Christiana Bank og Kreditkasse
The Chuo Trust & Banking Co. Ltd
Citibank NA
Commercial Bank of Korea Ltd
Commerzbank AG
Commonwealth Bank of Australia
Confederacion Española de Cajas
  de Ahorros
Continental Bank, National
  Association
Copenhagen Handelsbank A/S
Crédit Commercial de France
Crédit du Nord
Crédit Lyonnais

Crédit Lyonnais Bank Nederland
  NV
Crédit Suisse
Creditanstalt – Bankverein
Credito Italiano
Cyprus Credit Bank Ltd
The Cyprus Bank Ltd
The Cyprus Popular Bank

The Dai-Ichi Kangyo Bank, Ltd
The Daiwa Bank, Ltd
Den Danske Bank af 1871
  Aktieselskab
Deutsche Bank AG
Deutsche Genossenschaftsbank
The Development Bank of
  Singapore Ltd
Discount Bank and Trust Company
Dresdner Bank AG

Fidelity Bank NA
First Bank National Association
First Bank of Nigeria Ltd
First City National Bank of
  Houston
First Commercial Bank
First Interstate Bank of California
The First National Bank of Boston
The First National Bank of Chicago
First Wisconsin National Bank of
  Milwaukee
Fleet National Bank
French Bank of Southern Africa Ltd
The Fuji Bank, Ltd

Generale Bank
Ghana Commercial Bank
Girozentrale und Bank der
  österreichischen Sparkassen AG
Götabanken
Gulf International Bank BSC

Habib Bank AG Zurich
Habib Bank Ltd
Hanil Bank
Harris Trust and Savings Bank
Hessische Landesbank –
  Girozentrale
The Hokkaido Takushoku Bank,
  Ltd

The Hongkong and Shanghai Banking Corporation

The Industrial Bank of Japan, Ltd
The Investment Bank of Ireland Ltd
Irving Trust Company
Istituto Bancario San Paolo di Torino

Jyske Bank

Kansallis-Osake-Pankki
Keesler Federal Credit Union
Korea Exchange Bank
Korea First Bank
Kredietbank NV
The Kyowa Bank, Ltd

The Long-Term Credit Bank of Japan, Ltd

Malayan Banking Berhad
Manufacturers Hanover Trust Company
Mellon Bank, NA
Middle East Bank Ltd
The Mitsubishi Bank, Ltd
The Mitsubishi Trust and Banking Corporation
The Mitsui Bank, Ltd
The Mitsui Trust & Banking Co. Ltd
Monte dei Paschi di Siena
Morgan Guaranty Trust Company of New York
Multibanco Comermex SNC
Muslim Commercial Bank Ltd

NCNB National Bank of North Carolina
NCNB Texas National Bank
National Australia Bank Ltd
National Bank of Abu Dhabi
National Bank of Canada
National Bank of Detroit
The National Bank of Dubai Ltd
National Bank of Egypt
National Bank of Greece SA
The National Bank of Kuwait SAK

The National Bank of New Zealand Ltd
National Bank of Nigeria Ltd
The National Commercial Bank
National Bank of Pakistan
Nedbank Ltd
Nederlandsche Middenstandsbank NV
New Nigeria Bank Ltd
The Nippon Credit Bank, Ltd
Norddeutsche Landesbank Girozentrale
The Northern Trust Company

Osterreichische Landerbank AG
Oversea-Chinese Banking Corporation Ltd
Overseas Trust Bank Ltd
Overseas Union Bank Ltd

Philadelphia National Bank
Philippine National Bank
Provinsbanken A/S

Qatar National Bank SAQ

Rabobank Nederland
(Coöperatieve Centrale Raiffeisen-Boerenleenbank BA)
Rafidain Bank
Republic National Bank of New York
Reserve Bank of Australia
The Riggs National Bank of Washington, DC
Riyad Bank
The Royal Bank of Canada
The Rural and Industries Bank of Western Australia

The Saitama Bank, Ltd
The Sanwa Bank, Ltd
Saudi American Bank
Seattle – First National Bank
Security Pacific National Bank
Shanghai Commercial Bank Ltd
The Siam Commercial Bank, Ltd
Skandinaviska Enskilda Banken
Société Générale
Sonali Bank

State Bank of India
State Bank of New South Wales
State Bank of South Australia
State Bank of Victoria
State Street Bank and Trust
  Company
Südwestdeutsche Landesbank
  Girozentrale
The Sumitomo Bank, Ltd
The Sumitomo Trust & Banking Co.
  Ltd
Svenska Handelsbanken
Swiss Bank Corporation
Swiss Cantobank (International)
Swiss Volksbank
Syndicate Bank

TC Ziraat Bankasi
TDB American Express Bank
The Taiyo Kobe Bank, Ltd
The Thai Farmers Bank Ltd
The Tokai Bank, Ltd
The Toronto-Dominion Bank
The Toyo Trust & Banking
  Company, Ltd
The Trust Bank of Africa Ltd
Turkish Bank Ltd

Türkiye Is Bankasi ASA

Uco Bank
Ulster Investment Bank, Ltd
Union Bank of Finland Ltd
Union Bank of Nigeria Ltd
Union Bank of Norway
Union Bank of Switzerland
United Bank Ltd
United Mizrahi Bank Ltd
United Overseas Bank (Banque
  Unie pour les Pays d'Outre Mer)
United Overseas Bank Ltd

Volkskas Ltd

Westdeutsche Landesbank
  Girozentrale
Westpac Banking Corporation

The Yasuda Trust & Banking Co.,
  Ltd

Zambia National Commercial Bank
  Ltd
Zivnostenská Banka National
  Corporation

Appendix V

Banking Ombudsman

The Banking Ombudsman scheme became operational on Thursday, 2 January 1986 (1 January being a bank holiday). The first Banking Ombudsman, indeed the first in the world, was Mr Ian Edwards-Jones, QC. He has now retired from this post and his place has been taken by Mr Laurence Shurman, a leading London solicitor. Mr Shurman like his predecessor is responsible to a Council headed by Dame Mary Donaldson, CBE.

While it was originally envisaged that the scheme was open to any bank 'recognized' by the Bank of England, the Banking Act, 1987, abolished the definition of 'recognized bank'. Over 500 financial institutions are now authorized by the Bank of England and are permitted to call themselves banks.

The constitution of the scheme has been changed to enable any deposit-taking business authorized as a bank by the Bank of England to apply for membership, subject to the approval of the board. So far no other banks, other than those listed below are members.

It should be noted that quite a number of banks are involved almost totally in the business of dealing with securities and investments, so that any complaints after 29 April 1988 against them must be channelled through the appropriate SRO.

Member banks

Bank of Scotland	Barclays Bank
Clydesdale Bank	Co-operative Bank
Coutts & Co.	Lloyds Bank
Midland Bank	Girobank
National Westminster Bank	The Royal Bank of Scotland

Standard Chartered Bank
TSB England and Wales
TSB Scotland
TSB Northern Ireland
Ulster Bank

Yorkshire Bank
Bank of Ireland
Allied Irish Banks
Northern Bank

Designated associates

Joint Credit Card Company*
National Westminster Home
  Loans
Barclays Bank Trust Company
Midland Bank Trust Company
Bank of Scotland Insurance
  Services
Barclays Insurance Brokers
  International
Barclays Insurance Services
  Company
Clydesdale Bank Insurance
  Services
Unity Trust

Yorkshire Bank Home Loans
TSB Trustcard
Coutts Finance Company
Northern Bank Executor and
  Trustee Co.
Ulster Bank Trust Co.
Lloyds Bank Insurance
  Services
Midland Bank Insurance
  Services
National Westminster
  Insurance Services
Royal Bank Insurance Services
Girobank Insurance Services

* Normally called Access. Barclaycard, as part of Barclays Bank, is also within the scheme.

The task of the Ombudsman is to consider any eligible complaints from personal bank customers after it has been established that existing procedures for dealing with complaints have been exhausted. The Ombudsman has powers to make an award that is binding on a bank with an upper limit of £100,000 for events on or after 25 January 1988 and up to £50,000 as regards complaints about events pre-25 January 1988. If a customer decides not to accept the decision he or she will retain the full right to take legal action.

The free service provided by the Ombudsman covers most personal banking services, although finance house, travel agent and estate agent subsidiaries of banks will be excluded, as well as commercial decisions relating to lending.

Analysis by subject matters of specific complaints received, for twelve months ended 30 September 1988

Description	No.	%
ATM Cashcard disputed withdrawals	269	12.9
Bank Charges (all aspects)	187	8.9
Irregular Conduct of account by Bank	123	5.9
Unauthorised debits (Not ATM or cashcard)	74	3.5
Misrepresentation	65	3.1
Guarantee cards dishonoured (non customer)	64	3.1

Appendix VI

The Jack Committee Report

The revision of this book cannot be complete without a mention of the report of the committee chaired by Professor Robert Jack, whose brief it was to review the state of banking services law and to make recommendations to the government.

The complete review of the report has no place in this book as it contained 83 recommendations, of which 26 were addressed to banks and the remainder to the government, suggesting that there should be three new banking laws.

It may be some time before these recommendations are accepted either in full or with some amendments, but it is worth considering the thoughts of a committee that took some two years to do its survey and give its report.

The following are the key recommendations of the committee:

(1) Banks should produce their own voluntary Code of Banking Practice. This would be imposed statutorily by the government if the banks dragged their feet.

(2) Under the Code banks should explain to their customers the basis of charging for the normal operation of their account.

(3) Banks should explain to their customers how the system of bankers' opinions (references) works and should ask customers for their consent before supplying opinions on them in answer to status enquiries.

(4) Banks should explain some of the 'mysteries' of banking to customers, notably the timing of the clearing cycle.

(5) ATM disputes about 'unauthorised' transactions should be settled by 'equitable allocation' of loss rather than the present 'winner takes all' system.

(6)The rules of confidentiality should be updated and codified in a new Banking Services Act.

(7) Customers' liability to losses from unauthorized ATM withdrawals should be limited to £50, in line with the law on credit cards.

(8) The Banking Ombudsman should be given statutory powers to bring him in line with the Building Societies Ombudsman and 'underpin his independence'.

(9) A Banking Services Act should ban the unsolicited mailing of all payment cards by banks to their customers, apart from credit cards already covered by the Consumer Credit Act, 1974.

(10) The law relating to cheques should be re-enacted in a new act, the Cheques and Bankers Payment Orders Act.

(11) The Cheques and Bankers Payment Orders Act should allow banks to 'truncate' cheques and payment orders; that is, obtain payment by presentment of electronic information rather than the instrument itself.

(12) A non-negotiable, non-transferable payment instruction called the Bank Payment Order should be created to reduce fraud.

(13) A negotiable Instruments Act should be introduced to cover bills of exchange, promissory notes, and all other negotiable instruments.

The author would like to thank the *Banking World* for permission to reproduce the key recommendations of the Jack Committee Report.

Answers to tests

Tests	1	2	3	4	5	6	7	8	9	10
					Questions					
1	b	c	c	a	c	a	b	b	a	b
2	c	a	b	b	c	a	a	c	a	b
3	b	c	a	a	b	c	b	c	b	b
4	b	a	c	b	a	c	b	c	b	c
5	c	c	a	a	c	b	b	c	a	a
6	b	a	c	b	b	a	c	a	b	c
7	a	c	c	a	b	c	a	b	a	a
8	c	b	c	b	b	c	a	b	a	a
9	c	b	b	a	c	c	b	a	b	a
10	b	a	b	c	a	c	a	b	c	a
11	a	c	c	a	b	a	b	a	c	b
12	b	b	c	a	b	a	a	c	b	b
13	a	b	c	a	b	b	c	c	a	c
14	b	c	c	c	a	c	b	a	c	a
15	c	b	c	b	a	a	c	b	b	a

Index